CORPORATE FINANCIAL REPORTING AND ANALYSIS

FOURTH EDITION

S. David Young,

Jacob Cohen

and

Daniel A Bens

WILEY

VP AND EDITORIAL DIRECTOR	George Hoffman
EDITORIAL DIRECTOR	Veronica Visentin
EXECUTIVE EDITOR	Lise Johnson
SPONSORING EDITOR	Jennifer Manias
EDITORIAL MANAGER	Judy Howarth
CONTENT MANAGEMENT DIRECTOR	Lisa Wojcik
CONTENT MANAGER	Nichole Urban
SENIOR CONTENT SPECIALIST	Nicole Repasky
PRODUCTION EDITOR	Ameer Basha
COVER PHOTO CREDIT	© AhLamb / iStockphoto

This book was set in 10/12 TimesLTStd by SPi Global and printed and bound by Quad/Graphics.

Founded in 1807, John Wiley & Sons, Inc. has been a valued source of knowledge and understanding for more than 200 years, helping people around the world meet their needs and fulfill their aspirations. Our company is built on a foundation of principles that include responsibility to the communities we serve and where we live and work. In 2008, we launched a Corporate Citizenship Initiative, a global effort to address the environmental, social, economic, and ethical challenges we face in our business. Among the issues we are addressing are carbon impact, paper specifications and procurement, ethical conduct within our business and among our vendors, and community and charitable support. For more information, please visit our website: www.wiley.com/go/citizenship.

ISBN: 978-1-119-49457-7 (PBK)
ISBN: 978-1-119-49472-0 (EVAL)

Library of Congress Cataloging-in-Publication Data

Names: Young, S. David, 1955- author. | Cohen, Jacob, 1973- author. | Bens, Daniel A., author.
Title: Corporate financial reporting and analysis / S. David Young, Jacob Cohen and Daniel A Bens.
Description: Fourth Edition. | Hoboken : Wiley, [2019] | Revised edition of Corporate financial reporting and analysis, [2013] | Includes index. | Identifiers: LCCN 2018021868 (print) | LCCN 2018025342 (ebook) | ISBN 9781119494591 (Adobe PDF) | ISBN 9781119494638 (ePub) | ISBN 9781119494577 (pbk.) | ISBN 9781119494720 (eVal)
Subjects: LCSH: Financial statements. | Corporations—Accounting. | Corporation reports.
Classification: LCC HF5681.B2 (ebook) | LCC HF5681.B2 Y68 2019 (print) | DDC 657/.3—dc23
LC record available at https://lccn.loc.gov/2018021868

The inside back cover will contain printing identification and country of origin if omitted from this page. In addition, if the ISBN on the back cover differs from the ISBN on this page, the one on the back cover is correct.

V087784_110518

To Diane – S. David Young

To my parents – Jacob Cohen

To Katrina, Lincoln and Lydia – Daniel Bens

ABOUT THE AUTHORS

S. David Young is Professor of Accounting and Control at INSEAD, based in Fontainebleau (France) and Singapore. He has been there since 1989. Professor Young holds a PhD from the University of Virginia and is both a Certified Public Accountant (USA) and a Chartered Financial Analyst. His primary areas of expertise are corporate financial reporting and value-based management, with works published in a wide variety of academic and professional journals, including several articles in the *Harvard Business Review*.

Professor Young is the author or coauthor of several books, including *EVA and Value-Based Management: A Practical Guide to Implementation* (McGraw-Hill, 2001), *Profits You Can Trust: Spotting and Surviving Accounting Landmines* (Financial Times, Prentice Hall, 2003), and *Attracting Investors: A Marketing Approach to Finding Funds for Your Business* (John Wiley & Sons, 2004). His most recent book is *The Blue Line Imperative: What Managing for Value Really Means* (John Wiley & Sons, 2013).

Professor Young is also the recipient of several Outstanding Teaching Awards from the INSEAD MBA program and the Distinguished Alumni Scholar Award from his undergraduate alma mater, The George Washington University. He has consulted extensively for companies in Europe, the United States, and Asia, mainly on issues related to value-based management and financial analysis.

Jake Cohen is Senior Associate Dean for Undergraduate and Masters' Programs at MIT Sloan School of Management and Senior Lecturer in Accounting and Law, where he has been since 2012. In his role, he oversees strategy for eight programs. From 2003 to 2011, Jake was an Affiliate Professor of Accounting and Control at INSEAD and was based in France and Singapore. He served as Director of the INSEAD-PricewaterhouseCoopers Research Center from 2004 to 2008 and as Dean of the MBA Program from 2008 to 2011.

He teaches courses in financial and managerial accounting, financial statements analysis, mergers and acquisitions, corporate restructuring, and business law. Cohen is a recipient of Outstanding Teaching Awards from the INSEAD MBA for both core and elective courses.

Prior to joining INSEAD, Cohen was a Senior Teaching Fellow in the Accounting and Control group at the Harvard Business School, where he was a founding member of the MBA Analytics Program. Prior to teaching at Harvard, he taught at Syracuse University as an assistant professor and was named "Professor of the Year."

Jake Cohen received a Bachelor of Science degree in accounting from Lehigh University, where he graduated with honors, a Master of Science degree in accounting, and a Juris Doctor degree in law from Syracuse University.

Prior to his academic career, he worked as a tax accountant at KPMG LLP in Philadelphia and as a mergers and acquisition consultant for PricewaterhouseCoopers LLP in New York City.

Daniel Bens is a Professor at INSEAD, currently serving as the Chair of the Accounting and Control area. Previously, he was a faculty at the University of Arizona serving as Associate Dean of MBA programs. Prior to that he was a faculty at the University of Chicago, Booth School of Business from 1999 to 2005.

Professor Bens received his PhD from the Wharton School at the University of Pennsylvania, his MBA from Indiana University, and his BS from Penn State University. He was a licensed Certified Public Accountant (CPA) in Pennsylvania, working for Price Waterhouse and then Westinghouse prior to graduate school.

He has taught in full-time, evening, and executive MBA programs, as well as non-degree executive education programs throughout his career. His teaching has received special recognition at INSEAD in 2014 and 2015, and at the University of Arizona with awards in 2011 and 2007. His research has been cited or he has been quoted in *Fortune, Business Week*, and various newspapers via the Associated Press and Reuters news services. His research has appeared in the leading academic journals including *Accounting Horizons, The Accounting Review, Contemporary Accounting Research, Journal of Accounting, Auditing & Finance, Journal of Accounting and Economics*, and *Journal of Accounting Research*.

CONTENTS

3 A Brief Overview of GAAP and IFRS: The Framework for Financial Accounting 45

4 Revenue Recognition 52

5 The Statement of Cash Flows 80

6 FINANCIAL STATEMENT ANALYSIS 115

7 BUSINESS VALUATION AND FINANCIAL STATEMENT ANALYSIS 154

8 ACCOUNTING FOR RECEIVABLES AND BAD DEBTS 168

9 ACCOUNTING FOR INVENTORY 192

10 ACCOUNTING FOR PROPERTY, PLANT, AND EQUIPMENT 209

11 LEASES AND OFF-BALANCE-SHEET DEBT 225

12 ACCOUNTING FOR BONDS 236

13 PROVISIONS AND CONTINGENCIES 248

14   ACCOUNTING FOR PENSIONS   260

15   ACCOUNTING FOR INCOME TAX   274

16   ACCOUNTING FOR SHAREHOLDERS' EQUITY   293

17 INVESTMENTS 313

An Introduction to Financial Statements

Imagine that you're a banker, and you have to determine which companies to lend to and on what terms. Or you're an investor who wants to know which companies are likely to outperform the market averages over the next year or two. In short, where should you invest your capital? To answer this question, investors turn to corporate financial statements.

Financial statements exist to provide useful information on businesses to people who have, or may have, an economic stake in those businesses. These statements should help:

- *investors*, to make more intelligent decisions on where to put their scarce capital;
- *bankers*, to determine whether or not a company will be able to service its debts;
- *suppliers*, to assess whether or not a potential customer is a good credit risk;
- *customers*, to determine whether or not the company is strong enough financially to deliver on long-term promises of service and warranty coverage;
- *tax authorities*, to determine whether or not a company is paying its fair share of taxes;
- *trade union representatives*, in forming their negotiating positions with management;
- *competitors*, to benchmark their performance;
- *courts of law*, to measure, for example, the damage caused by one firm to another as a result of alleged unfair trade practices;
- *antitrust regulators*, to measure market share and profits relative to competitors;
- *prospective employees*, to determine whether the company is worth pursuing as a long-term employer.

You may notice one important constituency missing from this list of financial statement users: corporate management. Financial statements are the responsibility of management, but are not designed to meet their own informational needs. Financial statements are a means for company managers to communicate the financial strength and profitability of their businesses to investors and other groups, but are not really intended for internal management use. To understand why, let's take a brief look at the financial statements (shown in Exhibits 1.1–1.3) of Taiwan Semiconductor Manufacturing Company (TSMC), one of the world's largest manufacturers of integrated circuits and semiconductors. Based in Taiwan, they supply components for a variety of consumer and industrial electronic devices.

The three principal financial statements – the balance sheet, the income statement, and the statement of cash flows – are highly aggregated documents: masses of detail accumulated in a small number of line items. Without this aggregation, the statements would be unreadable; however, a lot of details are missing. While this lack of detail might be appropriate for potential investors, who have to compare financial data across many different companies, the information found in these financial statements is not sufficiently detailed to be of any practical use to managers in corporate decision-making.

This is not to say that managers shouldn't care about the financial statements. Managers must understand their financial statements because these are the most important sources of information used by the investing community to determine where to invest capital. Managers who don't understand the signals that their financial statements are sending to investors are not in a position to compete effectively in the global capital markets. However, internal decision-making and management control require data that are far more detailed (by product line, region, cost categories, etc.) than the data found in annual reports.

In addition, financial statements are mainly historical. The balance sheet reflects the financial position at a precise moment in the recent past. The income statement shows profits over a period of time in the recent past – for example, the year just completed. Similarly, the statement of cash flows reports on the sources and uses of cash over a period of time already past. But while appreciating the insights of these statements is critical to managers in understanding their business and its competitiveness in the capital markets, they need information systems that are forward-looking in nature. Managers plan, budget, and forecast – and they therefore need systems that help them to perform these critical functions.

Another problem with financial accounting from a management perspective is that accounting rules that are designed to measure costs or value assets can result in misleading figures, even when calculated in good faith by managers. For example, when a manufacturing company measures the cost of its inventory, it must include not only direct costs of production, such as labor and materials, but also manufacturing overhead (such as depreciation on equipment, power and electricity, and maintenance costs). In contrast with direct costs, overhead cannot be directly traced to individual units of production. Instead, they are assigned to individual products (and to inventory accounts) using an arbitrary allocation technique. The resulting inventory figures may be acceptable for the broad overview that an investor wants from the financial statements, but can be seriously misleading if management intends to use them to calculate product-line profitability, to set pricing policy, or to make product-mix decisions. In short, managers need cost-accounting systems that provide more detailed, and more accurate, costing data.

The Three Principal Financial Statements

The corporate financial reporting process focuses on the three principal financial statements – the balance sheet, the income statement, and the statement of cash flows.

The Balance Sheet[1]

Take glance at TSMC's balance sheet (Exhibit 1.1). One of the first things you should notice is that the balance sheet reports on the company's financial position at a moment in time, in this case the end of 2015 and 2016. In other words, it's a snapshot, taken at the end of each period, of the assets owned by the company and the financing for those assets. Assets are economic resources with the ability or potential to provide future benefits to a business, such as profits or cash flow.

The financing of assets occurs in two basic forms: liabilities and shareholders' equity. Liabilities are the company's debts or obligations. They are the claims on the assets held by a firm's creditors. Shareholders' equity shows the amount of financing provided by owners of the business, both in the form of direct investment (when shareholders contribute cash in exchange for shares) and indirect investment (when profits are reinvested in the firm).

Exhibit 1-1 | **TSMC Consolidated Balance Sheet (in NT$ millions)**

	December 31	
	2016	**2015**
CURRENT ASSETS		
Cash and equivalents	541,254	562,689
Financial assets	94,957	27,779
Notes and accounts receivable, net	128,335	85,060
Inventories	48,682	67,052
Other	4,502	4,164
Total current assets	817,730	746,744
NONCURRENT ASSETS		
Financial assets	26,411	10,902
Investments accounted for using the equity method	19,585	23,971
Property, Plant and Equipment	997,778	853,470
Intangible assets	14,615	14,066
Deferred income tax assets	8,271	6,385
Other	1,908	1,860
Total noncurrent assets	1,068,568	910,654
TOTAL ASSETS	1,886,298	1,657,398
CURRENT LIABILITIES		
Short term loans and financial liabilities	58,149	39,547
Accounts payable	26,062	18,575
Salaries, bonus, and profit sharing payables	36,576	32,661
Payables to contractors and suppliers	63,155	26,012
Income tax payable	70,353	60,445
Provisions	18,038	10,164
Long-term liabilities - current portion	38,110	23,518
Accrued expenses and other	37,844	28,851
Total Current Liabilities	348,287	239,773
NONCURRENT LIABILITIES		
Bonds payable and long term bank loans	153,116	191,998
Deferred income tax liabilities	141	31
Net defined benefit liability	8,551	7,448
Guarantee deposits	14,670	21,565
Other	1,687	1,613
Total Noncurrent Liabilities	178,165	222,655
TOTAL LIABILITIES	526,452	462,428

(Continued)

Exhibit 1-1	(Continued)		

		December 31	
		2016	**2015**
SHAREHOLDERS' EQUITY			
Capital stock		259,304	259,304
Capital surplus		56,272	56,300
Retained earnings		1,041,811	866,630
Other		1,664	11,774
Noncontrolling interests		795	962
TOTAL SHAREHOLDERS' EQUITY		1,359,846	1,194,970
TOTAL LIABILITIES AND SHAREHOLDERS' EQUITY		1,886,298	1,657,398

The accompanying notes are an integral part of these consolidated financial statements.

The organization of the balance sheet can thus be summarized like this:

$$\text{Assets} = \text{Liabilities} + \text{Shareholders' Equity}$$

The term "balance sheet" is derived from this equation. It simply reminds us that the right side and the left side must always equal, for all companies, in all industries, in all countries, without exception. Simply put, the balance sheet must balance. The reason why this is can be seen from the right side of the equation. Liabilities and shareholders' equity don't just represent financing, they also represent claims on the assets from the left side. In the event of liquidation (i.e., when a company goes out of business), the first claim on resources belongs to creditors. The claims held by shareholders are residual in nature, which means that they are entitled to whatever is left over after the creditors have been paid off. Because shareholders' equity represents a residual claim on the assets, it will be whatever size it needs to be in order to ensure that the two sides of the balance sheet are equal.

TSMC's balance sheet confirms this equality. Total assets at the end of 2016 of NT$1,886 billion equal the sum of liabilities, NT$526 billion, and shareholders' equity, NT$1,360 billion.

The Income Statement

The income statement reports on a company's profits, or revenues less expenses, during the accounting period. Unlike the balance sheet, it's not a snapshot, but rather reflects what a firm has accomplished over a period of time. In the case of TSMC, the income statement (Exhibit 1.2) reports on the company's performance for the years 2014, 2015, and 2016. Notice that the accounting year (sometimes called the "fiscal year") is the same as the calendar year (1 January–31 December). This is not required, however. For example, most major retailers in the United States have accounting years that end between late January and the end of March. This is done to avoid having to close the books and prepare financial statements at the busiest time of the year.

The top line of the income statement, _revenues_ (also called "sales" or "sales revenues"), represents the monetary value of goods or services sold to customers. Expenses represent the cost of resources used by the company to earn revenues during the period.

Exhibit 1-2	TSMC Consolidated Income Statements (in NT$ millions)

	Year Ended December 31		
	2016	2015	2014
Revenue	947,938	843,497	762,807
Cost of revenue	473,106	433,103	385,084
Gross profit	474,832	410,394	377,723
Research and development	71,208	65,546	56,829
General and administrative	19,796	17,257	18,933
Marketing	5,901	5,665	5,087
Other operating expenses (income)	(30)	1,881	1,002
Income from operations	377,957	320,045	295,872
Share of profits of associates and joint ventures	3,458	4,196	3,920
Finance costs	(3,306)	(3,190)	(3,236)
Foreign exchange gain	1,161	2,481	2,111
Other income	6,651	26,943	3,408
Income before income tax	385,921	350,475	302,075
Income tax expense	54,124	47,645	47,890
Net income	331,797	302,830	254,185

The accompanying notes are an integral part of these consolidated financial statements.

Profit (also known as "earnings" or "income") is shown in several ways on an income statement. For example, gross profit, sometimes called "gross margin," measures revenues, net of manufacturing costs. For a nonmanufacturing company, such as a retailer or distributor, gross profit equals revenues net of the cost of merchandise sold during the year.

Operating income equals sales net of all operating expenses, excluding taxes. It measures how well the company has done in a given period from its normal, recurring, day-to-day activities of producing and selling its products. For TSMC, gross profit and operating income in 2016 were NT$475 billion and NT$378 billion, respectively.

When taxes and the nonoperating sources of income and expense are added or subtracted from operating income, as appropriate, the result is net income, the "bottom line" of the income statement. For 2016, TSMC reports net income of NT$332 billion. Note that companies have discretion in how they categorize these costs. This discretion, otherwise known as accounting choice, is a theme we will return to throughout the book. In the case of TSMC, there are significant income items listed as "nonoperating" that might be classified as operating by other companies. Such choices can have significant effects. In this case, for example, TSMC's nonoperating income was nearly 10% of income before tax in 2015.

The Statement of Cash Flows

The statement of cash flows summarizes the inflows and outflows of cash that arise from the three primary activities of a typical business: operations, investing, and financing. For TSMC, operating activities refer mainly (but not exclusively) to the routine, recurring actions involved in the design, manufacture, and distribution of semiconductors and integrated circuits. Investing activities involve the buying and selling of long-term assets such as machinery and equipment, companies or parts of companies, and financial securities such as government bonds. Financing activities refer mainly to actions involving the capital markets such as borrowing, paying off loans, issuing shares, share buybacks, and the payment of dividends.

The statement is structured in such a way that the net cash flows during the period for all three activities must equal the change in cash. In other words, the net cash flows from operating, investing, and financing activities must equal the net increase or decrease in the cash balance for the year. You can easily confirm this reconciliation in TSMC's statement of cash flows.

What makes this statement so interesting is not just that it summarizes cash flows, and in so doing reconciles beginning and ending cash, but that it also reveals the sort of activities that gave rise to those cash flows. In short, the statement reveals where a company's cash came from during the year, and what the company did with it.

For example, TSMC's statement of cash flows (Exhibit 1.3) shows operating cash flow of nearly NT$540 billion in 2016. Much of this cash generated from TSMC's day-to-day operations was reinvested in the company. We know this is true because of the negative cash flows from investing activities (shown in parentheses). Of those investments, most (NT$329 billion) was committed to property, plant, and equipment. From the financing section, we see that TSMC returned significant amounts of cash to its shareholders in the form of dividends (NT$155.5 billion in 2016).

Exhibit 1-3	TSMC Consolidated Statements of Cash Flows (in NT$ millions)		

	Year Ended December 31		
	2016	**2015**	**2014**
Cash flows from operating activities			
Income before income tax	385,921	350,475	302,075
Adjustments for:			
Depreciation expense	220,085	219,303	197,645
Amortization expense	3,743	3,202	2,606
Finance costs	3,306	3,190	3,236
Share of profits of associates and joint venture	(3,458)	(4,196)	(3,920)
Interest income	(6,318)	(4,129)	(2,731)
Gain on disposal of property, plant and equipment, net	(47)	(434)	(15)
Asset impairments	122	2,759	1,187
Loss (gain) on financial assets	(2,707)	(19,585)	3,742
Loss (gain) on disposal of equity method investments and subsidiaries	325	(2,369)	(2,084)
Dividend income	(137)	(622)	(650)
Changes in operating assets and liabilities:			
Financial instruments at fair value through profit and loss, and other financial assets	(6,368)	492	(2,269)
Notes and accounts receivable, net	(49,828)	26,491	(43,128)
Inventories	18,370	(655)	(28,872)
Other assets	(251)	265	(743)

Exhibit 1-3 (Continued)

	Year Ended December 31		
	2016	**2015**	**2014**
Accounts payable	7,295	(2,693)	6,634
Accrued expenses and other current liabilities	3,833	(4,147)	8,238
Salary, bonus and profit sharing payables	3,913	3,805	7,595
Provisions	7,932	(383)	2,837
Net defined benefit liability	46	53	60
Cash generated from operations	585,778	570,822	451,442
Income taxes paid	(45,943)	(40,943)	(29,918)
Net cash generated by operating activities	539,835	529,879	421,524
Cash flows from investing activities			
Acquisitions of:			
Financial assets	(117,435)	(44,656)	(6,518)
Property, plant and equipment	(328,851)	(257,517)	(288,540)
Intangible assets	(4,243)	(4,284)	(3,860)
Proceeds from disposal or redemption of:			
Financial assets	40,753	74,665	4,139
Investments accounted for using equity method	0	5,172	3,472
Property, plant and equipment	98	817	200
Interest received	6,353	3,642	2,579
Proceeds from government grants	1,537	0	0
Net cash flow from disposal and acquisition of subsidiaries	0	549	0
Dividends received from investments using equity method	5,479	3,407	3,223
Other dividends received	137	617	646
Refundable deposits refunded (paid)	732	342	2,239
Net cash used in investing activities	(395,440)	(217,246)	(282,421)
Cash flows from financing activities			
Increase in short-term loans	18,969	3,139	18,564
Repayment of bonds, long-term bank loans, and finance leases	(23,480)	(29)	(28)
Interest paid	(3,302)	(3,156)	(3,193)
Guarantee deposits received net refunds	5,831	12	30,135
Cash dividends	(155,582)	(116,684)	(77,786)
Proceeds from exercise of stock options	0	34	47
Decrease in noncontrolling interests	(236)	(50)	(67)
Net cash used in financing activities	(157,800)	(116,734)	(32,328)

(Continued)

| Exhibit 1-3 | (Continued) |

	Year Ended December 31		
	2016	**2015**	**2014**
Effect of exchange rates on cash and equivalents	(8,030)	8,259	9,060
Net increase (decrease) in cash and equivalents	(21,435)	204,158	115,836
Cash and cash equivalents included in other noncurrent assets, beginning of year	0	82	0
Cash and equivalents beginning of year	562,689	358,449	242,695
Cash and equivalents end of year	541,254	562,689	358,531
Cash and cash equivalents included in other noncurrent assets	0	0	(82)
Cash and equivalents per the balance sheet	541,254	562,689	358,449

The accompanying notes are an integral part of these consolidated financial statements.

How the Financial Statements Relate to Each Other

Although each statement is a separate, discrete entity, it is also linked with the other two. For example, the net income from the income statement (e.g., NT$332 billion in 2016 for TSMC Group) is reflected in both retained earnings (from the shareholders' equity section of the balance sheet) and in the operations section of the statement of cash flows. Also, the net cash flows from the statement of cash flows (see final line) plus beginning cash (on the balance sheet) must equal ending cash. These relationships should come as no surprise because, logically, we would expect a company's performance, as reflected in its income statement, to influence its cash flows, and for both profit and cash flows to influence its financial position (i.e., the balance sheet).

To illustrate these relationships, let's take another look at TSMC's financial statements. Net income in 2016 was NT$332 billion. As revealed in the statement of cash flows, the company paid NT$156 billion in dividends that year. Retained earnings (on the balance sheet in the shareholders' equity section) represent all of the net income a company has ever earned in its history that has not yet been paid to shareholders as a dividend. In other words, it measures all of the profits retained by the business for reinvestment. We would expect retained earnings to change each year by an amount equal to the year's net income, less any dividends paid in that year. In the case of Taiwan Semiconductor, we should see an increase of NT$332 billion minus NT$156 billion, or NT$176 billion. And that is very close to the amount by which the company's retained earnings increased from the end of 2015 to the end of 2016 NT$1,042 billion - NT$867 billion, i.e., NT$175 billion.

Note also that cash flows from operating, investing and financing activities (plus effect of foreign exchange rates on cash and cash equivalent in 2016, i.e., -NT$8 billion) result in a net decrease in cash of NT$21 billion, which is equal to the difference between the cash balance at the end of 2016 (NT$541 billion) at the end of 2015 (NT$562 billion).

Other Items in the Annual Report

As mentioned earlier, the balance sheet, income statement, and statement of cash flows are highly condensed. For this reason, firms are required to provide supplemental information in the form of supporting schedules and notes. An opinion on the accuracy of the financial statements from a firm of independent public accountants must also be furnished. Depending on its country of origin, a company may also include a "management discussion and analysis" of recent performance and future prospects.

The Statement of Changes in Shareholders' Equity

There is, in fact, a fourth financial statement presented in many annual reports, although it functions more like a supporting schedule, and thus is not usually accorded the same status as the other three. This schedule, called the statement of changes in **shareholders' equity** (although it sometimes goes under different names), explains changes to all accounts in the shareholders' equity section of the balance sheet.

The Notes

In addition to the principal financial statements, companies must also provide extensive supplemental disclosures known as "notes" or "footnotes." You will see these at the back of any annual report. The importance of these notes can be seen from the statement at the bottom of each of TSMC's financial statements: "The accompanying notes are an integral part of the consolidated financial statements." This reminds us that the financial statements cannot be fully understood without reading the notes. In fact, the term "footnotes" is somewhat misleading, though widely used, because it may lead you to think that they serve the same function as footnotes in a book. This is not true because footnotes in the annual report are an indispensable part of the story. The story doesn't really hold together without them.

Most notes fall into either of two categories:

- The first type describes the accounting policies used by the company to prepare its financial statements. For example, the first note in most annual reports is a summary of key accounting principles and policies.

- The second type of note presents additional, clarifying detail about one or more financial statement line items. Examples of this type include notes that elaborate on debt balances, investments, pensions, and taxes. Companies are also expected to provide financial details on major business segments either broken down by industry or geography. TSMC reports that it operates in a single industry segment that includes integrated circuits and semiconductors. However, in its segment note, TSMC breaks down its revenues by geographic region. In 2016, the United States accounted for 64% of its revenues, followed by Asia excluding Taiwan (15%), Taiwan (13%), and the rest of the world (8%). Interestingly, in the same segment note, TSMC reveals that its two largest customers account for 28% of its sales in 2016. However, for competitive reasons, it does not identify these customers by name.

The Auditor's Opinion

Annual reports must include an opinion from an independent public accounting firm, attesting to whether or not the financial statements were correctly prepared and can therefore be relied on by investors and other parties in making decisions regarding the business. The opinion shown in Exhibit 1.4 follows a standard format, with occasional variations.

Exhibit 1-4	Independent Auditor's Report

REPORT OF INDEPENDENT REGISTERED PUBLIC ACCOUNTING FIRM

To the Board of Directors and Shareholders of
Taiwan Semiconductor Manufacturing Company Limited

We have audited the accompanying consolidated statements of financial position of Taiwan Semiconductor Manufacturing Company Limited (a Republic of China corporation) and subsidiaries (the "Company") as of December 31, 2015 and 2016, and the related consolidated statements of profit or loss and other comprehensive income, changes in equity, and cash flows for each of the three years in the period ended December 31, 2016 (all expressed in New Taiwan dollars). These financial statements are the responsibility of the Company's management. Our responsibility is to express an opinion on these financial statements based on our audits.

We conducted our audits in accordance with the standards of the Public Company Accounting Oversight Board (United States). Those standards require that we plan and perform the audit to obtain reasonable assurance about whether the financial statements are free of material misstatement. An audit includes examining, on a test basis, evidence supporting the amounts and disclosures in the financial statements. An audit also includes assessing the accounting principles used and significant estimates made by management, as well as evaluating the overall financial statement presentation. We believe that our audits provide a reasonable basis for our opinion.

In our opinion, such consolidated financial statements present fairly, in all material respects, the financial position of Taiwan Semiconductor Manufacturing Company Limited and subsidiaries as of December 31, 2015 and 2016, and the results of their operations and their cash flows for each of the three years in the period ended December 31, 2016, in conformity with International Financial Reporting Standards as issued by the International Accounting Standards Board.

Our audits also comprehended the translation of New Taiwan dollar amounts into U.S. dollar amounts and, in our opinion, such translation has been made in conformity with the basis stated in Note 3 to the consolidated financial statements. Such U.S. dollar amounts are presented solely for the convenience of the readers outside the Republic of China.

We have also audited, in accordance with the standards of the Public Company Accounting Oversight Board (United States), the Company's internal control over financial reporting as of December 31, 2016, based on the criteria established in *Internal Control — Integrated Framework (2013)* issued by the Committee of Sponsoring Organizations of the Treadway Commission and our report dated April 13, 2017 expressed an unqualified opinion on the Company's internal control over financial reporting.

/s/ Deloitte & Touche
Taipei, Taiwan
The Republic of China

April 13, 2017

The first paragraph indicates the scope of the opinion and also states that the responsibility for the financial statements rests with management. This responsibility has been reinforced by legislation in the United States (known as Sarbanes–Oxley) that requires chief executive officers and chief financial officers to certify, under oath, the truthfulness of their companies' financial statements. This means that while auditors attest to the reliability of the accounts, the ultimate responsibility rests with senior managers.[2] TSMC produces a similar declaration, signed by the two co-CEOs and the CFO that includes, among other language, the following:

> *Based on my knowledge, the financial statements, and other financial information included in this report, fairly present in all material respects the financial condition, results of operations and cash flows of the company as of, and for, the periods presented in this report.*

The second paragraph affirms that the auditor followed generally accepted auditing principles. In other words, the audit was conducted according to the standards of the auditing profession. In the case of TSMC, because its shares are traded on the New York Stock Exchange, they state that they followed auditing standards from the United States. The auditor then expresses the opinion in the third paragraph. It is here that the auditor states that the financial statements "present fairly in all material respects" the company's financial position, and results of operations for each of the years presented in the annual report. Audit standards outside the United States often use the terminology that the financial statements provide a "true and fair view" of the company.

Most opinions are unqualified, or "clean," which means that there are no exceptions, reservations, or qualifications. In effect, the auditor is telling you, the reader, that the financial statements can be trusted in making investment and other decisions related to this business. But while the overwhelming majority of audit opinions are clean, there are some exceptions.

A qualified opinion may arise because of serious uncertainties regarding the realization or valuation of assets (which can sometimes occur when companies are financially distressed), outstanding litigation, or tax liabilities that might compromise the firm's financial health. Inconsistencies between periods caused by changes in accounting rules or policy can also result in a qualified opinion.

An auditor may also disclaim an opinion (i.e., issue no opinion at all) or even issue an adverse opinion. Disclaimers may arise, for example, because of pending bankruptcy. The uncertainties regarding the truthfulness of financial statement numbers are so profound, the auditor is reluctant to issue any opinion on the financial statements. This happened to Parmalat, the Italian dairy company, after it was embroiled in a massive financial scandal. Adverse opinions are rare, because an auditor is likely to resign or be fired by a client before an adverse opinion would ever appear in a published annual report. The opinion provided by TSMC's auditor was indeed "clean" and thus fairly limited in content. This "boilerplate" approach to audit opinions has long been criticized as being too generic and not alerting users to the more subjective parts of the financial statements. Recently, global audit standards have been changed that compel the auditor to state the items in the financial statements that required more of their attention and how they designed procedures to reach their conclusion. In the United States (which governs TSMC's audits), the changes take effect in 2019, while in the United Kingdom and Ireland, they have been in effect since 2013; in much of the rest of the world, these changes took effect in 2016.

Management Discussion and Analysis

Most annual reports include a management discussion and analysis section, often called the MD&A or "review of operations". This section is an extended letter from the firm's management that summarizes the significant factors affecting the firm's operating results, financial strength, and cash flows for the past three years. It also contains an extensive discussion of business risks and forward-looking statements regarding the company's expectations for future operations, earnings, and prospects.

The review in TSMC's 2016 financial statements consists of detailed explanations for the company's performance and financial condition, with emphasis on changes from the previous year. Important events from 2016 are also discussed, including acquisitions and product development. Management contrasts financial figures from 2016 with 2015, explaining why these numbers improved or worsened. For example, management reveals that of the 12.4% growth in revenue, 9.6% is due to increased product shipments while the remainder is largely due to the depreciation of the NT$ against the currencies in which it sells its semiconductors. It also discusses the specific product where volumes increased the most (i.e., the "12-inch equivalent wafer"). Considerable attention is also given to liquidity, which is defined here as the ability of the company to obtain the cash resources it needs for growth and debt repayment.

Generally Accepted Accounting Principles: The Rules of the Game

When auditors declare that financial statements "present fairly" a company's financial condition, profitability, and cash flows, what they really mean is that the statements were prepared in accordance with Generally Accepted Accounting Principles (hereafter, GAAP). GAAP comprises the rules and principles that guide managers in the preparation of their companies' accounts. These rules provide the filter through which potentially millions of data points pass to produce the highly summarized financial statements we see in corporate annual reports.

GAAP sets the "rules of the game" under which financial statements are prepared. When these rules are implemented in good faith, the chances are high, though far from assured, that the resulting financial statements can be relied on by users to make important economic decisions regarding the business.

Here, we focus on two GAAP regimes: the one that prevails in the United States, otherwise known as US GAAP, and International Financial Reporting Standards (IFRS). Although many other accounting regimes exist around the world, capital markets have come to be dominated by these two approaches. Important differences exist between the two, but their primary objectives are the same. Moreover, there was a serious ongoing effort at convergence that would have led to a single set of global financial accounting standards. But as of this writing, that effort has stalled, meaning that for the foreseeable future, we are left with two dominant regimes instead of one.

US GAAP comes from a variety of sources, but the dominant player is the Financial Accounting Standards Board (FASB), based in Norwalk, Connecticut. The FASB is a private-sector body that is tasked with determining the appropriate financial reporting responses to an ever-changing business climate. Its official pronouncements are called "Financial Accounting Standards." In some cases, these standards are supplemented by "Interpretations" that augment or clarify key aspects of the standards.

IFRS is the product of the International Accounting Standards Boards (IASB), based in London. Since 2005, compliance with IFRS has been required for all publicly traded companies based in the European Union. It is also widely used in Asia. Today, 135 countries either require or allow the use of IFRS.

The Barriers to Understanding Financial Statements

Businesses can be complex, and if annual reports are to capture economic reality, they too must be complex. Analyzing and interpreting financial statements can be highly rewarding for readers who take the time to understand this complexity and the nature of the problems they are likely to encounter. The following discussion introduces the major barriers you can expect to face in trying to make sense of corporate financial reports.

The Volume of Data

The most obvious problem encountered by the reader of financial statements is the sheer volume of information available, especially for businesses traded on a major stock exchange. In addition to the principal financial statements, footnotes, management discussion and analysis, and auditors' reports, there are also financial filings with stock exchange and regulatory authorities (such as the Securities and Exchange Commission in the United States). The result can be a veritable mountain of information. Although capital markets run on information, the risk is that a reader can be easily overwhelmed.

A variety of analytical tools, such as financial statement ratios, exist to help readers overcome this problem. These tools are discussed in detail in later chapters.

Accounting Choice

Although GAAP and IFRS prescribe a set of rules and guidelines for preparing financial statements, they also afford corporate executives a broad range of choice. From the viewpoint of the financial statement reader, accounting choice adds greatly to the complexity of the task at hand. To some extent, this choice is a logical outcome of the diversity we observe in the business world. What might be an appropriate accounting treatment for a steel company might not be appropriate for a biotechnology firm or an Internet service provider. GAAP/IFRS must be flexible enough to accommodate all sorts of businesses and all types of business models. But even within the same industry, significant differences across companies in their accounting policies are often observed. For example, Coca-Cola's approach to translating the financial statements of its foreign subsidiaries into US dollars is different from that of PepsiCo, its major industry competitor.

To get a flavor for the nature of accounting choice, consider the following example. A machine with an expected, but still uncertain, life of five years is purchased for $500,000. For long-term assets like this, we must decide on a depreciation method. Depreciation is the process by which the cost of an asset is allocated to the future periods that will benefit from its use. The most common method is called "straight-line." Under this approach, each of the next five years (the periods expected to benefit from the use of the asset) will be assigned $100,000 of depreciation ($500,000 ÷ 5). This means that in the first year, the income statement will include $100,000 of depreciation expense. The balance sheet will show machinery with a net book value of $400,000 at the end of the year, the acquisition cost net of the depreciation charge.

But suppose we elect to use another depreciation method, as GAAP and IFRS allow us to do. For example, we may choose the "double-declining balance" method, in which depreciation is charged to the income statement in an accelerated fashion. Under this approach, we take the straight-line rate of 20% (the annual rate of depreciation on the asset) and multiply it by 2. The resulting figure, 40%, is then multiplied by the net book value of the asset at the beginning of each year to determine that year's depreciation expense. This means that depreciation in the first year is $200,000, instead of the $100,000 recognized under the straight-line method. Therefore, as a result of choosing double declining balance, depreciation expense in the first year would be $100,000 higher, and operating income $100,000 lower. In addition, the net book value of the asset at the end of the first year would be $300,000, instead of $400,000.

What this example shows is that the simple choice of one depreciation method over another can have a profound impact on both the balance sheet and the income statement. Which set of numbers is better? It's hard to say. Under some conditions, the straight-line approach may be better, but under other conditions it might not be. What's important to recognize is that both methods are allowed. Indeed, other methods are allowed too. Now imagine having to decide how all of the company's long-term assets are to be depreciated. Further, note that the useful lives are not known with certainty, and thus are another management estimate (five years in the example above). Also, management must assess if it will sell the asset when it is done using it (say a new airplane by a premium airline that is eventually sold to a low cost airline). In this case management estimates a "salvage value" and does not depreciate the asset below this amount. Now imagine the range of choices offered to corporate executives in how they measure other balance sheet items – or how they measure any transaction that arises in the normal course of their business.

Quite simply, differences in accounting choice can yield huge differences in financial statement numbers. One of the ways that a reader copes with this challenge is by carefully scrutinizing the notes to the financial statements.

In most annual reports, the first note summarizes the significant principles and policies chosen by the company's managers, helping the reader to understand the context under which the financial statements were prepared and key transactions measured. These disclosures allow analysts and other interested parties to compare a company's accounting policies with industry competitors and to make judgments on the quality of the numbers produced in the annual report.

Earnings Management

Accounting choice doesn't just make financial statements more complicated. It also provides a powerful weapon for managers who wish to mislead the capital markets, for whatever motive. Accounting policy requires judgment, and whenever there is scope for judgment, there is also scope for manipulation.

"Earnings management" is the term commonly used to describe efforts by corporate managers to distort or bias their companies' reported results. "Creative accounting" is also used. Both terms imply a conscious effort by managers to mislead readers of financial statements.

Although the opportunities for earnings management are practically limitless, the most serious efforts fall into either of two categories: faulty revenue recognition, and the improper recognition of losses and expenses. The Enron fiasco brought to light another area prone to mischief: off-balance-sheet financing. This accounting game also featured prominently in the global financial meltdown of 2008.

Incompleteness

TSMC was one of the world's first large-scale manufacturers that specialized in only making semiconductors. As a consumer, you may not have the awareness of their branded products. Yet equipment manufacturers, such as Apple, and other semiconductor companies, such as Intel, certainly are. These companies are two customers of TSMC. But while their products and customer relationships obviously carry great value for TSMC, you won't see them in the company's balance sheet. This fact may seem odd given that these products and customers may be the most valuable resources the company has.

The above example shows that important attributes of a business, attributes with potentially profound effects on financial performance, may not always find their way into corporate balance sheets, at least not directly.

Reliability is a key characteristic of financial statements. To be reliable, financial statements should be verifiable: auditors must be able to check the numbers to ensure an acceptable degree of accuracy. This is not to say that all numbers have to be perfectly accurate; such a standard is not feasible. But it does require at least some degree of objectivity, otherwise there is little for the auditors to observe and verify. In the example of TSMC, the company's products are well known by the electronics companies it sells to, and it has a significant market share. Yet such brand recognition will not be reported as an asset - unless it has been purchased via the acquisition of an entire company or an individual product line. In other words, intangibles acquired from other companies are included, but internally generated intangibles are not.

Sophisticated readers of financial statements are fully aware of this inconsistency, and of the need to cast a wide net when gathering information about a company. In short, they understand that not everything you need to know about a company in order to value its shares or to assess its creditworthiness is revealed in the accounts.

KEY LESSONS FROM THE CHAPTER

- There are many users of financial statements including: investors, bankers, suppliers, customers, tax authorities, trade unions, competitors, courts of law, government regulators, and prospective employees. Capital providers (i.e., shareholders, bankers, bondholders, and prospective investors) are arguably the most important constituencies.

- Although financial accounting is not targeted to the needs of corporate managers per se, financial statements are the outside world's "window" on the company. Therefore, managers need to know what signals are being sent to investors about their companies and how those signals are interpreted. Otherwise, their companies will be at a competitive disadvantage in the global capital markets.

- The notes at the back of the annual report complement the three principal financial statements – the balance sheet, the income statement, and the statement of cash flows – and provide extensive supplemental disclosures. The notes describe the accounting policies used by the company and present additional clarifying detail about financial statement line items.

- Annual reports must include an opinion from an independent public accounting firm, attesting to whether or not the financial statements were correctly prepared.

- US companies prepare their financial statements in accordance with Generally Accepted Accounting Principles (GAAP). GAAP sets the "rules of the game" under which financial statements are prepared. Most non-US companies prepare their financial statements in accordance with International Financial Reporting Standards (IFRS).

- A serious effort to achieve convergence between US GAAP and IFRS made some progress, but has recently. Convergence between the two financial reporting regimes is not imminent.

KEY TERMS AND CONCEPTS FROM THE CHAPTER

Investors	Statement of cash flows	Audit opinions	Generally Accepted	International Financial
Creditors	Shareholders' equity	Management	Accounting	Reporting Standards
Balance sheet	Notes to the financial	discussion and	Principles (GAAP)	(IFRS)
Income statement	statements	analysis		Earnings management

QUESTIONS

1. The balance sheet (or statement of financial position) is often referred to as a "snapshot." Why?

2. If the balance sheet is a snapshot, how would you describe the income statement and the statement of cash flows?

3. Why must the statement of financial position (i.e., the balance sheet) balance?

4. What is the purpose of the auditor's opinion?

5. What is Sarbanes–Oxley, and how has it affected corporate financial reporting?

6. Describe the limitations of the financial reporting process.

7. Financial accounting = Economic truth + error + manipulation. Explain.

8. Can you think of instances in which the creation of bias or error in the financial statements might be justified?

9. Describe how the three principal financial statements are linked.

10. What role is played by the notes in the financial reporting process?

11. What is the primary purpose of the statement of changes in shareholders' equity?

12. What is meant by the term "accounting choice," and why is the concept so important in financial accounting?

13. What is meant by the term "earnings management?"

PROBLEMS

1.1 Balance Sheet Terminology

Below is the statement of financial position (balance sheet) for the global brewing company, AB InBev. Identify the major differences in format and terminology between this balance sheet and the one introduced in this chapter for TSMC.

Consolidated Statement of Financial Position

As at 31 December Million US dollar	2011	2010
Assets		
Noncurrent assets		
Property, plant and equipment	16,022	15,893

As at 31 December Million US dollar	2011	2010
Goodwill	51,302	52,493
Intangible assets	23,818	23,359
Investments in associates	6,696	7,295
Investment securities	244	243
Deferred tax assets	673	744
Employee benefits	10	13
Trade and other receivables	1,339	1,700
	100,04	101,745
Current assets		
Investment securities	103	641
Inventories	2,466	2,409
Income tax receivable	312	366
Trade and other receivables	4,121	4,638
Cash and cash equivalents	5,320	4,511
Assets held for sale	1	32
	12,323	12,597
Total assets	112,427	114,342
Equity and Liabilities		
Equity	1,734	1,733
Issued capital	17,557	17,535
Share premium	381	2,335
Reserves	17,820	13,656
Retained earnings	37,492	35,259
Equity attributable to equity holders of AB InBev	3,552	3,540
Noncontrolling interest	41,044	38,799
Noncurrent liabilities	34,598	41,961
Interest-bearing loans and borrowings	3,440	2,746
Employee benefits	11,279	11,909
Deferred tax liabilities	1,548	2,295
Trade and other payables	874	912
Provisions	51,739	59,823
Current liabilities	8	14
Bank overdrafts	5,559	2,919
Interest-bearing loans and borrowings	449	478
Income tax payable	13,337	12,071
Trade and other payables	241	238
Provisions	19,644	15,720
Total equity and liabilities	112,427	114,342

1.2 Understanding Balance Sheet Relationships

Stora Enso is a large pulp and paper company headquartered in Finland. The company uses IFRS and reports its results in millions of euros (€). Compute the missing balance sheet amounts for each of the three years.

	2011	2010	2009
Current assets	€4,610	€4,494	?[b]
Noncurrent assets	?	8,543	?
Total liabilities	?	?	?
Total assets	?	?	€11,593
Current liabilities	2,786	2,569	2,619
Noncurrent liabilities	4,253	?	?
Total shareholders' equity	?	?	5,183
Share capital	?	3,150	?
Retained earnings	3,301	?[a]	1,200
Total liabilities and shareholders' equity	12,999	?	?

[a] Net income for 2010 is €766 and dividends are €158.
[b] Current assets – Current liabilities = €1144.

1.3 Interpreting an Auditor's Opinion

Excerpts are provided below from the auditor's opinion in the 2011 Annual Report of Creative Technology, Ltd., a Singapore-based consumer electronics company.

Required

a. Describe the audit opinion rendered by PwC. Is this opinion "unqualified" or "qualified?"

b. What is meant by the term "true and fair?"

c. What is the economic significance of this opinion for investors and other interested parties?

d. In what ways does management's responsibility for the financial statements differ from that of the auditor's?

We have audited the accompanying financial statements of Creative Technology Ltd. (the "Company") and its subsidiaries (the "Group") … which comprise the consolidated balance sheet of the Group and the balance sheet of the Company as at 30 June 2011, the consolidated statement of comprehensive income, the consolidated statement of changes in equity and the consolidated statement of cash flows of the Group for the financial year then ended, and a summary of significant accounting policies and other explanatory information.

Management's responsibility for the financial statements

Management is responsible for the preparation of financial statements that give a true and fair view in accordance with the provisions of the Singapore Companies Act (the "Act") and Singapore Financial Reporting Standards, and for devising and maintaining a system of internal accounting controls sufficient to provide a reasonable assurance that assets are safeguarded against loss from unauthorized use or disposition, that transactions are properly authorized and that they are recorded as necessary to permit the preparation of true and fair profit and loss accounts and balance sheets and to maintain accountability of assets.

Auditor's responsibility

Our responsibility is to express an opinion on these financial statements based on our audit. We conducted our audit in accordance with Singapore Standards on Auditing. Those Standards require that we comply with ethical requirements and plan and perform the audit to obtain reasonable assurance about whether the financial statements are free from material misstatement.

An audit involves performing procedures to obtain audit evidence about the amounts and disclosures in the financial statements. The procedures selected depend on the auditor's judgment, including the assessment of the risks of material misstatement of the financial statements, whether due to fraud or error. In making those risk assessments, the auditor considers internal controls relevant to the entity's preparation of financial statements that give a true and fair view in order to design audit procedures that are appropriate in the circumstances, but not for the purpose of expressing an opinion on the effectiveness of the entity's internal controls. An audit also includes evaluating the appropriateness of accounting policies used and the reasonableness of accounting estimates made by management, as well as evaluating the overall presentation of the financial statements.

We believe that the audit evidence we have obtained is sufficient and appropriate to provide a basis for our audit opinion.

Opinion

In our opinion, the consolidated financial statements of the Group and the balance sheet of the Company are properly drawn up in accordance with the provisions of the Act and Singapore Financial Reporting Standards so as to give a true and fair view of the state of affairs of the Group and of the Company as at 30 June 2011, and the results, changes in equity and cash flows of the Group for the financial year ended on that date.

PricewaterhouseCoopers LLP
Public Accountants and Certified Public Accountants
Singapore

Case Study

1-1 Apple: An Introduction to Financial Statement Analysis

Apple is a global leader in the computing industry, with an emphasis on personal computing, mobile communication devices, and portable digital music players. It designs, manufactures, and markets both hardware and software. At the time of this writing (autumn 2012), Apple is the largest company in history in terms of market capitalization (i.e., the market value of the company's equity).

As recently as the late 1990s, however, Apple was perceived as mainly a niche player in the personal computer business, where the emphasis was on commoditized, low-margin products. The return of Steve Jobs, ousted in the 1980s from the company he cofounded, is now legendary in corporate history. He is credited for refocusing the company on the customer experience with products that emphasize not only performance and technology, but also aesthetics.

The excerpts from the company's financial statements included in this case will give you a summary view of recent financial performance. As you review these disclosures, think about what information is *excluded*, and how the absence of this information affects the reports' ability to communicate the true value of Apple.

Required

Balance sheet

a. What was the magnitude and direction of the change to total assets for 2010?

b. What was the magnitude and direction of the change to total liabilities for 2010?

c. What was the magnitude and direction of the change to total shareholders' equity for 2010?

d. Verify that the sum of your answers to (b) and (c) equals your answer to (a).

e. What specific accounts explain most of the change to total assets?

f. Based on your own experience, think about what makes Apple a valuable company. Does this "asset" that you've imagined appear on Apple's balance sheet? Are you

(Continued)

satisfied that the balance sheet accurately reflects this value? Why or why not?

Income statement ("consolidated statement of operations")

a. What was the magnitude and direction of the change to net sales?

b. What was the magnitude and direction of the change to net income?

c. Do the changes above seem consistent with the changes in total assets you calculated previously?

d. Based on your own experience, think about the various product lines that generate these revenues (i.e., "sales") for Apple. Do you see the revenue from the individual product lines on the statement? Are you satisfied that the income statement accurately reflects these revenues? Why or why not?

Statement of cash flows

a. What are the names of the three subsections that present the different sources of cash flow for the year?

b. Note that net income is the first figure used in calculating cash generated by operating activities. How does net income compare to cash generated by operating activities?

c. What does Apple appear to be doing with the cash that it generates from its day-to-day operations? (Hint: review investing activities.)

d. Does Apple appear to have significant financing activities to report?

The auditor's opinion

a. Describe Ernst & Young's role as Apple's external auditor?

b. How useful is this opinion in helping an investor to value Apple's shares?

Apple's financial statements: Consolidated statements of operations (in millions, except share amounts which are reflected in thousands and per share amounts), three years ended September 25, 2010

	2010	2009	2008
Net sales	$65,225	$42,905	$37,491
Cost of sales	39,541	25,683	24,294
Gross margin	25,684	17,222	13,197

	2010	2009	2008
Operating expenses			
Research and development	1,782	1,333	1,109
Selling, general and administrative	5,517	4,149	3,761
Total operating expenses	7,299	5,482	4,870
Operating income	18,385	11,740	8,327
Other income and expense	155	326	620
Income before provision for income taxes	18,540	12,066	8,947
Provision for income taxes	4,527	3,831	2,828
Net income	$14,013	$8,235	$6,119
Earnings per common share			
Basic	$15.41	$9.22	$6.94
Diluted	$15.15	$9.08	$6.78
Shares used in computing earnings per share			
Basic	909,461	893,016	881,592
Diluted	924,712	907,005	902,139

Consolidated balance sheets (in millions, except share amounts)

	September 25, 2010	September 26, 2009
Assets		
Current assets		
Cash and cash equivalents	$11,261	$5,263
Short-term marketable securities	14,359	18,201
Accounts receivable, less allowances of $55 and $52, respectively	5,510	3,361
Inventories	1,051	455
Deferred tax assets	1,636	1,135

	September 25, 2010	September 26, 2009
Vendor nontrade receivables	4,414	1,696
Other current assets	3,447	1,444
Total current assets	41,678	31,555
Long-term marketable securities	25,391	10,528
Property, plant, and equipment, net	4,768	2,954
Goodwill	741	206
Acquired intangible assets, net	342	247
Other assets	2,263	2,011
Total assets	$75,183	$47,501
Liabilities and Shareholders' Equity		
Current liabilities		
Accounts payable	$12,015	$5,601
Accrued expenses	5,723	3,852
Deferred revenue	2,984	2,053
Total current liabilities	20,722	11,506
Deferred revenue – noncurrent	1,139	853
Other noncurrent liabilities	5,531	3,502
Total liabilities	27,392	15,861
Commitments and contingencies		
Shareholders' equity:		
Common stock, no par value; 1 800 000 000 shares authorized; 915 970 050 and 899 805 500 shares issued and		
outstanding, respectively	10,668	8,210
Retained earnings	37,169	23,353
Accumulated other comprehensive (loss)/income	(46)	77
Total shareholders' equity	47,791	31,640
Total liabilities and shareholders' equity	$75,183	$47,501

Consolidated statements of cash flows (in millions), three years ended September 25, 2010

	2010	2009	2008
Cash and cash equivalents, beginning of the year	$5,263	$11,875	$9,352
Operating activities:			
Net income	14,013	8,235	6,119
Adjustments to reconcile net income to cash generated by operating activities:			
Depreciation, amortization, and accretion	1,027	734	496
Stock-based compensation expense	879	710	516
Deferred income tax expense	1,440	1,040	398
Loss on disposition of property, plant and equipment	24	26	22
Changes in operating assets and liabilities:			
Accounts receivable, net	(2,142)	(939)	(785)
Inventories	(596)	54	(163)
Vendor non-trade receivables	(2,718)	586	110
Other current assets	(1,514)	163	(384)
Other assets	(120)	(902)	289
Accounts payable	6,307	92	596
Deferred revenue	1,217	521	718
Other liabilities	778	(161)	1,664
Cash generated by operating activities	18,595	10,159	9,596
Investing activities:			
Purchases of marketable securities	(57,793)	(46,724)	(22,965)
Proceeds from maturities of marketable securities	24,930	19,790	11,804
Proceeds from sales of marketable securities	21,788	10,888	4,439
Purchases of other long-term investments	(18)	(101)	(38)
Payments made in connection with business acquisitions, net of cash acquired	(638)	0	(220)

(Continued)

	2010	2009	2008
Payments for acquisition of property, plant, and equipment	(2,005)	(1,144)	(1,091)
Payments for acquisition of intangible assets	(116)	(69)	(108)
Other	(2)	(74)	(10)
Cash used in investing activities	(13,854)	(17,434)	(8,189)
Financing activities:			
Proceeds from issuance of common stock	912	475	483
Excess tax benefits from stock-based compensation	751	270	757
Taxes paid related to net share settlement of equity awards	(406)	(82)	(124)
Cash generated by financing activities	1,257	663	1,116
Increase/(decrease) in cash and cash equivalents	5,998	(6,612)	2,523
Cash and cash equivalents, end of the year	$11,261	$5,263	$11,875
Supplemental cash flow disclosure:			
Cash paid for income taxes, net	$2,697	$2,997	$1,267

Report of Ernst & Young LLP, Independent Registered Public Accounting Firm

The Board of Directors and Shareholders of Apple Inc.

We have audited the accompanying consolidated balance sheets of Apple Inc. as of September 25, 2010 and September 26, 2009, and the consolidated statements of operations, shareholders' equity and cash flows for the years then ended. These financial statements are the responsibility of the Company's management. Our responsibility is to express an opinion on these financial statements based on our audits.

We conducted our audits in accordance with the standards of the Public Company Accounting Oversight Board (United States). Those standards require that we plan and perform the audit to obtain reasonable assurance about whether the financial statements are free of material misstatement. An audit includes examining, on a test basis, evidence supporting the amounts and disclosures in the financial statements. An audit also includes assessing the accounting principles used and significant estimates made by management, as well as evaluating the overall financial statement presentation. We believe that our audits provide a reasonable basis for our opinion.

In our opinion, the financial statements referred to above present fairly, in all material respects, the consolidated financial position of Apple Inc. at September 25, 2010 and September 26, 2009, and the consolidated results of its operations and its cash flows for the years then ended, in conformity with US generally accepted accounting principles.

We also have audited, in accordance with the standards of the Public Company Accounting Oversight Board (United States), Apple Inc.'s internal control over financial reporting as of September 25, 2010, based on criteria established in *Internal Control – Integrated Framework* issued by the Committee of Sponsoring Organizations of the Treadway Commission and our report dated October 27, 2010 expressed an unqualified opinion thereon.

/s/ Ernst & Young LLP

San Jose, California
October 27, 2010

Case Study

1-2 PepsiCo: Communicating Financial Performance*

The Chairman's letter to the shareholders from PepsiCo's 2007 Annual Report is presented below.

Delivering Performance with Purpose in 2007

Dear Shareholders:

We have titled this year's annual report "Performance with Purpose: The Journey Continues." That's because in 2007 PepsiCo made great progress toward the long-term corporate objectives we set for ourselves last year: To achieve business and financial success while leaving a positive imprint on society.

Once more, our extraordinary associates around the world delivered terrific performance, and I am delighted to share with you the following 2007 financial results:

• Net revenue grew 12%, roughly three times the rate of global GDP growth.

*Source: 2007 PepsiCo Annual Report

- Division operating profit grew 10%.
- Earnings per share grew 13%.
- Total return to shareholders was 26%.
- Return on invested capital was 29%.
- Cash flow from operations was $6.9 billion.

In 2007 PepsiCo took important steps to support future growth.

What makes me particularly proud is that our 2007 performance was strong – not just measured by these short-term metrics – but also with the long-term equally in mind:

- We increased capital expenditures in plant and equipment worldwide to enable growth of core brands and expand into new platforms such as baked and crisp-bread snacks and non-carbonated beverages.
- We added several tuck-in acquisitions in key markets and segments, and we further expanded our successful coffee and tea joint ventures.
- We created the Chief Scientific Officer position to ensure our technical capabilities keep pace with increasingly sophisticated consumer demand; and we funded incremental investment to explore breakthrough R&D opportunities.
- We maintained focus on building next-generation IT capabilities with Project One Up, to support our long-term growth prospects worldwide.

Our brands once again demonstrated competitive strength.

On the ground, in cities and towns around the world, good brand strategies were implemented with operational excellence. I'd like to share a few notable examples of the big marketplace wins we enjoyed in 2007:

- Our carbonated soft drink and savory snack brands gained market share in the United States and in many of our top international markets.
- In the United Kingdom, Baked Walkers crisps was named "New Product of the Year" by *Marketing Week* magazine.
- SunChips snacks delivered double-digit growth in the United States as a result of great, innovative marketing and in-store execution.
- 7UP H2Oh! was our fastest-growing brand in value and volume share in Brazil in its launch year.
- Pepsi Max came of age as a global brand, with outstanding performance in the United States as Diet Pepsi Max, after successes in Northern Europe and Australia and 2007 launches across Asia.

- PepsiCo beverage brands crossed the $1 billion mark in Russia retail sales.
- We posted double-digit volume growth in China beverages and high-single-digit beverage volume growth in India.

And we did all of this while battling increased commodity inflation and more macroeconomic volatility than in previous years.

Required

In her review of PepsiCo's performance in 2007, Indra Nooyi, PepsiCo's Chairman and CEO, claims that, "Net revenue grew by 12%, roughly three times the rate of global GDP growth." What message is she trying to convey in this statement? After reviewing the disclosure "Results of Operation – Division Review," which is found in the notes to the financial statements, do you agree with Mrs. Nooyi's assertions about PepsiCo's growth?

Consolidated Statement of Income

PepsiCo, Inc. and Subsidiaries: Fiscal years ended December 29, 2007, December 30, 2006, and December 31, 2005

(in millions except per share amounts)	2007	2006	2005
Net Revenue	$39,474	$35,137	$32,562
Cost of sales	18,038	15,762	14,176
Selling, general and administrative expenses	14,208	12,711	12,252
Amortization of intangible assets	58	162	150
Operating Profit	7,170	6,502	5,984
Bottling equity income	560	553	495
Interest expense	(224)	(239)	(256)
Interest income	125	173	159
Income before Income Taxes	7,631	6,989	6,382
Provision for Income Taxes	1,973	1,347	2,304
Net Income	$5,658	$5,642	$4,078
Net Income per Common Share			
Basic	$3.48	$3.42	$2.43
Diluted	$3.41	$3.34	$2.39

(Continued)

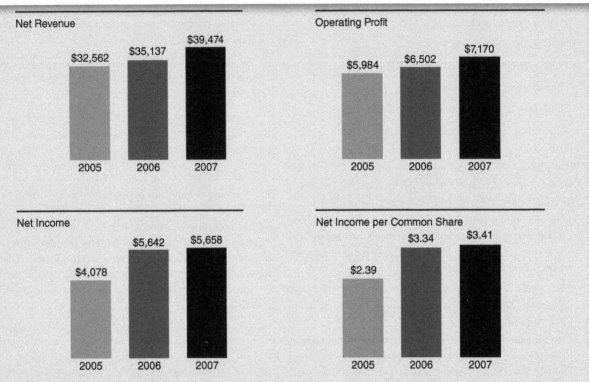

Net Revenue

2005	2006	2007
$32,562	$35,137	$39,474

Operating Profit

2005	2006	2007
$5,984	$6,502	$7,170

Net Income

2005	2006	2007
$4,078	$5,642	$5,658

Net Income per Common Share

2005	2006	2007
$2.39	$3.34	$3.41

Results of Operations—Division Review

The results and discussions below are based on how our Chief Executive Officer monitors the performance of our divisions.

	FLNA	PBNA	PI	QFNA	Total
Net Revenue, 2007	$11,586	$10,230	$15,798	$1,860	$39,474
Net Revenue, 2006	$10,844	$9,565	$12,959	$1,769	$35,137
% Impact of:					
Volume[a]	3%	(2)%	7%	2%	3%
Effective net pricing[b]	4	6	3.5	3	4
Foreign exchange	0.5	–	6	1	2
Acquisitions/divestitures	–	2	6	–	3
% Change[c]	7%	7%	22%	5%	12%
Net Revenue, 2006	$10,844	$9,565	$12,959	$1,769	$35,137
Net Revenue, 2005	$10,322	$9,146	$11,376	$1,718	$32,562
% Impact of:					
Volume[a]	1%	3%	6%	1%	3%
Effective net pricing[b]	3	1	4	2	3
Foreign exchange	0.5	–	1	1	1
Acquisitions/divestitures	0.5	–	3	–	1
% Change[c]	5%	5%	14%	3%	8%

(a) Excludes the impact of acquisitions and divestitures. For PBNA and PI, volume growth varies from the amounts disclosed in the following divisional discussions due primarily to non-consolidated joint venture volume and temporary timing differences between BCS and CSE. Our net revenue for PBNA and PI excludes non-consolidated joint venture volume and is based on CSE.
(b) Include the year-over-year impact of discrete pricing actions, sales incentive activities and mix resulting from selling varying products in different package sizes and in different countries.
(c) Amounts may not sum due to rounding.

NOTES

1. The balance sheet is also known as the statement of financial position. Although the latter is the official term, business people everywhere continue to use the term "balance sheet." We will do likewise in this book.

2. In some countries, such as the United Kingdom, principal responsibility for the financial statements rests with the board of directors.

2

The Balance Sheet and Income Statement

In Chapter 1, we introduced the three principal financial statements – the balance sheet, income statement, and statement of cash flows – and the role they play in the financial reporting process. In this chapter, we discuss the first two statements in greater depth, focusing on the statements from Taiwan Semiconductor's 2016 Annual Report. (Cash flows are examined in Chapter 5.)

A Further Look at the Balance Sheet

The balance sheet reports the financial position of a company at a particular point in time. By "financial position," we mean the resources available to managers to run the business (i.e., "assets") and the financing that made the acquisition of those resources possible (liabilities and shareholders' equity).

In Exhibit 1.1, you will have noticed the word "consolidated" at the top of TSMC's balance sheet. This means that the document before you represents not just the balance sheet of "Taiwan Semiconductor Manufacturing Company Limited", the parent company, but also the balance sheet of any entity controlled by the parent. It's not the balance sheet of any one company, but rather that of a group of companies known to the investing world as "TSMC."

To understand this idea, imagine that you buy shares in the company. What do you get for your investment? Not only do you obtain ownership rights over the legal entity whose shares you are buying, but also you gain indirect ownership rights over any business or entity effectively controlled by that company. This means that when you want to know the financial position of TSMC, it's not the balance sheet of the parent that you care about, but rather the balance sheet that includes all companies within the TSMC Group. In fact, the standard practice in Europe and much of Asia is to refer to consolidated financial statements as "group accounts."

This example introduces us to an important concept in corporate financial reporting: *economic substance is more important than legal form*. Consider the aforementioned example. There is no legal entity anywhere that can rightly claim ownership of the TSMC Group balance sheet because the document represents a consolidation, or aggregation, of many balance sheets. For a company of this size, the number of individual balance sheets included in the consolidated statement can easily run into the hundreds. But the consolidated balance sheet does correspond to an economic entity, namely, what you as an investor get when you buy shares in, or lend money to, this company. And from the investor's point of view, this economic perspective is more useful than the legal perspective. To put it another way, although the shareholders of TSMC own shares only in the parent company, the parent's financial statements will tell them little about what they are really getting from their ownership interest. For this, they need consolidated accounts.

TSMC's balance sheets are dated 31 December 2015 and 2016. This tells us that financial position is measured at a specific point in time. In fact, balance sheets are sometimes referred to as "snapshots" in that they reflect financial position on a particular date; they say nothing directly about what the company did in the previous year. To find out how the company performed over a period of time, we need to look to the income statement and the statement of cash flows.

Assets

At the end of 2016, TSMC reported total assets of NT$1,886 billion (see Exhibit 1.1). This does not mean that the company's assets were worth this much. The market, or fair, value of a company's assets can be less than, or greater than, their balance sheet value. This divergence occurs for two reasons:

- Many assets, such as land and buildings, are recorded at their acquisition, or historical, cost (i.e., what the company paid for the assets when they were acquired). Over time, these costs can sharply diverge from market values. This is particularly true for real estate. In some countries, companies are permitted periodically to restate real estate to market values. This treatment is permitted, though not required, under International Financial Reporting Standards (IFRS). American companies are constrained by the "historical cost rule," at least for nonfinancial assets. This is the valuation principle that says that assets should appear on the balance sheet at the price paid for them (historical or acquisition cost), less depreciation (if applicable). For property, plant, and equipment, they deviate from this rule only when the value of assets is impaired (i.e., fair value is significantly less than acquisition cost).

- Some assets (especially those of an intangible nature) might not even appear on a balance sheet and, therefore, will not be reflected in total assets. For example, TSMC's intellectual capital – arguably one of its most valuable assets – is missing from the balance sheet. Most intangibles appear on balance sheets only when acquired from other firms. This rule permits a reasonably objective valuation of the asset, but in knowledge-intensive companies, important assets are left out. Although this treatment may seem inconsistent (reporting assets only when bought from other firms, and ignoring them if created internally), it is important to recognize the role it plays in causing a divergence between the book (or balance sheet) value of assets and what they are really worth.

Current Assets

Current assets are short-term assets. An asset is short term if we expect to consume it or convert it into cash within one year or one operating cycle, whichever is longer. "Operating cycle" refers to the process of converting raw materials into finished products, selling them, and collecting cash from customers. In the case of TSMC, this includes the process of purchasing inputs, for example, silicon, from its suppliers; directing its employees to use production facilities to manufacture semiconductors; engaging a sales force to sell the finished product to manufacturers of electronics; and finally, collecting cash from the sales. For the overwhelming majority of businesses, TSMC included, the amount of time required for this cycle to turn is less than one year. Therefore, for TSMC, the criterion for "current" is one year.

Total current assets at the end of 2016 are NT$818 billion. One way to interpret this figure is that it represents the sum of all TSMC's assets that (1) were already in the form of cash, or

(2) were expected to be consumed or converted into cash some time in 2017. All other assets are classified as "noncurrent."

TSMC follows the American convention, also used in Canada and Japan, of listing current assets in descending order of liquidity ("liquidity" refers to the speed and ease with which an item can be converted into cash):

- Because it is already in the form of cash, cash is the most "current" or liquid of all assets and is the first to appear in the balance sheet.

- "Financial assets" are comprised of financial securities held for short-term, cash management purposes. Government bond investments are common examples.

- "Notes and accounts receivable" are the amounts owed by the company's customers.

- "Inventories" reflect finished goods that TSMC has manufactured, as well as raw materials and partially completed products. While these are "current" in that they are expected to be sold within the next year, they are less liquid than receivables as it will take the company longer to convert these assets into cash.

- "Other current assets" consist mainly of prepaid expenses, such as rent and insurance. These are examples of current assets that will not be converted into cash, but rather are expected to be consumed in the short term.

Noncurrent (Long-Term) Assets

Most of TSMC's noncurrent assets fall into three broad categories:

- Investments ("other financial assets")

- Property, plant and equipment

- Intangibles (including "goodwill").

"Investments" are those that management intends to hold for the long term, including securities in other firms. Some of these investments might represent excess cash, while others may be more strategic in nature. For example, a company might acquire shares of stock in one of its suppliers to ensure continued availability of raw materials. In TSMC's case, the category "Investments accounted for using the equity method" reflects companies where TSMC holds a stake between 20 and 50%, which gives them significant influence, but not control. We discuss this issue in detail in Chapter 17.

"Property, plant and equipment" (PP&E) are tangible, long-term assets used in a firm's operations over a period of years and generally not acquired for resale. This category includes land, buildings, machinery, equipment, vehicles, and computers.

TSMC records all such assets in the balance sheet at acquisition cost, net of accumulated depreciation. All tangible assets, apart from land, are depreciated because their service potential (i.e., their contribution to the firm's operations) gradually erodes over time. The notes to the company's financial statements reveal that plant and equipment at cost was NT$2,773 billion at the end of 2016. Accumulated depreciation, which represents all depreciation ever recognized on any asset still owned by the company, was NT$1,775 billion. This amount is offset against the acquisition cost to yield the net amount of NT$998 billion that you see on the balance sheet. This amount is sometimes called "net book value."

Accumulated depreciation is an example of a contra-account, in that its balance is offset against that of another account to yield a net amount that goes into the balance sheet total. Allowance for uncollectible accounts is another common example. Although we don't see any mention of this account in TSMC's balance sheet, you can be sure it's there. The company reports NT$128 billion of accounts receivable at the end of 2016. Technically, this is not the amount of cash owed by the company's customers at that date, but rather the amount of cash owed that management believes will actually be paid. To illustrate, if we are owed €500,000 by our customers, but believe that only €460,000 will be collected, the balance sheet total should reflect the latter number. We would arrive at that figure by netting an allowance for uncollectable accounts of €40,000 (the contra-asset) against the €500,000 of gross receivables. For TSMC, the allowance for doubtful accounts had a balance of NT$480 million, meaning that the gross amount of receivables owed to TSMC at the end of 2016 was NT$129 billion, or NT$128.5 billion ("net" receivables) + NT$0.5 billion.

"Intangible assets" are resources, apart from financial assets such as investments, that do not have any physical substance. Common examples include patents, copyrights, customer lists, brand names, and goodwill. The typical practice employed by most companies is that intangibles do not appear on balance sheets unless a market price has been paid for them. As a result, intangibles that are developed in-house typically are not included (with some exceptions), while intangibles that are bought from other firms are.

The term "goodwill" is often taken to represent reputation, management quality, and other qualitative aspects of a business firm that give rise to value but that cannot be directly observed and separately measured. But like most other intangibles, goodwill is not recognized unless it is bought. And it cannot be bought unless there is an acquisition of one company by another. Accountants assume that goodwill is acquired any time the purchase price for a company is greater than the sum of the fair value of all other assets (tangible, intangible, and financial), net of the fair value of the target company's debt. For example, if a company's assets (apart from goodwill) have a value of €10 million on the date it is acquired, and its debts have a fair value of €1.5 million, a purchase price of €12 million would require the buyer to recognize €3.5 million of goodwill [€12m – (€10m – €1.5m)]. TSMC combines its Goodwill account with other intangibles to report a single "Intangible assets" line on the balance sheet in the amount of NT$14 billion. According to the notes, approximately 41% of this amount relates to technology that TSMC has purchased from third parties via patents or licensing fees.

TSMC reports other noncurrent assets, including long-term financial assets and deferred tax assets. We will discuss deferred taxes later in the chapter.

Liabilities

A liability arises when a firm receives benefits and in exchange promises to pay the provider of those benefits a reasonably definite amount at a reasonably definite future date. Broadly speaking, liabilities fall into four broad categories:

- current operating liabilities
- debt ("financial liabilities")
- provisions
- deferred tax liabilities

Current Liabilities

Just as there are current assets, there are also current liabilities. These are obligations that must be paid within one year, or one operating cycle, whichever is longer. In the case of TSMC, any liability listed as current as of the end of 2016 will have to be paid sometime in 2017.

TSMC has financial debt, funds borrowed from banks, bond investors or other lenders, which must be repaid with interest. The lenders in this case are debt investors in TSMC and the amounts owed are both current and noncurrent liabilities. In the current section we see borrowings that were for less than one year at inception reported as "Short-term loans". Also under current liabilities are "Long-term liabilities current portion." These are borrowings that initially were to be repaid beyond one year, and now time has elapsed and the maturity date is within a year. "Accounts payable" (also known as "trade payables") shows the amount owed by the company to its suppliers.

In addition to accounts payable, TSMC lists amounts owed to suppliers of labor (i.e., employees) for work completed in 2016 but not yet paid for as "Salary and bonus payable." They also distinguish a payable to their suppliers of long-term assets as "Payables to contractors and equipment suppliers."

Tax liabilities appear twice on the balance sheet. The difference between the two accounts is based on when the tax payments are due. Some payments, classified as "Income tax payable", are due within the next year. The rest are due later and classified as "Deferred income tax liabilities" in the noncurrent section.

"Provisions capture a broad range of obligations that a firm may have to other parties. For example, suppose a company decides to close some of its facilities over the next two years. When companies restructure like this, they incur significant shutdown costs, such as the redundancy payments that must be made to employees. Accounting rules require firms to estimate what these shutdown costs might be in the period in which the decision is made, and to then recognize in that period a loss the income statement and a liability on the balance sheet. A firm does not wait until the actual payments are made to employees and other parties before acknowledging the financial effects of the restructuring decision. Other common sources of provisions include the cost of environmental cleanup and litigation. Provisions can either be current or noncurrent, depending on when the payments are expected to occur. In TSMC's case, they expect to honor all of their provisions within the next year. Hence, they are classified as current liabilities.

The final current liabilities account results from miscellaneous expenses that have been incurred by the firm but not yet paid, for example, marketing costs or rent on facilities. TSMC classifies these as "Accrued expenses and other current liabilities."

"Bonds payable and long-term bank loans" indicate how much the company owes to holders of debt instruments issued in the capital markets. Because these are noncurrent, they are not expected to be paid until 2018 or later.

"Net defined benefit liability" represents the retirement benefits earned by employees of TSMC that have not yet been funded.

"Guarantee deposits" represents payments made by customers for products or services not yet delivered. For example, a mobile phone manufacturer may want to ensure a supply of integrated circuits if they plan on ramping up the manufacture of a popular model. To ensure supply, they prepay TSMC. TMSC is then obligated to deliver the product on demand. This account is also referred to as "deferred revenue", "unearned revenue", or "advances from customers."

Shareholders' Equity

Shareholders' equity comprises the final section of the balance sheet. This section reports on the net amounts invested in the firm by its owners. Owners invest in their businesses in two ways: directly and indirectly.

Direct Investment

This occurs when investors contribute cash or other consideration in exchange for shares of stock that represent ownership stakes in the business. A long-standing convention in some countries, such as the United States, is to report this investment in two separate accounts:

- one that represents the "par value," "stated value," or "nominal value" of the shares (TSMC calls it "Capital stock") and

- a "capital surplus" amount, but sometimes called "capital in excess of par" or "additional paid-in capital."

To illustrate, imagine that a company issues shares for €10, with a par value of €1. For each share of stock sold, the company would report common stock of €1 and additional paid-in capital of €9.

An alternative approach, common in European countries, is to combine these two accounts into a single-line item on the balance sheet. In such cases, the account may be called "share capital," "paid-in capital," or "contributed capital."

Indirect investment is made by owners in the form of "retained earnings." This account represents all earnings ever earned in the history of the business that have not yet been paid out as dividends (and, hence, have been "retained" in the business). Because earnings are the property of shareholders, any earnings that have been retained, and presumably reinvested, have been reinvested on the behalf of shareholders. In fact, some companies call this account "reinvested earnings."

TSMC also reports an account titled "Others." This account consists of gains and losses that, for reasons we discuss later in this book, bypassed the income statement and, therefore, retained earnings.

Although not applicable to TSMC, many companies report a "Treasury stock" account that reflects stock bought back by the company from its shareholders, and retained in corporate treasury for possible reissue. These shares may be reissued as part of an employee stock ownership plan, to provide shares to employees exercising stock options, or to raise additional equity finance. Treasury stock appears as negative shareholders' equity on the balance sheet.

A Further Look at the Income Statement

The income statement reports on a company's performance during an accounting period. It is here that we find "net income." TSMC's income statement (Exhibit 1.2) begins with the "net revenue" figure. The term "net" refers to rebates and returns of product. For example, TSMC is required to estimate how much of its "gross" sales will be returned by customers. This amount, and any rebates paid to customers during the year, is subtracted from the gross amount to yield net sales. Revenue recognition will be explored in detail in Chapter 4.

The various expense categories that follow on the income statement represent the amounts, in monetary terms, of the resources used by the business to earn revenues during the period.

The first major expense item is the "cost of revenue."

In a manufacturing, retail, or distribution company, this is usually the most prominent expense category and is often referred to as "cost of goods sold," or "COGS." This figure includes all of the costs incurred to manufacture or acquire the inventory sold to customers, including (in the case of manufacturers) labor, materials, and factory overhead. In the case of retailers, such as Wal-Mart or Carrefour, cost of sales comes from the merchandise inventory sold in stores.

A preliminary profit measure called "gross profit" appears next. It is calculated by subtracting cost of sales from revenues.

"Research and development," "general and administrative," and "marketing" also feature prominently among TSMC's expenses. When all expenses are subtracted from revenue, the result is "operating profit," also known as "operating income." Operating profit is an important number because it reveals how successful the company has been in generating profit from its operating cycle (i.e., the process of producing and selling its goods and services). In other words, it tells us how much profit the company returns from its normal, day-to-day operating activities.

Operating profit is followed by "other non-operating income/expense," which is a catchall category consisting of many miscellaneous increases or decreases to profit. "Finance costs" represents TSMC's interest expense. "Share of profits of associates and joint ventures" reflects TSMC's income from affiliates, that is, large holdings that do not qualify for consolidation because TSMC does not control them. The default cut-off for making this determination is 50%. If TSMC owns more than 50% of the other company's common stock, the financial statements of the latter are consolidated with those of Taiwan Semiconductor. Otherwise, a separate method of accounting, known as the equity method, is required. We discuss this point in detail in Chapter 17.

After reporting "income before tax," TSMC subtracts its income tax expense of NT$54 billion. "Net income" equals NT$332 billion for 2016. When we speak of the "bottom line" in the context of a company's financial performance, this is the number we are referring to. However, the analyst community tends to focus on net income on a per share basis, otherwise known as "earnings per share." When the net income is divided by the number of TSMC shares outstanding (i.e., the number of shares of stock held by all owners), the result is NT$12.79. Because their point of reference is the price of a single share of stock, most securities analysts would say that TSMC "earned NT$12.79 in 2016."

Other Things You Should Know About the Balance Sheet and the Income Statement

Deferred Taxes

TSMC reports deferred tax assets of NT$8,271 million and deferred tax liabilities of NT$141 million at the end of 2016. These assets and liabilities arise because the amount that the firm reports as profit before tax (NT$386 billion) differs from the amount of taxable income that appears on its income tax return. This difference implies that the rules that TSMC uses to calculate its earnings under IFRS may not be the same as the rules that govern how earnings are calculated for tax purposes. At first glance, this difference may seem odd. Why doesn't the company simply use the same accounting for its income statement as it uses for its tax return? There is a logical reason why it doesn't.

The main purpose of IFRS (and US GAAP) is to help companies produce a set of accounts that captures the underlying economic reality of their businesses. In this way, it can guide investors and other relevant parties to make better, more value-enhancing decisions when they allocate resources, such as capital, or make any decisions related to the company. At its most basic, accounting exists to promote the efficient allocation of capital, and IFRS exists first and foremost to advance this goal.

In contrast, tax law exists mainly to allow governments to assess and collect tax revenues from businesses in a manner consistent with the public-policy priorities of the country's lawmakers. In the United States, for example, tax law is made in the Congress. When tax laws are written and amended, the efficient allocation of capital may have been the last thing on the minds of the politicians responsible for them. They are moved by other priorities. For example, tax law may be written to encourage investment in capital goods or personnel hiring in an economically depressed region. Or it may be written to discourage excessive management pay. The point here is that politicians deliberately inject bias into tax law, and thus into the measurement of corporate performance under tax law, to promote public policy goals. While such efforts may be laudable (or not), we can say with certainty that the result is bias and distortion in profit measurement from an investor's perspective.

To cope with this problem, accountants came up with the idea of separating tax reporting from the financial reports used to raise funds in the capital markets. In short, this means that firms calculate their earnings in two ways:

- in accordance with tax law ("tax earnings") and

- in accordance with GAAP or IFRS (often called "book earnings").

As a result, companies can conform with tax law, with all of the bias and distortion therein, while at the same time producing financial statements that are true and fair for the investment community. Deferred tax assets and liabilities reconcile the two approaches.

In most countries the biggest source of deferred tax liabilities is depreciation. Companies tend to use straight-line depreciation for book earnings, while using accelerated approaches for tax earnings. To illustrate, suppose a company buys a machine for $100,000, which it will depreciate over the next five years. In the first year, it will recognize $20,000 of depreciation expense for book earnings ($100,000 ÷ 5 years). Tax law in nearly all countries allows companies to depreciate assets using an accelerated approach, so that depreciation for tax purposes might be, say, $30,000. If the company's tax rate is 30%, income tax expense under IFRS will be $3,000 greater than the taxes it owes to the government that year [($30,000 − $20,000) × 30%]. This $3,000 of tax savings in the current year is not a permanent gift, but merely a temporary tax saving. The company will have to pay more tax in the future to make up the difference. That's why the $3,000 is called a deferred tax *liability*. We expect that at some point in the future, the additional taxes will have to be paid. Any time a company uses an accounting method under IFRS that leads to such temporary differences between profits and taxes under IFRS and under tax law, the difference is reconciled using deferred tax.

As we noted earlier, TSMC also has deferred tax *assets*. These assets arise when expenses are recognized for book purposes (per IFRS or GAAP) before they are recognized under tax law. The most common source of such assets is the provisioning for restructuring, litigation, warranties, etc. For example, when a company decides to restructure part of its business, the resulting loss is recognized immediately under IFRS. However, governments allow such losses to be deducted only after actual payments have been made. In effect, deferred tax assets represent future tax deductions on losses or expenses already recognized under IFRS. This topic is discussed in greater detail in Chapter 15.

Expenditure vs. Expense

To most people, these words are interchangeable, but not to accountants. When an expenditure is made, the firm can account for it in either of two ways: capitalization or expensing. To "capitalize" an expenditure is to record the amount as an asset. This treatment implies that the expenditure is expected to benefit a future period. For example, when a company buys a building, the cost appears as an asset on the balance sheet, only gradually finding its way into the income statement through the process of depreciation. When an expenditure is "expensed," the amount is charged in the current period to expense, and thus reduces earnings. The guiding principle is that if an expenditure is expected to benefit more than just the current period, it should be capitalized, thus appearing on the balance sheet. All other expenditures should be "expensed," that is, charged immediately to earnings on the income statement. However, as you proceed in your study of financial accounting, you will see that this guiding principle is sometimes violated.

Comprehensive Income

A widely accepted axiom in accounting states that changes in shareholders' equity, from the beginning of a period to the end, should equal the change in retained earnings for the year, apart from new share issues, dividends, and share buybacks. To put it another way, assuming that a company is not issuing new shares or buying back old shares, the change in shareholders' equity during the period should equal earnings in that period, net of any dividends paid to shareholders. This relationship is known as "clean surplus accounting."

When earnings are defined as "profit after tax" or "net income," the final line item on the income statement, this relationship usually does not hold. You can see this with a quick glance at the balance sheet and income statement of TSMC. Retained earnings increase from NT$867 billion to NT$1,042 billion. Even if we control for changes in issued capital, changes in the share premium (i.e., additional paid-in capital), and changes in treasury shares, we can't reconcile the change in shareholders' equity (from NT$1,195 billion to NT$1,360 billion). This happens because companies sometimes recognize gains or losses that impact on shareholders' equity, but which bypass the income statement. To restore the clean surplus relationship, accounting regulators developed the concept of "comprehensive income." This measure includes net income, but also any gains or losses that, for whatever reason, were not included in the income statement and therefore are not reflected in retained earnings.

These other gains or losses are shown on the balance sheet as "other components of equity." This line item covers a variety of gains or losses that do not figure in net income calculations because their true impact on earnings is not yet certain, irreversible, or realized. Items that might appear in this account include:

- unrealized (or "paper") gains and losses on most investments in financial securities;

- some gains and losses on derivatives transactions (options, futures, swaps, etc.) used to hedge risks; and

- most gains or losses incurred when translating the financial results of subsidiaries from local currency to the parent company's currency.

Comprehensive income for the year equals net income, plus or minus changes in the "other components of equity" account. When income is defined in this way, clean surplus accounting is restored.

KEY LESSONS FROM THE CHAPTER

- The balance sheet reports the financial position of a company at a particular point in time.

- The equation underlying the balance sheet is: Assets = Liabilities + Shareholders' Equity. This equation must hold for all companies.

- Most nonfinancial assets are carried on the balance sheet at their acquisition cost, net of accumulated depreciation (if applicable). Thus, the balance sheet does not necessarily reflect the true economic value of the company's assets.

- Total assets are classified into current and noncurrent assets. Current assets are expected to be consumed or converted into cash within one year or one operating cycle, whichever is longer. Noncurrent assets fall into three broad categories: investments, property plant and equipment, and intangibles.

- Liabilities fall into four broad categories: current liabilities, long-term debt, provisions, and deferred taxes.

- Shareholders' equity reports on the net amounts invested in the firm by its owners. It assumes that owners invest in the business directly and indirectly.

- Direct investment occurs when investors contribute cash or other consideration in exchange for shares of stock that represent ownership stakes in the business. The relevant amount is represented by "issued capital" or "share capital." The convention is some countries, such as the United States, is to separate share capital into two accounts: one for par value and another for additional paid-in capital.

- Indirect investment occurs in the form of retained earnings. Because earnings are the property of shareholders, any earnings that have been retained, and presumably reinvested, have been reinvested on the behalf of shareholders.

- When an expenditure is made, the firm can account for it either as an expense in the current period or as a capitalized asset on the balance sheet. Capitalized assets are future expenses.

KEY TERMS AND CONCEPTS FROM THE CHAPTER

Assets	Liabilities	Expenses and	Gains and losses	Cost of goods sold
Current assets	Current liabilities	expenditures	Revenues	Comprehensive income
Noncurrent assets	Shareholders' equity			

QUESTIONS

1. What are "consolidated financial statements?"

2. What is meant by the term "group financial statements?"

3. Describe the difference between current assets and noncurrent assets.

4. True or false: The criterion that determines whether or not an asset is current is 12 months.

5. How are current assets listed on the balance sheet?

6. What is meant by "prepaid expenses" and why is this item classified as an asset?

7. What is the dominant valuation basis for property, plant and equipment?

8. Why is share capital described as "direct" investment and retained earnings as "indirect" investment?

9. What does the term "net" mean in the context of net sales or net revenues?

10. Why do deferred income taxes exist?

11. What is the difference between "expensing" an item and "capitalizing" it?

12. What is "comprehensive income" and what is it designed to achieve?

Appendix 2.1 The Mechanics of Financial Accounting: The Double-Entry System

Financial statements are the primary end-products of the financial accounting process. To produce financial statements, all transactions that occur during a given period must be recorded and classified. The process of recording and classifying transactions is accomplished through journal entries prepared under the double-entry system. This chapter looks at how this system is used to prepare income statements and balance sheets. (Cash flow statements are addressed in Chapter 5.)

The origins of double-entry accounting have been traced as far back as the 12th century. By the end of the 15th century, the system was widely used by Venetian merchants. In 1494, Luca Pacioli, a monk who traveled in the same circles as Leonardo da Vinci, formalized the double-entry system in the chapter of a book on mathematics. The system used today in practically every country of the world is nearly identical to that described by Pacioli over 500 years ago.

Under the double-entry system, every transaction recorded in the accounts has an equal amount, in monetary terms, of debits and credits. Each line item on the balance sheet and income statement has its own account. These accounts can be graphically depicted as a "T," hence the commonly used term, "T-account." For example,

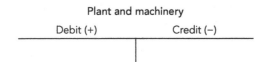

Plant and machinery

Debit (+)   Credit (−)

Notice the space at the top for the account name (in this case, plant and machinery), a left side to record debits, and a right side to record credits. Asset accounts are increased by making debit entries, liabilities and shareholders' equity accounts are increased through credit entries. Because sales, all else being equal, increase earnings (and earnings enter retained earnings, a shareholders' equity account), sales are recorded as credits. Expenses, on the other hand, are debited. Similarly, gains (from, for example, the sale of assets at a price exceeding book value) are recorded as credits; losses are recorded as debits. These rules may appear arbitrary, but their simplicity has contributed to their constant use over the centuries. They are summarized in Table 2A.1.

When the debit–credit equality is satisfied for each transaction, the total amount in monetary terms (i.e., dollars, euro, etc.) for all accounts with debit balances should equal the total for all accounts with credit balances. Also, when this equality holds, the balance sheet equation (Assets = Liabilities + Shareholders' Equity) is satisfied.

To illustrate the double-entry system, assume that plant and machinery is bought on credit for $55,000. The "journal entry" is an opportunity for the accountant to provide a detailed explanation for *why* the entry took place. It might be accompanied by an explanation such as "acquisition of machinery to replace obsolete equipment." The T-accounts would not include such a description, but any entry therein can be linked back to the journal so that the accountant can look for an explanation for the entry. The journal entry is recorded like this:

Plant and machinery $55,000
  Liability $55,000

Plant and machinery, an asset account, increases by $55,000 (debit), and a liability is recognized for the same amount (credit). Notice that while the debit entry appears on the left margin, the credit entry is indented. The debit and credit are then posted to the relevant T-accounts:

Plant and machinery		Liability	
$55,000			$55,000

At the end of each accounting period, and after every transaction that took place during the year is recorded, the balances in the T-accounts are posted to a "trial balance." This document lists

Table 2A.1   **Accounts**

Accounts	Increase	Decrease
Assets, expenses and losses	Debit	Credit
Liabilities, sh. equity, revenues and gains	Credit	Debit

every account in the balance sheet and income statement, and helps to ensure that total debit balances in the system equal total credit balances.

Adjusting entries are then posted, mainly to implement the matching principle. This principle says that any costs incurred to generate revenues must be recognized in the same period as the revenues. Revenues are "matched" with the costs that were incurred to generate them. Estimates are made of any revenues earned or expenses incurred for which cash has not yet been received or paid. The "accrual method" of accounting exists for the purpose of implementing this principle.

At the end of each accounting period, a standard set of accruals will be made before the financial statements are prepared. For example, nearly all companies must adjust for:

- interest income earned but not yet received;

- interest expense incurred but not yet paid;

- depreciation of tangible assets;

- amortization of intangibles;

- use of prepaid assets such as rent and insurance, and

- any unpaid benefits earned by employees (including salaries, bonuses, and pensions).

Other adjustments may also be needed. These entries are made whenever a company wishes to prepare a balance sheet and income statement and adhere to the matching principle.

After the adjustments, balances are recalculated for each account, and a postadjustment, preclosing trial balance is prepared. This document ensures that the system is still in balance, and is ready for the final steps in the process: the preparation of the financial statements.

The sequence works like this: the income statement is prepared from the preclosing trial balance. All income statement accounts (e.g., revenues, expenses, etc.) are then closed to retained earnings. The closing process performs two important functions. First, it transfers the company's profits (or losses) to the balance sheet. Second, it brings the balance of each income statement account to zero, allowing the "slate to be wiped clean" for the next accounting period.

After the closing process is complete, a postclosing trial balance is prepared. Because all income statement accounts have zero balances, only balance sheet accounts appear in this version of the trial balance. The accounts can then be recast in the form of a proper balance sheet, and the accounting process is now completed.

The accounting process in practice

To see how the accounting process works, we draw on the example of Truly Books & Co.

1. Misha establishes Truly Books at the beginning of 2018, investing $100,000 in the business.

| Cash | $100,000 | |
| Share capital | | $100,000 |

Cash (A)		Share capital (SE)	
$100,000			$100,000
$100,000			$100,000

where (A) = assets, and (SE) = shareholders' equity.

2. A bank loans Truly Books $50,000, to be paid in five years with an interest rate of 10% payable annually. The funds are used to purchase inventory and shop equipment, and to cover rent on the shop.

Cash $50,000
  Bank loan $50,000

Cash (A)			Bank loan (L)	
$100,000 50,000				$50,000
$150,000				$50,000

where (L) = liability.

3. Misha signs a two-year lease for a store paying the full amount, $12,000, in advance.

Prepaid rent $12,000
  Cash $12,000

Prepaid rent (A)			Cash (A)	
$12,000			$150,000	$12,000
$12,000			$138,000	

4. In early January, Misha spends $1,000 on bookshelves for her store.

Bookshelves $1,000
  Cash $1,000

Bookshelves (A)			Cash (A)	
$1,000			$138,000	$1,000
$1,000			$137,000	

5. Books are bought on credit for $50,000.

Inventory $50,000
  Accounts payable $50,000

Inventory (A)			Accounts payable (L)	
$50,000				$50,000
$50,000				$50,000

6. Before the end of 2018, Misha pays cash for half of the inventory purchased earlier in the year.

| Accounts payable | $25,000 | |
| Cash | | $25,000 |

Accounts payable (L)				Cash (A)	
$25,000	$50,000			$137,000	$25,000
	$25,000			$112,000	

7. In 2018, the business sells books costing $40,000 for $100,000. By the end of the year, 90% of the sales have been paid in cash; the remaining 10% are still unpaid.

Cash	$90,000	
Accounts receivable	$10,000	
Revenues		$100,000

Cash (A)				Accounts receivable (A)	
$112,000				$10,000	
$90,000					
$202,000				$10,000	

Revenues (R)	
	$100,000
	$100,000

| Cost of goods sold | $40,000 | |
| Inventory | | $40,000 |

Cost of goods sold (E)				Inventory (A)	
$40,000				$50,000	$40,000
$40,000				$10,000	

where (E) = expense.

8. Utilities expense for 2018 is $3,600. By the end of the year, $2,700 of the expense has been paid. The final quarterly bill is unpaid, but the cost is recognized as both an expense and an accrued liability.

Utilities expense	$3,600	
Cash		$2,700
Accrued utilities liability		$900

Utilities expense (E)	
$3,600	
$3,600	

Cash (A)	
$202,000	$2,700
$199,300	

Accrued utilities liability (L)	
	$900
	$900

At year end, a trial balance is prepared listing the balances for each balance sheet and income statement account – see Table 2A.2. As expected, the total debits and total credits are equal.

Table 2A.2   Misha's Trial Balance: Preadjusted Trial Balance, 31 December 2018

Balances

Balance Sheet Accounts	Debit	Credit
Cash	$199,300	
Accounts Receivable	10,000	
Inventory	10,000	
Prepaid Rent	12,000	
Bookshelves	1,000	
Bank Loan		$50,000
Accounts Payable		25,000
Accrued Utilities Liability		900
Share Capital		100,000
Income statement accounts		
Cost of Goods Sold	40,000	
Utilities Expense	3,600	
Revenues		100,000
Total	$275,900	$275,900

After each transaction is posted to the relevant accounts, Misha makes a series of adjusting entries to implement the matching principle. Unlike the entries made up to this point, the following entries do not arise because of transactions. Instead they are adjustments required under accrual accounting. In this example, adjustments are required for the use of prepaid rent, unpaid interest on the bank loan Misha took out at the beginning of the year, and depreciation on the bookshelves.

9. Two years' worth of lease payments were made at the beginning of the year. An adjustment is required at the end of the year to acknowledge that half of the asset acquired (prepaid rent) has been consumed.

Rent expense	$6,000	
Prepaid rent		$6,000

Rent expense (E)			Prepaid rent (A)	
$6,000			$12,000	$6,000
$6,000			$6,000	

10. Interest on the bank loan is acknowledged, even if actual payment will not take place until the beginning of the following year. Given the $50,000 loan, and a 10% interest rate, the following entry is required.

Interest expense	$5,000	
Accrued interest liability		$5,000

Interest expense (E)			Accrued interest liability (L)	
$5,000				$5,000
$5,000				$5,000

11. Depreciation on the bookshelves must be recognized. A common practice in retailing is to depreciate such assets over 4 years, using the straight-line method. Given the initial investment of $1,000, the annual depreciation charge is $250.

Depreciation expense	$250	
Accumulated depreciation		$250

Depreciation expense (E)			Accumulated depreciation	
$250				$250
$250				$250

Accumulated depreciation is a contra-asset account. All contra-assets have a credit balance, which is then offset against the asset account (in this case, Bookshelves) to yield the asset's net book value. The postadjustment, preclosing trial balance can now be prepared – see Table 2A.3. The income statement emerges from this trial balance – see Table 2A.4.

Table 2A.3 The Postadjusted, Preclosing Trial Balance:
Postadjusted, Preclosing Trial Balance, 31 December 2018

Balances Balance Sheet Accounts	Debit	Credit
Cash	$199,300	
Accounts receivable	10,000	
Inventory	10,000	
Prepaid rent	6,000	
Bookshelves	1,000	
Accumulated depreciation		$250
Bank loan		50,000

(Continued)

Table 2A.3 (Continued)

Balances

Balance Sheet Accounts	Debit	Credit
Accounts payable		25,000
Accrued utilities liability		900
Accrued interest liability		5,000
Share capital		100,000
Income statement accounts		
Cost of goods sold	40,000	
Utilities expense	3,600	
Rent expense	6,000	
Interest expense	5,000	
Depreciation expense	250	
Revenues		100,000
Total	$281,150	$281,150

Table 2A.4 Misha's Income Statement: Truly Books & Co. Income Statement for Year Ending 31 December 2018

Revenues		$100,000
Less cost of goods sold		(40,000)
Gross profit		60,000
Less expenses:		
Utilities expense	$3,600	
Rent expense	6,000	
Interest expense	5,000	
Depreciation expense	250	
		(14,850)
Net income		$45,150

12. The income statement accounts are closed to Retained Earnings. This process is accomplished with offsetting entries to each account. For example, because the Revenues account has a credit balance of $100,000, a debit for the same amount is required. The account balance is brought to zero, and the balancing entry is always to Retained Earnings.

Revenues	$100,000		
Retained earnings		$100,000	

Revenues (R)		Retained earnings (SE)	
$100,000	$100,000		$100,000
	$ __		$100,000

Similar entries are required for the expenses, only now the accounts are credited, and Retained Earnings is debited.

Retained earnings	$54,850	
Cost of goods sold		$40,000
Utilities expense		3,600
Rent expense		6,000
Interest expense		5,000
Depreciation expense		250

Retained earnings (SE)				Cost of goods sold (E)	
$54,850	$100,000			$40,000	$40,000
	$45,150			$__	

Utilities expense (E)				Rent expense (E)	
$3,600	$3,600			$6,000	$6,000
$__				$__	

Interest expense (E)				Depreciation expense (E)	
$5,000	$5,000			$250	$250
$__				$__	

A postclosing trial balance, consisting entirely of balance sheet accounts, is then prepared. This document will serve as the basis for the end-of-year balance sheet, and as the beginning trial balance for the next period – see Table 2A.5.

Finally, Misha can prepare the balance sheet for Truly Books and Co. – see Table 2A.6.

Table 2A.5   Postclosing Trial Balance as at 31 December 2018

Balances		
Account	**Debit**	**Credit**
Cash	$199,300	
Accounts receivable	10,000	
Inventory	10,000	
Prepaid rent	6,000	
Bookshelves	1,000	
Accumulated depreciation		$250
Bank loan		50,000
Accounts payable		25,000
Accrued utilities liability		900
Accrued interest liability		5,000
Share capital		100,000
Retained earnings		45,150
Total	$226,300	$226,300

Table 2A.6   Truly Books & Co. Balance Sheet: Truly Books and Co. Balance Sheet as at 31 December 2018

Assets		
Cash		$199,300
Accounts receivable		10,000
Inventory		10,000
Prepaid rent		6,000
Bookshelves	$1,000	
Less accumulated depreciation	(250)	750
Total assets		$ 226,050
Liabilities and stockholders' equity		
Bank loan		$50,000
Accounts payable		25,000
Accrued utilities liability		900
Accrued interest liability		5,000
Share capital		100,000
Retained earnings		45,150
Total liabilities and stockholders' equity		$226,050

KEY TERMS AND CONCEPTS FROM THE APPENDIX

Double-entry accounting	Accounts T-account	Debit Credit	Journal entry Trial balance	Adjusting entries

KEY LESSONS FROM THE APPENDIX

- The process of recording and classifying transactions is accomplished through journal entries prepared under the double-entry system. This system has been in continuous use for over 500 years.

- Under the double-entry system, every transaction recorded in the accounts has an equal amount, in monetary terms, of debits and credits.

- The income statement accounts are "temporary," meaning that they are closed at the end of the accounting period to the retained earnings account on the balance sheet. The closing process achieves two purposes. First, it removes any balances from income statement accounts, allowing the income measurement process to start from zero at the beginning of the following period. Second, it transfers net income or net loss to the balance sheet.

- Balance sheet accounts are "permanent" in the sense that they are not closed at the end of the accounting period. Permanent simply means that account balances can straddle two accounting periods.

PROBLEM

2.1 Preparing a Balance Sheet and an Income Statement

The following information is based on accounting data for 2017 and 2018 for PetroLim, a petrochemicals company based in Malaysia. It reports its results in thousands of Malaysian Ringgits.

	31 December	
Statement of Financial Position Items	**2018**	**2017**
Cash	177,178	108,140
Accounts receivable	36,838	16,976
Advances to suppliers	40,772	25,328

Statement of Financial Position Items	31 December 2018	2017
Inventories	176,934	152,076
Other current assets	40,734	26,914
Property, plant and equipment (net)	495,606	463,180
Oil and gas properties	652,656	540,992
Intangible assets	40,044	32,254
Other noncurrent assets	327,422	264,428
Accounts payable	208,920	155,872
Advances from customers	24,866	23,180
Other current liabilities	169,522	181,878
Long-term debt	70,610	60,802
Other noncurrent liabilities	84,124	73,366
Common shares	889,054	708,680
Retained earnings	541,088	426,510

Income Statement Items	2018
Net operating revenues	1,670,074
Interest and other revenues	6,196
Cost of sales	974,224
Selling expenses	82,690
General and administrative expenses	98,648
Other operating expenses	129,320
Interest expense	5,738
Income taxes	98,662

Required

a. Prepare an income statement for PetroLim for the year ending 31 December 2018.

b. Prepare statements of financial position for PetroLim as of 31 December 2017 and 31 December 2018.

Case Study

2-1 JanMar Fabrics: Preparing the Balance Sheet and Income Statement*

The adjusted, postclosing trial balance of JanMar Fabrics on 30 June 2012 appears on the next page.

JanMar Fabrics adjusted, postclosing trial balance June 30, 2012

Cash	$221,000	
Accounts Receivable	136,250	
Merchandise Inventory	340,750	
Prepaid Insurance	2,000	
Equipment	1,050,000	
Accumulated Depreciation		$420,000
Accounts Payable		165,500
Notes Payable		25,000
Salaries Payable		6,250
Common Stock		750,000
Retained Earnings		383,250
	$1,750,000	$1,750,000

The firm made the following transactions during July:

1. Sold merchandise on account for a total selling price of $425,000.
2. Purchased merchandise inventory on account from various suppliers for $231,500.
3. Paid rent for the month of July of $58,750.
4. Paid salaries to employees during July of $103,000.
5. Collected accounts receivable of $170,750.
6. Paid accounts payable of $194,750.
7. Paid miscellaneous expenses of $16,000.

Adjusting entries required at the end of July relate to the following:

8. The company paid the premium on a one-year insurance policy on 1 March 2012, with coverage beginning on that date. This is the only insurance policy in force on 30 June 2012.
9. The firm depreciates its equipment over a 10-year life. The equipment is not expected to have any residual value.

---

* Note that this case assumes that students are familiar with the double-entry system of accounting, the subject of this chapter's appendix.

(Continued)

10. Employees earned salaries of $8,000 during the last three days of July but were not paid. These are the only unpaid salaries at the end of July.

11. The note payable is a 90-day, 12% note issued on 30 June 2012.

12. Merchandise inventory on hand on 31 July 2012 was $389,750.

Required

Using a trial balance and T-accounts, prepare an income statement for the month of July 2012, and prepare a balance sheet dated 31 July 2012. Cross-reference entries in the T-accounts using the numbers of the transactions shown above.

A Brief Overview of GAAP and IFRS: The Framework for Financial Accounting

3

The primary objective of Generally Accepted Accounting Principles (GAAP) and International Financial Reporting Standards (IFRS) is to guide companies in producing economic information that helps external users make better decisions. To put it another way, the main purpose of corporate financial reporting from a broad economic perspective is to promote the efficient allocation of capital in the global capital markets. If accountants and auditors are doing their jobs properly, financial statements should facilitate the movement of capital to where it is likely to earn its highest risk-adjusted returns, thus maximizing wealth creation.

To achieve this goal, GAAP and IFRS are governed by a set of (1) core principles, (2) qualitative characteristics, (3) underlying assumptions, and (4) modifying conventions.

The Core Principles of GAAP and IFRS

Several principles exert a broad influence over the standards produced by the Financial Accounting Standards Board (FASB) and the International Accounting Standards Board (IASB) and on the way in which financial statements are prepared. The most important of these principles deal with: **asset valuation, revenue recognition**, and the **matching principle**.

Asset Valuation

For an asset to appear on a balance sheet, some basis must be chosen for assigning a value to it. The default option, and the dominant approach for certain classes of assets, is known as "acquisition (or historical) cost." As the term implies, value is measured as the cash or cash-equivalent price of the asset on the date it was acquired. Assets such as buildings, machinery, equipment, and vehicles are usually valued on this basis.

What happens subsequent to acquisition depends on whether an asset's value increases or decreases, on whether the company uses US GAAP or IFRS, and on the nature of the asset. As of now, IFRS is more flexible than US GAAP in the valuation of nonmonetary assets, such as land. While companies such as TSMC keep land and buildings on the balance sheet at acquisition price, businesses preparing balance sheets under IFRS have the option of using "fair value." Fair value is the price that would be received for an asset in an arm's-length (i.e., genuine market) transaction. It represents what the firm could get for the asset on the balance sheet date, assuming an orderly sale, not a fire sale or sale out of desperation. The assets are initially recorded at acquisition cost, but as market values change, so too will the balance sheet amounts *if* the firm opted to use fair values to report these assets as they are permitted to do under IFRS. For example, if land acquired at $20 million is now worth $30 million, the latter amount might appear on the balance sheet. Although IFRS allows for this treatment, most IFRS-compliant companies do in fact use acquisition cost for such assets anyway.

What happens if the value of the asset falls below its acquisition cost? The rule that prevails under both IFRS and US GAAP is that if an asset's value is deemed to be permanently impaired (i.e., a decline in value below acquisition cost appears irreversible), the asset must be written down to its fair value. For example, if land bought for $20 million is now worth only $8 million, and recovery is unlikely, the balance sheet must now say $8 million. The $12 million reduction in value appears as a loss in the income statement for the period in which the asset impairment is recognized.

The nature of an asset also influences its measurement. For example, in the case of monetary assets – such as shares of stock, bonds, and positions in options and futures – fair value is the dominant measurement basis, under both US GAAP and IFRS. In other words, while nonmonetary assets, such as land and equipment, are usually measured at acquisition cost, most monetary assets appear on balance sheets at fair value.

Revenue Recognition

Before companies are permitted to recognize revenue from the sale of goods or services to customers, three criteria must be met. The revenues must measurable and realizable, and the goods and services must have been transferred to the customer.

"Measurable" implies that a reasonable basis exists for determining the amount of revenues earned. For routine sales, measurability is rarely a concern. But imagine a construction contract in which work is performed, and revenue earned, gradually over a period of years. The possibility of error, deliberate or otherwise, is far greater in such circumstances than in the semiconductor sales that comprise most of the revenues for TSMC. However, TSMC is not immune to measurement issues, particularly when another manufacturer licenses some of TSMC's production technology for use in its own processes. In such cases, TSMC must determine whether it needs to put in effort to upgrade the technology over time. If so, it should defer a portion of the licensing revenue regardless of whether or not it has been collected.

"Realizable" means that the seller can reasonably expect to get paid for the revenue earned. If there are serious doubts about the financial health of a customer, revenue shouldn't be recognized. Or if revenue is recognized, an adequate provision for bad debts should be included in the accounts.

Standard setters of both IFRS and US GAAP have recognized that identifying *when* revenue is earned is becoming more difficult in the 21st century economy. As a result, in 2018, companies reporting under these regimes were forced to adopt new revenue recognition rules. The most important feature of the new rules is that revenue cannot be recognized until the good or service in question has been transferred to the customer. Numerous issues arise in trying to determine precisely when this act occurs and how much revenue should be recognized. The challenges in implementing this standard are especially acute when a company sells a product and a service at the same time and in cases where product delivery can extend for years via the Internet.

Consider the mobile phone. On the retail end, frequently a phone is purchased from a shop operated by a telecom provider such as Vodafone. The customer purchases a phone, often at a discount, but signs up for a long-term service plan that may last up to two years. Assigning value to both the phone and the service can be difficult, yet new rules will require the seller to do so.

Or consider the phone itself, exclusive of the telecom contract. When a customer purchases a smartphone, they can expect that product to change its functionality over time as the manufacturer, say Apple or Samsung, sends regular operating system updates over the Internet to keep the phone current. We must now ask over what period and at what rate should the manufacturer recognize the revenue after the initial sale, knowing that it still has to earn a portion of the revenue by upgrading the equipment?

We will discuss the new rules further in Chapter 4. For now, note that this is a vital financial reporting issue as revenue is the first component of the income statement.

The Matching Principle

This principle says that any costs incurred to generate revenues must be recognized as expenses in the same period as the revenues. Revenues must be "matched" with the costs that were incurred to generate them. Much of contemporary accounting practice is the direct result of applying this principle. So, too, are many of its controversies.

Notice that the word "cash" is missing from the above definition of expense, because the expenditure of cash does not necessarily drive the recognition of expenses, just as the receipt of cash does not necessarily determine when revenue is recognized. To illustrate, imagine that employees are paid on the 10th of every month. If financial statements are prepared at the end of each month, the matching principle requires an estimate be made of any salaries and benefits earned by employees for the final three weeks. In short, expenses are recorded as incurred, regardless of when cash is paid.

The Key Qualitative Characteristics of Financial Information

If the financial information produced by application of the aforementioned principles is to be of practical use to investors, it should possess certain characteristics, including:

Relevance

Information should be capable of making a difference in decisions. This implies that the information has at least some predictive value (i.e., it helps the reader to forecast the target company's future with more accuracy than if the information did not exist), and that it is released in a timely manner (i.e., quickly enough to help investors and other interested parties).

Reliability

Investors must be able to trust financial statements. This means that the statements should be "representationally faithful" (i.e., they capture economic reality), neutral (i.e., unbiased), and verifiable. The neutrality condition implies that while financial statement measurements may be incorrect, any errors that do arise are made in good faith and are not deliberately biased in one direction or the other. Verifiability implies that the information must be subject to audit by independent experts, such as a public accounting firm.

Consistency

To facilitate comparison of a company's performance over time, financial statement measurements must be consistent. This means that a company should employ the same measurement approaches from one year to the next. If there are changes in accounting methods, the effects of such changes must be discussed in detail in the notes to the financial statements. And if these changes are significant, a qualification of the auditor's opinion may be required. In addition, financial information should be comparable across firms, to enable comparison of performance between a company and its industry competitors.

The Key Assumptions of Financial Information

In addition to the aforementioned qualitative characteristics, there are several fundamental assumptions that underlie financial statements prepared under US GAAP or IFRS. For example, the entity assumption requires that the activities of a business be accounted for separately from those of its owners. This assumption is obvious enough for a corporation, because it operates as a legal person, separate and apart from its owners. But the entity assumption applies equally to nonincorporated businesses, such as partnerships, that may be considered inseparable from their owners from a legal or tax point of view.

There is also a "going concern" assumption, which states that the entity in question will remain in business for the foreseeable future. This doesn't mean that the business is expected to last forever, but there is no reason to believe that its immediate survivability is threatened. Much of contemporary financial reporting practice is based on this assumption. For example, when a long-term asset, such as land or a building, is reported on the balance sheet at its acquisition cost, the implication is that the company will be in business long enough to recover that cost in some way. In most cases, the cost will be recovered indirectly through the normal, day-to-day activities of the business in which materials and labor are converted into products, products into sales, and sales into cash. When this assumption no longer holds, as would be the case for a business on the verge of bankruptcy, the measurement rules for assets can change. Additionally, in such cases the independent auditor will likely issue a "going concern" opinion that explicitly highlights that this assumption may not be descriptive of reality.

Modifying Conventions

The financial reporting process is also governed by a set of "modifying conventions," or practical constraints. The two most important are "materiality" and "conservatism."

Materiality

This is the term accountants use to denote "significance." It means that relatively small amounts that are not likely to influence decisions should be recorded in whatever manner is most cost-efficient. For example, if a company were to buy office supplies, the expenditure can be treated in either of two ways: as the acquisition of an asset or as an expense. If the former option is chosen, the cost of the supplies will be gradually transferred from an asset account on the balance sheet to an expense account on the income statement as the supplies are consumed. This is a lot of work for what may be a trivial sum of money. The materiality principle reminds us that because the amounts involved are small, the company should choose the approach that is most cost-efficient. This means that the expenditure would be charged immediately to the current year's income statement, even though (technically) an asset has been acquired.

It also means that accounts with insignificant balances (i.e., amounts that are not large enough to influence readers of the annual report) can be lumped together with other accounts. Typically, accounting systems include many more asset and liability accounts than we see in the balance sheet or income statement, but for the sake of convenience and readability these accounts are aggregated into broad summary accounts. Otherwise, the financial statements would be swamped by a mountain of useless detail.

Materiality is a subjective concept. What may be large enough to make a difference to one investor may be irrelevant to another. Hence, companies, when reporting their results and making judgments of materiality, must rely on professional expertise, including their external auditors. But while the auditors certainly have input on application of the materiality concept, ultimately the financial statements are the responsibility of management.

Conservatism

This means that companies should exercise care not to overstate assets and revenues or to understate liabilities and expenses. This convention is applied to a wide range of measurement issues. For example, inventories are reported on the balance sheet at the lower of cost or net realizable value. In other words, inventories should be measured at acquisition cost, unless fair, or market, value is lower. But note that fair value is not used for balance sheet purposes if, as is usually the case, the inventory is worth more than acquisition cost. Applying the conservatism convention reduces the likelihood that an asset will be overvalued. The flip side, however, is that because fair value is ignored when greater than acquisition cost, conservatism increases the likelihood that an asset will be undervalued.

Another way to view how conservatism is applied in practice is that it means bad economic news *should be* recognized more quickly in the financial statements than good news. Continuing with the inventory example, if a company realizes that it has a product with very high demand and thus it could charge a higher price, it must wait until it actually makes those sales. Effectively, the good news is delayed at least with respect to the accounting reports. Conversely, if a company realizes that its products are no longer in demand, they should recognize the loss as soon as management views the situation as unlikely to change. Therefore, the bad news is recognized immediately rather than deferred until the sales take place and the losses are realized.

For example, in each year from 2014 to 2016 TSMC reported an inventory impairment charge. These impairments amounted to 5% of beginning inventory in 2014, 1% in 2015, and 2% in 2016. Obsolescence is a key risk in an industry with rapid technological change, and TSMC's management is required, via the conservatism convention, to communicate the outcome of that risk annually. It should be noted, however, that the practice we just described is driven, at least in part, by managerial discretion. As we will discuss throughout the remainder of the text, managers do not always follow such principles exactly, which can lead to allegations of earnings management (i.e., manipulation).

The Future of Financial Reporting

In addition to the principles already discussed, other concepts of relatively recent vintage have emerged as part of an ongoing joint project of the IASB and the FASB. The project's aim is to establish a common standard that would improve how information is organized and presented in the financial statements. For this purpose, two principles have emerged, both of which have lurked in the background of standards setting for a long time, but only recently have been discussed in an explicit fashion: The cohesiveness principle and the disaggregation principle. Both are worth knowing because of the influence they are likely to exert on future changes to the presentation of financial information in corporate annual reports.

Cohesiveness

Cohesiveness refers to the use of consistent labeling and ordering of items *across* the financial statements. The aim is to enhance the usefulness and understandability of the financial statements and to ensure that an entity's financial statements complement each other as much as possible. It reflects the idea that a company's traditional financial statements should be closely related, because they all contribute to the same goal of understanding its financial performance. For example, as we explore in a later chapter, the statement of cash flows is organized into three major sections – operations, investing, and financing. Because this statement is of more recent vintage than the balance sheet and income statement, these categories reflect contemporary thinking on how to categorize and order financial information. One practical consequence of the cohesiveness principle is that, in the not too distant future, the balance sheet and income statement could be reorganized into a format that more closely resembles that of the cash flow statement, providing a consistent and seamless view of an entity's performance.

Disaggregation

The financial statements already take highly aggregated items, such as total assets, and disaggregate them into smaller categories for display on the face of the statements. The idea behind the disaggregation principle is to extend this practice by providing a noticeably greater level of detail in the financial statements than before. The challenge is to ensure that the level of disaggregation for each component, such as property, plant, and equipment (PP&E), responds to user needs without distracting users from an overall view of performance. It's a delicate balancing act: greater detail vs. understandability, with appropriate consideration given to materiality and clarity. The goal is not disaggregation *per se*, but rather sufficient information to help the reader understand the company's financial performance. Also, we shouldn't forget the role of the notes, which allows further disaggregation of line items while maintaining the understandability and clarity of the financial statements. That's one reason why the application of this principle is controversial. To what extent should information traditionally relegated to the notes be brought into the financial statements proper? What this means to the financial statement reader is that, in future, some increased detail in the principal statements can be expected. The balance sheet, the income statement, and possibly the statement of cash flows will almost certainly carry more account details than they do now. How much more is a matter of conjecture as of this writing.

KEY LESSONS FROM THE CHAPTER

- The main purpose of corporate financial reporting from a broad economic perspective is to promote the efficient allocation of capital in the global capital markets.

- Historical (or acquisition) cost is the default valuation approach for nonfinancial assets.

- IFRS is more flexible in allowing property, plant & equipment (PP&E) to be adjusted both upwards and downwards in value. US GAAP is more conservative and generally does not allow for an upward revaluation of fixed assets. However, most IFRS companies choose to rely on acquisition cost anyway.

- Before companies are permitted to recognize revenues from the sale of goods or services to customers, three criteria must be met. The revenues must be: measurable and earned, and the good or services in question must have been transferred to customers.

- The matching principle states that any cost incurred to generate revenues must be recognized in the same period as the revenues.

- The "going concern" assumption states that the entity in question will remain in business for the foreseeable future. This assumption has important implications for financial reporting practice.

- The materiality concept means that relatively small amounts that are not likely to influence decisions should be recorded in whatever manner is the most efficient.

- The conservatism principle (known as "prudence" in the United Kingdom) states that companies should exercise care not to overstate assets and revenues and not to understate liabilities or expenses. Moreover, they should recognize bad news on a more timely basis than good news.

KEY TERMS AND CONCEPTS FROM THE CHAPTER

Asset valuation	The matching	Reliability	Conservatism	Disaggregation
Revenue	principle	Consistency	Cohesiveness	principle
recognition	Relevance	Materiality	principle	

QUESTIONS

1. Describe the basic criteria that must be met before revenue can be recognized under US GAAP or IFRS.

2. What is the "matching principle" and what role does it play in the financial reporting process?

3. True or false: The criteria describing the key characteristics of financial information (relevance, reliability, and consistency) are contradictory.

4. What is meant by the term "conservatism?" Doesn't it create biased financial reporting?

5. Describe the "materiality" concept and its influence on the financial statements.

6. What do the concepts of "cohesiveness" and "disaggregation" mean and what is their significance for the future of corporate financial reporting?

4

Revenue Recognition

Introduction

This chapter discusses revenue-recognition practices under US GAAP and IFRS. Revenue is one of the most important figures in a company's financial statements and is often the largest. Not only is it the starting point for calculating profit, but also sales forecasts are typically the first step in performing corporate valuations. But what exactly is "revenue" and how should companies measure and report it?

For decades, questions have been raised about how to determine when revenue should be recognized under various circumstances. US GAAP was, to a large extent, based on industry-specific guidance, created piecemeal to address individual questions as they arose. The result was a lack of consistency in the recognition of revenue across industries, and sometimes even within industries. Just as troublesome were the differences in practice between companies reporting under US GAAP and those reporting under IFRS, at times resulting in different accounting for similar transactions.

In response to these problems, the IASB and the FASB created a single, unifying framework for determining when revenue should be recognized—a framework that could be applied to any industry and provide similar results for similar facts. The result was ASC Topic 606, "Revenue from Contracts with Customers." At the same time the IASB issued its equivalent standard, IFRS 15. Although the two standards are not entirely identical, they are close enough such that the discussion that follows in this chapter applies to both. Also, both took effect in 2018.

The underlying principle is that a business recognizes revenue when the goods or services have been transferred to the buyer. The new standards provide a five-step model for evaluating how and when revenue should be recognized, rather than providing detailed industry-by-industry guidance. Another important difference is that the new standards focus on when the control of goods and services is transferred to the customer, rather than when the firm has earned the consideration to which it is entitled. Under the principles that prevailed before the new standards, revenue was recognized when the seller "earned" the revenue, not necessarily when the goods or services were transferred to the buyer. One practical effect of the change is that in some industries, revenue will be recognized later than it was before, while in others revenue might be recognized earlier. Simply put, the timing of revenue in countless companies throughout the world is changing because of the new standards.

This chapter focuses on the five-step model that serves as the centerpiece of the two standards. As we present each of the steps, we will explore a number of complexities that may arise as companies try to apply the model.

The Five-Step Revenue Recognition Model

The five-step model is as follows:

1. Identify the contract(s) with a customer.

2. Identify the performance obligations in the contract.

3. Determine the transaction price.

4. Allocate the transaction price to the performance obligations in the contract.

5. Recognize revenue when (or as) the entity satisfies a performance obligation.

A contract contains a promise (or promises) to transfer goods or services to a customer. A performance obligation is a promise (or a group of promises). Identifying performance obligations can be relatively straightforward, such as an electronics store's promise to provide a television. But it can also be more complex, such as a contract to provide a new computer system with a three-year software license, a right to upgrades, and technical support. Businesses must determine whether to account for performance obligations separately, or as a group.

Transfer means that control has passed from seller to buyer. Control implies the ability to direct the use of and obtain substantially all of the benefits from the asset or service. The following are some indicators that may, though not necessarily will be, indicators of control:

- The seller has a present right to payment for the asset.

- The customer has legal title to the asset.

- The seller has transferred physical possession of the asset.

- The seller has the ability to prevent others from directing the use of, and obtaining the benefits from, the asset or service.

- The customer has the risks and rewards of ownership of the asset.

The transaction price is the amount of consideration an entity expects to be entitled to from a customer in exchange for providing the goods or services. In other words, how much is the customer expected to pay if the performance obligations are met? Sounds easy enough, but several factors must be considered, including whether there is variable consideration, a significant financing component, or noncash consideration.

The transaction price is then allocated to the separate performance obligations based on relative standalone selling prices. Determining the relative standalone selling price can be challenging when goods or services are not sold on a standalone basis. The revenue standard sets out several methods that can be used to estimate a standalone selling price when one is not directly observable. Allocating discounts and variable consideration must also be considered.

Revenue is recognized when (or as) the performance obligations are satisfied. The revenue standard provides guidance to help determine if a performance obligation is satisfied at a point in time or over time. Where a performance obligation is satisfied over time (for example, in a long-term construction contract), the related revenue is also recognized over time.

The revenue standard applies to all contracts with customers, except for contracts that are within the scope of other standards, such as leases, insurance, and financial instruments. Other items might also be presented as revenue because they arise from a company's ordinary activities, but are not within the scope of the revenue standard, including interest and dividends. Changes in the value of biological assets or investment properties under IFRS do not come under the revenue standard, as are changes in regulatory assets and liabilities for certain rate-regulated entities under US GAAP.

In the discussion that follows, we explore each of the five steps in more detail.

Step 1: Identifying the contract with a customer

The first step is to identify the "contract," which IFRS 15 defines as "an agreement between two or more parties that creates enforceable rights and obligations." A contract can be written, oral or implied by a company's customary business practices. A contract does not exist if each party has a unilateral right to terminate a wholly unperformed contract without compensating the other party.

A customer is defined as "a party that has contracted with an entity to obtain goods or services that are an output of the entity's ordinary activities in exchange for consideration." The reference to "the entity's ordinary activities" eliminates transactions that are not part of the firm's regular operations, such as sales of used equipment, from the scope of the standard. In other words, selling used assets constitutes gains or losses that must appear on the income statement, but are not considered revenue. This practice is largely unchanged from earlier standards.

All of the following conditions must be met for a firm to account for a contract with a customer as revenue under the new standard:

- All parties to the contract have approved the contract and are legally obligated to perform their obligations under the contract.

- Each party's rights regarding the goods or services being exchanged can be identified.

- Payment terms can be identified, although consideration may include a variable component.

- The contract has commercial substance. Commercial substance means that the amount, timing, and/or the uncertainty of the firm's future cash flows have changed as a result of the contract.

- Collection is probable. "Probable" under IFRS means "more likely than not," resulting in a threshold of 50% probability. Under US GAAP, "probable" means "likely to occur," which is a higher threshold than 50%, such as 75% or even higher.

Step 1 seems, on the face of it, to be relatively straightforward, but when there are multiple parties to a contract, identifying the customer can be complex. For example, a health care provider, especially in the United States, often has contracts with both the patient and a third-party insurer. Judgment is required to assess the substance of each contract to determine which party is the customer.

Further complications can arise when a contract undergoes later modifications. These modifications can be treated as new contracts or as part of existing contracts. The former applies if both of the following conditions are met:

- The modification adds distinct goods or services to the agreement.

- The increase in the contract price reflects the standalone selling price of the additional goods or services.

The five-step model is then applied to the contract modification in the same way it would be if the additions to the contract were a new contract.

Another factor to consider is when a payment is received from a customer before the contract even exists. In such a case, revenue is recognized when the payment is nonrefundable and any of the following events has occurred:

- There are no remaining obligations to transfer goods or services to the customer.

- The contract has been terminated.

- The seller has transferred the goods or services to which the payment received relates, and it has no further obligation to transfer goods or services.

If payment is received after a contract has come into existence, but the payment occurs before the seller has satisfied its performance obligation under the contract, the discrepancy between when the payment is received and when the obligation is satisfied is considered a "significant financing component." This topic is discussed under Step 3.

Step 2: Identify the performance obligations in the contract

At the inception of a contract, the selling firm must determine its performance obligations. Each obligation is a promise to provide goods or services. To put it another way, a performance obligation is what the buyer is paying the seller to deliver. This step requires a seller to identify what it has promised. It then determines whether a promise or multiple promises represent one or more performance obligations to the customer. To accomplish this task, the seller should determine whether the promises in the contract are distinct. ASC 606 notes that "a good or service that is promised to a customer is distinct if both of the following criteria are met":

- The customer can benefit from the good or service either on its own or together with other resources that are readily available to the customer (that is, the good or service is capable of being distinct).

- The entity's promise to transfer the good or service to the customer is separately identifiable from other promises in the contract (that is, the promise to transfer the good or service is distinct within the context of the contract).

In most cases, a performance obligation is easy to identify. For instance, when a contract simply states that an automobile dealer will sell a car to a customer, we expect that delivering the car is the performance obligation. But some obligations can be harder to spot. As already noted, a performance obligation can be implicit, meaning that it doesn't have to be stated in the contract. Some performance obligations can be implied by the seller's past behavior creating a valid expectation of performance in the mind of a customer.

Each distinct good or service that an entity promises to transfer is a performance obligation. Goods and services that are not distinct are bundled with other goods or services in the contract until a bundle of goods or services that is distinct is created. The bundle of goods or services in that case is a single performance obligation.

For example, a promise to provide hotel management services for a specified contract term could be treated as a single performance obligation, even though a series of different activities are performed. This is because the company is providing the same service of "hotel management" each period, even though some of the underlying activities may vary each day. The underlying activities (for example, reservation services, room cleaning, property maintenance) are activities to fulfill the hotel management service rather than separate promises.

When there are multiple promises in a contract, management needs to determine whether goods or services are distinct and, therefore, separate performance obligations. A good or service that is promised to a customer is distinct if both of the following criteria are met:

- The customer can benefit from the good or service either on its own or together with other resources that are readily available to the customer. In other words, the good or service is capable of being distinct.

- The seller's promise to transfer the good or service to the customer is separately identifiable from other promises in the contract. This criterion means that the promise to transfer the good or service is distinct within the context of the contract.

Factors indicating that two or more promises to transfer goods or services are not separately identifiable include:

- The seller provides a significant service of integrating the goods or services with other goods or services promised in the contract.

- One or more of the goods or services significantly modifies or is significantly modified by other goods or services promised in the contract.

- The goods or services are highly interdependent or interrelated.

To illustrate the first of these factors, ASC 606 provides an example based on a software developer. The developer agrees to license the software, and provide updates and technical support. In this case, each performance obligation is highly integrated with the others, and therefore none is separately identifiable. In other words, the components of this contract are considered a single performance obligation.

Complicating matters still further, contracts frequently include options for customers to purchase additional goods or services in the future. Customer options that provide a material right to the customer (such as a free or discounted good or service) give rise to a separate performance obligation. In this case, the performance obligation is the option itself, rather than the underlying goods or services. Management will allocate a portion of the transaction price to such options, and recognize revenue allocated to the option when the additional goods or services are transferred to the customer, or when the option expires unused.

Warranties are another issue that come under Step 2. Sellers must now distinguish between warranties representing assurance of a product's performance and service-type warranties. Assurance warranties would continue to be accounted for as before the new revenue-recognition standard – accrued as expenses and liabilities in the period of sale. A warranty is a service-type warranty if the customer has the option to purchase it separately or if it provides a service to the customer beyond fixing defects existing at the time of sale. Service-type warranties are accounted for as separate performance obligations. If an entity promises both assurance and service-type warranties but cannot reasonably account for them separately, it would account for both together as a single performance obligation.

The standard offers three factors that should be considered in each evaluation:

a. **Legal requirement.** Is the warranty required by law? If the intention is to protect the customer from purchasing a defective product, it likely does not represent a separate performance obligation.

b. **Warranty term.** The longer the coverage period, the more likely it covers repairs that were not caused by unseen defects at the time of sale.

c. **Services required under the warranty.** If the seller must perform certain tasks to assure that the product complies with agreed-upon specifications, those services likely would not constitute a separate performance obligation. An example would be offering return shipping for a defective product.

Borrowing from an example offered by the FASB staff who worked on the new standard, imagine a luggage company that provides a lifetime warranty that states, "If your baggage is broken or damaged, we will repair it free of charge." The seller should determine whether the substance of the warranty reflects additional service, considering the promises made. It would first review the three factors for assessing whether a warranty provides a customer with a service in addition to the assurance that the product satisfies agreed-upon specifications:

a. **Legal requirement.** Since there is no law requiring an entity to make a lifetime promise, this suggests the warranty is a performance obligation.

b. **Length of coverage.** The lifetime promise suggests the warranty is a performance obligation.

c. **Nature of promise.** Since the baggage warranty goes beyond the promise that the baggage complies with agreed-upon specifications, this suggests the warranty is a performance obligation.

The FASB determined that based on the promise made and the three indicators provided in the standard, the warranty provided by the baggage company in the above example goes beyond mere assurance that the product complies with agreed-upon specifications, meaning it should be accounted for as a separate performance obligation.

Gift cards

When a customer purchases a gift card, it is prepaying for goods or services to be delivered in the future. The seller should recognize a liability for the amount of the prepayment. The journal entry is as follows:

```
Cash                        xx
    Gift card liability              xx
```

When the performance obligation is fulfilled – for example, when the card is redeemed for merchandise – the liability is removed and revenue is recognized:

```
Gift card liability         xx
    Revenue                          xx
```

Any portion of the card that is unused by the customer is known as "breakage." In cases where there is significant breakage, the unused portion of the card is recognized as revenue when the likelihood of the customer exercising its rights becomes remote. For example, if a retailer knows from experience that cards with unused balances tend not to redeemed after 2 years from purchase, the unused portion of the card can be recognized as revenue at that time.

There is an important exception to the above rule. Where "escheat" laws apply, the seller cannot recognize breakage revenue because it is required to remit the funds to a third party. In several American states, for instance, unused portions of gift cards must be remitted to a government body. If so, the company should not recognize revenue related to unexercised rights.

Step 3: Determine the transaction price

The third step is determining the transaction price. The transaction price in a contract reflects the amount of consideration to which an entity expects to be entitled in exchange for goods or services transferred. The transaction price includes only those amounts to which the entity has rights under the present contract. Management must take into account any consideration that is variable, noncash consideration, and amounts payable to a customer to determine the transaction price. Management also needs to assess whether a significant financing component exists in arrangements with customers.

The revenue standard provides the following guidance on determining the transaction price: "An entity shall consider the terms of the contract and its customary business practices to determine the transaction price. The transaction price is the amount of consideration to which an entity expects to be entitled in exchange for transferring promised goods or services to a customer, excluding amounts collected on behalf of third parties (for example, sales taxes). The consideration promised in a contract with a customer may include fixed amounts, variable amounts, or both. The transaction price is the amount that an entity allocates to the performance obligations identified in the contract and, therefore, represents the amount of revenue recognized as those performance obligations are satisfied. The transaction price excludes amounts collected on behalf of third parties, such as sales taxes the entity collects on behalf of the government." This final provision means that value added taxes are not consider part of the transaction price, a practice that is unchanged from earlier standards.

Determining the transaction price can be straightforward, such as where a contract is for a fixed amount of consideration in return for a fixed number of goods or services over a reasonably short time period. Complexities arise where a contract includes, for example, variable consideration and a significant financing component.

Variable consideration

Some contracts contain an element of consideration that is variable or contingent upon certain thresholds or events being met or achieved. The variable consideration included in the transaction price is measured using a probability-weighted or most likely amount.

Contractually stated prices for goods or services might not represent the amount of consideration that an entity expects to be entitled to as a result of its customary business practices. For example, management should consider whether the entity has a practice of providing price concessions to customers. Or the amounts to which the seller is entitled to could in some cases be paid by other parties. For example, a manufacturer might offer a coupon to end customers that will be redeemed by retailers. The retailer should include the consideration received from both the end customer and any reimbursement from the manufacturer in determining the transaction price.

Management should assume that the contract will be fulfilled as agreed upon and not cancelled, renewed, or modified when determining the transaction price. The transaction price also generally does not include estimates of consideration from the future exercise of options for additional goods and services, because until a customer exercises that right, the seller does not have a right to consideration. An exception is made, however, for customer options that meet certain criteria (for example, some contract renewals) that allows management to estimate goods or services to be provided under the option when determining the transaction price.

If the consideration promised in a contract includes a variable amount, the seller will estimate the amount of consideration to which it is entitled in exchange for transferring the promised goods or services to a customer. Variable consideration is common and takes various forms, including (but not limited to) price concessions, volume discounts, rebates, refunds, credits, incentives, performance bonuses, and royalties. An entity's past business practices can cause consideration to be variable if there is a history of providing discounts or concessions after goods are sold.

Consideration is also variable if the amount an entity will receive is contingent on a future event occurring or not occurring, even though the amount itself is fixed. This might be the case, for example, if a customer can return a product it has purchased. The amount of consideration the entity is entitled to receive depends on whether the customer retains the product or not. Similarly, consideration might be contingent upon meeting certain performance goals or deadlines.

The revenue standard provides two methods for estimating variable consideration. An entity shall estimate an amount of variable consideration by using either of the following methods:

- **The expected value.**   The expected value is the sum of probability-weighted amounts in a range of possible consideration amounts. An expected value may be an appropriate estimate of the amount of variable consideration if an entity has a large number of contracts with similar characteristics.

- **The most likely amount.**   The most likely amount is the single most likely amount in a range of possible consideration amounts (that is, the single most likely outcome of the contract). The most likely amount may be an appropriate estimate of the amount of variable consideration if the contract has only two possible outcomes (for example, an entity either achieves a performance bonus or does not).

Management should use the method that it expects best predicts the amount of consideration to which the entity will be entitled based on the terms of the contract. The method used should be applied consistently throughout the contract.

The following example illustrates how customer rebates affect the transaction price. A manufacturer sells electric razors to retailers for €75. A rebate coupon is included inside the package that can be redeemed by end consumers for €15 per unit. The manufacturer estimates that about 25% of eligible rebates will be redeemed based on its experience with similar programs. It therefore concludes that the transaction price should incorporate an assumption of a 25% rebate redemption. How then should the seller determine the transaction price?

The manufacturer records sales to the retailer at a transaction price of €71.25 [€75 − (25% × €15)]. The difference between the per unit cash selling price to the retailers and the transaction price is recorded as a liability.

Significant financing components

Sellers are required to identify any significant financing components in their contracts with customers. The accounting aims to recognize revenue in the amount that would have been paid in cash if the timing of the payment coincided with the timing of the revenue recognition. In other words, a financing component exist when the timing of a payment does not coincide with the time when the performance obligation is satisfied. Financing components can be either financing of the customer by the seller or vice versa.

When the customer is financed by the seller (i.e., payment is made after the performance obligation is satisfied), the recognition of revenue results in the simultaneous recognition of a contract asset. Interest income accrues on the contract asset until the payment is made. When the seller is financed by the customer (i.e., payment is made before the performance obligation is satisfied), a contract liability is recognized when the payment is received and interest expense accrues until the revenue is recognized.

What if the customer has a right of return?

In many business settings, customers are entitled to a full or partial credit if they return a product within a specified period. In such cases, the variable consideration discussed above applies. For example, suppose a discount retailer sells goods for an aggregate price of $250,000 and a cost of $180,000. Customers have a right of return within 30 days. Based on recent history, the retailer estimates that goods representing 5% of the total sales will be returned. Revenue for the period is 95% × $250,000 = $237,500, resulting in the recognition of a refund liability of $12,500:

Cash	$250,000	
Sales revenue		$237,500
Refund liability		$12,500

The estimated returns also affect cost of goods sold (COGS). COGS is recognized only on that portion of the total sales for which revenue has been recognized. In this example, COGS is $180,000 × 95% = $171,000. The difference between the inventory that is removed from the balance sheet ($180,000) and the amount charged to COGS is recognized as an asset, which represents the right to recover the inventory if and when it is returned:

COGS	$171,000	
Inventory recovery asset	$9,000	
Inventory		$180,000

Slotting fees

Slotting fees are an issue that often arises in retailing, especially supermarket chains. Here, a food processing company is charged by the retailer for having their products placed on the retailer's shelves. To illustrate, suppose a manufacturer sells products to a retailer for $10 million. The manufacturer also makes a $1 million nonrefundable upfront payment for favorable product placement. Because the service (access to store shelves) is of no value without selling products to the retailer, the two components of the transaction cannot be considered separate performance obligations. Instead, the manufacturer should recognize a reduction in the transaction price of $1 million and, therefore, recognize $9 million in revenue when control of the products transfers to the retailer. From the retailer's perspective, the $1 million upfront payment is not a payment for satisfying a distinct performance obligation and, therefore, should not be accounted for as revenue. Instead, it should be recognized as a reduction in cost of goods sold.

Price protection guarantees

Another common issue that arises in retailing is a price guarantee. Here, the retailer promises to reimburse a customer if the same product is found to sell at a lower price. For example, an electronics retailer sells a television to a customer for $300 and agrees to reimburse the customer for the difference between the purchase price and any lower price offered by a direct competitor during the three-month period following the sale. Based on prior experience with similar promotions in the past the retailer estimates it will reimburse the customer $15. The expected reimbursement should be excluded from revenue and recorded as a liability at the time of sale:

Cash	$300	
Revenue		$285
Liability		$15

Step 4: Allocate the transaction price to the performance obligation(s)

The fourth step in the model is to allocate the transaction price to the separate performance obligations identified in Step 2. The objective when allocating the transaction price is for a seller to allocate the transaction price to each performance obligation (i.e., each distinct good or service) in an amount that represents the payments expected by the seller in exchange for transferring the promised goods or services to the customer.

As we noted earlier in this chapter, many contracts involve the sale of more than one good or service. Such contracts might involve the sale of multiple goods, goods followed by related services, or multiple services. The transaction price must be allocated to each separate performance obligation so that revenue is recorded at the right time and in the right amounts. To complicate matters, the allocation could be affected by variable considerations or discounts.

The overriding principle of Step 4 is that the transaction price should be allocated to each performance obligation based on the relative standalone selling prices of the goods or services being provided to the customer. Management should determine the standalone selling price for each item and allocate the transaction price based on each item's relative value to the total value of the goods and services in the arrangement. For example, if a contract has three distinct performance obligations – we'll call them A, B, and C – with standalone selling prices of €60, €30 and €10, respectively, 60% of the total transaction price will be allocated to performance obligation A, 30% to B, and 10% to C.

The best evidence of standalone selling price is the price a seller charges for that good or service when the good or services is sold separately in similar circumstances to similar customers. However, goods or services are not always sold separately. If so, the standalone selling price needs to be estimated or derived by other means. This estimate often requires judgment, such as when specialized goods or services are sold only as part of a bundled arrangement. In any case, the relative standalone selling price of each performance obligation is determined at contract inception. The transaction price is not reallocated after contract inception to reflect subsequent changes in standalone selling prices.

Discounts

A contractually stated price or list price for a good or service may be, but should not be presumed to be, the standalone selling price for the good or service. Sellers often provide discounts. The seller's customary business practices should be considered, including adjustments to list prices, when determining the standalone selling price of an item.

To illustrate, assume a dealer in marine equipment sells boats and provides mooring facilities for its customers. It sells the boats for $50,000 each and provides mooring facilities for $8,000 per year. The boats and mooring facilities are deemed to be distinct and, therefore, the seller accounts for them as separate performance obligations. It enters into a contract to sell a boat and one year of mooring services to a customer for $53,000 (a discount of $5,000 over the combined prices). The seller should allocate the transaction price of $53,000 to the boat and the mooring services based on their relative standalone selling prices ($50,000 and $8,000):

$$\text{Boat: } \$45,690 \left[\$53,000 \times \left(\$50,000 \div \$58,000 \right) \right]$$
$$\text{Mooring services: } \$7,310 \left[\$53,000 \times \left(\$8,000 \div \$58,000 \right) \right]$$

The allocation results in the $5,000 discount being allocated proportionately to the two performance obligations.

In the above example, the standalone selling price of both performance obligations is directly observable. If a directly observable price does not exist, one must be estimated. The revenue standard does not prescribe or prohibit any particular method, as long as the method results in an estimate that faithfully represents the price the seller would charge for the goods or services if they were sold separately. These prices can be estimated in a number of ways. One approach is to estimate the expected cost of the good or service, and then add a profit margin. But other methods are acceptable too.

Loyalty programs

An issue that often arises in implementing Step 4 is the accounting for loyalty programs. Retailers, for example, often use such programs to build brand loyalty and increase sales volume. Airlines, too, have their frequent flyer programs. Each time a customer makes a purchase, they are rewarded with points that they can later redeem for free or discounted goods or services. The awards are considered a separate performance obligation and therefore some portion of the transaction price must be allocated to them. Implementing this requirement is complicated because companies need to make credible estimates of redemption rates, breakage, and the value of the award.

To illustrate how the accounting for loyalty programs works, consider a retailer with a program that rewards customers one point for every dollar spent. Points are redeemable for $0.10 off future purchases. A customer spends $500 on products and earns 500 points redeemable for $50 off future purchases. The retailer expects that 450 points will be redeemed, which means 10% of the points will expire unredeemed. The retailer then estimates a standalone selling price for the incentive of $0.09 per point ($0.10, less 10% breakage).

The retailer will allocate the transaction price of $500 between the product and points based on the relative standalone prices of $500 for the product and $45 for the loyalty reward:

$$\text{Product}: \quad \$459 \quad = \quad \left[\$500 \times (\$500 \div \$545) \right]$$
$$\text{Points}: \quad \$41 \quad = \quad \left[\$500 \times (\$45 \div \$545) \right]$$

At time the product is transferred to the customer:

Cash	$500	
Revenue		$459
Liability		$41

When the points are redeemed or expire unused:

Liability	$41	
Revenue		$41

The revenue allocated to the product ($459) is recognized upon transfer to the customer, and the revenue allocated to the points ($41) is recognized upon the redemption or expiration of the points, whichever comes first. The estimate of the breakage is updated at the end of each period and the contract liability adjusted accordingly.

Step 5: Recognize the revenue

Revenue is recognized when or as performance obligations are satisfied by transferring control of a promised good or service to a customer. A customer obtains control of a good or service if it has the ability to direct the use of and obtain substantially all of the remaining benefits from that good or service. A customer could have the future right to direct the use of the asset and obtain substantially all of the benefits from it (for example, upon making a prepayment for a specified product), but the customer must have actually obtained those rights for control to have transferred.

Directing the use of an asset refers to a customer's right to deploy that asset, allow another entity to deploy it, or restrict another entity from using it. An asset's benefits are the potential cash inflows (or reduced cash outflows) that are expected from its use. Examples include using the asset to produce goods or provide services, selling or exchanging the asset, and using the asset to settle liabilities or reduce expenses. Another example is the ability to pledge the asset (such as land) as collateral for a loan or to hold it for future use.

Management should evaluate transfer of control primarily from the customer's perspective. Considering the transaction from the customer's perspective reduces the risk that revenue is recognized for activities that do not transfer control of a good or service to the customer.

"Point in time" vs. "over time"

Management needs to determine, at contract inception, whether control of a good or service transfers to a customer over time or at a point in time. Arrangements where the performance obligations are satisfied over time are not limited to services arrangements. Complex assets or certain customized goods constructed for a customer, such as a complex refinery or specialized machinery, could also transfer over time, depending on the terms of the arrangement.

An entity transfers control of a good or service over time and, therefore, satisfies a performance obligation and recognizes revenue over time, if one of the following criteria is met:

- The customer simultaneously receives and consumes the benefits provided by the entity's performance as the entity performs.

- The entity's performance creates or enhances an asset (for example, work in process on a construction project) that the customer controls.

- The entity's performance does not create an asset with an alternative use to the entity, and the entity has an enforceable right to payment for performance completed to date.

The first of these criteria mainly applies to contracts for the provision of services, such as security or cleaning services. An entity transfers the benefit of the services to the customer as it performs and therefore satisfies its performance obligation over time. This criterion also applies to arrangements such as contracts to deliver electricity or natural gas.

For the second criterion, management should apply the principle of control to determine whether the customer obtains control of an asset as it is created. Like so much in this new standard, determining if the customer controls the work in process often requires judgment. For example, a government entity might control work in process if a contractor is building a specialized military aircraft, while a commercial airline might not control the work in process.

Measuring progress for "over time" contracts

Once management determines that a performance obligation is satisfied over time, it must measure its progress toward completion to determine the timing of revenue recognition. For each performance obligation satisfied over time, an entity shall recognize revenue over time by measuring the progress toward complete satisfaction of that performance obligation. The objective when measuring progress is to depict a business's performance in transferring control of goods or services promised to a customer (that is, satisfaction of its performance obligation).

The purpose of measuring progress toward satisfaction of a performance obligation is to recognize revenue in a pattern that reflects the transfer of control of the promised good or service to the customer. Management can employ various methods for measuring progress, but whichever method is selected should be the one that best depicts the transfer of control of the goods or services.

Methods for measuring progress fall into two broad categories:

- **Output methods**, that recognize revenue based on direct measurements of the value transferred to the customer, and

- **Input methods**, that recognize revenue based on the entity's efforts to satisfy the performance obligation.

Output methods recognize revenue on the basis of direct measurements of the value to the customer of the goods or services transferred to date relative to the remaining goods or services promised under the contract. Examples include surveys of work performed, units produced, units delivered, and contract milestones. Output methods directly measure performance and can be the most faithful representation of progress. However, it can be difficult to obtain directly observable information about the output of performance without incurring undue costs in some circumstances, in which case use of an input method might be necessary.

Input methods recognize revenue based on the entity's effort to satisfy the performance obligation relative to the total expected effort to satisfy the performance obligation. For example, resources consumed, labor hours expended, costs incurred, time elapsed, or machine hours used.

However, wasted costs should not be included in estimating progress toward completion. If the entity's efforts are expended evenly throughout the performance period, it may be appropriate to recognize revenue on a straight-line basis.

Each of these methods has advantages and disadvantages which should be considered in determining which is the most appropriate in a particular arrangement. Management should select the method of measuring progress that best depicts the transfer of goods or services to the customer.

"Over time" accounting illustrated

Accounting for revenue over time is common in any sector with long-term contracts. Construction is one obvious example.

Under the new standards, a portion of the contract price as revenue during each accounting period over which the work is performed. For example, if 40% of the total work was accomplished in a given year, 40% of the contract price is recognized as revenue. The proportion of total work carried out in any period is usually based on either engineers' estimates of the degree of completion (as mentioned above, an output-based approach) or from the ratio of costs incurred to date to the total costs expected for the entire contract (an input-based approach).

The actual schedule of cash collections does not affect the revenue-recognition process under this method. In fact, this approach is used even in cases where the entire payment comes at the end of the contract, as long as the firm is able to reasonably estimate total revenues and total expenses over the life of the contract, the amount of work completed in any given period, and the collection of cash is reasonably assured.

To illustrate, assume that a firm has signed a three-year contract to construct a building. Total expected revenues are $10 million, and total expected costs are $8 million (with $4 million in the first year, and $2 million in each of the final two years). Revenue and expense recognition would look like this (assuming the work proceeds as expected) – see Table 4.1.

Suppose progress payments are made by the client as follows: $4.5 million at the end of the first year, $2.5 million at the end of the second year, and the remaining $3 million upon the project's completion. The contractor would make the following journal entries to record the progress payments:

Year 1

Cash	4.5	
Accounts receivable	0.5	
Revenue		5.0
Expenses	4.0	
Cash		4.0

Table 4.1 **Revenues and Expenses Under the Percentage-of-Completion Method**

Year	% of completion	Revenue	Expense	Profit
1	$4m/$8m = 50%	$5.0m	$4m	$1.0m
2	$2m/$8m = 25%	2.5m	2m	0.5m
3	$2m/$8m = 25%	2.5m	2m	0.5m
		$10m	$8m	$2m

Year 2

Cash	2.5	
Revenue		2.5
Expenses	2.0	
Cash		2.0

Year 3

Cash	3.0	
Accounts rec.		0.5
Revenue		2.5
Expenses	2.0	
Cash		2.0

Note that the receipt of cash has no influence on the recognition of either revenues or expenses. It should also be noted that the above example was based on an input approach: the proportion of expenses incurred in a given year as a percentage of the total determined the percentage of work done. Alternatively, the firm could have chosen an output-based measure in which independent engineers certify a particular percentage of the total work as being completed. For example, if the engineers had certified that 55% of the total work was completed in the first year, the contractor could have recognized more revenue.

One factor to consider is the effect of cost overruns. For example, materials costs prove to be higher than budgeted, or inefficiencies result in higher labor costs. The important point here is to isolate the overruns and ensure that they have no influence on estimates of the percentage of work completed. If cost increases do not result from the performance of additional work, but rather from costs exceeding budgets, the increases should not result in the recognition of additional revenue. Many companies have found themselves in deep trouble because project managers obscured overruns, and maybe even theft, by citing higher percentages of completion, and therefore higher revenue. When the day of reckoning comes, and it must, the consequences can be devastating. For example, in early 2017 the Japan based Toshiba recorded losses on its United States nuclear power plant construction subsidiary that wiped out all of the retained earnings of the company. The loss was needed to admit that there were massive cost overruns at the nuclear unit.

Another factor to note is what to do in the case of an onerous contract. This term refers to a contract in which losses are inevitable for the reporting entity. In such cases, the losses must be recognized immediately, even if the contract is far from being completed and the magnitude of the losses is not known with certainty. This treatment results from the conservatism principle introduced in Chapter 3.

Revenue-Recognition Controversies

In some businesses, the revenue-recognition decision is fairly straightforward. But in many others, especially those with unique or unusual business models, the decision is not always so obvious. Even in relatively simple businesses, there may be enough latitude available to management to mislead investors on how much revenue has really been earned in a given year.

One of the major tasks of the financial statement reader is to understand the chosen policy, to determine if that policy is reasonable given the underlying economics of the business, and if the reported revenue figures are supported by economic reality. For example, if a company reports 10% revenue growth in a stagnant industry, can this figure be defended?

Improper revenue recognition is often the cause of spectacular, high-profile financial reporting controversies. The SEC reports that over half of all financial reporting frauds in the United States involving publicly traded companies result from the deliberate overstatement of revenue. The practice has become so widespread that the chief accountant of the Commission's Enforcement Division felt compelled to say that improper revenue recognition is the "recipe of choice for cooking the books."[1]

Indeed, the problem is truly global. One of Japan's most prominent internet companies – Livedoor – was caught out in a major accounting scandal involving the inappropriate recognition of revenue. Lernout & Hauspie, a Belgian voice-recognition software company with a market capitalization of $9 billion at the peak of the dot-com boom of the late 1990s, collapsed when it was discovered that nearly all of its revenues resulted from fictitious transactions with Asian affiliates. The shares of India's Satyam Computer Services collapsed in 2009 when it was discovered that most of the company's reported revenues were fictitious. Also, the notorious collapse of Parmalat, the Italian dairy company, was triggered in part by the discovery of fraudulent revenue-recognition practices.

In this section, we address some of the more common issues, controversies, and scandals that arise in revenue recognition.

Channel Stuffing

Sometimes sellers use their power over customers to induce them to purchase more goods than is necessary to satisfy demand, thus allowing the sellers to report higher sales and profits. For example, automobile manufacturers have often been charged by dealers with pushing products through the distribution chain before the dealers really want them. The temptation for the automobile company to pursue such a strategy can be difficult to overcome when sales or profit figures for the year fall just short of targets. Bristol-Myers Squibb, a large pharmaceuticals company, was charged with boosting sales in 2000 and 2001 by offering discounts to wholesalers to purchase more drugs than patients needed. However, in early 2002, wholesalers stopped building up inventories, and the game was up. The company was forced to restate results, wiping out $2 billion of previously recognized revenue.

Although this practice is discouraged, US GAAP and IFRS are somewhat ambiguous on how to treat it. Generally, the seller can get away with it as long as there is no agreement for product returns. But even if the company gets away with it, and most do, channel stuffing catches up with them eventually because it effectively moves sales forward from future periods. At some point in the future, sales will take a hit because sales that should have been recognized in the current period had already been recognized in previous periods.

Gross vs. Net

Some companies use their distribution systems or auction platforms to act as "go-betweens," or agents, for buyers and sellers. In effect, other companies' goods are sold at a slight markup. The reporting entity can easily inflate revenues by choosing to report the transactions on a gross basis, instead of reporting only the markup or commission. This practice became especially popular during the dot-com boom, as start-ups searched for ways to report the highest revenue numbers possible. One motive for such behavior was the belief that share prices are driven by revenue growth and not profitability. The dot-com meltdown in 2000 disproved this notion, but the temptation has not disappeared.

According to the new revenue-recognition standards, a company should record revenue on a gross basis if it controls the specified good or service before it is transferred to the customer.

Round Trips

This practice is similar to barter transaction except that one company sells a product for cash to another company, which in turn sells an equivalent product back to the initial seller for a similar price. Each recognizes revenue on the sale. Although round trips are not allowed under US GAAP or IFRS, companies may try to disguise them by running transactions through a third party.

One variant is to sell inventory to third parties in one period, agreeing to buy it back in the next. Delphi, an auto-parts company carved out of General Motors, was accused of this practice. Symbol Technologies, a maker of barcode readers and mobile computing equipment, was charged with pushing unwanted products on distributors, promising to buy them back at a 1% premium. The transactions were really loans, disguised as sales.

Deferred Payments

In some industries, payments for goods sold are made over an extended period (sometimes lasting several years). Revenue can be recognized on a discounted cash-flow basis at the point of sale, but are collections reasonably assured and what discount rates are being used? For example, Xerox's Mexican subsidiary was found to use artificially low discount rates to boost present values, and thus the amount of revenue recognized from equipment leasing. The company was later forced to restate results.

Bill and Hold

Here, the seller invoices the buyer but does not ship the product. In effect, it's a special case of channel stuffing. Revenue can be recognized under such circumstances, but only if certain criteria are met:

- the reason for the arrangement is substantive;
- the product has been identified separately as belonging to the customer;
- the product is ready for delivery; and
- the seller does not have the ability to use the product or sell it to another customer.

If all of these criteria are met, control is deemed to have been transferred to the customer and revenue can be recognized. The seller is simply providing temporary storage until the customer is ready to accept delivery. If any of the aforementioned criteria are not met, the customer has not yet obtained control and the seller may not recognize revenue.

In extreme (i.e., criminal) cases, companies have been found to create false bill-and-hold letters from customers to justify premature revenue recognition.

Holding the Books Open

The idea here is to capture sales in one period that actually occur in the next. One variant of this practice: a company deliberately ships the wrong products at the end of the quarter or year when the products requested by the customer are not yet available. After booking the revenue, the company cancels the order in the next period, and ships the correct products. This practice is strictly forbidden under US GAAP and IFRS, but tempting to ethically challenged executives desperate to inflate revenues.

KEY LESSONS FROM THE CHAPTER

- The FASB and IASB implemented new standards on revenue recognition. These standards took effect in 2018. The standards provide a five-step model for evaluating how and when revenue should be recognized.

- The overriding principle of the new standards is that revenue should not be recognized until the good or service in question has been transferred to the buyer.

- Revenue recognition may seem like a straightforward exercise, but it is not always obvious when revenue should be recognized and in what amount.

- A performance obligation is a promise in a contract to transfer a distinct good or service to a customer. In essence, it is what a customer is paying for.

- Revenue can be recognized over time or at a point in time.

- The transaction price determined in Step 3 of the model should be allocated to all of the performance obligations in the arrangement based on standalone prices.

- Revenue recognition is probably the single greatest source of financial statement manipulation. The number of games that companies play is practically endless, but perhaps the most common is channel stuffing.

KEY TERMS AND CONCEPTS FROM THE CHAPTER

The five-step method	Transfer of control	Revenue recognition	Round trips
Performance obligation	Input method	Gross vs. net	Bill and hold
Transaction price	Output method	Barter transactions	Channel stuffing

QUESTIONS

1. Describe the 5-step revenue recognition model.

2. What is a "performance obligation"?

3. Describe the difference between revenues recognized at a point in time and those recognized over time?

4. What is the major difference between "output-based" methods and input-based methods for estimating over-time revenue?

5. How is the transaction price allocated for contracts with two or more performance obligations?

6. What is channel stuffing and how does it impact revenue recognition?

7. Describe the "gross vs. net" controversy. Why might a company prefer to recognize revenues on a gross basis?

PROBLEMS

4.1 Revenue Recognition at and After Time of Sale

Suite Novotel is an all-suites hotel chain owned and operated by the Accor Group. Most of the hotels in this chain are found in France, Spain, and Germany.

On the company website, customers are offered a nonrefundable special rate at €160 per night, or a refundable rate at €225 per night. In either case, the entire amount is charged to the customer's account at the time of booking. For the refundable room, if the reservation is cancelled prior to 16.00 on the date of arrival, a full refund of the amount charged is made. If the cancellation occurs after 16.00 the customer forfeits one day at the reserved rate (€225).

Required

Determine the appropriate journal entries for each of the following transactions:

a. On 6 March, a customer makes a nonrefundable reservation for three nights beginning 24 March. The customer arrives as scheduled and checks out on 27 March.

b. On 6 March, a customer makes a reservation identical to the one in part (a). On 21 March, the customer cancels the reservation.

c. On 6 March, a customer makes a refundable reservation for three nights beginning 24 March. The customer arrives as scheduled and checks out on 27 March.

d. On 6 March, a customer makes a reservation identical to the one in part (c). On 21 March the customer cancels the reservation.

e. On 6 March, a customer makes a reservation identical to the one in part (c). On 24 March, at 19.30, the customer cancels the reservation.

4.2 Recognizing Revenue Over Time

On 1 April 2018, Roller Construction entered into a fixed-price contract to construct an office building for €18 million. Roller recognizes revenue as the job is performed (i.e., over time). Information related to the contract appears below.

	December 31, 2018	December 31, 2019
Percentage completed	20%	60%
Estimated total cost	€13,500,000	€14,400,000
Profit recognized to date	€900,000	€2,160,000

Required

a. Calculate the revenues and expenses recognized for both 2018 and 2019.

b. What impact did the €900,000 increase in estimated total cost in 2019 have on revenue recognition in that year?

4.3 Journal Entries for Gift Cards

Subway is a global food retailer with stores located throughout the world. Suppose a customer at one of its Paris stores purchases a sandwich for €5.00, a brownie for €2.00 and a soft drink for €1.50. The customer pays with cash. Ignore any potential breakage.

Required

a. What journal entry will Subway record for this transaction? (Ignore expenses.)

b. Suppose that in addition to the above items, the customer buys a Subway gift card for €50.00. What journal entry would Subway record for this transaction?

c. Now suppose that the customer buys the same items listed above, but uses a previously purchased gift card to pay for the purchases. Also assume that there is a sufficient balance on the card to cover the entire cost. What journal entry would Subway make now to record the transaction?

4.4 Recognizing Revenue Over Time

On 1 September 2018, Tan Construction Company contracted to build a shopping complex on the east coast of Singapore. The total contract price was $90 million. As required by Singapore's Financial Reporting Standards (which are based on IFRS), Tan Construction uses the percentage-of-completion method in accounting for long-term contracts. The Company uses an input-based (i.e., cost-based) approach to determine the percentage of completion.

The schedule of expected and actual cash collections and contract costs is follows:

Year	Cash Collections from Customer	Estimated and Actual Cost Incurred
2018	$18.0 million	$6.0 million
2019	22.5 million	18.0 million
2020	22.5 million	24.0 million
2021	27.0 million	12.0 million
	$90.0 million	$60.0 million

Required

a. Calculate the amount of revenue, expense, and net income for each of the four years.

b. Show the journal entries that Tan Construction will make in 2018, 2019, 2020, and 2021 for this contract. Tan accumulates contract costs in a Construction in Progress account. The costs involve a mix of cash payments, credits to various other asset accounts, and credits to liability accounts. But for the sake of simplicity, assume that all costs are credited to Accounts Payable.

4.5 Revenue Recognition in Different Types of Businesses

Determine when Step 5 of the revenue recognition process is complete for each of the following types of businesses:

a. A bank lending money for home mortgages.

b. A firm that grows and harvests oranges.

c. A hair salon.

d. A professional football team that sells season tickets before the season begins.

e. A dress shop.

f. A cattle rancher.

g. An airline. Customers can accumulate frequent flyer miles, which earn them a free flight if enough miles are accumulated.

h. A producer of port wine that is aged from 10 to 15 years.

i. A real estate developer selling lots on long-term contracts with down payments equal to 10% of the selling price.

j. A real estate developer who constructs houses and then sells them near or at completion.

k. A printer who prints custom-order announcements (for weddings, etc.) and brochures.

l. A military contractor constructing fighter aircraft.

Case Study

4-1 Kiwi Builders, Ltd.

In May 2018, Kiwi Builders, Ltd. was employed by the government of Hamilton, New Zealand, to erect a municipal office building on the outskirts of the city. The contract called for work to begin a few weeks later. Kiwi took on the role of general contractor. Most of the work would be done by subcontractors.

Under the terms of the contract, Kiwi Builders was to receive $24 million in cash payments to be paid as follows: 25% when the work was 30% complete, another 25% when the work was 60% complete, and the remaining 50% when the work was fully completed. The contract stipulated that completion percentage estimates had to be certified by an independent engineering consultant before progress payments would be made.

In preparing its bid, the company estimated that the total cost to complete the project would be $21.6 million, assuming no cost overruns. Hence, the company expected a profit of $2.4 million.

During the first year of the contract, the company incurred costs of $6.48 million. In late June 2019, the engineering consulting firm of C. McMillan & Associates determined that the project was at least 30% complete, and on 30 June the first progress payment was made.

In the following year, the company incurred additional costs of $7.02 million. In late June 2020 the engineers certified that at least 60% of the project had been completed, and the second progress payment was made at the end of the month.

In their report, the engineers noted that the company might be facing significant cost overruns. The directors of Kiwi Builders responded by saying that anticipated efficiency improvements in the final phases of construction would offset any prior cost overruns. Subsequent results suggest that some, but not all, of the cost overruns were recovered.

By the end of May 2021, Kiwi's work was done. Actual costs incurred during the fiscal year ending 30 June 2021 were $8.4 million. The firm received certification for the fully completed building, and the final cash payment was made.

Required

a. Ignoring any other sources of revenues and expenses, determine the level of profits to be reported by Kiwi Builders, Ltd. for the years ended 30 June 2019, 2020, and 2021.

b. Kiwi experienced cost overruns in the second year of the project. In hindsight, the overruns proved modest. But assume that the magnitude of the problem was severe enough so that by the end of fiscal year 2020 it was apparent that Kiwi would suffer a loss on the project of approximately $700,000. What impact would such information have had on the accounting for the project?

Case Study

4-2 Revenue Recognition at Starbucks Corporation*

Introduction

On 2 February 2005, Starbucks Corporation's stock price plummeted 8.2% after the company released its latest revenue numbers (see Exhibit 4.1 for the company's stock graph). In a

*This case was adapted by S. David Young, Professor of Accounting and Control, INSEAD, from a case written by Jacob Cohen, Affiliate Professor of Accounting & Control and Business Law and Chad Myers, Research Associate. This case is intended to be used as a basis for class discussion rather than to illustrate either effective or ineffective handling of an administrative situation.

Exhibit 4.1   **Starbuck Stock Graph Performance Compared to the NASDAQ**

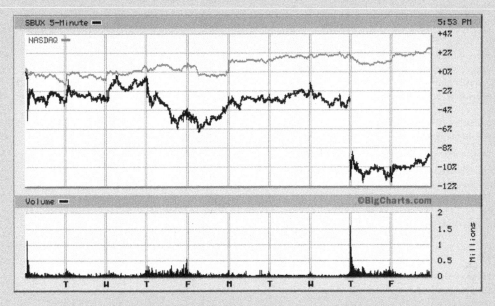

Stock performance for the week ending February 4, 2005

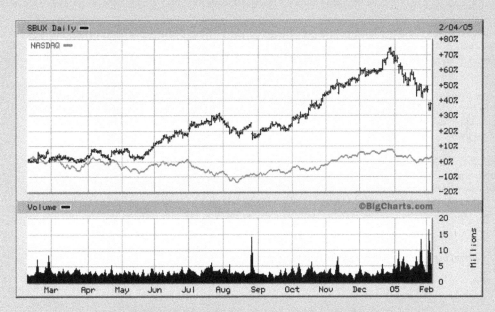

Stock performance for the year ending February 4, 2005

Source: www.BigChart.com, a service of Market Watch.

press statement, the specialty coffee company said sales rose 23% to $452 million from $368 million[2] for the four-week period ended 30 January 2005. Moreover, consolidated net revenues for the quarter were $2 billion, a 24% increase from $1.6 billion a year earlier.[3] Same-store sales, however, rose a disappointing 7%.[4] Starbucks' financial statements are shown in Exhibits 4.2–4.4.

(Continued)

Exhibit 4.2   **Starbucks Corp. Balance Sheet**

Diluted (In millions US$)	2004	2003
Assets		
Current assets:		
Cash and cash equivalents	$299.13	$200.91
Short-term investments – available-for-sale securities	329.08	128.91
Short-term investments – trading securities	24.80	20.20
Accounts receivable, net of allowances of $2.2 and $4.8, respectively	140.23	114.45
Inventories	422.66	342.94
Prepaid expenses and other current assets	71.35	55.17
Deferred income taxes, net	81.24	61.45
Total current assets	1,368.49	924.03
Long-term investments – available-for-sale securities	135.18	136.16
Equity and other investments	171.75	144.26
Property, plant and equipment, net	1,471.45	1,384.90
Other assets	85.56	52.11
Other intangible assets	26.80	24.94
Goodwill	68.95	63.34
Total Assets	$3,328.17	$2,729.75
Liabilities and Shareholders' Equity		
Current liabilities:		
Accounts payable	$199.35	$168.98
Accrued compensation and related costs	208.93	152.61
Accrued occupancy costs	65.87	56.18
Accrued taxes	63.04	54.93
Other accrued expenses	123.68	101.80
Deferred revenue	121.38	73.48
Current portion of long-term debt	0.74	0.72
Total current liabilities	782.98	608.70
Deferred income taxes, net	46.68	33.22
Long-term debt	3.62	4.35
Other long-term liabilities	8.13	1.05
Shareholders' equity:		
Common stock and additional paid-in capital	956.69	959.10
Other additional paid-in-capital	39.39	39.39
Retained earnings	1,461.46	1,069.68
Accumulated other comprehensive income	29.22	14.25

Source: Starbucks Corp. 10-K filing with Securities and Exchange Commission for fiscal year ended 3 October 2004.

Exhibit 4.3   **Starbucks Corp. Income Statement**

(In millions US$)	2004	2003	2002
Net revenues:			
Company-operated retail	$4,457.38	$3,449.62	$2,792.90
Specialty:			
Licensing	565.80	409.55	311.93
Foodservice and other	271.07	216.35	184.07
Total specialty	836.87	625.90	496.00
Total net revenues	5,294.25	4,075.52	3,288.91
Cost of sales including occupancy costs	2,198.65	1,685.93	1,350.01

(In millions US$)	2004	2003	2002
Store operating expenses	1,790.17	1,379.57	1,109.78
Other operating expenses	171.65	141.35	106.08
Depreciation and amortization expenses	280.02	237.81	205.56
General and administrative expenses	304.29	244.55	234.58
Subtotal operating expenses	4,744.79	3,689.21	3,006.02
Income from equity investees	60.66	38.40	33.45
Operating income	610.12	424.71	316.34
Interest and other income, net	14.14	11.62	9.30
Gain on sale of investment	-	-	13.36
Earnings before income taxes	624.26	436.34	339.00
Income taxes	232.48	167.99	126.31
Net earnings	$391.78	$268.35	$212.69
Weighted average shares outstanding:			
Basic	397.17	390.75	385.58
Diluted	411.47	401.65	397.53

Source: Starbucks Corp. 10-K filing with Securities and Exchange Commission for fiscal year ended 3 October 2004.

Exhibit 4.4　Starbucks Corp. Statement of Cash Flows

(In millions US$)	2004	2003	2002
Operating Activities			
Net earnings	$391.78	$268.35	$212.69
Adjustments to reconcile net earnings to net cash provided by operating activities:			
Depreciation and amortization	304.82	259.27	221.14
Gain on sale of investment	-	-	(13.36)
Provision for impairments and asset disposals	13.57	7.78	26.85
Deferred income taxes, net	(3.07)	(5.93)	(6.09)
Equity in income of investees	(33.39)	(22.81)	(19.58)
Tax benefit from exercise of nonqualified stock options	63.41	36.59	44.20
Net accretion of discount and amortization of premium on marketable securities	11.60	6.00	-
Cash provided/(used) by changes in operating assets and liabilities:			
Inventories	(77.66)	(64.77)	(41.38)
Prepaid expenses and other current assets	(16.62)	(12.86)	(12.46)
Accounts payable	27.95	24.99	5.46
Accrued compensation and related costs	54.93	42.13	24.09
Accrued occupancy costs	8.90	4.29	15.34
Deferred revenue	47.59	30.73	15.32
Other accrued expenses	16.47	9.47	31.90
Other operating assets and liabilities	(16.41)	(16.78)	(26.44)
Net cash provided by operating activities	$793.85	$566.45	$477.69
Investing Activities			
Purchase of available-for-sale securities	(566.65)	(323.33)	(339.97)
Maturity of available-for-sale securities	163.81	180.69	78.35
Sale of available-for-sale securities	190.75	88.89	144.76
Acquisitions, net of cash acquired	(7.52)	(69.93)	-
Net additions to equity, other investments and other assets	(64.75)	(47.26)	(15.84)
Distributions from equity investees	38.33	28.97	22.83
Net additions to property, plant and equipment	(386.18)	(357.28)	(375.47)
Net cash used by investing activities	($632.19)	($499.26)	($485.34)

(Continued)

(In millions US$)	2004	2003	2002
Financing Activities			
Proceeds from issuance of common stock	137.59	107.18	107.47
Principal payments on long-term debt	(0.72)	(0.71)	(0.70)
Repurchase of common stock	(203.41)	(75.71)	(52.25)
Net cash provided/(used) by financing activities	($66.55)	$30.76	$54.52
Effect of exchange rate changes on cash and cash equivalents	3.11	3.28	1.56
Net increase in cash and cash equivalents	98.22	101.23	48.43
Cash and Cash Equivalents			
Beginning of period	200.91	99.68	51.25
End of period	$299.13	$200.91	$99.68
Supplemental Disclosure of Cash Flow Information			
Cash paid during the year for:			
Interest	0.37	0.27	0.30
Income taxes	172.76	140.11	105.34

Source: Starbucks Corp. 10-K filing with Securities and Exchange Commission for fiscal year ended 3 October 2004.

Background

In 1971, Starbucks Coffee, Tea and Spice opened its first location in Seattle's Pike Place Market. In 1982, Howard Schultz joined the company as director of retail operations and marketing. Inspired by the popularity of espresso bars in Italy, he developed and launched a plan to bring the coffeehouse concept to the United States. In 1987, Schultz and other investors acquired the company's assets and renamed it Starbucks Corporation. The company went public in 1992 on the NASDAQ listed under the ticker symbol SBUX.

Starbucks' business consisted of purchasing, roasting, and selling high-quality whole bean coffees and coffee drinks, primarily through company-operated retail stores. The company also sold noncoffee beverages, a variety of complementary food items, value cards, coffee-related accessories and equipment, and a line of compact discs (CDs) (see Exhibit 4.5). In addition, Starbucks sold coffee and tea products through its equity investees and other channels.

The company's objective was to establish Starbucks as the most recognized and respected brand in the world. To achieve this goal, the company's strategy was threefold. First, it would continue rapid expansion of its retail operations. Secondly, it planned to grow its specialty operations (licensing, foodservices, and other initiatives). Finally, it would selectively pursue other opportunities, aiming to leverage the Starbucks brand through the introduction of new products and the development of new distribution channels. By the end of 2004, the company had over 8500 stores worldwide, strong alliances with established corporations, and one of the world's strongest brands.

Revenue recognition

Starbucks reported net revenues of $5.2 billion in 2004. The company derived that figure from five distinct revenue streams: company-operating retail stores, specialty operations, licensing, foodservice accounts, and a catch-all category called "other initiatives."

Company-Operated Retail Stores

By the end of fiscal 2004, Starbucks had 5215 company-operated retail stores. These stores were typically situated in high-traffic, high-visibility locations in countries such as the United States, United Kingdom, Singapore, and Thailand (see Exhibit 4.6) and sold beverages, food, CDs, and coffee-related equipment.

In November 2001, Starbucks introduced the Starbucks card, which allowed customers to purchase prepaid cards that ranged in value from $5 to $500. These cards were intended to provide quicker, convenient transactions; build loyalty; reduce company costs; increase revenues; and improve customer data.

In fiscal 2004, the company opened the Starbucks Hear Music™ Coffeehouse, a first-of-its-kind music store, in Santa Monica, California. This café/music-store concept combined the Starbucks coffeehouse experience with an innovative retail environment. In addition to offering the usual Starbucks

Exhibit 4.5 Starbucks Corp. Net Revenues, Specialty Operations Revenues, and Retail Sales for 2004

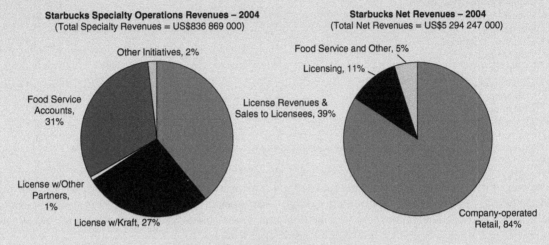

Starbucks Specialty Operations Revenues – 2004
(Total Specialty Revenues = US$836 869 000)

Other Initiatives, 2%
Food Service Accounts, 31%
License w/Other Partners, 1%
License w/Kraft, 27%
License Revenues & Sales to Licensees, 39%

Starbucks Net Revenues – 2004
(Total Net Revenues = US$5 294 247 000)

Food Service and Other, 5%
Licensing, 11%
Company-operated Retail, 84%

Starbucks Retail Sales by Product Type – 2004

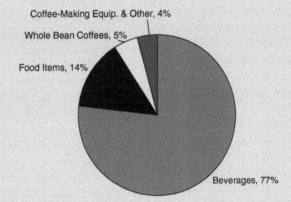

Coffee-Making Equip. & Other, 4%
Whole Bean Coffees, 5%
Food Items, 14%
Beverages, 77%

Source: Starbucks Corp. 10-K filing with Securities and Exchange Commission for fiscal year ended 3 October 2004.

products, the store gave customers a hands-on guide to music discovery with an interactive listening bar and allowed customers access to CD burning technology to create personalized CDs from a digital music library.

Specialty Operations

The company's specialty operations aimed to develop the Starbucks brand outside the company-operated retail store environment. Starbucks' strategy was to reach customers where they worked, traveled, shopped, and dined by establishing relationships with prominent and reputable third parties. These relationships took various forms, including licensing arrangements, foodservice accounts, and other initiatives related to the

company's core businesses. In some cases, Starbucks had an equity ownership interest in the licensee operations. During fiscal 2004, specialty revenues, which included royalties and fees from licensees and product sales derived from specialty operations, accounted for 16% of total net revenues (see Exhibit 4.5).

Licensing

Starbucks did not franchise or generally relinquish operational control of its retail stores in the United States, nor did it plan to in the foreseeable future. However, in situations where a master concessionaire or another company controlled or could provide improved access to desirable retail space, the company licensed its operations.[5]

(Continued)

Exhibit 4.6   Starbucks Corp. Company-Owned Retail Stores Categorized by Region

Company-operated stores

United States	4,293
International:	
United Kingdom	422
Canada	372
Thailand	49
Australia	44
Singapore	35
Total International	922
Total Company-operated	**5,215**

Source: Starbucks Corp. 10-K filing with Securities and Exchange Commission for fiscal year ended 3 October 2004.

As part of these arrangements, Starbucks sold coffee and related products in the licensed locations and received license fees and royalties. Employees working in the locations were required to follow Starbucks' detailed store operating procedures and attend training classes similar to those given to company-operated store managers and employees.

In 2004, Starbucks had 1839 licensed stores in the United States. Internationally the company's licensed stores totaled 1515, arranged primarily with prominent local retailers.

Starbucks' licensing operations generated a number of revenue streams, including product sales, royalties, and license fees. In total, these stores accounted for 39% of specialty revenues in fiscal 2004 (see Exhibit 4.5).

In 2004, the company expanded its licensing agreement with Kraft Foods, Inc. ("Kraft") to provide a larger selection of Starbucks whole bean and ground coffees, Seattle's Best Coffee and Torrefazione Italia branded coffees, and a selection of premium Tazo teas in grocery and warehouse club stores throughout the United States. Kraft managed all distribution, marketing, advertising, and promotion and paid a royalty to Starbucks. Revenues from this category accounted for 27% of specialty revenues in fiscal 2004.

Foodservice Accounts

Starbucks sold whole bean and ground coffees, including the Starbucks, Seattle's Best Coffee, and Torrefazione Italia brands, as well as a selection of premium Tazo teas, to institutional foodservice companies that serviced business, industry, education and healthcare accounts, office coffee distributors, hotels, restaurants, airlines, and other retailers. At the start of fiscal 2003, the company transitioned the majority of its US foodservice accounts to SYSCO Corporation's national broad line distribution network, aligning its foodservice sales, customer service, and support resources with those of SYSCO Corporation. This alliance greatly improved customer service

levels and was expected to continue to generate new foodservice accounts over several years. The company's revenues from these accounts accounted for 31% of total specialty revenues (see Exhibit 4.5).

Other initiatives

The company maintained a website at www.starbucks.com where customers could purchase, register, or reload Starbucks stored value cards as well as apply for the Starbucks Card Duetto Visa, issued through an agreement with Bank One Corporation and Visa. The Duetto card was the first of its kind, combining the functionality of a credit card with the convenience of a reloadable Starbucks card. The website also contained information about the company's coffee products, brewing equipment, and store locations.

In fiscal 2004, Starbucks entered into a strategic marketing alliance with XM Satellite Radio, debuting the 24-hour Starbucks Hear Music channel 75 for all XM Satellite Radio subscribers. Starbucks started providing the Hear Music satellite channel in more than 4000 company-operated locations in the United States during fiscal 2005. Collectively, the operations of these other initiatives accounted for 2% of specialty revenues in fiscal 2004 (see Exhibit 4.5).

Required

a. In terms of timing for the recognition of revenue relative to the receipt of cash, three revenue-recognition models are possible. In the first, revenue is recognized as cash is received. In the second, revenue is recognized before cash is received (hence, accounts receivable, or A/R). In the third, cash is received before the revenue is recognized (hence, the deferred revenue account). These models are summarized by the journal entries below.

```
(1)  Cash              X
        Revenue              X

                                        Later

(2)  A/R               X          Cash       X
        Revenue              X       A/R              X

(3)  Cash              X          Dfd. rev    X
        Dfd. revenue         X       Revenue          X
```

Your task is to determine which of the above models is most appropriate for each of the following revenue streams:

- retail sales

- the "Starbucks" card

- the "Duetto" card

- food service operations

- licensing.

b. Assume that Starbucks creates a loyalty card. Any customer can get the card free of charge. The way it works is that every time a customer buys a cup of coffee, the purchase is registered on the card. After 10 cups are purchased, the card can be turned in for a free cup of coffee. Assuming that the selling price for a cup of coffee is $3.30, how would you account for the loyalty program?

Case Study

4-3 Network Associates (McAfee): A Case of "Channel Stuffing"

Network Associates (hereafter, NA, later renamed McAfee) designed computer hardware and software to combat viruses, improve network security, and manage network operations.

Like many other high-tech companies of that era, NA rode a wave of high stock market valuation in the late 1990s (see Exhibit 4.7). The company achieved high revenue growth through 1998, some of it organic, some via acquisitions (see Exhibit 4.8).

However, in early 1999, the stock price took a big hit. After peaking at a split-adjusted $335.39 per share in December 1998, the first four months of 1999 saw significant declines: −21% in January; −10% in February; −35% in March; and −57% in April. The closing price at the end of April was $67.08, or an 80% drop in just four months.

In its prerelease of 1998 earnings (made in January 1999 for the purpose of providing guidance to the analyst community), management gave no indication of sales declines on the horizon. On the contrary, they stated that they were on track to meet analysts' expectations for the year. Yet three months later, they reversed their previous announcement. In April 1999, several shareholder lawsuits against the company and its senior management were filed.

Management's explanation for the reduced forecasts of future sales blamed a shift in customer preferences, as explained in this 7 April 1999 article from *Dow Jones Business Service*:

"Our sales cycle is more complex," said Network Associates' Chairman and Chief Executive Officer William Larson. Only a year or so ago, corporations would buy security software by picking a socalled firewall, encryption software and then cobbling their purchases together as a security umbrella. Today, companies are seeking integrated suites of security products, taking longer periods of time to evaluate the product and paying more attention to price.

Network Associates has begun integrating offerings from its many acquisitions into a suite. But the move toward a broader, enterprise-wide sales posture has meant longer evaluation cycles. "Be careful what you ask for, you just might get it," Larson said of its enterprise focus.

Yet at the time management was making these claims to the investing community, they were actually dealing with the effects of several quarters of **channel stuffing**. Inventory was backing up at the distributor level, and distributors could not pay off the amounts owed to NA.

On 26 December 2000 the CEO (Larson) resigned without explanation, as did the CFO and President. The company's share price fell by 68% that month, which followed a loss of 32% in November.

Eventually, the SEC filed a complaint in the US federal court system, which sought monetary penalties from the company. Among other charges, the Commission claimed that the company:

- created a subsidiary to buy back inventory it had previously sold to distributors, in order to avoid characterizing the transaction as a return of merchandise;

- secretly paid distributors significant amounts so that funds could be cycled back to the company and be portrayed as "payments";

- used other unrelated reserve accounts to draw upon (i.e., debit) when transferring cash to the distributors as mentioned above;

(Continued)

- timed sales with a significant customer (Ingram Micro) with a fiscal quarter date that often followed McAfee's by several days – McAfee would pass the inventory along at the end of its quarter as a "sale," yet Ingram would return it after McAfee's new quarter started but before Ingram's current quarter ended;

- sold inventory to distributors *on consignment*, where the distributor only paid for the receivable when the product was passed along to an end customer; and

- conducted sham sales of its accounts receivable by transferring them to a financial institution for up-front cash, yet guaranteeing the institution that the receivables would be paid (thus McAfee retained the risk of collection).

NA, now called McAfee, settled these claims, without admitting or denying the allegations, in early 2006, by paying a fine of $50 million.[6]

Before the settlement, the company recorded a series of accounting restatements related to the above issues, most notably in June 2002 and October 2003. Those two restatements focused on the year 1998, and resulted in a reduction in revenues in that year of $562 million as well as a reduction in net income of $356 million. Overall, cumulative restatements during the early 2000s reduced revenue by $622 million and net income by $353 million over the period 1998 to 2000.

Required

a. Describe in one or two sentences the concept of "channel stuffing."

b. Can a company stuff its distribution channels forever? If not, how does the practice come to an end?

c. After McAfee restated their accounts, what was the "true" number for 1998 sales?

d. What indicators can you find in Exhibit 4.8 that might indicate channel stuffing?

e. Not all of the allegations made by the SEC are easily detected from the analysis of financial statements. Which ones might be more difficult to detect?

Exhibit 4.7   Cumulative Stock Returns: McAfee vs. S&P 500

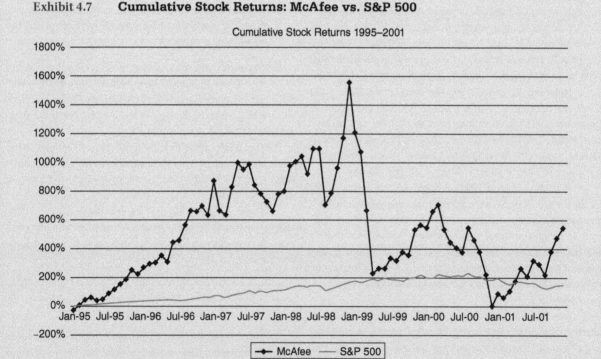

Source: Center for Research in Security Prices (University of Chicago).

f. What is the pattern of operating cash flows that is likely to occur when a company stuffs its channel? In NA's (McAfee's) case, where was it getting the cash that enabled it to carry out the strategy?

g. What sort of forces do you suppose pressure managers into opting for a strategy of channel stuffing?

Selected Financial Information and Ratios from 1996 to 2001

Exhibit 4.8 Selected Financial Data for McAfee

	1996	1997	1998	1999	2000	2001
Revenue and income statement data						
Sales	181,126	612,193	990,045	683,668	745,692	834,478
Pre-tax Operating Income	67,269	18,221	119,966	−138,199	−151,967	−81,966
NOPAT	40,361	10,933	71,980	−82,919	−91,180	−49,180
Net Income	39,017	−28,356	36,438	−159,901	−102,721	−102,381
Balance sheet data						
Net A/R	25,930	125,284	260,784	174,646	122,315	136,366
Allowance	3,027	3,662	11,682	16,249	15,332	8,394
Gross A/R	28,957	128,946	272,466	190,895	137,647	144,760
Allowance % of Gross A/R	0.105	0.028	0.043	0.085	0.111	0.058
A/R turnover	7.737	8.097	5.129	3.140	5.022	6.452
Days A/R outstanding	47	45	71	116	73	57
Total Assets	194,485	601,931	1,536,721	1,479,394	1,384,848	1,627,132
Cash Flow Statement Data						
Cash from Operations	46,530	90,686	52,466	−23,335	26,672	145,706
Cash from Investing	−46,863	−134,704	−318,823	−168,549	10,443	20,775
Cash from Financing	46,397	43,391	533,330	96,597	−39,403	158,904
Significant financing items:						
Cash from exercise of employee stock options	14,290	43,188	151,099	27,471	46,548	51,067
Cash from tax benefits of employee stock options	32,107	39,941	43,500			
Cash used in repurchasing shares		−39,738		−12,443	−100,416	−53,800
Cash from issuance of convertible debt			337,624			335,081
Cash from IPO of subsidiary				78,945		
Cash used in repurchasing convertible debt						−173,708

Source: Company SEC filings

NOTES

1. *Fact Sheet: Staff Accounting Bulletin No. 101 – Revenue Recognition*, US Securities and Exchange Commission, 3 December 1999.

2. All dollar amounts are in US$.

3. Anjali Cordeiro, "Starbucks Jan Same-Store Sales Rose 7%," *CNN Money*, 2 February 2005.

4. Same-store sales, which compare sales performance at stores open for at least one year, are an important metric in the retail industry.

5. Attractive retail real estate in the United States that would have otherwise been unavailable included airports, national grocery chains, major food services corporations, college and university campuses, and hospitals. Internationally, Starbucks employed three business strategies: joint ventures, licenses, and company-owned operations.

6. After the name change, in April 2004, McAfee divested its computer network management division. From that point onward, its strategic focus would be on the antivirus software business.

5 The Statement of Cash Flows

Introduction

The accrual method of accounting is a fundamental feature of corporate financial reporting. Under this method, revenues are recognized when earned and expenses when incurred, even if cash is received or paid at some other time. But determining precisely when revenues are earned and expenses incurred requires judgment, and where there is judgment there is also the possibility of manipulation. One way for financial statement readers to deal with the possibility of manipulation is to analyze performance with the effects of accruals stripped from the accounts. That's what the statement of cash flows is for.

The statement of cash flows provides a view of the firm's performance independent of accruals. It summarizes cash inflows and cash outflows and, in so doing, reconciles beginning and ending cash. But the statement does more than just summarize cash flows. It reveals the nature of the activities that gave rise to those cash flows. To understand how this works, let's examine how the statement is organized. Once again, we'll use Taiwan Semiconductor as an example (see Exhibit 1.3).

The cash flow statement is prepared on the assumption that all cash flows result from just three types of activities – operating, investing, and financing. Operating activities refer mainly, though not exclusively, to the company's recurring, day-to-day activities of producing and selling its products. Investing activities refer to the buying and selling of assets other than inventory, including property, plant & equipment, and shares in other companies. It also includes the purchases and sale of marketable securities such as government bonds. Financing activities refer to capital changes that impact the liabilities and equity portions of the balance sheet, including loans, repayment of loans, issuance of new equity, the repurchase of the company's own shares, and dividend payments. When the year's net cash flows (inflows, minus outflows) from each of these three types of activities are added, the result should equal "delta cash," that is, the change in cash from the beginning of the year to the end.

The Reporting of Cash Flows from Operations

Cash flows from operating activities are reported in either of two equivalent ways: the direct method or the indirect method.

The Direct Method

Under the direct method, the firm reports gross cash receipts and cash payments related to operations. Receipts include cash received from customers, dividends, and interest. Payments include cash paid to employees and suppliers, interest paid to banks, and income taxes. This approach is shown in Exhibit 5.1(a) for CVS Health, an American retail pharmacy and health care company headquartered in the state of Rhode Island. The sources of operating cash reported by the company consist entirely of actual cash receipts from customers and other parties, just as the uses of operating cash consist entirely of cash actually paid out to suppliers, employees, and others.

Exhibit 5.1(a)	CVS Health Cash Flows: Direct Method

	YEAR ENDED DECEMBER 31.		
IN MILLIONS	2016	2015	2014
Cash flows from operating activities:			
Cash receipts from customers	$172,310	$148,954	$132,406
Cash paid for inventory and prescriptions dispensed by retail network pharmacies	(142,511)	(122,498)	(105,362)
Cash paid to other suppliers and employees	(15,550)	(14,162)	(15,344)
Interest received	20	21	15
Interest paid	(1,140)	(629)	(647)
Income taxes paid	(3,060)	(3,274)	(2,931)
Net cash provided by operating activities	10,069	8,412	8,137
Cash flows from investing activities:			
Purchases of property and equipment	(2,224)	(2,367)	(2,136)
Proceeds from sale-leaseback transactions	230	411	515
Proceeds from sale of property and equipment and other assets	37	35	11
Acquisitions (net of cash acquired) and other investments	(539)	(11,475)	(2,439)
Purchase of available-for-sale investments	(65)	(267)	(157)
Maturity of available-for-sale investments	91	243	161
Net cash used in investing activities	(2,470)	(13,420)	(4,045)
Cash flows from financing activities:			
Increase (decrease) in short-term debt	1,874	(685)	685
Proceeds from issuance of long-term debt	3,455	14,805	1,483
Repayments of long-term debt	(5,943)	(2,902)	(3,100)
Purchase of noncontrolling interest in subsidiary	(39)	—	—
Payment of contingent consideration	(26)	(58)	—
Dividends paid	(1,840)	(1,576)	(1,288)
Proceeds from exercise of stock options	224	299	421
Excess tax benefits from stock-based compensation	72	127	106
Repurchase of common stock	(4,461)	(5,001)	(4,001)
Other	(5)	(3)	—
Net cash (used in) provided by financing activities	(6,689)	5,006	(5,694)
Effect of exchange rate changes on cash and cash equivalents	2	(20)	(6)
Net increase (decrease) in cash and cash equivalents	912	(22)	(1,608)
Cash and cash equivalents at the beginning of the year	2,459	2,481	4,089
Cash and cash equivalents at the end of the year	$3,371	$2,459	$2,481

Exhibit 5.1(b)	CVS Health Operating Cash Flows: Indirect Method

	YEAR ENDED DECEMBER 31.		
IN MILLIONS	2016	2015	2014
Reconciliation of net income to net cash provided by operating activities:			
Net income	$5,319	$5,239	$4,644
Adjustments required to reconcile net income to net cash provided by operating activities:			
Depreciation and amortization	2,475	2,092	1,931
Stock-based compensation	222	230	165
Loss on early extinguishment of debt	643	—	521
Deferred income taxes and other noncash items	153	(266)	(58)
Change in operating assets and liabilities, net of effects from acquisitions:			
Accounts receivable, net	(243)	(1,594)	(737)
Inventories	(742)	(1,141)	(770)
Other current assets	35	355	(383)
Other assets	(43)	2	9
Accounts payable and claims and discounts payable	2,189	2,834	1,742
Accrued expenses	59	765	1,060
Other long-term liabilities	2	(104)	13
Net cash provided by operating activities	$10,069	$8,412	$8,137

See accompanying notes to consolidated financial statements.

The Indirect Method

Under the more popular indirect method, operating cash flows are calculated by removing all noncash items that went into the calculation of net income. In effect, all of the accruals embedded in net income are reversed through a series of adjustments. The end result should be the same figure calculated using the direct method. For example, notice that cash flow from operating activities for CVS Health is $10,069 million in 2016 under both methods.[1]

Preparing the Statement of Cash Flows

Corporate accounting systems are designed to accumulate the information needed to prepare balance sheets and income statements. In other words, accounting systems are geared to the accrual method of accounting, not the cash basis. Therefore, companies must find a way to transform information from the balance sheet and the income statement into a cash flow statement. We illustrate how this process works using the T-accounts introduced in the appendix to Chapter 2.

In essence, the statement is prepared by showing how cash changes in relation to changes in noncash accounts. To understand this point, consider the basic accounting equation:

$$\text{Assets (A)} = \text{Liabilities (L)} + \text{Shareholders' Equity (SE)}$$

Exhibit 5.2(a)	Morris Distributors Inc., Balance Sheets for December 31, 2017 and 2018

	December 31	
	2017	2018
Assets		
Current assets		
Cash	$90,000	$18,000
Accounts receivable	60,000	165,000
Inventories	120,000	150,000
Total Current assets	$270,000	$333,000
Noncurrent assets		
Property, plant and equipment	$300,000	$675,000
Accumulated depreciation	90,000	120,000
Total Noncurrent assets	$210,000	$555,000
Total Assets	$480,000	$888,000
Liabilities and shareholders' equity		
Current liabilities		
Accounts payable	$90,000	$150,000
Salaries payable	15,000	18,000
Other short-term payables	30,000	36,000
Total Current liabilities	$135,000	$204,000
Noncurrent liabilities		
Long-term loans	$0	$300,000
Shareholders' equity		
Common stock	$300,000	$300,000
Retained earnings	45,000	84,000
Total Shareholders' equity	$345,000	$384,000
Total Liabilities and shareholders' equity	$480,000	$888,000

It therefore follows that

$$\Delta A = \Delta L + \Delta SE$$

where Δ, or delta, is the change in an item. This equation tells us that changes in assets during the period must equal the sum of changes in liabilities and changes in shareholders' equity.

If we divide assets into two categories, cash and noncash assets (NCA),

$$\Delta Cash + \Delta NCA = \Delta L + \Delta SE$$

Exhibit 5.2(b)	Morris Distributors Inc., Income Statement for 2018	

Sales revenue	$375,000
Cost of goods sold	180,000
Depreciation expense	30,000
Salary expense	60,000
Operating income	$105,000
Interest expense	12,000
Income before taxes	$93,000
Income taxes	33,000
Net Income	$60,000
Statement of retained earnings, 2009	
Retained earnings, beginning	$45,000
Net income	$60,000
Dividends, declared and paid	$21,000
Retained earnings, ending	$84,000

Rearranging the terms in this equation, we get the equation for changes in cash (or "delta cash"):

$$\Delta Cash = \Delta L + \Delta SE - \Delta NCA$$

This equation tells us that changes in cash can be explained by reference to changes in all other balance sheet accounts and thus provides the underlying logic for preparing the statement of cash flows. Any transaction that changes cash must be accompanied by a change in liabilities, shareholders' equity, or noncash assets.

The preparation of the cash flow statement is shown using information for a company we call Morris Distributors Corporation. Exhibit 5.2(a) presents the balance sheets for the beginning and the end of 2018, and Exhibit 5.2(b) the income statement for 2018. Morris Distributors declared and paid $21,000 in dividends during the year.

We begin with the T-account worksheet from Exhibit 5.3(a). At the top of the worksheet is a master T-account for Cash. This account is divided into three sections – operations, investing, and financing – to correspond to the three sections of the cash flow statement.

The beginning and ending balances have been recorded for each balance sheet account, including cash. The beginning balance is found at the top of each T-account; the ending balance is shown on the bottom.[2] Morris Distributors' beginning and ending cash balances were $90,000 and $18,000, respectively. For the statement of cash flows to balance, this $72,000 reduction in cash must be reconciled.

All changes in the master T-account are explained by accounting for the changes during the year in each noncash account. In essence, the entries originally recorded in the accounts during the year are reconstructed and entered into the same accounts on the T-account worksheet. This process may seem complicated at first, but you will soon see that it's really quite easy.

The only additional requirement is that each entry in the cash T-account must be classified as operating, investing, or financing. Once the net change in each noncash account has been accounted for, all of the data are there to prepare a complete and proper cash flow statement.

| Exhibit 5.3(a) | T-account Worksheet for Morris Distributors |

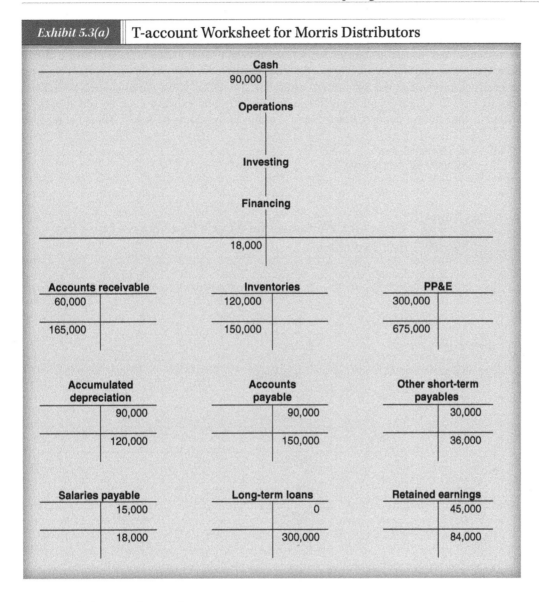

We begin by recording net income:

(1)   Cash (operations)   60,000
      Retained earnings   60,000

As shown in Exhibit 5.3(b), both the debit to cash and the credit to retained earnings are crossreferenced by a (1) to indicate that this is the first reconciling entry.

However, after this entry is recorded, the ending balance of retained earnings ($84,000) has not yet been reconciled to the beginning balance. What's missing is a $21,000 debit that corresponds to the dividends declared and paid in 2018:

(2)   Retained earnings   21,000
      Cash (financing)   21,000

At this point, the difference between the beginning and ending balances for retained earnings has been explained. We signal this reconciliation with a check mark on the top line of the T-account.

The next set of entries, shown in Exhibit 5.3(c), adjusts net income for the effects of items that reflect differences in the timing of the accrued-based net income figure and cash flows. For example, net income is adjusted for depreciation and amortization expense. This expense is subtracted in computing net income but does not involve an outlay of cash (the outlays occurred in previous years when the assets were acquired). Therefore, if we are to convert net income into its cash flow equivalent, depreciation and amortization expense must be added back. In this case, the effect of depreciation expense is removed by adding back $30,000 to net income:

(3)	Cash (operations)	30,000	
	Accumulated depreciation		30,000

Exhibit 5.3(b)	T-account Worksheet for Morris Distributors (after the first two entries)

Cash

90,000		

Operations

Net income (1)	60,000	

Investing

Financing

	21,000	(2) Dividends paid
18,000		

Accounts receivable		**Inventories**		**PP&E**	
60,000		120,000		300,000	
165,000		150,000		675,000	

Accumulated depreciation		**Accounts payable**		**Other short-term payables**	
	90,000		90,000		30,000
	120,000		150,000		36,000

Salaries payable		**Long-term loans**		**Retained earnings** ✓	
	15,000		0	(2) 21,000	45,000
					60,000 (1)
	18,000		300,000		84,000

Exhibit 5.3(c)	T-account Worksheet for Morris Distributors (completed version)

Cash

		90,000			
Operations					
		105,000		(4)	Increase in accounts receivable
Net income	(1)	60,000			
Depreciation expense	(3)	30,000	30,000	(5)	Increase in merchandise Inventory
Increase in accounts payable	(6)	60,000			
Increase in other short-term payables	(7)	6,000			
Increase in salaries payable	(8)	3,000			
Investing					
			375,000	(9)	Acquisition of buildings and equipment
Financing					
Long-term bond Issue	(10)	300,000	21,000	(2)	Dividends paid
Ending balance		18,000			

(Continued)

Exhibit 5.3(c) | **Continued**

Accounts receivable ✓		Inventories ✓		PP&E ✓	
60,000		120,000		300,000	
(4) 105,000		(5) 30,000		(9) 375,000	
165,000		150,000		675,000	

Accumulated depreciation ✓		Accounts payable ✓		Other short-term payables ✓	
	90,000		90,000		30,000
	30,000 (3)		60,000 (6)		6,000 (7)
	120,000		150,000		36,000

Salaries payable ✓		Long-term loans ✓		Retained earnings ✓	
	15,000		0	(2) 21,000	45,000
	3,000 (8)		300,000 (10)		60,000 (1)
	18,000		300,000		84,000

Net income is then adjusted for changes in all current assets and current liabilities, apart from cash (which is already accounted for in delta cash) and short-term debt (which is accounted for as a financing cash flow). When converting net income into its cash flow equivalent, we apply the following general rules:

> *Add the change when a current asset decreases or current liability increases; and subtract the change when a current asset increases or current liability decreases.*

If you follow the logic and mechanics of the T-account approach, these rules will be implemented automatically. (In our later discussion on the analysis of cash flow statements, we elaborate on the economic reasoning behind these rules.)

For example:

(4) Accounts receivable   105,000
      Cash (operations)   105,000

To understand the logic behind this entry, remember that the sales revenues shown on the income statement are recognized when earned, not necessarily when cash is paid. For cash flow purposes, however, cash collected from customers is what matters. Sales revenues were $375,000 in 2018 (see Exhibit 5.2(b)). When these revenues were earned (from the sale of products), two entries were made: a credit to sales revenue and a debit to accounts receivable. Accounts receivable is then credited as collections are made. The fact that accounts receivable increased by $105,000 in 2018 means that debits to the account must have exceeded credits by the same amount. To put it another way, sales revenues recognized in 2018 must have exceeded cash collected from customers by $105,000. This amount is subtracted from net income (hence the credit to cash, under operations) to convert it into its cash flow equivalent.

The same logic is used to adjust for the other current assets and liabilities. For example, the $30,000 increase in inventories implies that purchases of inventory in 2018 (debits to the inventory account) must have exceeded the amount of inventory sold (credits to the account). This increase must be subtracted from net income to convert it into operating cash flow:

(5)	Inventories	30,000	
	Cash (operations)		30,000

Now consider accounts payable. Cash flow from operations (CFFO) must reflect cash purchases, but not all purchases are for cash. The $60,000 increase in accounts payable for 2018 means purchases on account (credits to accounts payable) must have exceeded payments to suppliers (debits to the account). In other words, the purchases amount that went into the calculation of costs of goods sold includes $60,000 of purchases for which cash payment has not yet been made. This amount must be *added* to net income:

(6)	Cash (operations)	60,000	
	Accounts payable		60,000

The increases in the next two current liability accounts, Other short-term payables and salaries payable, imply that accrued-based expenses exceeded cash paid for the expenses and must be added back to net income:

(7)	Cash (operations)	6,000	
	Other short-term payables		6,000
(8)	Cash (operations)	3,000	
	Salaries payable		3,000

Two accounts remain to be reconciled: property, plant, and equipment (PP&E) and long-term loans. The $375,000 increase in PP&E means that assets were acquired during the year. Of course, it is possible that the company bought, say, $400,000, while raising $25,000 in cash from disposing of other assets. In other words, $375,000 is a net increase. But in the absence of additional information, it is reasonable to assume that the company must have invested that amount in property, plant, and equipment. The credit to cash is under the investing section:

(9)	Property, plant, and equipment	375,000	
	Cash (investing)		375,000

The increase in long-term loans tells us that the company borrowed $300,000 from its bankers. This cash flow is debited to cash, under financing:

(10)	Cash (financing)	300,000	
	Long-term loans		300,000

As we can see from Exhibit 5.3(c), after recording entry 10, all of the balance sheet accounts have been reconciled.

The final step is to take the information provided in the cash T-account and prepare a formal statement of cash flows, which is shown in Exhibit 5.4. The completed master T-account is a worksheet that provides us with all of the information needed to prepare the statement. In effect, the master T-account performs the same function for the statement of cash flows as the adjusted, preclosing trial balance does for the balance sheet and income statement.

Exhibit 5-4	Morris Distributors Statement of Cash Flows for the Year Ended December 31, 2018

Net income	$60,000	
Add: Depreciation	30,000	
Adjustments for working capital		
Increase in accounts receivable	–105,000	
Increase in inventories	–30,000	
Increase in accounts payable	60,000	
Increase in salaries payable	3,000	
Increase in other short-term payables	6,000	
Cash flow from operating activities		**$24,000**
Acquisition of buildings and equipment	–$375,000	
Cash flow used in investing activities		**–$375,000**
Borrowings	$300,000	
Dividends paid	–21,000	
Cash flow from financing activities		**$279,000**
Net change in cash		**–$72,000**

IFRS and the Statement of Cash Flows

The IFRS approach to preparing the statement is largely the same as the format presented in this chapter, although there can be differences. The most important difference is that IFRS is more flexible in defining operating, investing, and financing cash flows than US GAAP. For example, interest and dividends received can be classified as operating cash flows (as under US GAAP) *or* as investing cash flows. Interest paid can be classified as operating *or* financing cash flows.

Generally speaking, if a cash flow statement is prepared in accordance with US GAAP, it is likely to be IFRS-compliant. However, the reverse is not necessarily true.

Analyzing the Statement of Cash Flows

The analysis of the cash flow statement focuses on two fundamental issues:

- the relationship between net income and CFFO, and

- the relationship between operating, investing, and financing cash flows.

We'll examine these issues by drawing again on the cash flow statements of Taiwan Semiconductor Manufacturing Company (TSMC) (Exhibit 1.3, Chapter 1).

Net Income and Cash Flow from Operations

The operating activities section focuses on the firm's ability to generate cash internally from its recurring, day-to-day operating activities. To put it another way, it addresses how successful the company has been at generating cash from producing and selling its products and services.

Table 5.1   The Operating Activities Section of TSMC's Statement of Cash Flows

in millions of NT$	Year Ended December 31		
	2016	2015	2014
Cash flows from operating activities			
Income before income tax	385,921	350,475	302,075
Adjustments for:			
Depreciation expense	220,085	219,303	197,645
Amortization expense	3,743	3,202	2,606
Finance costs	3,306	3,190	3,236
Share of profits of associates and joint venture	−3,458	−4,196	−3,920
Interest income	−6,318	−4,129	−2,731
Gain on disposal of property, plant and equipment, net	−47	−434	−15
Asset impairments	122	2,759	1,187
Loss (gain) on financial assets	−2,707	−19,585	3,742
Loss (gain) on disposal of equity method investments and subsidiaries	325	−2,369	−2,084
Dividend income	−137	−622	−650
Changes in operating assets and liabilities:			
Financial instruments at fair value through profit and loss, and other financial assets	−6,368	492	−2,269
Notes and accounts receivable, net	−49,828	26,491	−43,128
Inventories	18,370	−655	−28,872
Other assets	−251	265	−743
Accounts payable	7,295	−2,693	6,634
Accrued expenses and other current liabilities	3,833	−4,147	8,238
Salary, bonus and profit sharing payables	3,913	3,805	7,595
Provisions	7,932	−383	2,837
Net defined benefit liability	46	53	60
Cash generated from operations	585,778	570,822	451,442
Income taxes paid	−45,943	−40,943	−29,918
Net cash generated by operating activities	539,835	529,879	421,524

The operating activities section shown in Table 5.1 reveals that NT$539,835 million (about US$16.87 billion) of cash was provided by operations in 2016, a marginal increase from the previous year and a more sizable increase — about 28% — from 2014. Because TSMC uses the indirect method, the starting point for the calculation of CFFO is the profit after tax from the income statement. One of the most important tasks for the analyst is to understand how these two figures – net income and CFFO – are reconciled.

The reconciliation of the accrual-basis profit figure (net income) and CFFO begins with the adding back of depreciation and amortization.[3] These expenses are added back to net income because they did not result in a cash outlay. For the same reason, increases in provisions are added back to net income, while reductions are subtracted.[4]

The final major adjustment to net income is for changes in working capital. To understand how to interpret these changes, consider a typical manufacturing company.[5] As shown in Figure 5.1, the operating cycle begins with the acquisition of the materials used in the company's products.

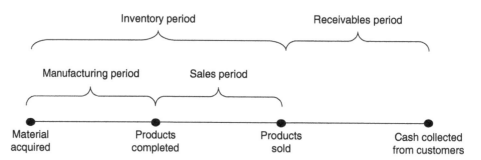

FIGURE 5.1
The operating cycle.

These materials are transferred to production facilities, where workers and various elements of manufacturing overhead (such as public utilities and maintenance) combine to convert the materials into a finished product.

The length of time from acquisition of raw materials to finished product is the manufacturing period. A sales period marks the time from completion of the manufacturing process to sale of the product.

The operating cycle does not end with the sale of the product, however. Most companies extend credit to their customers. The length of a company's operating cycle is thus the sum of its manufacturing period, sales period, and receivables period. We call this process a "cycle" because a portion of the cash collected from customers is used to pay suppliers and acquire more materials, which, in turn, enables the process to repeat itself.

Getting this cycle to turn requires investment, mainly in receivables and inventory. Other types of investment may be needed too, such as prepaid rent and insurance. Also, companies must maintain a certain level of cash to support their day-to-day operations. For example, retailers need to keep some cash in the register. We call this type of investment "operating cash" to distinguish it from more discretionary balances, or excess cash.

Therefore, we can think of the total investment in a company's operating cycle as the sum of inventories, receivables, prepaid expenses and other current assets, and operating cash. It is crucial to note, however, that this amount does not represent the company's own investment in the cycle, but rather the total investment made by the company and others, including suppliers, employees, and the government. The extent to which other parties invest in the company's operating cycle is the extent to which the company itself does not have to.

When suppliers grant credit to a company, they are really investing in its operating cycle. The same can be said for employees when they have not yet been paid for work already performed, for the government, in the form of owed but unpaid taxes, and for customers when they make advance payments. We can estimate the company's *net* investment in the operating cycle by subtracting the sum of accounts payable (supplier finance), accrued liabilities (which include unpaid wages and taxes), and advance payments, from the *total* investment in the operating cycle. We call this net investment the working capital requirement (WCR):

$$\text{WCR} = \left(\text{inventories} + \text{receivables} + \text{other current assets} + \text{operating cash}\right) -$$
$$\left(\text{accounts payable} + \text{accrued liabilities} + \text{advances from customers}\right)$$

Increases in the WCR reflect increases in the cash tied up in the operating cycle and are therefore subtracted from net income in calculating CFFO. Decreases in the WCR have the opposite effect.

In the case of TSMC in 2016 working capital adjustments included (amounts in millions of New Taiwan dollars) notes and accounts receivable (−$49,828), inventories (18,370), other current assets (−$251), accounts payable (7,295), accrued expenses and other current liabilities (3,833), and salary, bonus, and profit sharing payables (3,913). The net effect was an increase in the WCR, and a corresponding decrease in CFFO.

Operating, Investing, and Financing Cash Flows

The second major area of interest in the analysis of cash flow statements centers on the relationship between operating, investing, and financing cash flows. This relationship is most conveniently expressed using the notion of free cash flow. Free cash flow can be defined in many ways, but perhaps the easiest way is to add cash flow from investing (CFFI) to CFFO. Because CFFI is usually a negative number (in most years, companies buy more fixed assets than they sell), the effect of adding CFFI is to subtract investment. The investing and financing sections of Taiwan Semiconductor's statements of cash flows for 2014, 2015 and 2016 are shown in Table 5.2.

Table 5.2   The Investing and Financing Sections of TSMC's Statements of Cash Flows (all amounts in millions of NT$), for the year ended December 31

	2016	2015	2014
Cash flows from investing activities			
Acquisitions of:			
Financial assets	−117,435	−44,656	−6,518
Property, plant and equipment	−328,851	−257,517	−288,540
Intangible assets	−4,243	−4,284	−3,860
Proceeds from disposal or redemption of:			
Financial assets	40,753	74,665	4,139
Investments accounted for using equity method		5,172	3,472
Property, plant and equipment	98	817	200
Interest received	6,353	3,642	2,579
Proceeds from government grants	1,537	0	0
Net cash flow from disposal and acquisition of subsidiaries	0	549	0
Dividends received from investments using equity method	5,479	3,407	3,223
Other dividends received	137	617	646
Refundable deposits refunded (paid)	732	342	2,239
Net cash used in investing activities	−395,440	−217,246	−282,421
Cash flows from financing activities			
Increase in short-term loans	18,969	3,139	18,564
Repayment of bonds, long-term bank loans, and finance leases	−23,480	−29	−28
Interest paid	−3,302	−3,156	−3,193
Guarantee deposits received net refunds	5,831	12	30,135
Cash dividends	−155,582	−116,684	−77,786
Proceeds from exercise of stock options	0	34	47
Decrease in noncontrolling interests	−236	−50	−67
Net cash used in financing activities	−157,800	−116,734	−32,328

Free cash flow for TSMC in 2016 equals NT$539,835 million − NT$395,440 million, or NT$144,395 million (about US$4.5 billion). This figure tells us how much operating cash the company has left over, net of all investing activities, and therefore, the amount of cash flow generated in that year available for either financing activities or increasing cash balances. Because TSMC's free cash flow is positive, the company is in a position to return cash to its investors, which it does in the form of dividend payments.

An alternative definition of free cash flow, known as free operating cash flow, deducts only capital expenditures from CFFO, ignoring other investing transactions such as company acquisitions and the sale or purchase of financial securities. The appeal of this approach is that these other types of investing transactions are more discretionary in nature. To include them is to produce free cash flow figures that are not truly reflective of the company's success in generating cash from its ongoing business activities. In the case of TSMC, operating free cash flow for 2016 is higher than the free cash flow figures reported earlier [(NT$539,835 million − NT$328,851 million) = NT$210,984 million, vs. NT$144,395 million for the previous definition of free cash flow].

A critical assumption underlying the above analysis is that operating, investing, and financing cash flows are easily and neatly defined. Unfortunately, cash flows do not always fit clearly into one of the three categories. For example, there is some ambiguity over the proper treatment of securitized receivables. Many companies package their receivables and sell them in the capital markets as securities, hence the term "securitized." In essence, a firm that securitizes its receivables is borrowing from investors, using the receivables as collateral for the loan. Given the financial nature of this transaction, it should be treated as a financing cash flow. But if the transaction is structured in the right way, securitization can be treated as a reduction in receivables (and in the working capital requirement), and thus as an increase in CFFO. What this example teaches us is that cash flow statements can be manipulated, principally by redefining the boundaries that separate operations from investing and financing activities.

KEY LESSONS FROM THE CHAPTER

- The statement of cash flows provides a view of the firm's performance independent of accruals.

- The statement summarizes cash inflows and outflows and, in so doing, reconciles beginning and ending cash. Because the statement is grounded in beginning and ending cash, two figures that are easy to verify, it is thought that the cash flow statement is harder to manipulate than the income statement or the balance sheet.

- The cash flow statement is prepared on the assumption that all cash flows result from three types of activities: operating, investing, and financing.

- Cash flows from operating activities are reported in either of two equivalent ways: the direct method or the indirect method. As of this writing, the overwhelming majority of companies use the indirect approach.

- The analysis of the statement of cash flows focuses on two fundamental issues: the relationship between net income and cash flow from operations and the relationship between operating, investing, and financing cash flows.

- An alternative definition of free cash flow, known as free operating cash flow, deducts only capital expenditures from CFFO, ignoring other investing transactions. This metric is generally preferred to free cash flow for internal control purposes.

- Although beginning and ending cash must be reconciled, the cash flow statement can be manipulated. Efforts to manipulate focus on redefining the boundaries between operating cash flows on one hand and investing or financing cash flows on the other.

KEY TERMS AND CONCEPTS FROM THE CHAPTER

Direct method	Operating cash flows	Financing cash flows	Working capital	Free cash flows
Indirect method	Investing cash flows	Operating cycle	requirement	

QUESTIONS

1. What are the primary uses of the statement of cash flows? Why aren't the statement of financial position (or balance sheet) and the income statement sufficient?

2. Define operating, investing, and financing cash flows.

3. Describe the major elements of a "cash flow profile."

4. What is the indirect method for determining CFFO, and how does it differ from the direct method? Which method is more common?

5. What are the primary causes for differences between net income and CFFO?

6. How can a company report positive net income, but CFFO for the same year is negative?

7. How can a company report a net loss, but CFFO for the same year is positive?

8. Which figure would you expect to be higher for most companies most of the time: net income or CFFO? Why?

9. One argument given for the statement of cash flows is that it is less subject to manipulation than the income statement. Do you agree with this view?

10. Under US GAAP, cash spent on interest is classified as an operating activity, but cash spent on dividends is classified as a financing activity. Explain the paradox.

11. What is meant by the terms "negative free cash flow" and "positive free cash flow"? What are the managerial implications in either case?

12. True or false: a firm in a strong growth stage of development is more likely to have negative free cash flow than a more mature firm.

13. Why might an investor not put much weight on a firm's current free cash flow as an indicator of future free cash flow?

14. Why might changes in provisions appear as an item in the operations section of the statement?

15. What does "working capital requirement" mean, and what impact does it have on the statement of cash flows?

16. When total cash inflows exceed total cash outflows, or vice versa, how is the difference reflected on the statement of cash flows?

PROBLEMS

5.1 Interpreting the Statement of Cash Flows

Exhibit 5.5 contains three years of cash flow statements from Massa Corporation.

Required

Answer the following questions:

a. For each year:
   1. What were the firm's major sources of cash? Its major uses of cash?
   2. Was CFFO greater or less than net income? Explain in detail the major reasons for the difference between these two figures.
   3. Was the firm able to generate enough cash from operations to cover its capital expenditures?
   4. Did the CFFO cover both the capital expenditures and the firm's dividend payments?
   5. If it did, what did Massa do with its excess cash?
   6. If not, what were the sources of cash the firm relied on to cover its capital expenditures and/or dividends?
   7. Were the working capital accounts primarily sources of cash, or users of cash? Explain.

b. Based on the evidence in the statement of cash flows alone, what is your assessment of the financial strength of this business? Be as specific as possible in your assessment.

5.2 Adjustments on the Statement of Cash Flows

The 2003 Annual Report of McDonald's includes the following note:

In 2003, the $272.1 million of charges consisted of: $237.0 million related to the loss on the sale of Donatos Pizzeria, the closing of Donatos and Boston Market restaurants outside the US and the exit of a domestic joint venture with Fazoli's; and $35.1 million related to the revitalization plan actions of McDonald's Japan, including headcount reductions, the closing of Pret A Manger stores in Japan, and the early termination of a long-term management services agreement.

In 2002, the $266.9 million of net charges consisted of: $201.4 million related to the anticipated transfer of ownership in five countries in the Middle East and Latin America to developmental licensees and ceasing operations in two countries in Latin America; $80.5 million primarily related to eliminating approximately 600 positions (about half of which were in the US and half of which were in international markets), reallocating resources and consolidating certain home office facilities to control costs; and a $15.0 million favorable adjustment to the 2001 restructuring charge due to lower employee-related costs than originally anticipated.

Exhibit 5.5 | **Massa Corporation Consolidated Statements of Cash Flows ($millions)**

	2018	2017	2016
Operating activities			
Loss from continuing operations	$(377.9)	$(623.5)	$(320.6)
Depreciation	168.4	220.1	263.4
Amortization of capitalized software	41.4	58.2	39.1
Gain from sale of investments and other assets	(16.6)	(119.0)	–
Restructuring and other unusual items, net	135.5	384.1	125.3
Changes in other accounts affecting operations			
Accounts receivable	160.8	73.4	(45.2)
Inventory	80.2	100.9	(3.0)
Other current assets	17.0	(1.2)	(13.0)
Accounts payable and other current liabilities	(91.3)	(21.3)	41.0
Other	2.8	14.1	(10.5)
Net cash provided by continuing operations	120.3	85.8	76.5
Net cash provided by (used in) discontinued operations	4.9	3.5	(29.7)
Net cash provided by operating activities	125.2	89.3	46.8
Investing activities			
Investment in depreciable assets	(129.7)	(174.4)	(303.6)
Proceeds from disposal of depreciable and other assets	157.0	242.0	94.1
Proceeds from the sale of discontinued operations	25.3	407.3	–
Investment in capitalized software	(27.8)	(43.1)	(59.5)
Other	(6.0)	(13.0)	14.2
Net cash provided by (used in) investing activities	18.8	418.8	(254.8)
Financing activities			
(Decrease) increase in short-term borrowings	(2.6)	(222.6)	139.8
Proceeds from long-term debt	44.4	167.7	305.0
Payments of long-term debt	(126.5)	(544.8)	(91.7)
Proceeds from sale of common stock	5.0	8.7	17.5
Purchase of treasury stock	(0.3)	(0.6)	(18.8)
Dividends paid	–	(7.2)	(26.0)
Net cash provided by (used in) financing activities	(80.0)	(598.8)	325.8
Effect of changes in foreign exchange rates	0.1	1.1	(3.9)
Increase (decrease) in cash equivalents	64.1	(89.6)	113.9
Cash and equivalents at beginning of year	169.1	258.7	144.8
Cash and equivalents at end of year	$233.2	$169.1	$258.7

Required

a. McDonald's reports cash flows from operating activities using the indirect method. How would the $237 million loss in 2003 for the sale of Donatos and other be reported on the company's statement of cash flows? Why?

b. Explain how the $15 million favorable adjustment to the 2001 restructuring charge is accounted on each of the three principal financial statements for 2002.

5.3 Preparing and Analyzing a Statement of Cash Flows

Allen Company produces roofing supplies and insulation materials for use in home and commercial construction. Although Allen has been growing, recent lack of production capacity has caused production delays, some stockouts of finished goods, and a shift in the inventory mix from finished goods to raw materials and work in process. Allen Company's comparative balance sheet data and additional information follow:

Allen Company Comparative Balance Sheets

	2017	2016
Assets		
Cash	$108,000	$60,000
Accounts receivable, net	320,000	235,000
Inventory	450,000	510,000
Prepaid expenses	27,000	30,000
Total current assets	905,000	835,000
Investments in affiliates	200,000	100,000
Property, plant, and equipment	1,100,000	950,000
Less accumulated depreciation	(440,000)	(370,000)
Intangible assets	35,000	45,000
Total assets	$1,800,000	$1,560,000
Liabilities and shareholders' equity		
Accounts payable	$554,000	$400,000
Accrued liabilities	36,000	38,000
Total current liabilities	590,000	438,000
Long-term notes payable	380,000	100,000
Contributed capital	710,000	750,000
Retained earnings	120,000	272,000
Total liabilities and shareholders' equity	$1,800,000	$1,560,000

The following additional information is available:

- The company's stock has no par or stated value. Contributed capital is shown as one amount (i.e., no distinction between common stock and capital in excess of par).

- Net loss for the year was $110,000.

- The intangible assets have limited lives and were amortized by $10,000 during the year.

- Investment in affiliates represents equity method investments. The income statement reported $80,000 income from equity method investments. $10,000 dividends were received from affiliates. Remaining changes in the account relate to additional investments.

- Less efficient equipment with an original cost of $200,000 was sold during the year for $40,000. The accumulated depreciation on that equipment was $130,000.

- Cash dividends of $12,000 were declared and paid during the year. The company also declared and distributed a $30,000 stock dividend during the year.

- The company repurchased the stock of a dissident shareholder during the year and retired the shares. The company paid $70,000 (which was the original issue price of the shares).

- No long-term notes were retired during the year.

Required

a. Prepare a statement of cash flows for 2017.

b. Discuss the relationship between net income and CFFO and the relationship among cash flow from operating, investing, and financing activities during the two years. Be as specific as the data allow.

c. Identify two conditions in the operating section of the statement which point to the possibility that CFFO might decline next year.

5.4 Interpreting the Role of Accounts Payable in Cash Flow from Operations

AB InBev is the world's largest brewer. An abbreviated version of the operating activities section of the company's statement of cash flows appears below:

Cash flows from operating activities (million US dollars)	2011	2010
Profit	7,959	5,762
Interest, taxes, and noncash items included in profit	7,420	8,503
Cash flow from operating activities before changes in working capital and use of provisions	15,379	14,265
Change in working capital	1,409	226
Pension contributions and use of provisions	(710)	(519)
Interest and taxes (paid)/received	(3,998)	(4,450)
Dividends received	406	383
Cash flow from operating activities	12,486	9,905

Elsewhere in the annual report, management reveals that trade payables increased in 2011 because of higher capital expenditures. Also, these payables have, on average, longer payment terms than payables from previous years.

Required

Explain why the increase in payables and the change in payment terms contributed to the increased in CFFO in 2011. What other factors contributed to the increase?

5.5 Manipulating the Statement of Cash Flows

You are the company's chief financial officer. It is early December, and your accountants have produced financial statements showing provisional results for the year. (Your company's fiscal year ends on 31 December.) You show these to the CEO who then expresses concern about several figures. One figure in particular, cash flow from operations (CFFO), appears low. The CEO wonders if anything can be done before the end of the year to increase it.

Which of the following actions will increase CFFO this year? Which of these actions do you consider appropriate, which are inappropriate, and why?

a. The company sells €2 million of accounts receivable for 97% of face value to a bank. The receivables are sold "with recourse," which means that the company must reimburse the bank for any amount not collected beyond 3% of total receivables.

b. Social charges are due on employees' wages at the end of the year. The firm can delay these payments by a few days so that they are made at the beginning of the following year.

c. The company can work out a deal with some of its customers in which the customers buy goods now, for cash, but they can receive a full refund after the beginning of the next year.

d. A training program is moved from the final month of the current year to the first month of the following year.

e. Routine maintenance is delayed on machinery and equipment until early next year.

f. The company delays the purchase of a new forklift until the beginning of next year.

5.6 Analysis of the Statement of Cash Flows

The statements of cash flows shown below are from an anonymous IFRS-compliant Swedish company:

	Notes	2017 SKK 000s	2016 SKK 000s
Profit before tax		3,398,589	8,280,786
Adjustments to reconcile profit before tax to net cash provided by operating activities			

	Notes	2017 SKK 000s	2016 SKK 000s
Depreciation, depletion, amortization, and impairment		2,960,276	3,044,376
Amortization of government grants and assets acquired free-of-charge	19	(38,395)	(52,375)
Write-off of inventories and reversal of impairment of inventories		(42,350)	11,844
Increase/(decrease) in provisions for liabilities and charges, net		8,885	(334,580)
Profit from the sale of intangible assets and property, plant and equipment	19	(18,452)	(334,412)
Write-off of receivables		10,727	14,998
Profit from the sale of available-for-sale financial assets and subsidiaries		–	(108,503)
Impairment of available-for-sale financial assets	23	826,305	–
Unrealized foreign exchange gain on receivables and payables		(70,332)	(35,702)
Other unrealized foreign exchange losses	23	138,509	128,892
Interest revenue	23	(63,913)	(148,142)
Interest expense on borrowings	23	42,267	9,481
Other financial (profit)/loss, net		(39,127)	21,865
Dividends received	23	(1,063,522)	(70,165)
Other noncash terms		(20,458)	10,030
Operating cash flow before changes in working capital		**6,029,009**	**10,438,393**
Decrease/(increase) in inventories		1,970,942	(418,799)
Decrease/(increase) in trade receivables		4,156,154	(1,013,185)
Decrease/(increase) in other current assets		784,466	(1,614,350)
(Decrease)/increase in trade payables		(4,702,919)	2,015,695
Increase in other current liabilities		57,158	182,186
Corporate income tax paid		(1,563,485)	(536,326)
Net cash provided by operating activities		**6,731,325**	**9,053,614**
Capital expenditures		(4,227,547)	(2,891,865)

	Notes	2017 SKK 000s	2016 SKK 000s
Proceeds from disposals of intangible assets and property, plant and equipment		34,168	395,845
Acquired subsidiaries	4	(200)	(263,856)
Acquired associated companies and joint ventures	5	–	(29,679)
Purchase of available-for-sale financial assets	6	(2)	–
Net cash inflow on sale of subsidiary undertakings		–	7,229
Short-term loans repaid, net		876,116	1,377,293
Interest received and other financial income		68,293	154,345
Dividends received and income from the decrease of share capital		1,526,861	105,973
Net cash used in investing activities		**(1,722,311)**	**(1,144,715)**
Proceeds from long-term bank borrowings		2,000,000	–
Repayments of long-term bank borrowings		(2,000,000)	–
Proceeds from/(repayments of) short-term bank borrowings, net		32,763	(85,200)
Net proceeds from short-term nonbank borrowings		–	6,698
Net proceeds/(payments) from derivative transactions	23	39,125	(20,542)
Interest paid and other financial costs		(40,118)	(8,051)
Dividends paid to shareholders of the parent company		(5,419,287)	(7,367,795)
Dividends paid to minority shareholders		(83,422)	(112,735)
Net cash used in financing activities		**(5,470,939)**	**(7,587,625)**

	Notes	2017 SKK 000s	2016 SKK 000s
(Decrease)/increase in cash and cash equivalents		**(461,925)**	**321,274**
Cash and cash equivalents at the beginning of the period	11	1,935,789	1,672,716
Effects of exchange rate changes		(66,064)	(58,201)
Cash and cash equivalents at the end of the period	11	1,407,800	1,935,789

Required

a. What are the company's major sources of cash?

b. What are the company's major uses of cash?

c. Were "depreciation, depletion, amortization, and impairment" sources or uses of cash in each of the two years shown? Explain.

d. Does the company's productive capacity appear to be increasing or declining in each of the two years depicted on the statement? Support your answer.

e. Were the components of the working capital requirement a net source or use of cash in the most recent year? Support your answer.

f. What does the amount (42,350) shown in the 2017 column (i.e., the fourth line item) refer to? Explain.

g. What is your overall assessment of the company's situation (e.g., its apparent lifecycle stage, recent performance, changes to its financial structure) for the years presented?

5.7 Cash Flow and Credit Risk

Taipei-based Tang Manufacturing has a $1.45 million bank loan that starts coming due in a year, and the loan officer at the local bank has asked for cash budgets to be reassured that the company can repay the debt on schedule. Management has prepared quarterly cash flow forecasts for each of the next six quarters, excerpts of which are produced in the table below. Also worth noting is that much of Tang's equipment and machinery is dated, and therefore long overdue for replacement.

	Q1	Q2	Q3	Q4	Q5	Q6
Scheduled loan payments					$725,000	$725,000
Forecasted cash flows						
Cash flow from operations	$290,000	$362,500	$435,000	$348,000	$290,000	$319,000
Capital expenditures	217,500		217,500		253,750	
Dividends					72,500	

Required

a. Why might Tang's loan officer be concerned about the company's ability to repay the loan?

b. What steps can Tang management take to reduce the bank's risk on the loan?

5.8 Preparing and Interpreting the Statement of Cash Flows

The annual reports from Year 7 and Year 8 of The GAP, a global clothing retailer, indicate the following changes in its balance sheet accounts (amounts in millions):

	Year 7	Year 8
Cash	$2 decrease	$428 increase
Marketable securities (current asset)	46 decrease	46 decrease
Merchandise inventories	96 increase	154 increase
Prepaid expenses	1 increase	56 increase
Property, plant and equipment (at cost)	372 increase	466 increase
Accumulated depreciation	215 increase	270 increase
Other noncurrent assets	51 increase	15 increase
Accounts payable	114 increase	134 increase
Notes payable to banks (current liability)	18 increase	45 increase
Income taxes payable	26 increase	7 decrease
Other current liabilities	90 increase	123 increase
Bonds payable	—	577 increase
Common stock	360 decrease	524 decrease
Retained earnings	369 increase	455 increase

Abbreviated income statements for The GAP appear below:

	Year 7	Year 8
Sales	$5,284	$6,508
Cost of goods sold	−3,285	−4,022
Selling and administrative expenses	−1,250	−1,632
Income tax expense	−296	−320
Net income	$453	$534

Additional data:

- The cash balance was $486 at the end of Year 7 and $914 at the end of Year 8.

- The firm did not sell property, plant and equipment in either year.

- Changes in other noncurrent assets resulted from investing activities.

Required

a. Prepare statements of cash flows for Year 7 and Year 8.

b. Comment on the relationship between net income and CFFO, and on the relationship between operating, investing, and financing cash flows. Compare Year 7 with Year 8.

Case Study

5-1 Blockbuster, Inc.: Movie Rentals, Profits, and Operating Cash

Ronald Baker, a US equities analyst in the London office of Homeguard Investments, has a problem. The stock of Blockbuster, Inc., the video rental chain, has done well over the last six months. (See Exhibit 5.6.) Because this company is not one that Ronald tracks on a routine basis, he barely noticed the move. But a brief correction over the past two weeks has led several clients to ask if the recent dip in price created a good buying opportunity.

Ronald's dilemma is caused by one simple fact: Blockbuster is not a profitable company and hasn't been for years. (See Exhibit 5.7.) Still, the operating cash flows are positive and, from first appearances, strongly so. Blockbuster's cash flow performance is what appears to be supporting the share price. But Ronald's intuition is telling him that negative earnings and positive operating cash cannot go on forever. If earnings incorporate cash flows and accruals, and accruals are really nothing more than future cash flows, shouldn't we be seeing negative cash flows too? Or are the losses the result of

Exhibit 5.6   Blockbuster, Inc., daily stock prices, October 1, 2004–April 1, 2005

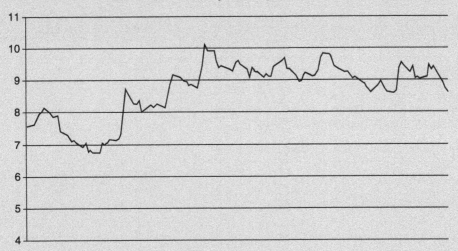

Exhibit 5.7   Financial Statements Blockbuster, Inc.: From the 2004 Annual Report

BLOCKBUSTER INC.
CONSOLIDATED STATEMENTS OF OPERATIONS
(In millions, except per share amounts)

	Year ended December 31		
	2004	**2003**	**2002**
		Restated	Restated
Revenues:			
Base rental revenues	$3,806.2	$3,811.4	$3,720.9
Extended viewing fee revenues	622.4	722.1	739.5
Total rental revenues	4,428.6	4,533.5	4,460.4
Merchandise sales	1,532.6	1,281.6	1,019.7
Other revenues	92.0	96.6	85.8
	6,053.2	5,911.7	5,565.9
Cost of sales:			
Cost of rental revenues	1,250.7	1,362.1	1,513.8
Cost of merchandise sold	1,190.7	1,027.7	844.9
	2,441.4	2,389.8	2,358.7
Gross profit	3,611.8	3,521.9	3,207.2
Operating expenses:			
General and administrative	2,835.2	2,605.9	2,369.5
Share-based compensation	18.3	—	—
Advertising	257.4	179.4	249.2
Depreciation	247.4	266.0	239.1
Impairment of goodwill and other long-lived assets	1,504.4	1,304.9	—
Amortization of intangibles	2.3	2.4	1.7
	4,865.0	4,358.6	2,859.5
Operating income (loss)	(1,253.2)	(836.7)	347.7
Interest expense	(38.1)	(33.1)	(49.5)
Interest income	3.6	3.1	4.1
Other items, net	1.6	(0.4)	2.9

(Continued)

Exhibit 5.7 (continued)

	2004	2003	2002
		Year ended December 31	
		Restated	Restated
Income (loss) before income taxes	(1,286.1)	(867.1)	305.2
Benefit (provision) for income taxes	37.3	(106.5)	(107.1)
Equity in loss of affiliated companies, net of tax	—	(0.7)	(2.2)
Income (loss) before cumulative effect of change in accounting principle	(1,248.8)	(974.3)	195.9
Cumulative effect of change in accounting principle, net of tax	—	(4.4)	(1,817.0)
Net loss	$(1,248.8)	$(978.7)	$(1,621.1)
Income (loss) per share before cumulative effect of change in accounting principle:			
Basic	$(6.89)	$(5.41)	$1.10
Diluted	$(6.89)	$(5.41)	$1.08
Cumulative effect of change in accounting principle per share:			
Basic	$—	$(0.02)	$(10.17)
Diluted	$—	$(0.02)	$(10.01)
Net loss per share:			
Basic	$(6.89)	$(5.43)	$(9.08)
Diluted	$(6.89)	$(5.43)	$(8.93)
Weighted average shares outstanding:			
Basic	181.2	180.1	178.6
Diluted	181.2	180.1	181.6
Recurring cash dividends per common share	$0.08	$0.08	$0.08
Special distribution per common share	$5.00	$—	$—

BLOCKBUSTER INC.
CONSOLIDATED BALANCE SHEETS
(In millions, except per share amounts)

	December 31	
	2004	2003
		Restated
Assets		
Current assets:		
Cash and cash equivalents	$330.3	$233.4
Receivables, less allowances of $14.5 and $13.0 for 2004 and 2003, respectively	177.8	183.7
Merchandise inventories	516.6	415.1
Prepaid and other current assets	193.0	128.1
Total current assets	1,217.7	960.3
Rental library	457.6	354.4
Receivable from Viacom, net	2.6	3.5
Property and equipment, net	854.0	787.3
Deferred tax asset	87.0	—
Intangibles, net	34.5	34.4
Goodwill	1,138.5	2,627.7
Other assets	71.5	54.4
	$3,863.4	$4,822.0
Liabilities and Stockholders' Equity		
Current liabilities:		
Accounts payable	$721.8	$565.1
Accrued expenses	697.3	610.2
Current portion of long-term debt	5.8	124.1

	December 31	
	2004	**2003**
		Restated
Current portion of capital lease obligations	19.7	20.7
Deferred taxes	4.8	3.3
Total current liabilities	1,449.4	1,323.4
Long-term debt, less current portion	1,044.9	0.7
Capital lease obligations, less current portion	74.8	74.4
Deferred taxes	—	9.3
Deferred rent liability	69.2	71.1
Other liabilities	162.2	154.7
	2,800.5	1,633.6
Commitments and contingencies (Note 6)		
Stockholders' equity:		
Preferred stock, par value $0.01 per share: 100.0 shares authorized; no shares issued or outstanding	—	—
Class A common stock, par value $0.01 per share; 400.0 shares authorized; 111.7 and 36.9 shares issued and outstanding for 2004 and 2003, respectively Class B common stock, par value $0.01 per share; 500.0 shares authorized;	1.1	0.4
72.0 and 144.0 shares issued and outstanding for 2004 and 2003, respectively	0.7	1.4
Additional paid-in capital	5,336.7	6,227.3
Retained deficit	(4,248.3)	(2,999.5)
Accumulated other comprehensive loss	(27.3)	(41.2)
Total stockholders' equity	1,062.9	3,188.4
	$3,863.4	$4,822.0

BLOCKBUSTER INC.
CONSOLIDATED STATEMENTS OF CHANGES IN STOCKHOLDERS' EQUITY AND COMPREHENSIVE LOSS (In millions)

	Year ended December 31					
	2004		2003		2002	
	Shares	Amount	Shares	Amount	Shares	Amount
			Restated		Restated	
Class A common stock:						
Balance, beginning of year	36.9	$0.4	35.6	$0.4	32.8	$0.3
Exercise of stock options	0.3	—	1.3	—	2.8	0.1
Issuance upon vesting of restricted shares	2.5	—	—	—	—	—
Conversion from Class B common stock	72.0	0.7	—	—	—	—
Balance, end of year	111.7	1.1	36.9	0.4	35.6	0.4
Class B common stock:						
Balance, beginning of year	144.0	$1.4	144.0	$1.4	144.0	$1.4
Conversion to Class A common stock	(72.0)	(0.7)	—	—	—	—
Balance, end of year	72.0	$0.7	144.0	$1.4	144.0	$1.4
Additional paid-in capital:						
Balance, beginning of year		$6,227.3		$6,220.8		$6,181.1
Issuance of Class A common stock		0.1		0.1		0.1
Exercise and expense of share-based compensation, net of tax benefit		10.0		20.8		53.9
Net issuance of Class A common stock upon vesting of restricted shares		10.7		—		—

(Continued)

Exhibit 5.7 (continued)

		Year Ended December 31				
	2004		**2003**		**2002**	
	Shares	Amount	Shares	Amount	Shares	Amount
				Restated		Restated
Acceleration of Viacom stock options		1.7		—		—
Viacom capital contribution		7.0		—		—
Recurring cash dividends		(14.5)		(14.4)		(14.3)
Special distribution		(905.6)		—		—
Balance, end of year		$5,336.7		$6,227.3		$6,220.8
Accumulated other comprehensive loss:						
Balance, beginning of year		$(41.2)		$(100.9)		$(107.0)
Other comprehensive income (loss):						
Change in fair value of interest rate swaps, net of taxes		—		6.3		2.0
Foreign currency translation		13.9		53.4		4.1
Balance, end of year		$(27.3)		$(41.2)		$(100.9)
Retained deficit:						
Balance at December 31, 2001, as previously reported						$(327.1)
Cumulative effect of restatement for lease accounting (see Note 1)						(72.6)
Balance, beginning of year, as restated		$(2,999.5)		$(2,020.8)		$(399.7)
Net loss		$(1,248.8)		$(978.7)		$(1,621.1)
Balance, end of year		$(4,248.3)		$(2,999.5)		$(2,020.8)
Total stockholders' equity		$1,062.9		$3,188.4		$4,100.9
Comprehensive loss:						
Net loss		$(1,248.8)		$(978.7)		$(1,621.1)
Other comprehensive income (loss):						
Change in fair value of interest rate swaps, net of taxes		—		6.3		2.0
Foreign currency translation		13.9		53.4		4.1
Total comprehensive loss		$(1,234.9)		$(919.0)		$(1,615.0)

BLOCKBUSTER INC.
CONSOLIDATED STATEMENTS OF CASH FLOWS (In millions)

	Year ended December 31		
	2004	**2003**	**2002**
		Restated	Restated
Cash flows from operating activities:			
Net loss	$(1,248.8)	$(978.7)	$(1,621.1)
Adjustments to reconcile net loss to net cash flow provided by operating activities:			
Depreciation and amortization	249.7	268.4	240.8
Impairment of goodwill and other long-lived assets	1,504.4	1,304.9	—
Rental library amortization	748.0	954.8	1,024.3
Noncash share-based compensation expense	17.0	—	—
Excess tax benefit from share-based compensation	(5.1)	—	—
Cumulative effect of change in accounting principle, net of tax	—	4.4	1,817.0
Deferred taxes and other	(94.3)	(73.5)	18.3
Change in operating assets and liabilities:			
(Increase) decrease in receivables	8.6	5.9	(27.8)
Decrease in receivable from Viacom	0.8	14.0	82.9

Exhibit 5.7 (continued)

	Year ended December 31		
	2004	2003	2002
		Restated	Restated
(Increase) decrease in merchandise inventories	(84.2)	55.1	(221.8)
Increase in prepaid and other assets	(97.5)	(4.8)	(38.7)
Increase (decrease) in accounts payable	125.4	(221.9)	187.6
Increase in accrued expenses and other liabilities	91.4	101.7	0.8
Net cash flow provided by operating activities	1,215.4	1,430.3	1,462.3
Cash flows from investing activities:			
Rental library purchases	(798.4)	(836.6)	(1,060.9)
Capital expenditures	(289.1)	(191.0)	(151.7)
Cash used for acquisitions	(25.5)	(3.4)	(106.0)
Proceeds from notes receivable and other	1.2	4.5	3.6
Investments in affiliated companies	(0.5)	1.9	0.4
Net cash flow used for investing activities	(1,112.3)	(1,024.6)	(1,314.6)
Cash flows from financing activities:			
Proceeds from credit agreements	820.0	140.0	170.0
Proceeds from senior subordinated notes	300.0	—	—
Repayments on credit agreements	(170.0)	(450.0)	(360.0)
Net repayments on other notes and lines of credit	(23.8)	(5.8)	(10.1)
Net proceeds from the exercise of stock options	2.8	18.1	39.3
Cash dividends	(920.1)	(14.4)	(14.3)
Payment of debt financing costs	(18.7)	—	—
Capital lease payments	(21.0)	(23.4)	(24.1)
Capital contributions received from Viacom	6.9	—	—
Excess tax benefit from share-based compensation	5.1	—	—
Net cash flow used for financing activities	(18.8)	(335.5)	(199.2)
Effect of exchange rate changes on cash	12.6	10.7	3.8
Net increase (decrease) in cash and cash equivalents	96.9	80.9	(47.7)
Cash and cash equivalents at beginning of year	233.4	152.5	200.2
Cash and cash equivalents at end of year	$330.3	$233.4	$152.5
Supplemental cash flow information:			
Cash payments for interest	$23.2	$34.3	$45.8
Cash payments for taxes	44.4	98.1	12.6
Noncash financing and investing activities:			
Retail stores acquired under capital leases	20.4	15.4	15.3

excessively conservative accounting? Either way, Ronald needs an answer.

Blockbuster: A General Overview

Blockbuster (NYSE: BBI) is the world's largest video rental chain with about 9,000 company-owned and franchised stores in 25 countries. Founded in 1982, and headquartered in Dallas, Texas, the company rents more than 1 billion videos, DVDs, and video games each year. In 2004, the company launched Blockbuster Online, in response to the growing popularity of Netflix. Later that year, entertainment giant Viacom, Blockbuster's majority shareholder, spun off its entire stake in a

public sale.[9] But where Viacom had seen only chronic unprofitability, others saw value. Carl Icahn, the wellknown financier, still owns about 9% of the company. Ronald thought that if a famously uncompromising investor like Icahn had retained a large stake, there must be something positive about Blockbuster. But the closer he looked, the more worried he became.

In December 2004, Blockbuster announced the "end of late fees," effective 1 January 2005, which means no more extended viewing fees on any movie or game rental at more than 4,500 company-operated stores and approximately 550 participating franchise stores in the United States. A similar program was planned for its 426 stores in Canada. Ronald

(Continued)

viewed this move with some skepticism, believing that it was unlikely to improve the company's operating margins. First, the marketing campaign was costly. Second, late fees have been an important source of revenue. In fact, the company admits that between $250 million and $300 million of operating income would be lost as a direct result of the move. Ronald thought that the figure might even be higher. Of course, Blockbuster hoped the loss would be partially offset by growth in other revenues. Third, Ronald was concerned about the effect of the move on Blockbuster's relations with franchisees. If late fees were an important source of revenue for Blockbuster, the same must be true for franchise stores. Will franchisees continue to offer their cooperation in an effort that will clearly affect, in a significantly negative way, their own bottom line? Ronald suspects that many will opt out, including some who have already agreed to participate.

In Ronald's view, the end-of-late-fees initiative was a sign of weakness, prompted by stagnating sales in the United States. In addition, sales have declined in several international markets. On the plus side, video game rentals are growing, but the market is highly cyclical and prone to changes in technology. Also, video games have significantly higher prices than DVDs, which means that even hit game titles generate much lower volume than hit movies. These observations imply that game rentals are unlikely to make up for the flat growth in movie rentals.

Blockbuster's Rental Library

Ronald figured that if he was to understand the true profitability and cash flow generation of Blockbuster, he would have to learn something about Blockbuster's core product – namely, the video library that served as the basis for its rental income.

The company purchases its movie rental inventory directly from the film studios or from third-party distributors on both a title-by-title basis and through various revenue-sharing arrangements. The number of domestic movie rental inventory units purchased under revenue sharing increased during 2004 to approximately 2/3 of total units purchased, up from half in 2003.

Revenue sharing requires the company to share an agreed-upon percentage of rental revenues with a studio for a limited period of time. The advantage to Blockbuster is the low initial price for the product. In effect, the studio's price is paid gradually as customers rent the film. Without revenue sharing, Blockbuster, and its franchisees, would struggle to purchase enough copies of popular films to satisfy customer demand. The upfront cost would create major cash flow problems, because the cost would have to be paid immediately to the studio while the revenues earned from customers would be generated over the ensuing months.

The rental library is reported on the balance sheet as a long-term asset, and purchases are classified as investing activities on the statement of cash flows. Movies and games in the library are amortized over periods ranging from 3 to 12 months, down to an estimated residual value of $2 to $5 per unit. Estimates surrounding the useful lives and residual values are continually evaluated.

The revenue-sharing arrangements complicate the accounting to some extent. The cost of rental product purchased pursuant to these arrangements equals the sum of the low initial cost and an estimate of the revenues to be shared with the studios. The portion of the capitalized film cost attributable to revenue sharing is not amortized, but expensed as the related revenue is earned. All other amounts in the rental film library, including the upfront cost and the price paid for any films not acquired under revenue-sharing arrangements, are amortized in the manner described above.

Required

a. Focusing on the balance sheet and the statement of cash flows, do you agree with how Blockbuster accounts for its rental library? What logic might the company offer to defend its approach?

b. How else might the company account for the rental library? What effects would the alternative approach have on the financial statements? Be specific.

c. Regarding Blockbuster's cash flow performance, is Ronald right to worry, or is the company stronger than the earnings suggest?

5-2 Monahan Manufacturing: Preparing and
     Interpreting a Statement of Cash Flows

Balance sheets for Monahan Manufacturing, Inc., appear in
Exhibit 5.8. Additional information includes the following (all
amounts in thousands):

- Net income for 2012 was $2,840.

- Dividends declared and paid were $300.

- Depreciation expense on buildings and machinery was
  $2,550 for the year.

- The firm sold for $125 machinery originally costing $750
  and accumulated depreciation of $600.

- The firm retired bonds during the year at their book value.

Required

Prepare a statement of cash flows for Monahan Manufacturing
for 2012 using the indirect method to compute CFFO. Comment on the pattern of cash flows from operating, investing,
and financing activities.

Exhibit 5.8 Monahan Manufacturing, Inc.: Balance Sheets for December 31, 2011 and 2012 (in thousands of dollars)

	December 31	
	2011	2012
Assets		
Current assets		
Cash	$1,790	$1,620
Accounts receivables	4,730	5,260
Inventories	5,020	6,040
Total current assets	$11,540	$12,920
Noncurrent assets		
Land	$2,970	$3,150
Buildings and equipment	43,390	47,730
Accumulated depreciation	19,870	21,820
Total noncurrent assets	$26,490	$29,060
Total assets	$38,030	$41,980
Liabilities and shareholders' equity		
Current liabilities		
Accounts payable	$2,060	$2,790
Taxes payable	1,370	1,450
Other short-term payables	2,940	3,630
Total current liabilities	$6,370	$7,870
Noncurrent liabilities		
Long-term loans	$9,920	$9,670
Shareholders' equity		
Common stock	$8,360	$8,520
Retained earnings	13,380	15,920
Total shareholders' equity	$21,740	$24,440
Total liabilities and shareholders' equity	$38,030	$41,980

5-3 A Tale of Three Companies: Cash Flows at Sun Microsystems, Wal-Mart, and Merck

Exhibits 5.9, 5.10, and 5.11 present five years of cash flow statements for Sun Microsystems, Wal-Mart, and Merck, respectively. Sales figures are also provided.

In the 1980s, Sun Microsystems was mainly a producer of computer workstations. By 1988 it was the industry leader, thanks largely to superior operating efficiencies and an ability to bring innovative products to market faster than its competitors. Founded in 1982, Sun went public in 1986.

Wal-Mart, a discount retail chain, was founded in 1962, becoming a publicly traded company in 1970. The company achieved its first billion-dollar sales year in 1979. Strategies in the 1980s centered on innovative practices in supply chain management and in the use of information technology, combined with aggressive price competition. The company also embarked on a massive store-building campaign.

Merck was founded in 1891 as the US subsidiary of a German chemical and pharmaceutical company, becoming

independent of its parent during World War I. Over the ensuing decades, Merck became a fully integrated, multinational producer of pharmaceutical products. The company has long depended heavily on its research efforts, funded in-house and through joint ventures, to develop innovative, patent-protected drugs. Throughout the 1980s, Merck was consistently among the top three drugs companies in the world.

During the observation period, macroeconomic performance was robust, as shown by real GDP growth rates in the United States:

1984	7.2%
1985	4.1%
1986	3.5%
1987	3.4%
1988	4.1%

Exhibit 5.9   Sun Microsystems Statement of Cash Flows (amounts in millions)

	1984	1985	1986	1987	1988
Operations					
Net income	$3	$9	$12	$36	$66
Depreciation	1	4	6	25	51
Working capital provided by operations	$4	$13	$18	$61	$117
(Inc.) decr. in receivables	−9	−5	−24	−58	−117
(Inc.) decr. in inventories	−8	−8	−21	−32	−77
(Inc.) decr. in other current assets	−1	−1	−18	−31	−30
Inc. (decr.) in accounts payable – trade	4	4	21	33	58
Inc. (decr.) in other current liabilities	2	9	6	35	52
Cash flow from operations	$−8	$12	$−18	$8	$3
Investing					
Fixed assets acquired	$−5	$−15	$−36	$−76	$−117
Other investing transactions	0	−2	−2	−23	−32
Cash flow from investing	$−5	$−17	$−38	$−99	$−149
Financing					
Incr. short-term borrowing	$1	$3	$11	$21	$0
Incr. long-term borrowing	3	5	1	121	0
Issue of capital stock	11	21	47	96	63
Decr. short-term borrowing	0	0	0	0	−6
Decr. long-term borrowing	0	−1	−2	0	0
Other financing transactions	0	3	3	0	0
Cash flow from financing	$15	$31	$60	$238	$57
Change in cash	$2	$26	$4	$147	$−89
Sales (in millions of $)	NA	115	210	538	1,052

NA = not available.

Exhibit 5.10   Wal-Mart Statement of Cash Flows (amounts in millions)

	1984	1985	1986	1987	1988
Operations					
Net income	$271	$327	$450	$628	$837
Depreciation	67	90	124	166	214
Other addbacks	9	18	7	0	1
Other subtractions	0	0	0	−1	0
Working capital provided by operations	$347	$435	$581	$793	$1,052
(Inc.) decr. in receivables	−6	−12	−33	−6	−31
(Inc.) decr. in inventories	−368	−284	−643	−575	−700
(Inc.) decr. in other current assets	−77	−12	−8	−0	−6
Inc. (decr.) in accounts payable – trade	161	287	229	127	290
Inc. (decr.) in other current liabilities	22	16	139	120	129
Cash flow from operations	$79	$430	$265	$459	$734
Investing					
Fixed assets acquired	$−322	$−513	$−675	$−757	$−797
Other investing transactions	148	−160	−4	−51	9
Cash flow from investing	$−174	$−673	$−679	$−808	$−788
Financing					
Incr. short-term borrowing	$0	$0	$0	$104	$0
Incr. long-term borrowing	129	298	460	194	248
Issue of capital stock	6	5	6	7	4
Decr. short-term borrowing	0	0	0	0	−85
Decr. long-term borrowing	−16	−12	−13	−42	−21
Acquisition of capital stock	−1	−1	0	0	0
Dividends	−30	−40	−48	−68	−91
Cash flow from financing	$88	$250	$405	$195	$55
Change in cash	$−7	$7	$−9	$−154	$1
Sales (in millions of $)	6,401	8,451	11,909	15,959	20,649

Exhibit 5.11   Merck and Company Statement of Cash Flows (amounts in millions)

	1984	1985	1986	1987	1988
Operations					
Net income	$493	$540	$676	$906	$1,207
Depreciation and amortization	162	182	194	210	205
Other addbacks	130	86	37	0	0
Other subtractions	0	0	0	−66	−245
Working capital provided by operations	$785	$808	$907	$1,050	$1,167
(Inc.) decr. in receivables	−102	−53	−42	−170	−106
(Inc.) decr. in inventories	0	22	−35	−80	−14
(Inc.) decr. in other cash	29	1	0	0	0
Inc. (decr.) accounts payable – trade	78	81	98	144	−77
Inc. (decr.) in other current liabilities	−49	152	166	379	417
Cash flow from operations	$741	$1,009	$1,094	$1,322	$1,387
Investing					
Fixed assets sold	$0	$92	$0	$0	$0
Fixed assets acquired	−274	−238	−211	−254	−373
Other investing transactions	119	−278	−126	−206	262
Cash flow from investing	$−155	$−424	$−337	$−460	$−111

(Continued)

Exhibit 5.11 **(continued)**

	1984	1985	1986	1987	1988
Financing					
Incr. short-term borrowing	$38	$0	$43	$478	$0
Incr. long-term borrowing	0	0	0	0	1,997
Issue of capital stock	2	18	25	21	30
Decr. short-term borrowing	0	79	0	0	392
Decr. long-term borrowing	−206	8	3	0	1,991
Acquisition of capital stock	−164	−242	−500	−1,000	0
Dividends	−224	−235	−278	−335	−505
Other financing trans	0	0	0	0	31
Cash flow from financing	$−554	$−546	$−713	$−836	$−830
Change in cash	$32	$39	$44	$27	$446
Sales (in millions of $)	3,560	3,548	4,128	5,061	5,940

Required

a. Identify five distinctive characteristics for each of the three companies, based on their cash flow statements. Compare and contrast their cash flow profiles, focusing on free cash flow and on the relationship between CFFO and net income.

b. Which of these companies is the "most successful"? How did you arrive at your conclusion?

c. What factors might account for differences in the cash flow profiles of these three companies, apart from differences in financial performance or efficiency?

Case Study

5-4 Inditex: Analyzing the Statement of Cash Flows

Industria de Diseño Textil, SA (commonly known as "Inditex") is a global specialty retailer with eight major brands: Zara, Pull & Bear, Massimo Dutti, Bershka, Stradivarius, Oysho, Zara Home, and Uterque. Its first store opened in 1975.

Despite the recent global economic downturn, the company has recently enjoyed successful results and a rising share price. The company currently has slightly more than 100,000 employees worldwide, with stores in 77 countries, including recent expansion into Bulgaria, India, and Kazakhstan.

According to its 2010 annual report, Inditex has identified the following operating priorities:

1. Customers
2. Stores
3. Design/production
4. Logistics
5. Teams.

Required

a. In 2009 and 2010, which individual line item consumed the most cash according to the statement of cash flows?

b. Where did the company obtain the cash to pay for the item identified in part (a)?

c. Why is depreciation and amortization added back to income before taxes when calculating cash from operations?

d. Review the subsection titled changes in assets and liabilities within the statement of cash flows. Note for the individual line items listed as increase in inventories and increase in accounts receivable the signs of the adjustments flip from FY2009 to FY2010 (i.e., added back in 2009 but deducted in 2010). What was the firm doing differently across the two years that caused the sign of the adjustments to flip?

e. Review management's discussion of the historical results in 2010 as well as their forecast for 2011 and focus on their discussion of new store openings.

1. Does Inditex appear to be contracting or expanding its store presence?
2. Where on the statement of cash flows can one find information about the cash needed to open new outlets?
3. Focusing just on the historical data, compare the rate of depreciation and amortization to the level of capital expenditure. Does this analysis support the level of expansion described by management in the text disclosures?

f. Review management's discussion on dividend policy. Consider these dividend plans in light of the expansion plans from part (e). Do these two strategies appear consistent?

g. In the disclosures that follow, management makes the following statement:

"The operating working capital position remains negative, a consequence of the business model."

Then a table appears detailing this negative working capital position. How do you interpret this disclosure? That is, what operational decisions is management making and executing as part of their "business model" that leads to this result? Is it a good or a bad outcome?

1. Performance in FY2010

Figures expressed in millions of euros

Net sales reached €12,527 million in FY2010, with sales growth of 13% (10% in local currencies).

In FY2010 INDITEX **retail space** increased 10%. Total selling area at FYE reached 2,587,648 square meters:

	31 Jan 2011	31 Jan 2010	Chg % 10/09
ZARA	1,687,949	1,541,291	10%
PULL & BEAR	196,320	175,574	12%
MASSIMO DUTTI	143,023	138,001	4%
BERSHKA	262,009	232,319	13%
STRADIVARIUS	154,253	133,062	16%
OYSHO	60,474	54,930	10%
ZARA HOME	72,748	65,761	11%
UTERQÜE	10,871	7,770	40%
Total	2,587,648	2,348,709	10%

Net store openings in FY2010 amounted to 437, reaching a total of 5,044 stores in 77 countries. In FY2010 INDITEX has opened stores in 45 countries:

	Net openings	Total stores	
Concept	FY2010	31 January 2011	31 January 2010
ZARA	123	1,518	1,395
ZARA KIDS	(8)	205	213
PULL&BEAR	56	682	626
MASSIMO DUTTI	33	530	497
BERSHKA	69	720	651
STRADIVARIUS	78	593	515
OYSHO	40	432	392
ZARA HOME	23	284	261
UTERQÜE	23	80	57
Total	437	5,044	4,607

A list of quarterly openings and stores opened as at FYE by concept and by country is included in Annexes IV and V.

Like-for-like sales increased 3% in FY2010 (5% in 1H and 2% in 2H). The like-for-like calculation includes 81% of FY2010 store sales (i.e., sales in stores opened for the whole of fiscal years 2010 and 2009).

Net sales by concept in FY2010 and FY2009 are shown in the table below:

Concept	FY2010	FY2009	% Chg 10/09
ZARA	8,088	7,077	14%
PULL & BEAR	857	771	11%
MASSIMO DUTTI	897	790	14%
BERSHKA	1,247	1,177	6%
STRADIVARIUS	780	702	11%
OYSHO	304	280	9%
ZARA HOME	294	243	21%
UTERQÜE	59	44	36%
Total sales	12,527	11,084	13%

The ongoing expansion of the Group has led to a widely diversified sales platform. All the concepts have increased their sales demonstrating their global scalability.

(Continued)

Region	FY2010	FY2009
EUROPE EX-SPAIN	45%	46%
SPAIN	28%	32%
ASIA	15%	12%
AMERICAS	12%	10%
Total	100%	100%

Gross profit rose to €7,422 million, 17% higher than the previous year. The Gross margin has reached 59.3% of sales (57.1% in FY2009).

Operating expenses have been tightly managed over the year and have grown by 12.6%, mainly as a result of the new retail space added and include all the start-up costs for new openings and €12 million for the launch of Zara e-commerce.

In millions of euros	FY2010	FY2009	Chg % 10/09
Personnel expenses	2,009	1,792	12%
Rental expenses	1,272	1,134	12%
Other operating expenses	1,171	1,027	14%
Total	4,452	3,953	13%

At FYE2010 the number of employees was 100,138 (92,301 at FYE2009).

FY2010 **EBITDA** came to €2,966 million, 25% higher than the previous year, and EBIT to €2,290 million, 33% higher. The breakdown of EBIT by concept is shown below:

Concept	Ebit by concept (in millions of euros)				
	FY2010	FY2009	Chg % 10/09	% Sales FY2010	% Total FY2010
ZARA	1,534	1,104	39%	19.0%	67.0%
PULL&BEAR	139	101	37%	16.2%	6.1%
MASSIMO DUTTI	172	117	47%	19.2%	7.5%
BERSHKA	197	196	1%	15.8%	8.6%
STRADIVARIUS	176	149	18%	22.5%	7.7%
OYSHO	45	38	19%	14.9%	2.0%
ZARA HOME	39	25	60%	13.3%	1.7%
UTERQÜE*	−12	−2	–	–	–
Total ebit	2,290	1,728	33%	18.3%	100%

*Includes €12 million for accelerated depreciation of assets.

The following chart shows the breakdown of financial results.

In millions of euros	FY2010	FY2009
Net finance income (losses)	18	8
Foreign exchange gains (losses)	13	(5)
Total	31	4

Net income came to €1,732 million, 32% higher than the previous year.

INDITEX's Board of Directors will propose to the General Shareholders Meeting a dividend increase of 33%, composed of an ordinary dividend of €1.40 per share and a bonus dividend of €0.20 per share, equating to a total dividend of €1.60 per share. €0.80 will be payable on 2 May 2011 as interim ordinary dividend and €0.80 would be payable on 2 November 2011 as final ordinary and bonus dividend.

INDITEX continued to show a strong financial condition over Fiscal 2010:

	31 January 2011	31 January 2010
Cash & cash equivalents	3,433	2,420
Current financial debt	(3)	(35)
Noncurrent financial debt	(4)	(5)
Net financial cash (debt)	3,427	2,380

The **operating working capital** position remains negative, a consequence of the business model:

	31 January 2011	31 January 2010
Inventories	1,215	993
Receivables	482	422
Payables	(2,672)	(2,270)
Operating working capital	(976)	(856)

Funds from operations reached €2,540 million in FY2010, 23% higher than the previous year.

Capital expenditure for the FY2010 amounted to €754 million driven by 437 store openings in the year.

Dividends paid to shareholders reached €751 million.

2. Start of FY2011

Store sales in local currencies have increased by 10% from 1 February to 14 March 2011. The Spring–Summer season is influenced by the performance over the Easter period due to its significant sales volumes.

Expected Capital Expenditure in FY2011 is approximately €800 million as a result of the store opening plan for the year. Additionally, we have incurred an extraordinary, one-off investment of €230 million for the acquisition of unique retail premises at 666 Fifth Avenue, New York, for a global flagship for Zara.

Inditex expects to open between 460 and 500 net stores in FY2011. Approximately 70% of the new contracts have been signed, but in some cases openings may not take place in FY2011.

Concept	Range	
ZARA	125	130
PULL & BEAR	45	50
MASSIMO DUTTI	40	45
BERSHKA	70	75
STRADIVARIUS	80	85
OYSHO	40	45
ZARA HOME	35	40
UTERQÜE	25	30
Total	460	500

Inditex plans to open in Australia in April and will launch South Africa in Autumn–Winter 2011, demonstrating its global reach.

On the second of September 2010, Zara launched e-commerce and is now operating in 16 European markets. Zara plans to begin e-commerce sales in the United States and Japan in Autumn–Winter 2011.

Additionally, all Inditex concepts plan to be present in e-commerce in 2011 with the launch of Massimo Dutti, Bershka, Pull&Bear, Stradivarius, Oysho, and Uterqüe e-commerce operations in selected European markets over the second half of 2011.

3. Tables and Appendices to Follow

Consolidated financial statements

FY2010 income statement

In millions of euros	FY2010	FY2009
Net sales	12,527	11,084
Cost of sales	(5,105)	(4,756)
Gross profit	7,422	6,328
Gross margin	59.3%	57.1%
Operating expenses	(4,452)	(3,953)
Other net operating income (losses)	(4)	(1)
Operating cash flow (ebitda)	2,966	2,374
Ebitda margin	23.7%	21.4%
Amortization and depreciation	(676)	(646)
Operating income (ebit)	2,290	1,728
Ebit margin	18.3%	15.6%
Financial results	31	4
Income before taxes	2,322	1,732
Ebit margin	18.5%	15.6%
Taxes	(580)	(410)
Net income	1,741	1,322
	13.9%	11.9%
Noncontrolling interests	9	8
Net income attributable to the controlling company	1,732	1,314
Net income margin	13.8%	11.9%
Earnings per share, cents euro*	278	211

*Shares for EPS calculation 623.1 million for 2010 and 2009

(Continued)

Consolidated balance sheet as 31 January 2011

In millions of euros

Assets	31 January 2011	31 January 2010
Current assets	5,203	3,944
Cash & cash equivalents	3,433	2,420
Receivables	482	422
Inventories	1,215	993
Other	73	109
Noncurrent assets	4,624	4,392
Property, plant and equipment	3,414	3,307
Intangible assets	687	665
Financial investments	9	15
Other	513	404
Total assets	9,826	8,335
Total equity & liabilities		
Current liabilities	2,675	2,305
Payables	2,672	2,270
Financial debt	3	35
Noncurrent liabilities	728	660
Financial debt	4	5
Deferred taxes	173	173
Other	551	482
Equity	6,423	5,371
Equity attributable to the group	6,386	5,329
Noncontrolling interests	37	41
Total equity & liabilities	9,826	8,335

FY2010 Consolidated statement of cash flows

In millions of euros	FY2010	FY2009
Income before taxes	2,322	1,732
Adjustments to income		
Depreciation and amortization	636	625
Foreign exchange impact	(30)	31
Other	120	63
Corporate income tax	(508)	(391)
Funds from operations	2,540	2,060
Changes in assets and liabilities		
Increase in inventories	(227)	48
Increase in accounts receivable	(120)	163
Decrease in current liabilities	363	50
Changes in working capital	16	261
Cash from operations	2,556	2,321
Investments in intangible assets	(74)	(27)
Investments in property, plant and equipment	(617)	(461)
Addition to other long-term financial investments	(26)	–
Other assets investments	(37)	(13)
Other investing activities	–	(10)
Capital expenditure	(754)	(510)
Net decrease in long-term financial debt	(1)	(4)
Net decrease in other long-term debt	(33)	11
Net increase in current debt	(32)	(204)
Dividends	(751)	(662)
Other financing activities	(1)	–
Cash used in financing activities	(819)	(859)
Net increase in cash and cash equivalents	984	953
Foreign exchange impact on cash & cash equivalents	30	1
Cash and cash equivalents at beginning of the year	2,420	1,466
Cash and cash equivalents at end of the year	3,433	2,420

NOTES

1. Firms using the direct method must disclose the reconciliation between net income and CFFO (as in the indirect method).

2. The T-account for common stock is not included because there was no change in the accounting balance for 2018 (i.e., the ending balance is the same as the beginning balance).

3. Natural resources businesses, such as coalmines and oil companies, also add back depletion expense.

4. Provisions are routinely taken for the costs of restructuring, warranties and guarantees, environmental cleanup, and litigation.

5. The following discussion on working capital is adapted from S.D. Young and S.F. O'Byrne, *EVA and Value Based Management: A Practical Guide to Implementation*, 2001, McGraw-Hill.

6. Just prior to the sale, Blockbuster paid a special dividend of $5 per share. Most of the dividends went to Viacom.

Financial Statement Analysis

Introduction

Corporate financial reporting serves many purposes, but perhaps its most important role is to provide useful information to investors. In this chapter, we look at how to analyze financial statements in order to make better investment decisions.

Financial statement analysis unlocks the clues about a company's future from its recent past and, in so doing, makes possible intelligent forecasts of future performance. It helps investors to decide whether or not a company's shares are worth buying, or if the company is a creditworthy borrower. For the equity investor, the decision depends ultimately on perceptions of value. If the value of a company, based on forecasts of future performance, is perceived to be greater than its market price, we buy. Otherwise, we don't. In short, much of the usefulness of financial statement analysis comes down to the quality of the forecasts and company valuations it produces.

To produce forecasts and valuations that help investors determine where their capital is likely to earn its highest risk-adjusted returns, a thorough financial statement analysis must follow four sequential steps:

1. Business and industry analysis

2. Accounting analysis

3. Financial analysis

4. Valuation.

1. **Business and industry analysis** identifies the main competitive forces in the company's industry, its key business risks, and the sources and sustainability of competitive advantage.

2. **Accounting analysis** identifies the accounting policy choices made by management and evaluates the appropriateness of those choices.

3. **Financial analysis** evaluates the past performance of a firm using its financial statements and related information and seeks to determine the sustainability of that performance.

4. **Valuation** takes the inputs from the first three steps and translates them into a set of financial forecasts to produce estimates of company value.

In the sections that follow, we will be showing how to perform the first and third of these steps. Although there is also a brief discussion of accounting analysis (the second step), the topic is discussed in later chapters. Valuation is discussed in Chapter 7. Once again, we will draw on the financial statements produced by TSMC to illustrate how to perform a comprehensive financial statement analysis.

Business and Industry Analysis

The goal of business and industry analysis is to learn whatever we need to know about the business, its industry, and its competitors that might affect future profitability – including prospects for growth, how firms in the industry compete, the role of technology and innovation, marketing and distribution, and the relative power of key players in the value chain, e.g., suppliers and customers. This involves both:

- industry analysis (understanding the forces that drive profitability in the industry) and

- the analysis of competitive strategies (how the company positions itself in the industry to create and sustain competitive advantage).

Industry Analysis

The most popular approach to industry analysis is known as the "5-forces" or "Porter" model, as described by Michael Porter in his book *Competitive Strategy* (1998).

The Porter 5-forces model provides a systematic approach to studying the economic structure of an industry by analyzing the five basic competitive forces that affect industry returns. Any of these forces, if strong enough, can reduce or even eliminate industry profits.

At the center of the model is *rivalry among existing firms*, because it may be affected by each of the other forces. The term "rivalry" is used to reflect the jockeying for market share by firms within the industry. Questions then need to be posed, including

- How fast is the industry growing?

- Is it stagnant or declining?

- How many competitors are there?

- Do firms compete mainly on price or differentiation?

- Is there a history of cooperative pricing or is price competition more "cut-throat"?

- What are the key economic and regulatory issues faced by companies in this industry?

For example, slow growth, a large number of competitors, and intense price-based competition exert downward pressure on profit margins.

The *threat of new entrants* looks beyond existing rivalries and considers how the industry's competitive landscape might unfold in the future. Here we ask the following:

- Who are the *potential* competitors and how might their entry affect competitive rivalry?

- Are there strong barriers (such as patents, economies of scale, access to distribution channels, strong branding, legal constraints, or high capital needs) that limit the threat of new entrants?

- Does government policy protect incumbents?

- Are there first-mover advantages, such as an experience curve, that might put new entrants at a cost disadvantage and thus strongly favor existing businesses?

For example, the absence of strong barriers implies that incumbents will have to divide up market share among more sellers, leading ultimately to an erosion of profits.

The *threat of substitute products* considers whether the industry is under threat from other products. If customers perceive that substitutes may satisfy their needs, competing businesses will be drawn into price comparisons and price cutting.

In assessing the threat from substitutes, we ask the following questions:

- Are close substitutes available?
- What are the price/value characteristics of substitutes?
- How sensitive are buyers to changing prices?
- Are buyers able and willing to switch, and how costly is it to switch?

The availability of close substitutes, combined with low switching costs, exerts downward pressure on industry profits.

The *bargaining power of buyers* focuses on the ability of buyers to negotiate from a position of strength, thereby reducing industry profits. Questions to ask here include the following:

- Are buyers highly concentrated or diffuse?
- Do purchasers buy in large quantities?
- Are substitute products available?
- How costly is it for buyers to switch?

This power is likely to be greater when the number of buyers is relatively small, when the purchasing volume of individual buyers is high, when products or services are commoditized (i.e., difficult or impossible to differentiate), and the costs of switching from one seller to another are low. When any of these conditions are present, downward pressure can be exerted on prices and operating margins.

The *bargaining power of suppliers* is the flip side to buyers' bargaining power. It poses similar questions, but from the opposite end of the value chain. For example:

- How much power do suppliers have to raise price?
- How many suppliers are there, and are there available substitutes?
- How costly is switching to new suppliers?

Significant supplier power implies that sizable portions of the wealth-creating potential of a value chain may accrue to suppliers instead of companies in the target industry. For example, distributors of processors in the personal computer industry face severe downward pressure on profit margins because of the overwhelming power of Intel, their principal supplier (and both a competitor *and* customer of TSMC). So even if the value chain is highly profitable, the bargaining power of Intel ensures that the portion of that profitability available to distributors is highly constrained.

The 5-forces model is an enduring and adaptable approach to understanding industry economies, a necessary starting point to understanding firm-specific profitability. However, there is one obvious drawback to the framework, at least in the form in which it is commonly presented: it assumes that all industry players – competitors, buyers, sellers, etc. – are threats to profitability. As the growing use of strategic alliances suggest, interactions among firms in an industry can be positive, as well as negative. One famous example was the cooperation of Sony and Toshiba in establishing a global standard for DVDs. Such cooperation allowed the two firms, hitherto known for their fierce rivalry, to boost industry growth and profitability. Other, more recent examples include an agreement between automakers BMW and Fiat to jointly produce components and systems for some of their vehicles, arrangements by airlines to share check-in, gate management, and other facilities, and a contract between parcel delivery companies DHL and UPS to grant each other access to spare capacity.

Complementary products can also have a positive effect on profitability. For example, manufacturers of home cinema systems have benefited from the rapid growth in the market for big-screen televisions. In effect, the complementary product (e.g., big-screen TVs) boosts demand for the industry's product offerings, with correspondingly positive effects on profit margins. Product tie-ins between Hollywood studios and McDonald's for action films and animated features are another example in which companies in two ostensibly different industries benefit from the presence of the other.

These examples teach us that a comprehensive industry analysis doesn't just assess threats to profit, but also opportunities.

Competitive Strategy

The 5-forces analysis identifies the threats to profits for all firms in an industry. The analysis of competitive strategy focuses on how individual firms are likely to cope with these threats, and also any opportunities that may arise from cooperation with other players. In light of industry structure and profitability, we ask: "How does the company create a sustainable competitive advantage that might lead to abnormal profits?" Or to put it another way, "How does the firm position itself to capture at least some of the industry's profit-making potential?"

The existence of abnormal profits implies that the company generates returns greater than its cost of capital. In a competitive market, such profits are possible only if the company can do something better than its competitors. A fundamental truism of valuation states that value creation is not possible without abnormal profits, and abnormal profits are not possible without competitive advantage.

Broadly speaking, firms create a competitive advantage through cost leadership, differentiation, or some combination of the two.

Cost Leadership

This may be achieved because the company delivers the same product or service offered by its competitors at a lower cost. They may have attained this position through more efficient production, design improvements, lower input costs (e.g., cheaper labor or materials), economies of scale or scope, tighter cost control, or more efficient distribution. If a firm has truly achieved such an advantage, it can earn above-normal profits while charging the same prices as its competitors. Alternatively, it can lower prices, forcing its less efficient competitors to exit the industry.

Dell's strategy of executing "good enough" technology faster and cheaper than all of its key rivals in the computer business is a prime example of a company that pursued cost leadership with success.

Differentiation

A differentiation strategy implies that the firm seeks to be "different" along some dimension that customers care about. Whether it's different or "better" in an objective sense is less important than whether it is perceived by customers to be better. Companies might try to differentiate in terms of product quality, service quality, faster or more flexible delivery, product innovation, or strong brands. If a firm has truly succeeded in differentiating itself from competitors, it should be able to command a premium price from its customers. Think of powerful brand names, such as McDonald's or Gucci, that allow their owners to charge more than competitors for ostensibly similar products.

Appendix 6.1 provides a business and industry analysis and a competitive strategy analysis of TSMC. We will later draw on this analysis to show how such knowledge and insight about a company and its industry can be used to interpret the company's financial performance.

Accounting Analysis

As you will have become aware of by now, financial statements don't always provide a complete and truthful picture of a company's performance and financial condition. The data needed to form such a picture are filtered by GAAP/IFRS and by managerial discretion, both of which can distort the quality of the reported information. The reader must therefore know how to adjust the reported numbers, when necessary, in order to overcome these distortions. The result of such adjustments is that the financial figures used for analytical purposes may differ in material ways from the numbers that appear in the official financial statements.

Financial statement analysis is a "garbage in, garbage out" system: it's only as good as the quality of the numbers that go into it. The main purpose of accounting analysis is to assess the *quality* of the financial statements, and to adjust where necessary. Ultimately, it's about whether or not the numbers can be trusted. We therefore need to judge whether the accounting methods chosen appear appropriate, the estimates reasonable, and the accounting policy consistently applied.

Issues relating to financial reporting quality were addressed in Chapter 4 (revenue recognition) and will also be discussed from Chapter 8 onward.

Financial Analysis

In this phase, the performance of the firm is assessed in the context of its industry and competitive strategies. Financial statement ratios are the most common tools used for this purpose. (The ratios discussed in this section are summarized in Appendix 6.2.)

Ratio analysis focuses on the relationships between two or more financial statement numbers. How these ratios are then used depends largely on the purpose of the financial analysis. For example, trade creditors and banks offering short-term credit facilities are primarily interested in the short-term liquidity of the business, and will select a set of ratios that address this issue. Other creditors, such as bondholders and banks offering long-term loans, are interested in long-term liquidity and capital structure and in the company's ability to generate sufficient cash flow over the term of a loan to pay interest and principal. The range of financial ratios of interest to this group include the same ratios looked at by short-term creditors, but will also include ratios that deal with broader issues related to how the company finances its assets.

Equity investors care most about long-term earnings and the cash-flow-generating power of the firm. Because shareholders are residual claimants on the firm and its resources, equity analysis must address the same issues of concern to creditors. Unless a company can repay its loans, there is no residual cash for shareholders. But equity investors must also care about the size and risk of any residual earnings or cash flows, which are less relevant to lenders who receive a final payout that is capped at the principal amount. Thus, equity investors' perspective is the most comprehensive of any investor group.

For whatever purpose they're put to, ratios should tell a story. It's the story of the company's strategy, and whether or not that strategy is working. It confirms whether or not the company has a competitive advantage – some feature of the business that allows it to beat the competition – and whether or not that advantage is sustainable. Companies with a sustainable competitive advantage should have the means to service any and all debts, and to provide competitive returns to equity investors. Ratio analysis helps us to interpret business results and determine if such advantages have been achieved.

The insights gained are then used to forecast future performance and value the firm. In deciding whether or not to invest in a particular company, investors try to estimate the returns and the riskiness of returns expected from that investment. In short, they seek to maximize expected returns for a given level of risk, or minimize risk for a given level of expected returns. The goal is to maximize risk-adjusted returns. It stands to reason, therefore, that when using financial statements to analyze and value the firm, special emphasis is given to understanding profitability (the source of returns) and risk. Ratio analysis focuses on these two issues. In the discussion below, we illustrate how to perform such an analysis drawing on the financial statements of TSMC.

ROE and ROIC

Let's begin with profitability. To say that a company has achieved a certain level of profit is of little analytical interest unless we can also say something about the amount of capital used to generate it. We do this in two ways:

- **return on equity** (ROE) and

- **return on invested capital** (ROIC).

ROE

This measures earnings available to common shareholders as a percentage of equity capital.[1] To many analysts, this is the most important of all financial statement ratios because it measures the profitability of the firm from the owners' perspective.

$$ROE = \frac{Net\,Income}{Average\,Shareholders'Equity}$$

For TSMC in 2016 (see Exhibit 1.1),[2]

$$ROE = \frac{331,797}{1,227,408} = 26.0\%$$

Average shareholders' equity = $(1,194,970 + 1,359,846) \div 2$

2016:   26.0%
2015:   27.3%
2014:   27.4%

Average shareholders' equity equals the beginning balance plus the ending balance divided by two. Because balance sheet numbers are snapshot figures (i.e., measured at a point in time) the standard practice is to calculate average figures when a balance sheet account, such as shareholders' equity, is tied to an income statement or cash flow number as these latter amounts are measured over a period of time. An alternative approach is to use the beginning balance in the denominator.

TSMC's ROE of 26.0% is high, although it has declined slightly over the past two years. A quick review of the income statement reveals that TSMC's net income (in millions) has increased over the two years since 2014 (from NT$254,185 to NT$302,830 to NT$331,797). However, shareholders' equity has risen at a slightly faster rate, mainly from reinvested earnings. Taken together, these trends explain the small decline in ROE.

Although ROE is a popular measure of performance in the analyst community, there is a important drawback to it from an analytical point of view: ROE is a function of both operating profitability and the financing choices made by management. Therefore, if ROE increases or decreases, without further analysis we cannot say whether this change is a function of changes in the underlying profitability of the business or whether it is a function of changes in how the company finances its assets. For this reason, we believe that ROIC is a better place to start the analysis of a company's performance.

ROIC

An alternative approach to measuring profitability, return on invested capital (ROIC), looks at the firm from an "unlevered," or zero-debt, perspective. When the firm is viewed in this way, the influence of financing choice (debt vs. equity) is neutralized. ROIC is measured as follows:

$$ROIC = \frac{NOPAT}{Average\ Invested\ Capital}$$

NOPAT is net operating profit after tax. Invested capital measures assets independently of how they were financed. For this reason, ROIC is a measure of profitability from an operating and investment perspective, without regard to financing choices.

The balance sheets in Figure 6.1 clarify how invested capital is defined.[3] On the right we see a managerial, or operating, balance sheet in which short-term, noninterest-bearing liabilities are netted against short-term operating assets – inventories, receivables, and prepaid expenses. The sum from either side of this balance sheet is known as "invested capital." Other common terms for invested capital include "net operating assets" and "capital employed." Return on capital employed and return on net operating assets are simply alternative ways of expressing the same idea as ROIC and are thus conceptually equivalent.

Subtracting short-term, noninterest-bearing liabilities (NIBL) from the sum of receivables, inventories, and prepaid assets yields what is commonly known as the working capital requirement (WCR). The WCR is an integral part of invested capital.[4]

So why do we subtract noninterest-bearing current liabilities in calculating invested capital, when it might be easier to use total assets from the regular balance sheet?[5] The reason is subtle, but important to understanding what the term "invested capital" really means. Although accounts payable and other nondebt current liabilities are to some extent interest-bearing (if they weren't, suppliers extending credit in competitive markets would go bankrupt), digging out the interest

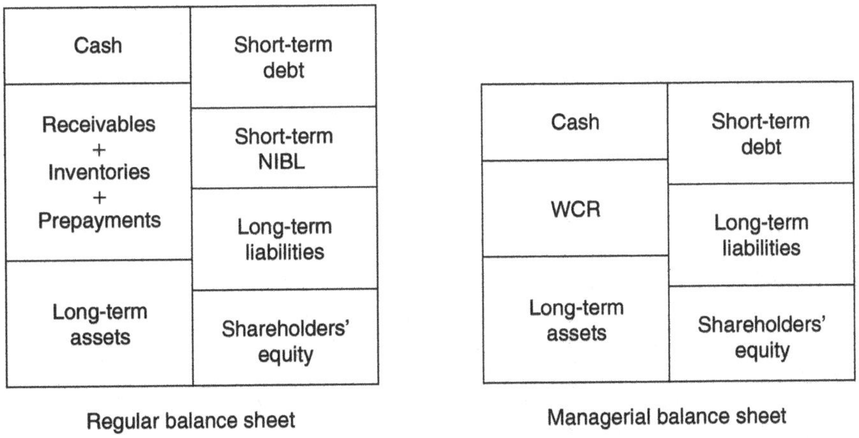

Regular balance sheet   Managerial balance sheet

FIGURE 6.1 The regular vs. managerial balance sheet.

component is seldom worth the effort. In addition, the entire cost of goods and services bought in from suppliers, including any interest component, is reflected in either cost of sales or selling, general, and administration (SG&A) expenses. Therefore, the company is charged, albeit indirectly, for these interest costs.

By including an item in invested capital (and thus in the denominator of ROIC), the implication is that the firm should earn a return on it for the capital provider. But in the case of short-term, noninterest-bearing liabilities, the interest component of the expense is already included in the numerator. Therefore, we exclude such items from the denominator when calculating the profitability of assets. Otherwise, the interest charges for these liabilities would be counted twice.

For TSMC, NOPAT and invested capital are calculated as follows:[6]

NOPAT (2016): Operating income $(1 - T)$ + Equity income, net of tax

$$377,957 (1 - 0.17) + 3,458 = 317,162$$

where T is the income tax rate. Equity income arises from the normal course of TSMC's operating and investing activities, and therefore should be included in NOPAT.

Invested capital: *Total assets Short-term noninterest-bearing liabilities*

(end of 2015) $1,886,297 - 252,028 = 1,634,269$

(end of 2016) $1,657,397 - 176,708 = 1,480,689$

(average 2016) $1,634,269 + 1,480,689 \div 2 = 1,557,479$

Therefore, ROIC for 2016 equals

$$\frac{317,162}{1,557,479} = 20.4\%$$

2016:   20.4%

2015:   19.2%

2014:   20.8%

ROIC has decreased slightly since 2014, but the decrease is smaller than that of ROE. This difference can be explained by TSMC's growing shareholders' equity (and reduced financial leverage). In short, TSMC is providing stable returns, with growing operating profits. The rate of return on shareholders' equity has declined slightly due to changes in the company's capital structure.

DuPont Analysis

To study changes in ROIC over time, and to better explain differences between a company's profitability and that of its competitors, ROIC can be disaggregated using DuPont analysis.[7]

DuPont analysis progressively disaggregates, or breaks down, broad measures of profitability such as ROIC into two or more constituent elements. As we will see, much of the benefit of ratio analysis is not just in understanding individual ratio values, but also in the relationships between and among key ratios. DuPont analysis provides the framework for examining such relationships.

To illustrate, consider the following:

$$\underset{\substack{\text{NOPAT} \\ \text{Margin}}}{\underbrace{\frac{\text{NOPAT}}{\text{Sales}}}} \times \underset{\substack{\text{Invested Capital} \\ \text{Turnover}}}{\underbrace{\frac{\text{Sales}}{\text{Average Invested Capital}}}}$$

Notice that the "sales" terms cancel out, resulting in the same numerator and denominator as ROIC, which means that ROIC is the product of NOPAT margin and invested capital turnover. The logic of the DuPont framework is to then break down these components of profitability into even more finely granulated measures of performance, helping us to identify the sources of profit and value creation in the business.

NOPAT margin is operating profit, net of tax, as a percentage of sales. Invested capital turnover measures how much revenue was generated during the year as a function of the assets available. If either ratio increases, holding the other constant, ROIC increases.

TSMC's 2016 NOPAT margin equals:

$$\frac{317{,}162}{947{,}938} = 33.5\%$$

2016:   33.5%

2015:   32.0%

2014:   32.7%

These figures show that TSMC's after-tax operating profit scaled by revenue dipped slightly in 2015, but recovered in 2016. Every NT$100 of revenue produced in 2016 yielded NT$33.50 in NOPAT, an improvement of NT$1.50 over the previous year.

TSMC's invested capital turnover for 2016 equals:

$$\frac{947{,}938}{1{,}557{,}479} = 0.61$$

2016:   0.61

2015:   0.60

2014:   0.64

Invested capital turnover is a measure of operating efficiency. Efficiency in this context refers to the company's ability to manage its operating assets. Companies acquire assets to produce and sell their products and services. However, as the balance sheet shows (remember, balance sheets must balance!), all assets have to be financed, and there is always an opportunity cost to financing. Therefore, assets should be acquired only if their incremental contribution to profit more than offsets the opportunity cost of capital. When measuring efficiency, we are gauging the company's ability to convert these costly resources into sales.

For every NT$100 of invested capital held by TSMC in 2014, NT$64 in revenue was produced, decreasing to NT$61 by 2016. We can now explain why TSMC's ROIC dropped by 0.4 percentage points from 2014 to 2016. The disaggregation of ROIC into constituent components reveals that the improvement in operating margins was offset by the decline in invested capital turnover. Overall, TSMC is delivering very consistent returns, so the decline in ROIC is slight and not a major concern. On the other hand, the DuPont analysis does demonstrate that the healthy margins the company generates are being somewhat undone by low asset efficiency. Further analysis of both the margin and invested capital turnover ratios will provide even more information about the execution of the company's strategy.

While NOPAT margin and invested capital turnover are both components of a higher-order ratio (e.g., ROIC), they too can be disaggregated. For NOPAT margin, the most common approach is to prepare a common-size income statement, in which all components of the statement are expressed as a percentage of sales. Exhibit 6.1 shows common-size income statements for TSMC.

A similar approach is to prepare base-year, or trend, financial statements. Instead of expressing income statement items as a percentage of sales, each item is expressed as a percentage of the value for the base year sales.[8] Exhibit 6.2 shows base-year income statements for TSMC. Each item for the 2015 and 2016 statements is shown as a percentage of the value for 2014.

Invested capital turnover is dissected by calculating a set of turnover ratios. For example, PP&E turnover can be used to measure the efficiency of the company's long-term productive assets in generating sales:

$$PP\&E\ Turnover = \frac{Sales}{Average\ Property,\ Plant,\ \&\ Equipment}$$

The expected value for this ratio is largely a function of industry, with companies in capital-intensive industries reporting the lowest. Ratio values are normally much higher in light industry, or in services. The nature of the semiconductor industry suggests that TSMC's PP&E turnover

Exhibit 6-1	TSMC Common-size Income Statements: 2014 in NT$million, 2015 and 2016 as a Percentage of Total Sales		

	Year ended December 31		
	2016	2015	2014
Revenue	100.0	100.0	762,807
Cost of revenue	(49.9)	(51.3)	385,084
Gross profit	50.1	48.7	377,723
Research and development	(7.5)	(7.8)	56,829
General and administrative	(2.1)	(2.0)	18,933
Marketing	(0.6)	(0.7)	5,087
Other operating expenses (income)	0.0	(0.2)	1,002
Income from operations	39.9	37.9	295,872
Share of profits of associates and joint ventures	0.4	0.5	3,920
Finance costs	(0.3)	(0.4)	-3,236
Foreign exchange gain	0.1	0.3	2,111
Other income	0.7	3.2	3,408
Income before income tax	40.7	41.6	302,075
Income tax expense	(5.7)	(5.6)	47,890
Net income	35.0	35.9	254,185

Exhibit 6-2	TSMC Base-year Income Statements: 2014 in NT$million 2015 and 2016 as a Percentage of 2014		

	2016	2015	2014
Revenue	124.3	110.6	762,807
Cost of revenue	122.9	112.5	385,084
Gross profit	125.7	108.6	377,723
Research and development	125.3	115.3	56,829
General and administrative	104.6	91.1	18,933
Marketing	116.0	111.4	5,087
Other operating expenses (income)	(3.0)	187.7	1,002
Income from operations	127.7	108.2	295,872
Share of profits of associates and joint ventures	88.2	107.0	3,920
Finance costs	102.2	98.6	–3,236
Foreign exchange gain	55.0	117.5	2,111
Other income	195.2	790.6	3,408
Income before income tax	127.8	116.0	302,075
Income tax expense	113.0	99.5	47,890
Net income	130.5	119.1	254,185

should be lower than companies that are more service based. TSMC is a capital-intensive company, and much of that capital will be deployed to fixed assets such as PP&E.

Depreciation and amortization policies impact this ratio too. Companies that use accelerated depreciation methods for their financial statements tend to report higher PP&E turnover because assets (the denominator of the ratio) are written down more quickly. In contrast, TSMC uses straight-line depreciation, which further contributes to a low turnover ratio.

TSMC's PP&E turnover for 2016 equals:

$$\frac{947,938}{925,624} = 1.02X$$

* [(997,778 + 853,470) ÷ 2]

2016:   1.02X

2015:   1.01X

2014:   0.95X

PP&E turnover has been improving, albeit slightly. Thus as we seek to understand why overall invested capital turnover has declined, we can rule out that it is due to changes in PP&E efficiency. This individual ratio has improved, contrary to the overall number.

We now turn our attention to the main components of working capital. A set of turnover ratios is calculated here too. We begin with the receivables turnover ratio:

$$\frac{\text{Net Sales on Account}}{\text{Average Accounts Receivable}}$$

For TSMC,

$$\frac{947,938}{106,698} = 7.39X$$

* $[(85,060 + 128,335) \div 2]$

2016:	7.39X
2015:	9.92X
2014:	6.65X

When calculating the ratio, the definition of receivables should be restricted to "trade" receivables, i.e., monies owed by customers only. Other receivables (monies owed to the company as a result of returns to suppliers, loans to employees, or the overpayment of taxes) should be included with prepaid expenses as "other current assets." Otherwise, the analysis of receivables turnover, and the management of customer accounts, will be distorted. The numerator should be based on credit sales, but because such information is usually not available to external readers, total sales are used instead.

Receivables turnover is easily converted into days. The resulting figure, the accounts receivable period, is also called the average collection period (ACP) or sometimes referred to as days of sales outstanding (DSO):

$$\frac{365}{\text{Average Receivable Turnover}}$$

For TSMC,

$$\frac{365 \text{ days}}{7.39} = 49 \text{ days}$$

2016:	49 days
2015:	37 days
2014:	55 days

As receivable turns increase, the ACP becomes shorter. This means that the company is speeding up the collection of cash from its customers. A decrease in receivable turns has the opposite effect. This ratio has varied quite a bit for TSMC over the three year period from a high of 55 days (reflecting less efficient collection) to a low of 37 days (more efficient collection). Its most recent level of 49 days appears reasonable for a business-to-business company.

The next significant component of working capital is inventory.

First, we calculate the inventory turnover ratio:

$$\frac{\text{Cost of Goods Sold}}{\text{Average Inventory}}$$

For TSMC,

$$\frac{473,106}{57,867^*} = 8.18X$$

* [(67,052 + 48,682) ÷ 2]

2016:   8.18X

2015:   6.49X

2014:   7.42X

Cost of goods sold is used in the numerator, instead of sales, because it excludes the profit margin. Using cost, instead of sales, provides a more accurate indicator of how quickly the inventory is converted into products and then sold.

Like PP&E turnover, this ratio is industry- and product-line specific. Therefore, considerable care is required when interpreting it. Mergers, acquisitions, spin-offs, and divestitures will cause product mix to change, resulting in changes to inventory turns, without respect to whether working capital management improved, deteriorated, or stayed the same.

Most analysts think of inventory in terms of days. This figure is easily calculated by dividing the inventory turnover ratio into 365, the number of days in the year:

$$\frac{365}{\text{Inventory Turnover}}$$

For TSMC, days of inventory equal:

$$\frac{365 \text{ days}}{8.18} = 45 \text{ days}$$

2016:   45 days

2015:   56 days

2014:   49 days

This ratio indicates that, on average, it takes TSMC 45 days from the acquisition of raw materials to the sale of finished products to customers.

An important advantage of converting inventory and receivables turnovers into days is that we can then easily calculate the length of the company's "operating cycle":

$$\text{Operating Cycle (in days)} = \text{Days Inventory Held} + \text{Accounts Receivable Period}$$

For TSMC, the average length of the operating cycle in 2016 equals:

$$45 \text{ days} + 49 \text{ days} = 94 \text{ days}$$

The length of the cycle is the amount of time, in days, from the acquisition of inventory (materials in the case of manufacturers, and merchandise in the case of retailers and distributors) to the collection of cash from customers. All else being equal, the shorter the cycle, the better. This qualifier is important, because technology and market competition impose limits on how short inventory and receivables periods can be. For example, once inventories drop below a certain level, efficiency might be compromised. The firm may face production bottlenecks because of shortages for key inputs. Also, low levels of finished goods inventories might lead to lost sales as frustrated customers go elsewhere. Similarly, competitive constraints may require a company to extend a certain level of credit; any efforts to reduce it may lead to lost sales.

But conditional on these competitive constraints, we prefer cycle times to be as short as possible. The shorter the cycle, the less investment, and the less cash, that a company has tied up in its operations. As the cash tied up in the cycle is reduced, the cash flow available for shareholders and other capital providers increases, thus increasing the value of the firm. In other words, more efficient working capital management creates value for shareholders.

The operating cycle reflects an estimate of how long it takes a company to collect its cash after it has acquired its inventory. These investments in inventory and receivables are viewed as costly because they must be financed, perhaps by a bank or by the owners themselves. Yet note that the company can also delay payment to its suppliers, and thus use that group as a source of financing. The accounts payable turnover ratio reveals the extent to which a company relies on its suppliers for financing:

$$\frac{\text{Purchases}}{\text{Average Accounts Payable}}$$

A slight complication with this formula is that purchases of inventory do not appear directly in the financial statements. For a retail or wholesale company they can be inferred fairly easily as

$$\text{Purchases} = \text{Cost of Goods Sold} + \text{Ending Inventory} - \text{Beginning Inventory}$$

If we apply this formula to TSMC in 2016, we can solve for purchases as

$$454,736 = 473,106 + 48,682 - 67,052$$

This yields an accounts payable turnover of

$$\frac{454,736}{22,319^*} = 20.37\text{X}$$

$^*[(18,575 + 26,062) \div 2]$

2016:   20.37X

2015:   21.45X

2014:   22.65X

As a manufacturer, as we discuss further in chapter 9, TSMC's cost of goods sold also includes significant depreciation and facilities which were not actually paid for in 2016. Therefore, if possible, these costs could be excluded from the purchases definition used above. However, for simplicity in this case, we just use the cost of revenue figure as reported on the income statement because it is easily obtained.

Like the previous working capital statistics, we can also convert the accounts payable turnover ratio into days payables outstanding:

$$\frac{365}{\text{Accounts Payable Turnover}}$$

For TSMC we get

$$\frac{365}{20.37} = 18 \text{ days}$$

2016:   18 days

2015:   17 days

2014:   16 days

Now we can calculate the Cash Conversion Cycle as

Cash Conversion Cycle = Days Inventory Held + Accounts Receivable Period – Accounts Payable Period

For TSMC this equals

$$76\,\text{days} = 45\,\text{days} + 49\,\text{days} - 18\,\text{days}$$

This figure reveals the net number of days for which TSMC will need to wait from the start of the operating cycle, taking into account that it can delay payment to its suppliers. Recall this is somewhat overstated because the payables turnover ratio includes depreciation charges that do not require current cash payments. From TSMC's notes we can identify and then exclude these costs from the purchases calculation. Under this assumption, the accounts payable period increases to 31 days, dropping the cash conversion cycle to 63 days.

Efficiency can further be evaluated using the cash conversion efficiency ratio, which measures a company's ability to convert sales into operating cash flow:

$$\frac{\text{CFFO}}{\text{Sales}} = \text{Cash Conversion Efficiency Ratio}$$

where CFFO is cash flow from operating activities.

TSMC's cash conversion efficiency ratio for 2016 is:

$$\frac{539,835}{947,938} = 56.9$$

2016:   56.9%

2015:   62.8%

2014:   55.3%

This means that for every NT$100 of sales in 2016, TSMC generated NT$56.9 of operating cash flow to cover capital investment and cash payments to capital providers. While the amount has fluctuated a bit over the three years, overall the ratios suggest that the company nets considerable amounts of cash on every sale.

ROE and the Analysis of Financial Risk

We can now extend the DuPont framework to include the influence of capital structure on profitability. This is accomplished by multiplying the components of ROIC – profit margin and invested capital turnover – by the product of the common earnings leverage ratio and the capital structure leverage ratio.

$$\frac{\text{NOPAT}}{\text{Sales}} \times \frac{\text{Sales}}{\text{Average Invested Capital}} \times \frac{\text{Net Income}}{\text{NOPAT}} \times \frac{\text{Average Invested Capital}}{\text{Average Shareholder's Equity}}$$

NOPAT Margin	Invested Capital Turnover	Common Earnings Leverage	Capital Structure Leverage

The first of these leverage ratios measures the percentage of unlevered profits that belong to the company's shareholders. For the all-equity firm (i.e., a firm that finances its net operating assets, or invested capital, entirely with equity), this ratio takes on a value of 1. In other words, if there is no debt, unlevered profit and net income must be the same. As the company levers up, levered and unlevered profits diverge and the value of the ratio declines.

The second leverage ratio is a measure of capital structure. Like common earnings leverage, it takes on a value of 1 for the unlevered firm. In such a case, invested capital must equal shareholders' equity, because invested capital is financed entirely with equity. As the company levers up, assets (and invested capital) are acquired while shareholders' equity is unchanged, resulting in an increase in the value of the ratio. In summary, for the unlevered firm, both leverage ratios equal 1, which means that ROIC must equal ROE. As firms lever up, common earnings leverage decreases while capital structure leverage increases. The product of these two ratios is call *adjusted leverage*. Multiplying this figure by ROIC yields ROE.

In the case of TSMC, we reconcile ROE to ROIC in 2016 as follows:

$$\text{ROE} = 26.0\% = 33.5\% \times 0.61 \times 1.05 \times 1.22$$

The breakdown reveals a slightly unusual pattern because common earnings leverage exceeds 1.0. Two factors explain this unusual result. First, although TSMC does maintain a certain amount of financial leverage, its overall interest costs are low (0.3% of revenue according to exhibit 6.1). Second, TSMC maintains "other" sources of income that, while not tied to core operations and thus not impacting NOPAT, do belong to shareholders.

Now that our analysis has been extended to include financing, we can turn our attention to financial risk. The analysis of risk is viewed from both a liquidity and capital structure perspective.

Liquidity refers to the ability of a company to raise cash from all sources, including operations, asset sales, and lines of credit from banks. Liquidity analysis tends to focus on the short term because it considers the company's ability to service current (i.e., short-term) obligations.

The capital structure perspective focuses on the mix of debt (both short- and long-term) and equity used to finance the company's assets, and asks whether or not the current level of debt, also known as *financial leverage*, is appropriate. This task is conducted by comparing various risk ratios such as debt–equity and interest coverage against industry benchmarks.

We'll begin with an analysis of TSMC's liquidity. Metrics such as the current ratio and quick ratio are popular ways to measure it. The current ratio is defined as follows:

$$\frac{\text{Current Assets}}{\text{Current Liabilities}}$$

Remember that current assets are those assets that will be used up or converted to cash within one year (or longer, if the operating cycle is longer than a year). The intuition behind the current ratio is that a company's ability to pay off its current liabilities is based on its current assets, because these are the assets that will be converted most quickly into cash. The higher the current ratio, it is said, the safer the company – at least in the short term.

TSMC's current ratio at the end of 2016 is:

$$\frac{817,730}{348,287} = 2.35$$

2016:   2.35

2015:   3.11

2014:   2.79

These values indicate that for every NT\$100 of short-term liabilities at the end of 2016, TSMC had NT\$235 in cash and other short-term assets.

The current ratio has been an important indicator of financial safety for over 100 years. But despite a venerable history, its relative importance has declined in recent years. One important weakness of this ratio is that it includes all current assets in the numerator, mixing the most liquid assets such as cash and marketable securities with less liquid assets such as inventories.

The quick ratio addresses this problem by excluding all but the most highly liquid current assets from the numerator, while using the same denominator as the current ratio. The ratio is defined as follows:

$$\frac{\text{Highly Liquid Assets}}{\text{Current Liabilities}}$$

Highly liquid assets are usually defined as the sum of cash, marketable securities, and accounts receivable.

For TSMC,

$$\frac{764,546}{348,287} = 2.20$$

2016:   2.20

2015:   2.82

2014:   2.47

The quick ratio for TSMC is consistently high. A ratio of 2.20 means that for every NT\$100 of short-term liabilities, TSMC has NT\$220 available in cash and other liquid assets to pay those liabilities. Compared to most companies, this figure is extremely high. While this analysis of short term financial health reveals a great deal of safety for TSMC, it also provides some insight into inefficiencies we identified in the DuPont analysis of ROIC. Invested capital turnover of 0.61 is negatively impacted by the high level of liquid assets.

Although the quick ratio solves one problem of the current ratio (by limiting the numerator to only the most liquid current assets), another problem with the current ratio is not solved. The numerator and denominator of both ratios come from the balance sheet, and balance sheet numbers reflect measurement at a point in time. These are static measures that do not provide a dynamic, or flow, perspective on liquidity.

Still, investors continue to use one or the other of these ratios as short-term risk measures. For example, some banks continue to use the current ratio as a statistical screen in credit granting decisions, especially those involving small businesses.

A more dynamic perspective on short-term liquidity is available from the same working capital ratios we examined earlier, and from cash flow analysis. For example, days of receivables is a liquidity measure because the shorter the period, the closer the receivables are to being realized as cash. A similar argument can be made for inventories.

Cash flow from operations (CFFO) is another important indicator of liquidity. Its CFFO of roughly NT$540 billion in 2016 suggests that TSMC easily generates the cash it needs to service all debts, short-term and long-term. The company generates operating cash flow of roughly NT$2.2 billion each working day.[9] This means that in a typical working day, TSMC collects cash from its customers, pays its suppliers, employees, marketing costs, administrative expenses, and taxes, and still has NT$2.2 billion (or US$73 million) in cash left over.

In contrast to short-term liquidity analysis, the capital structure perspective focuses on the extent to which the company relies on debt, short-term and long-term, to finance its assets. The more debt a company has, the greater its financial risk. By financial risk, we mean the risk of financial distress (i.e., the risk that a company will struggle to pay its debts). In its most extreme form, financial distress leads to bankruptcy. Therefore, when we evaluate the financial risk of a company, we examine the risk that debts will not be paid and the business will fail.

The analysis of financial risk focuses on two major questions:

- Does the company pursue appropriate financing strategies?

- Is there significant bankruptcy risk?

We answer these questions by focusing on the company's capital structure. Although a broad range of financing alternatives are available to corporate finance specialists, at its most basic the capital structure question centers on how much debt and how much equity a firm should use to finance its assets. This is commonly known in finance circles as "debt–equity choice." Once that decision is made, the firm can then determine which financial instruments – e.g., short-term debt, long-term debt, convertible bonds, warrants, preferred stock, common shares, etc. – are most appropriate for achieving the target capital structure. The two most important factors to consider in debt–equity choice are the tax shield from interest payments, and the costs of financial distress (or bankruptcy) that arise from too much debt.

Debt finance is cheaper than equity finance because it's less risky from the investors' perspective. Lenders are contractually entitled to interest and principal payments, while firms are under no such obligation to make payments to shareholders. Also, lenders have priority of claim over shareholders in the event that the firm is liquidated. Because their investment is riskier, equity investors require higher returns. It is commonly assumed, therefore, that a firm's cost of capital can be reduced simply by replacing equity with relatively cheaper debt. But the contributions of Nobel Economics Laureates Franco Modigliani and Merton Miller (often referred to as M&M) teach us that reality is more complicated.

They proved that in a world without taxes and bankruptcy costs (and other things), asset financing does not matter.[10] The intuition behind this insight is that as a firm increases its borrowings, and as debt thus comprises a larger portion of total financing, the equity that remains becomes riskier. To compensate shareholders for the added risk, firms must offer the expectation of correspondingly higher returns. Also, the debt itself becomes riskier because there is more of it. The result: whatever benefit the firm gets from replacing expensive equity with cheaper debt is offset by the increased cost of the debt and of the remaining equity. The cost of capital does not change and, as we will see in our discussion on valuation, neither does the value of the firm.

When asked, "Why do we borrow?," corporate managers often respond by saying, "because of leverage, and leverage has a magnifying effect on profits and ROE." But M&M proved that this benefit is illusory. The "adjusted leverage" factor observed in the DuPont disaggregation of

ROE offers no value-creating advantages (or value-destroying disadvantages) for the firm. Debt finance can still be beneficial, but not because of the leverage effect.

The M&M model assumes no taxes[11] and no bankruptcy costs. Of course, in the real world there are taxes and bankruptcy costs, and this simple fact changes everything. Interest on debt is tax-deductible, but the cost of equity is not. Therein lies the principal benefit of injecting debt into a company's capital structure. It explains why highly profitable companies that can easily finance all of their investments without borrowing still choose to borrow anyway. The tax deductibility of interest offers a valuable tax shield, allowing the company to reduce its tax bill.[12] For this reason alone, it is wrong to assume that the less debt a company has, the better. However, it can be said that the less debt a company has, the lower the risk of financial distress.

But just as it is wrong to assume that less debt is better than more debt, it is equally wrong to assume the reverse. The problem with debt is that the more of it a company has, the greater the risk that the company will encounter financial distress, or even bankruptcy. Outside the artificial M&M world, financial distress is costly. These costs include the direct out-of-pocket expenses paid to lawyers, accountants, and investments bankers to reorganize a firm, renegotiate its debts, or undertake other activities to fend off bankruptcy. Perhaps even more significant are the indirect costs of financial distress, costs that cannot be directly observed but have profound value implications. For example, in companies where after-sales service and warranty protection are critical attributes of the products they sell, customers may be reluctant to buy from companies that are thought to be in financial difficulty.

The key point here is that debt carries costs as well as benefits. When we examine the capital structure and financial risk of a firm, we are judging whether we believe the firm has achieved a proper balance of debt and equity, one that allows the exploitation of valuable tax shields without putting the firm in a position where debts might become overwhelming and the business fails. In short, are the company's financing policies appropriate, or do we believe the firm to be under- or overleveraged? And if the firm is overleveraged (i.e., it has too much debt), what is the likelihood that it will experience financial distress, if it hasn't already?

One popular way of measuring financial risk is the debt–equity ratio:

$$\frac{\text{Interest-bearing Debt}}{\text{Shareholders'Equity}}$$

Interest-bearing debt includes all bank loans, whether short-term or long-term, corporate bonds, capital leases, and any other form of financing a company might obtain from the money and capital markets. Trade payables and any other liabilities that arise spontaneously from operating activities are excluded.

For TSMC, the debt–equity ratio at the end of 2016 is:

$$\frac{249,375}{1,359,846} = 0.18X$$

2016: 0.18X

2015: 0.21X

2014: 0.26X

This means that for every NT$100 of shareholders' equity at the end of 2016, TSMC had NT$18 in debt finance, versus NT$21 in 2015 and NT$26 in 2014. The steady decline represents a relative deleveraging of the company as the shareholders' indirectly increase their investment via increased retained earnings.

An alternative approach to measuring financial risk is known as "times interest earned," which is measured as follows:

$$\frac{\text{Operating Income}}{\text{Interest Expense}}$$

The logic of this ratio is that a company's ability to pay interest charges derives from its pretax operating profits, sometimes called "interest coverage." Because these profits come from operations, they are potentially recurring. A rule of thumb is that interest coverage should be at least 5X for cyclical companies in the up-phase of the business cycle, which means that operating profits can later decline by as much as 80%, and still be sufficient to cover interest payments. The standard for companies with more stable earnings is about 3X. This is not to say that a company with interest coverage below these figures is unsafe or poorly managed, but rather that it is unlikely to get an investment grade rating from Moody's or Standard & Poor's (S&P) for its bond issues.[13]

For TSMC, interest coverage for 2016 equals:

$$\frac{377,957}{3,306} = 114.3X$$

2016:   114.3X
2015:   100.3X
2014:   91.4X

An interest coverage of 114.3X clearly puts TSMC among the ranks of safe, creditworthy companies.

Because of its utility in signaling the risk of default, the interest coverage ratio also plays a role in debt covenants. A debt covenant is a provision in a lending contract that is designed to reduce conflicts of interest between lenders and borrowers and, therefore, to reduce the likelihood that the latter will take actions that harm the former. Such covenants can take on many forms. For example, they may place limits on new borrowing, or prohibit share repurchases or dividend payments without the lender's approval. Covenants can also serve as signals of deteriorating financial performance, especially when expressed in the form of financial statement ratios. If deterioration occurs, a negotiation of the lending contract may be triggered. The practical effect of these provisions is that a firm can make all of the scheduled debt payments on time, and yet be judged to have violated the terms of the contract. For example, covenants might state a minimum value for interest coverage. If the condition is not met (i.e., the ratio value falls under the threshold), the result is "technical default." The lender can then decide whether to waive or modify the restrictions, ask for a higher interest rate to compensate for the perceived increase in risk, or terminate the relationship and demand immediate repayment.

A variant on interest coverage, EBITDA interest coverage, adds depreciation and amortization to operating income.[14] Depreciation and amortization are taken directly from the cash flow statement. The ratio is calculated as follows:

$$\frac{\text{EBITDA}}{\text{Interest Expense}}$$

For TSMC, EBITDA interest coverage for 2016 is:

$$\frac{608,511}{3,306} = 184.1X$$

2016:   184.1X

2015:   172.1X

2014:   155.3X

One criticism of interest and EBITDA coverage is that both rely on accounting earnings, whereas interest payments must be made with cash. Although EBITDA does add back depreciation and amortization, it ignores changes in working capital and is thus a flawed measure of cash flow. The cash coverage ratio was developed to address this weakness by focusing directly on operating cash. It is calculated as follows:

$$\text{Cash Coverage} = \frac{\text{Cash Flow from Operations} + \text{Interest Paid} + \text{Taxes}}{\text{Interest Paid}}$$

TSMC's cash coverage for 2016 equals (note that per the statement of cash flows the interest has already been added back in the operating section as TSMC reclassifies it as a financing cash flow):

$$\frac{539,835 + 54,124}{3,306} = 179.7X$$

2016:   179.7X

2015:   181.0X

2014:   145.1X

For TSMC, the interest coverage, EBITDA coverage, and cash coverage ratios tell similar stories. In 2016, TSMC generated over NT$179 in pretax operating cash flow for every NT$1 of interest paid. This figure, combined with ratio values for the two previous years, confirms that TSMC generates ample cash flows to meet its interest payments.

An important limitation of all coverage ratios, whether based on earnings or cash flow, is that they focus exclusively on interest. Principal, too, must be repaid. An alternative approach to risk measurement relates cash flow to levels of indebtedness (i.e., the principal on outstanding debts). One example is the ratio of free operating cash flows to total debt:

$$\frac{\text{Free Operating Cash Flows}}{\text{Total Debt}}$$

Free operating cash flows (FOCF) are defined as cash flow from operating activities, net of capital expenditures. The measure is used as a proxy for the amount of cash generated from core operations. TSMC had free operating cash flows in 2016 of NT$539,835 – NT$328,045, or NT$211,790.[15]

Total debt is defined as all debts, short-term and long-term, apart from short-term operating liabilities such as accounts payable. For TSMC, we include post-retirement benefits, long-term debt, deferred income taxes, and other long-term liabilities.[16] This yields total debt of NT$274,424 million at the end of 2016. Short-term bank loans should be included too, as should the capitalized value of any off-balance-sheet debts such as operating leases.

For TSMC, the ratio of FOCF to total debt for 2016 equals:

$$\frac{211,790}{274,424} = 77.2\%$$

2016:   77.2%
2015:   95.3%
2014:   44.2%

Although the above ratios are widely used to assess a firm's capital structure, none of these measures provides a probabilistic assessment of bankruptcy risk. We can say, for example, that a particular value for a given ratio is associated with a particular bond rating. But such insights do not provide an estimate of the likelihood that the company will default on its debts. For this reason, formal bankruptcy prediction models were developed. Altman's Z-score and Ohlson's O-score are two popular examples.[17] In contrast to the ratio-by-ratio approach discussed here, these models take a multivariate approach. Statistical techniques are used to discriminate between samples of bankrupt and nonbankrupt firms. An equation is derived from a set of financial statement ratios that are found to be the best discriminators. The coefficients for the chosen ratios and the ratio values for the subject firm are then used to produce a composite score that predicts the likelihood of future bankruptcy.

These and similar models continue to be employed, especially by banks and other credit granting institutions, but they have fallen out of favor in recent years with the bond-rating agencies. A more sophisticated approach has evolved, drawing on option pricing theory. It's based on the idea that the equity of a firm can be viewed as a call option on the value of the firm's assets. When the value of the assets is below the face value of liabilities, the call option is left unexercised and the bankrupt firm is turned over to its bankers and bondholders. In other words, the firm becomes bankrupt. An option pricing model, such as Black–Scholes–Merton, is used to convert equity prices and their volatility into a probability estimate that this eventuality (the value of assets falling below the value of debt) will happen. The great virtue of this approach is that it incorporates the myriad of insights and knowledge embedded in corporate share prices.

KEY LESSONS FROM THE CHAPTER

- A thorough financial analysis should follow four sequential steps: business and industry analysis, accounting analysis, financial analysis, and valuation.
- Business and industry analysis identifies the main competitive forces in the company's industry, its key business risks, and sources of competitive advantage. This analysis is critical because financial statement numbers have little meaning and defy interpretation unless they are placed in an economic and strategic context. Business and industry analysis is a necessary first step to the analysis of financial statements.
- Even the most sophisticated financial analysis cannot overcome unreliable financial statement numbers. That's why accounting analysis is so important. It begins by identifying critical accounting issues in the subject company's industry, and the key accounting policies adopted by the company. If needed, accounts should be adjusted before ratios are calculated and analyzed.

- Financial analysis evaluates the recent performance of the firm using its financial statements and related information, and seeks to determine the sustainability of that performance.
- Valuation takes the inputs from the first three steps and translates them into a set of financial forecasts to produce estimates of company value.
- Ratio analysis works best in a DuPont setting. Much of the story behind the ratios is revealed not just in the ratios themselves but in the interaction and interrelationships among the ratios. The DuPont framework provides an integrative framework that allows for a more holistic approach to the analysis of financial statements.

- Always begin a ratio analysis from the unlevered perspective. This permits an examination of operating and investing activities without being encumbered by financing issues. Only when knowledge of operating and investing activities is exhausted do we then think about financial risk and capital structure.
- Operating cycle in days equals the days inventory is held plus the accounts receivable period. This metric is indispensable for helping analysts to assess both the operating efficiency of the company and the liquidity of its working capital components, such as inventories and receivables.

KEY TERMS AND CONCEPTS FROM THE CHAPTER

Business and industry analysis
Accounting analysis
Financial analysis

Porter 5-forces model
Return on equity
Return on invested capital

NOPAT
Managerial balance sheet

DuPont analysis
Turnover ratios
Leverage ratios

Profitability ratios
Coverage ratios

QUESTIONS

1. What is the primary purpose of "accounting analysis"?
2. Explain how and why short-term creditors, long-term creditors, and shareholders approach ratio analysis differently.
3. What is the difference between ROIC and ROE?
4. Under what conditions is ROIC equal to ROE?
5. Explain why, all else being equal, an increase in accounts payable and other operating liabilities causes ROIC to increase.
6. True or false: A decrease in SG&A expenses as a percentage of sales will increase ROE and share price.
7. Many companies state ROE targets as important corporate goals. Do you agree with this practice? Why or why not?
8. What is DuPont analysis and what purposes does it serve?

9. True or false: The shorter the operating cycle, the better.
10. Describe the limitations of the current ratio and quick ratio as indicators of liquidity. What alternatives are available for assessing the liquidity of a firm?
11. Average current ratios in Europe and North America are noticeably lower today than they were 30 years ago. What might account for this change?
12. What is the primary purpose of turnover ratios?
13. Describe the major financial risk ratios and what they are designed to reveal.
14. True or false: The greater the interest coverage, the better.

Appendix 6.1 An Industry and Competitive Analysis of Taiwan Semiconductor Manufacturing Company (TSMC)

A 5-Forces Analysis of TSMC and the Foundry Semiconductor Industry – as of 2017

Rivalry among Existing Firms

Semiconductors are a necessary component to modern electronics and computing products. TSMC was one of the pioneering firms in the *foundry* segment of the semiconductor market. This segment does not design the function of the semiconductor, but rather manufactures the product to the specification of the designers. Such designers are referred to as *fabless manufacturers* and include companies such as Qualcomm, Broadcom, and AMD.

The *foundry* portion of the industry competes on elements of scale (large volumes) as well as quality, as the designers and ultimate device manufacturers (such as Apple) demand high performance from their components. TSMC is the largest of the foundry companies, many of which are located in Taiwan and other parts of Asia to take advantage of low labor costs. TSMC is essentially a pure-play company in that the manufacture of chips for further processing is its only business.

However, despite being the largest and oldest, TSMC still faces significant competition in the industry. Moreover, some firms that provide further processing of the semiconductors are also involved in the foundry activities. Thus, a company like Intel is both a customer of TSMC *and* a rival. This further intensifies the already high rivalry of the firms.

Threat of New Entrants

The scale and technological processes needed to compete in the foundry segment of semiconductor manufacturing raise significant barriers to entry. It would likely take an unforeseen change in production technology to lead to a new player in the market. Thus the threat of new entrants is low.

Threat of Substitute Products

The widespread technological adoption of the semiconductor makes it a ubiquitous component of many electronic appliances and tools that consumers and businesses use on a daily basis. Currently, there is not a meaningful substitute for the product. Therefore, the threat from substitutes is low.

The Bargaining Power of Buyers

Buyers of semiconductors from the foundry segment are going to further refine the product for final use. These buyers may be other semiconductor companies or original equipment manufacturers (OEMs) of electronic products.

As products utilize more and more computing technology – as we move to the "Internet of things" – we can expect that a greater number of customers for semiconductors will emerge. Such higher numbers would, on average, tend to weaken buyer power. At the same time, the inherent technical complexity and specialization of the product give the semiconductor company more power.

Conversely, in the foundry segment specifically, some customers are very large and are themselves specialized. As the foundry manufacturer seeks to meet their demands, sometimes on cost, it requires a large volume of sales to remain profitable. Overall, we consider the bargaining power of buyers to be moderate to strong.

The Bargaining Power of Suppliers

Suppliers to semiconductor foundry manufacturers include both companies providing raw materials, most notably silicon, and also specialized equipment. From a size standpoint, these suppliers are often smaller and do not pose a financial threat to the manufacturer. Yet, due to the unique nature of the inputs and the threat of supply chain disruptions, supplier power cannot be ignored. We classify supplier power for this industry as moderate.

A Competitive Strategy Analysis of TSMC

Sources of Competitive Advantage

The strategies of TSMC emphasize differentiation more than cost leadership. Differentiation is achieved mainly through: (1) technological leadership that constantly leads to breakthroughs in production of next generation chips; (2) a robust R&D program that feeds this technology leadership; (3) flexible manufacturing that can adjust quickly to demand fluctuations; (4) manufacturing processes that can be adapted to many different products and thus meet different customer needs; (5) large scale that enables a low average cost of production; and (6) a global network of manufacturing facilities that help decrease delivery times to customers.

The sustainability of these advantages is enhanced by global R&D partnerships to ensure that TSMC remains at the forefront of technological advancement. Further, while TSMC offers the latest technology from a product standpoint, they also emphasize adaptation of their manufacturing processes as well. Technology is emphasized that not only makes the processes more efficient but also helps to minimize costly defects.

Major Business Risks

Major risks include the following: (1) concentration of sales in a small number of customers – from 2014 to 2016 the 10 largest customers accounted for an average of 65% of sales, and the single largest customer an average of 18% over the period; (2) threats from technological shifts – despite this being a current competitive advantage of TSMC's, it requires constant attention and investment to maintain the strength; (3) cyclicality in customer markets of electronics and semiconductors; (4) currency risks from selling mostly to customers paying in US dollars (90% in 2016), while input costs are paid for in a wide range of currencies – only about 50% of which is NT$; and (5) political risks from operating in Asia, and especially with uncertainty regarding the relationship between Taiwan and mainland China.

Appendix 6.2 Summary of Financial Statement Ratios

$$\text{Return on Equity} = \frac{\text{Net Income Available to Common Shareholders}}{\text{Average Common Shareholders' Equity}}$$

$$\text{Return on Invested Capital} = \frac{\text{NOPAT}}{\text{Average Invested Capital}}$$

$$\text{NOPAT Margin} = \frac{\text{NOPAT}}{\text{Sales}}$$

$$\text{Invested Capital Turnover} = \frac{\text{Sales}}{\text{Average Invested Capital}}$$

$$\text{PP\&E Turnover} = \frac{\text{Sales}}{\text{Average Property, Plant and Equipment}}$$

$$\text{Inventory Turnover} = \frac{\text{Cost of Goods Sold}}{\text{Average Inventory}}$$

$$\text{Days Inventory Held} = \frac{365}{\text{Inventory Turnover}}$$

$$\text{Accounts Receivable Turnover} = \frac{\text{Net Sales on Account}}{\text{Average Accounts Receivable}}$$

$$\text{Accounts Receivable Period} = \frac{365}{\text{Accounts Receivable Turnover}}$$

$$\text{Accounts Payable Turnover} = \frac{\text{Purchases}}{\text{Average Accounts Payable}}$$

$$\text{Purchases} = \text{Cost of Goods Sold} + \text{Ending Inventory} - \text{Beginning Inventory}$$

$$\text{Accounts Payable Period} = \frac{365}{\text{Accounts Payable Turnover}}$$

$$\text{Cash Conversion Efficiency Ratio} = \frac{\text{Cash Flow from Operations}}{\text{Sales}}$$

$$\text{Common Earnings Leverage} = \frac{\text{Net Income}}{\text{NOPAT}}$$

$$\text{Capital Structure Leverage} = \frac{\text{Average Invested Capital}}{\text{Average Shareholders' Equity}}$$

$$\text{Current Ratio} = \frac{\text{Current Assets}}{\text{Current Liabilities}}$$

$$\text{Quick Ratio} = \frac{\text{Highly Liquid Assets}}{\text{Current Liabilities}}$$

$$\text{Debt/Equity Ratio} = \frac{\text{Interest-bearing Debt}}{\text{Shareholders' Equity}}$$

$$\text{Times Interest Earned} = \frac{\text{Operating Income}}{\text{Interest Expense}}$$

$$\text{EBITDA Coverage} = \frac{\text{EBITDA}}{\text{Interest Expense}}$$

$$\text{Cash Coverage} = \frac{\text{Cash Flow from Operations} + \text{Interest Paid} + \text{Taxes}}{\text{Interest Expense}}$$

$$\text{Free Operating Cash Flows to Total Debt} = \frac{\text{Free Operating Cash Flows}}{\text{Total Debt}}$$

PROBLEMS

6.1 Financial Statement Detective Exercise

Exhibit 6.3 shows common-size balance sheets and income statements for 12 companies, described below. Your job is to match each company with its financial statements.

Accor

One of the world's leading hotel operators, owning or managing almost 4000 properties throughout the world. It serves travelers in Europe through its flagship chains Mercure, Novotel, and Sofitel, and its economy chains Ibis and Formule 1. In the United States, it operates budget brands Motel 6 and Red Roof Inns. Accor has embarked on a sale and leaseback strategy for its upscale properties to reduce exposure to slowdowns in the market and is working to transition many of its midscale hotel leases to variable cost arrangements.

Arcelor

Arcelor was formed by the combination of three European steel companies and is now the second largest steel manufacturer in the world. The company produces carbon steel and stainless steel for the automotive, construction, appliance, and packaging industries.

Carrefour

Carrefour is the world's second largest retailer. Based in France, it operates more than 11 000 stores under two dozen brand names, including Carrefour (hypermarkets), Champion (supermarkets), and Shopi (convenience stores). Unable to build new stores in France, until recent changes in French law, Carrefour has expanded through acquisitions, at home and abroad.

Dell

Dell is the world's #1 direct-sale computer vendor. In addition to a full line of desktop and notebook PCs (about 80% of total sales), Dell also offers workstations, storage systems, network servers, and Ethernet switches. Dell's direct-sales, built-to-order model allows for lower inventories and lower operating costs, a necessity for the PC price wars and the occasional slump in corporate IT spending.

Deutsche Telekom

The #1 telecom company in Europe. Deutsche Telekom is Germany's leading fixed-line phone operator, its T-Mobile unit serves millions of wireless phone customers, and T-Online is one of the Europe's leading internet service providers. Although privatized in the 1990s, the German government still holds a 15% stake and an additional 22% through a state-owned development bank.

The FPL Group

The FPL Group is a holding company with operations across the United States. Most revenue comes from its utility subsidiary, the largest electricity provider in the state of Florida. The electricity is generated from the company's nuclear and fossil-fueled power plants.

Interpublic

Interpublic is one of the world's largest advertising and marketing services companies. Operating through offices in 130 countries, its flagship agencies include McCann Worldgroup, Lowe & Partners, and Hill Holliday. Like all of the global players in its industry, much of Interpublic's growth has come from acquisitions.

Exhibit 6-3   **Common-size Financial Statements**

	1	2	3	4	5	6	7	8	9	10	11	12
Balance sheet (year-end)												
Cash and marketable securities	2.1%	20.0%	22.5%	37.9%	13.4%	11.7%	4.0%	30.8%	17.6%	19.9%	42.7%	14.1%
Receivables	7.5	4.8	18.0	17.8	12.5	26.0	4.2	76.8	13.6	9.0	25.7	8.9
Inventories	3.7	2.1	0.1	17.7	22.5	7.3	8.6	—	8.1	0.9	0.1	2.4
Property, plant, and equipment	301.5	182.6	94.5	51.3	67.9	79.0	34.4	26.9	47.5	6.1	24.8	76.3
Accumulated depreciation	(99.7)	(49.0)	(38.6)	(16.3)	(30.7)	(46.4)	(16.6)	(15.6)	(27.7)	(2.7)	(11.5)	(25.4)
Investments	7.0	—	15.2	8.6	8.5	28.8	3.2	2.6	7.5	8.8	1.3	5.2
Other assets	47.2	13.1	51.1	123.5	9.4	30.4	15.8	70.6	33.8	5.2	17.8	104.8
Total assets	269.3%	173.6%	162.8%	235.5%	103.5%	136.8%	53.6%	192.1%	100.4%	47.2%	100.9%	186.3%
Current liabilities	40.4%	32.8%	53.1%	50.4%	34.4%	46.2%	26.4%	118.4%	33.6%	28.7%	34.3%	21.2%
Long-term debt	76.3	26.0	39.8	13.9	14.4	28.2	13.4	30.3	12.4	1.0	0.1	73.4
Other noncurrent liabilities	81.0	5.5	7.8	41.3	13.8	8.7	2.4	16.5	8.0	4.3	5.4	24.8
Shareholders' equity	71.6	109.3	62.1	129.9	40.9	53.7	11.4	26.9	46.4	13.2	61.1	66.9
Total liabilities and shareholders' equities	269.3%	173.6%	162.8%	235.5%	103.5%	136.8%	53.6%	192.1%	100.4%	47.2%	100.9	186.3%
Income statement												
Operating revenues	100.0%	100.0%	100.0%	100.0%	100.0%	100.0%	100.0%	100.0%	100.0%	100.0%	100.0%	100.0%
Other revenues	—	—	0.7%	—	1.4%	4.3%	—	—	—	—	—	—
Cost of goods sold (excluding depreciation) or operating expenses	58.7	75.4	74.4	11.1	86.5	73.8	74.9	98.3	45.1	80.9	31.6	33.1
Depreciation and amortization	11.4	6.6	7.8	9.7	4.3	5.6	2.9	3.2	4.7	0.7	2.8	21.2
Selling and administrative	15.9	16.2	—	32.2	—	11.3	16.2	—	36.0	8.7	25.1	31.0
Interest expense	4.6	1.3	1.1	0.7	1.4	0.1	0.7	2.5	1.3	—	0.1	7.9
Research and development	—	—	—	14.4	—	4.2	—	—	1.6	0.9	13.6	—
Income taxes	2.5	2.7	2.2	5.1	1.7	3.7	1.2	4.1	2.8	2.8	10.1	2.8
Other	(1.5)	(7.0)	11.5	5.2	(1.8)	(1.0)	1.8	0.6	0.8	(0.2)	(0.7)	(4.0)
Total expenses	91.6%	95.2%	97.0%	78.4%	92.1%	97.7%	97.7%	108.7%	92.3%	93.8%	82.6%	92.0%
Net income	8.4%	4.8%	3.7%	21.6%	9.0%	6.6%	2.3%	(8.7)	7.7%	6.2%	17.4%	8.0%
Cash flow from operations	25.2%	17.7%	7.9%	31.1%	10.6%	13.3%	5.8%	7.1%	12.0%	10.8%	24.3%	28.2%
Free operating cash flow	10.6	(9.5)	5.9	25.6	5.5	4.7	3.1	4.8	7.6	9.7	23.1	18.5

Nestlé

Nestlé is the world's #1 food company. It is the world leader in coffee (Nescafé), and is also one of the largest bottled water (Perrier) and baby-food manufacturers. At last count, it is the owner of over 9000 branded products worldwide. Nestlé's recent purchase of Ralston-Purina has made it a top player in the pet food business. In addition to its food business, Nestlé owns nearly 27% of cosmetic giant L'Oreal.

Pfizer

Pfizer is the world's largest research-based pharmaceutical company. Its best-known products include Viagra, Zoloft, and Lipitor. In addition to prescription drugs, Pfizer also makes a broad range of popular over-the-counter remedies, including Sudafed and Benadryl.

SAP

SAP is the world's leading provider of enterprise resource planning software used to integrate corporate back-office functions such as human resources, accounting, distribution, and manufacturing. The company also offers a range of products on supply chain and customer relationship management. SAP's large customer base provides a steady stream of recurring licensing and service revenue.

Southwest Airlines

Southwest Airlines offers low-cost, no-frills air travel to 60 cities in the United States. A model for low-fare upstarts the world over, the company has enjoyed over 30 straight years of profitability. Southwest's business model is simple: flights are short (most are under two hours), and the airline usually lands at small airports to avoid congestion at large hubs. Originally concentrated in the western part of the United States, Southwest has expanded into key eastern markets, such as Philadelphia.

Toyota

Toyota is the world's #2 car maker (by sales) and its most profitable. In addition to longstanding core brands – Camry, Land Cruiser, Celica, Corolla, and the luxury Lexus line – Toyota has pioneered the market for hybrid-powered sedans (Prius). While most of its North American and European competitors are downsizing operations, Toyota continues to pursue an aggressive growth strategy.

6.2 Effects of Transactions on Selected Balance Sheet Figures

	Total current assets	Total current liabilities	Working capital requirement	Current ratio
(a) Additional common stock is issued for cash				
(b) Merchandise is sold, above cost, for cash				
(c) A piece of equipment is sold for more than book value				
(d) Payment is made to trade creditors for previous purchases				
(e) A cash dividend is declared and paid				
(f) A stock dividend is declared and paid				
(g) Cash is obtained through long-term bank loan				
(h) A profitable firm increases the accumulated depreciation account for property, plant and equipment				
(i) Current operating expenses are paid				
(j) Ten-year notes are issued to pay off accounts payable				
(k) Accounts receivable are collected				
(l) Equipment is purchased with short-term notes				
(m) Merchandise is purchased on credit				
(n) Taxes payable are increased				
(o) Marketable securities are sold below cost				

Required

Indicate the effects of the previous transactions on each of the following: total current assets, total current liabilities, working capital requirement, and current ratio. Use + to indicate an increase, – to indicate a decrease, and 0 to indicate no effect. Assume an initial current ratio is greater than 1.

6.3 Calculating and Interpreting PP&E Turnover Ratios

Texas Instruments (TI) designs and manufactures semiconductor products for use in computers, telecommunications equipment, automobiles, and other electronics-based products. The manufacturing of semiconductors is highly capital intensive. Hewlett-Packard Corporation (HP) manufactures computer hardware and various imaging products, such as printers and fax machines. HP outsources the manufacture of a portion of the components for its products. HP acquired Compaq Computer in the middle of 2002. Exhibit 6.4 presents selected data for TI and HP for 2002, 2003, and 2004.

Required

a. Compute the PP&E turnover for each firm for 2002, 2003, and 2004.

b. Suggest reasons for the differences in the PP&E turnovers of TI and HP. Be specific.

c. Suggest reasons for the changes in the PP&E turnovers of TI and HP during the three year period. Be as specific as the data allow.

6.4 Financial Statement Detective Exercise in the Pharmaceutical Industry

Exhibit 6.5 presents common-size income statements and balance sheets for seven firms that operate at various stages in the value chain for the pharmaceutical industry. (The companies are real, but the names have been disguised.) These common-size statements express all amounts as a percentage of sales revenue. Exhibit 6.5 also shows the cash flow from operations to capital expenditures ratio for each firm. A dash for a particular financial statement item does not necessarily mean that the amount is zero. It merely indicates that the amount is not disclosed. The seven companies and a brief description of their activities follow.

Required

Match the financial statements with the company described below. Give the reasons for your choice. Be as specific as possible in explaining why you chose a particular set of financial statements for one of the below companies.

1. Wilson Pharma: Engages in the development, manufacture, and sale of ethical drugs (i.e., drugs requiring a prescription). Ethical drug companies must obtain approval of new drugs from government regulators, such as the US Food and Drug Administration (FDA). Patents protect such drugs from competition until either other drug companies develop more effective products or the patent expires.

2. American Biotech: Engages in the development, manufacture, and sale of drugs based on biotechnology research. The biotechnology segment is less mature than the ethical drug

| *Exhibit 6-4* | Selected Data for Texas Instruments and Hewlett-Packard (in millions) |

	2004	2003	2002
Texas Instruments			
Sales	$12,580	$9,834	$8,383
Cost of goods sold	6,902	5,728	5,313
Capital expenditures	1,298	800	802
Average PP&E	4,025	4,463	5,192
Percentage PP&E depreciated	59.1%	56.7%	49.6%
Percentage change in sales	+27.9%	+17.3%	−17.8%
Hewlett-Packard			
Sales	$79,905	$73,061	$56,588
Cost of goods sold	60,340	53,858	41,793
Capital expenditures	2,126	1,995	1,710
Average PP&E	6,894	6,703	5,661
Percentage PP&E depreciated	51.9	51.3	44.8
Percentage change in sales	+9.4	+29.1	+25.1

industry, with relatively few products having received regulatory approval.

3. **Mauborgne Laboratories:** Engages in the development, manufacture, and sale of generic drugs. Generics have the same chemical compositions as drugs that had previously benefited from patent protection. In recent years, generic drug companies have benefited from the patent expiration of several blockbuster ethical drugs. However, the big ethical drug companies have increasingly offered generic versions of their products to compete against generic drug companies.

4. **Morris & Morris:** A huge global enterprise that engages in the development, manufacture, and sale of over-the-counter health care products. Also, the company operates in consumer segments where brand recognition is important.

5. **Chang Labs:** Offers laboratory testing services and expedition of the drug approval process for ethical drug companies. Cost of goods sold for this company represents the salaries of personnel conducting the laboratory testing and drug approval services.

6. **Crimson Health:** Distributes drugs as a wholesaler to drugstores and primary care facilities, including hospitals and clinics. It also offers pharmaceutical benefit management services (PBMS) to help customers order more efficiently, contain costs, and monitor their purchases. Cost of goods sold includes the cost of drugs sold plus the salaries of personnel providing PBMS.

7. **Eberhard:** Operates a nationwide chain of drugstores, some of which are owned while others are leased.

Exhibit 6-5	Common-size Financial Statement Data						
	(1)	**(2)**	**(3)**	**(4)**	**(5)**	**(6)**	**(7)**
Income statement							
Sales	100.0%	100.0%	100.0%	100.0%	100.0%	100.0%	100.0%
Cost of goods sold	(47.0)	(11.0)	(24.0)	(58.4)	(28.9)	(73.3)	(92.5)
Selling and administrative	(18.8)	(24.2)	(36.7)	(31.0)	(36.3)	(21.0)	(4.2)
Research and development	(8.0)	(21.5)	(13.2)	–	(10.9)	–	–
Interest	–	(.3)	(1.0)	(2.6)	(1.6)	–	(.3)
Income taxes	(10.6)	(14.1)	(7.0)	(3.2)	(6.8)	(2.2)	(1.0)
Other	3.5	5.2	(1.5)	1.0	1.4	.1	(.2)
Net income	19.1%	34.1%	16.6%	5.8%	16.9%	3.6%	1.8%
Balance sheet							
Cash	33.7%	66.3%	21.4%	34.9%	24.2%	.1%	1.9%
Receivables	27.5	12.3	19.4	26.4	14.0	3.2	5.0
Inventories	19.1	8.9	12.4	–	9.1	14.1	13.1
Other current	7.6	8.6	15.9	5.4	8.7	.4	2.3
Investments	–	–	–	–	–	–	–
Property, plant, and equipment, net	19.9	48.5	44.6	22.4	23.4	17.7	3.8
Other noncurrent assets	49.9	15.9	48.9	31.2	37.2	.4	4.4
Total assets	157.7%	160.5%	162.6%	120.3%	116.6%	35.9%	30.5%
Current liabilities	34.4%	25.0%	51.4%	28.5%	24.4%	12.2%	13.7%
Long-term debt	2.8	5.6	11.4	2.0	6.5	–	3.9
Other noncurrent liabilities	2.2	–	23.8	–	2.3	2.6	1.6
Shareholders' equity	118.3	129.9	76.0	89.8	73.4	21.1	11.3
Total equities	157.7%	160.5%	162.6%	120.3%	116.6%	35.9%	30.5%
Cash flow from operations/capital expenditures	2.2	3.4	2.3	1.3	2.8	.6	1.3

6.5 Comprehensive Financial Ratio Analysis

Financial statements for Wertenbroch Company, a distributor of kitchenware, are presented below (all amounts in thousands of euro).

Statements of financial position

	2018	2017
Assets		
Land	€260	€260
Buildings and equipment (net)	360	350
Prepaid expenses	58	46
Inventories	250	270
Receivables (net)	196	160
Short-term investments	104	80
Cash	140	130
	€1,368	€1,296

Equities and liabilities

	2018	2017
Share capital	€400	€400
Retained earnings	272	232
Long-term debt	300	300
Short-term debt	200	200
Accounts payable	96	84
Accrued liabilities	100	80
	€1,368	€1,296

Income statements

	2018	2017
Revenues	€1,700	€1,580
Cost of goods sold	1,240	1,150
Gross profit	460	430
Other operating expenses	303	283
Operating profit	157	147
Interest expense	34	23
Income before taxes	123	123
Income taxes	37	36
Net Income	€86	€88

Additional information:

- All sales were on account.
- No share transactions took place in either year.
- Total assets at the beginning of 2017 were €1,260.
- Accounts payable and accrued liabilities at the beginning of 2017 totaled €146.
- Receivables (net) at the beginning of 2017 were €176.
- Inventory at the beginning of 2017 was €236.
- Shareholders' equity at the beginning of 2017 was €594.
- Cash flow from operations was €175 in 2017 and €198 in 2018.
- Capital expenditures were modest in both years.
- The tax rate is 30%.

Required

Using whatever ratios you need, analyze the liquidity, operating efficiency, and profitability of Wertenbroch Company for 2017 and 2018. Has Wertenbroch's performance improved or deteriorated over the two years? Be as specific as the data allow.

6.6 Profitability Analysis for The Home Depot

The Home Depot, Inc. operates as a home improvement retailer primarily in the United States, Canada, and Mexico. It operates The Home Depot stores, which sell building materials, home improvement supplies, and lawn and garden products to do-it-yourself customers, home improvement contractors, and building maintenance professionals.

The company also operates The Home Depot and EXPO Design Center stores that offer various installation services, which include products, such as carpeting, flooring, cabinets, countertops, and water heaters primarily to business-to-business customers. In addition, the company offers credit purchase programs through third-party credit providers. Meanwhile, The Home Depot has centralized purchasing and invested more than a billion dollars in state-of-the-art technology, including self-checkout aisles and in-store Web kiosks.

Since 2002, Home Depot's return on invested capital has risen from below 16% to nearly 21% last year. This profitability increase is impressive when one considers the severe competition in the industry from other big box stores (e.g., Lowes), the wellknown hardware coop Ace Hardware, lumber yards, and the host of other retailers who supply the products carried by Home Depot.

Key **profitability ratios** for Home Depot for the last three years are shown below:

	2004	2005	2006
ROIC	18.7%	19.7%	20.7%
NOPAT margin	6.6%	6.8%	7.2%
IC turnover	2.84X	2.88X	2.85X
A/R turnover	67.0X	66.3X	54.3X
Inventory turnover	5.3X	5.3X	5.3X
PP&E turnover	3.6X	3.6X	3.6X
COGS/sales ratio	68.2%	66.6%	66.5%
SGA/sales ratio	19.6%	20.9%	20.2%
Sales (in millions)	$64,816	$73,094	$81,511
Ending IC (in millions)	$25,392	$28,576	$32,994

Required

a. Explain how Home Depot has achieved an increase in ROIC over the three years. Be as specific as the data allow. Give likely reasons for changes in specific ratios.

b. Home Depot's accounts receivable turnover is very high. How does Home Depot achieve this turnover? What is the benefit of the high accounts receivable turnover in terms of profitability, liquidity, and cash flows?

6.7 Comparative Analysis of Receivables and Inventories

The following information is taken from the annual reports of The Coca-Cola Company and PepsiCo, Inc. The two companies are fierce competitors, but they differ in important respects.

Coca-Cola is more "cola-centric," which means that its core Coke and Diet Coke brands play a more dominant role in the company than Pepsi brand cola does in PepsiCo. Although Coca-Cola is the world leader in soft drinks, by a large margin, PepsiCo is the bigger company because of greater diversification. Both companies sell bottled water and other beverages (e.g., health and energy drinks), but these products feature more prominently in PepsiCo. Also, PepsiCo is the world leader in salty snacks through its Frito Lay business.

(in millions)		Coca-Cola	PepsiCo
Accounts receivable, net	31 Dec. 2010	$4,430	$6,323
	31 Dec. 2011	4,920	6,912
Inventories	31 Dec. 2010	2,650	3,372
	31 Dec. 2011	3,092	3,827
Net revenue	2010	35,119	57,838
	2011	46,542	66,504
Cost of goods sold	2010	12,693	26,575
	2011	18,216	31,593

Required

a. For both companies, calculate the receivables period, the inventory period, and the length of the operating cycle for 2011. Assume that all sales are on credit.

b. Comment on any differences you observe between the two companies. What reasons can you give for why the companies have different operating cycles?

Case Study

6-1 Profitability Analysis and WalMart's Suppliers

WalMart, the world's largest retailer, is legendary for squeezing price concessions and ever greater operating efficiencies from its suppliers. To what extent do such concessions hurt financial performance?[*] One recent study has found that suppliers identifying WalMart as a primary customer financially underperformed compared to companies that did not identify themselves in this way. Especially revealing is the observation that among the 10 largest suppliers to WalMart in 1994, four subsequently went bankrupt and a fifth was taken private as it was failing. But should suppliers just say "no" to WalMart? Or is it simply too big to ignore?

Consider the case of Dell, the computer maker. While the overall computer market has been growing, Dell's own share of that market is falling. In a first step toward transforming its model of direct selling to consumers, the company announced in May 2007 that it would begin selling two models of its low-end Dimension line through more than 3000 WalMart stores in the United States and Canada. Dell's share price fell by 1.4% on the news, partly because of analyst fears that the company might see a further deterioration of its already battered profit margins.

Still, some analysts viewed the move favorably. "They got products on the shelf of the No. 1 retailer in the world,"

---

[*]This case is adapted from material found in *The Wal-Mart Effect*, by Charles Fishman, London: Penguin Books, 2006. The following article was also consulted: "Dell, in shift, will offer PCs at Wal-Mart," by Matt Richtel, *The New York Times*, 25 May 2007.

(Continued)

according to one such analyst. "Dell is finally listening to its customers."

Bain & Company, the management consultants, have studied the effect of doing business with WalMart. "The fact of the matter is, the way WalMart is continuing to grow means that our clients cannot grow their business without finding a way to be successful with WalMart," according to Gib Carey, the partner in charge of the study. "We have clients out there who would like that not to be true. . . . But we think that WalMart is an essential retailer, in a way that no other retailer is."

To understand the effect of WalMart on supplier profitability, Bain staffers conducted an analysis of 38 publicly traded companies that did more than 10% of their business with WalMart. Bain also analyzed the performance of 20 companies in similar industries that were not significant WalMart suppliers, as a control group. The analysis produced a consistent pattern. For every percentage point of increased business these companies were doing with WalMart, operating margins declined to some extent. That is, the more business a company does with WalMart, the less profitable each sale is. "It may be pressure," says Carey, "or it may be that companies are intentionally letting some profit margins decline to aggressively grow their business with WalMart."

According to the Bain study, companies doing 10% or less of their business with WalMart had operating profit margins of 12.7%. Companies that became what Carey calls "captive suppliers" to WalMart – selling more than 25% of their output to WalMart – see their profit margin cut almost in half, to 7.3%. "What we've found as we've continued to work with clients," says Carey, "is that WalMart is really forcing companies to either get their act together, or get crushed."

Required

a. If "profitability" (i.e., operating margin) is lower for companies that derive a lot of their business from WalMart, why sell to WalMart? What logical reasons can a company give for such a practice if greater sales to WalMart are associated with lower margins?

b. How would a company know if an expected decline in profit margin was a price worth paying for WalMart's business? Be specific. What measures would need to be considered to address this issue?

Case Study

6-2 LVMH and Warnaco: Strategy and Financial Statement Analysis

LVMH was created in 1987 with the merger of Moët Hennessy and Louis Vuitton. However, the history of those merged companies goes back centuries. LVMH is diversified into a number of brands, with operations in five segments: wines and spirits; fashion and leather goods; perfumes and cosmetics; watches and jewelry; and selective retailing. The luxury brands they manage are among the world's most recognizable: Dom Pérignon champagne, Christian Dior perfume, and TAG Heuer timepieces, and several others.

Warnaco is a more focused group, with an emphasis on the design and manufacture of intimate apparel, sportswear, and swimwear. The brands that they supply products for include Calvin Klein and Speedo. While these brands are respected for their quality, they are not viewed as competing for the same high-end customers as LVMH.

The intent of this case is not to assess how the firms compete against each other. Rather, given that they likely have different operating strategies, how might an analyst detect these differences in the accounting numbers?

Required

a. Calculate ROIC for both companies for fiscal year 2011. For calculations requiring a tax rate, assume 33.3% for LVMH (the French corporate rate), and 35% for Warnaco (the US corporate rate). Based on this analysis alone, how do the companies compare in terms of their performance?

b. Review the description of each company above and think about the strategic positioning of their products. How are the two companies similar, and how do they differ?

c. Break down ROIC into its components, NOPAT margin and invested capital (IC) turnover.

d. Based on your calculations in part (c), and your analysis in part (b), does the breakdown for ROIC into NOPAT margin and IC turnover align with your expectations regarding company strategy? What does this say about management's ability to deliver performance in accordance with their stated objectives?

Excerpts from LVMH's financial statements

CONSOLIDATED BALANCE SHEET

Assets (EUR millions)	Notes	2011	2010	2009
Brands and other intangible assets – net	3	11,482	9,104	8,697
Goodwill – net	4	6,957	5,027	4,270
Property, plant and equipment – net	6	8,017	6,733	6,140
Investments in associates	7	170	223	213
Noncurrent available for sale financial assets	8	5,982	3,891	540
Other noncurrent assets		478	319	750
Deferred tax		716	668	521
Noncurrent assets		33,802	25,965	21,131
Inventories and work in progress	9	7,510	5,991	5,644
Trade accounts receivable	10	1,878	1,565	1,455
Income taxes		121	96	217
Other current assets	11	1,455	1,255	1,213
Cash and cash equivalents	13	2,303	2,292	2,446
Current assets		13,267	11,199	10,975
Total assets		47,069	37,164	32,106
Share capital		152	147	147
Share premium account		3,801	1,782	1,763
Treasury shares and LVMH-share settled derivatives		(485)	(607)	(929)
Cumulative translation adjustment		431	230	(495)
Revaluation reserves		2,689	1,244	871
Other reserves		12,798	11,370	10,684
Net profit, Group share		3,065	3,032	1,755
Equity, Group share	14	22,451	17,198	13,796
Minority interests	16	1,061	1,006	989
Total equity		23,512	18,204	14,785
Long-term borrowings	17	4,132	3,432	4,077
Provisions	18	1,400	1,167	990
Deferred tax		3,925	3,354	3,117
Other noncurrent liabilities	19	4,506	3,947	3,089
Noncurrent liabilities		13,963	11,900	11,273
Short-term borrowings	17	3,134	1,834	1,708
Trade accounts payable		2,952	2,298	1,911
Income taxes		443	446	221
Provisions	18	349	339	334
Other current liabilities	20	2,716	2,143	1,874
Current liabilities		9,594	7,060	6,048
Total liabilities and equity		47,069	37,164	32,106

(Continued)

CONSOLIDATED INCOME STATEMENT

(EUR millions, except for earnings per share)	Notes	2011	2010	2009
Revenue	22	23,659	20,320	17,053
Cost of sales		(8,092)	(7,184)	(6,164)
Gross margin		15,567	13,136	10,889
Marketing and selling expenses		(8,360)	(7,098)	(6,051)
General and administrative expenses		(1,944)	(1,717)	(1,486)
Profit from recurring operations	22–23	5,263	4,321	3,352
Other operating income and expenses	24	(109)	(152)	(191)
Operating profit		5,154	4,169	3,161
Cost of net financial debt		(151)	(151)	(187)
Other financial income and expenses		(91)	763	(155)
Net financial income (expense)	25	(242)	612	(342)
Income taxes	26	(1,453)	(1,469)	(849)
Income (loss) from investments in associates	7	6	7	3
Net profit before minority interests		3,465	3,319	1,973
Minority interests		(400)	(287)	(218)
Net profit, Group share		3,065	3,032	1,755
Basic Group share of net earnings per share (EUR)	27	6.27	6.36	3.71
Number of shares on which the calculation is based		488,769,286	476,870,920	473,597,075
Diluted Group share of net earnings per share (EUR)	27	6.23	6.32	3.70
Number of shares on which the calculation is based		492,207,492	479,739,697	474,838,025

Excerpts from Warnaco's financial statements

CONSOLIDATED BALANCE SHEETS

(Dollars in thousands, excluding per share data)

	December 31, 2011	January 1, 2011
Assets		
Current assets:		
Cash and cash equivalents	$232,531	$191,227
Accounts receivable, less reserves of $94,739 and $95,639 as of December 31, 2011, and January 1, 2011, respectively	322,976	318,123
Inventories	350,835	310,504
Assets of discontinued operations	—	125
Prepaid expenses and other current assets	99,686	100,389
Deferred income taxes	58,602	58,270
Total current assets	1,064,630	978,638

	December 31, 2011	January 1, 2011
Property, plant and equipment, net	133,022	129,252
Other assets:		
Licenses, trademarks and other intangible assets, net	320,880	373,276
Deferred financing costs, net	8,790	2,540
Deferred income taxes	21,885	11,769
Other assets	58,695	42,519
Goodwill	139,948	115,278
Total assets	$1,747,850	$1,653,272
Liabilities, Redeemable Noncontrolling Interest and Stockholders' Equity		
Current liabilities:		
Short-term debt	$47,513	$32,172
Accounts payable	141,797	152,714
Accrued liabilities	212,655	227,561
Liabilities of discontinued operations	6,797	18,800
Accrued income taxes payable	41,762	37,957
Deferred income taxes	1,476	262
Total current liabilities	452,000	469,466
Long-term debt	208,477	—
Deferred income taxes	37,000	74,233
Other long-term liabilities	137,973	136,967
Commitments and contingencies		
Redeemable noncontrolling interest	15,200	—
Stockholders' equity:		
Preferred stock (See Note 13)	—	—
Common stock: $0.01 par value, 112,500,000 shares authorized, 52,184,730 and 51,712,674 issued as of December 31, 2011, and January 1, 2011, respectively	522	517
Additional paid-in capital	721,356	674,508
Accumulated other comprehensive income	16,242	43,048
Retained earnings	625,760	501,394
Treasury stock, at cost 11,790,428 and 7,445,166 shares as of December 31, 2011, and January 1, 2011, respectively	(466,680)	(246,861)
Total stockholders' equity	897,200	972,606
Total liabilities, redeemable noncontrolling interest and stockholders' equity	$1,747,850	$1,653,272

(Continued)

CONSOLIDATED STATEMENTS OF OPERATIONS
(Dollars in thousands, excluding per share amounts)

	Fiscal 2011	Fiscal 2010	Fiscal 2009
Net revenues	$2,513,388	$2,295,751	$2,019,625
Cost of goods sold	1,412,446	1,275,788	1,155,278
Gross profit	1,100,942	1,019,963	864,347
Selling, general and administrative expenses	844,696	758,053	638,907
Amortization of intangible assets	47,957	11,549	11,032
Pension expense	26,744	2,550	20,873
Operating income	181,545	247,811	193,535
Other loss	631	6,238	1,889
Interest expense	16,274	14,483	23,897
Interest income	(3,361)	(2,815)	(1,248)
Income from continuing operations before provision for income taxes and noncontrolling interest	168,001	229,905	168,997
Provision for income taxes	36,006	82,107	64,272
Income from continuing operations before noncontrolling interest	131,995	147,798	104,725
Loss from discontinued operations, net of taxes	(4,802)	(9,217)	(6,227)
Net income	127,193	138,581	98,498
Less: Net income (loss) attributable to the noncontrolling interest	(257)	—	2,500
Net income attributable to Warnaco Group	$127,450	$138,581	$95,998
Amounts attributable to Warnaco Group common shareholders:			
Income from continuing operations, net of tax	$132,252	$147,798	$102,225
Discontinued operations, net of tax	(4,802)	(9,217)	(6,227)
Net income	$127,450	$138,581	$95,998
Basic income per common share attributable to Warnaco Group common shareholders (see Note 14):			
Income from continuing operations	$3.07	$3.26	$2.22
Loss from discontinued operations	(0.11)	(0.20)	(0.13)
Net income	$2.96	$3.06	$2.09
Diluted income per common share attributable to Warnaco Group common shareholders (see Note 14):			
Income from continuing operations	$3.01	$3.19	$2.19
Loss from discontinued operations	(0.11)	(0.20)	(0.14)
Net income	$2.90	$2.99	$2.05
Weighted average number of shares outstanding used in computing income per common share (see Note 14):			
Basic	42,425,750	44,701,643	45,433,874
Diluted	43,299,849	45,755,935	46,196,397

NOTES

1. If the company has preferred shares, preferred dividends are subtracted from net income. The numerator should equal the net income available to common shareholders only.

2. For this and the ratios to follow, values will be shown initially for 2016 and then for the years 2014–2016.

3. NIBL = noninterest-bearing liabilities; WCR = the working capital requirement.

4. The definition of invested capital used here applies at group level only. It is common practice to exclude cash when measuring invested capital at division or business unit levels. The reason for this treatment is that cash tends to be centrally managed and is therefore not the responsibility of division managers.

5. The discussion on how to calculate invested capital is adapted from S.D. Young and S.F. O'Byrne, *EVA and Value Based Management: A Practical Guide to Implementation*, McGraw-Hill, 2001.

6. TSMC uses the term "income from operations" in place of "operating income." The latter term is more common.

7. Readers familiar with the "ROIC trees" popularized by strategy consultants McKinsey should recognize DuPont analysis. ROIC trees and DuPont analysis are essentially the same.

8. Although we don't show it here, similar analyses can be performed for the balance sheet.

9. NT$540 billion ÷ 250 days (assuming five working days each week and 50 working weeks each year).

10. The following discussion on M&M is adapted from S.D. Young and S.F. O'Byrne, *EVA and Value Based Management: a Practical Guide to Implementation*, New York: McGraw-Hill, 2001.

11. More precisely, M&M assume that tax laws are nondiscriminatory, meaning that they don't favor one form of financing over another. Therefore, the M&M model still holds even if there are taxes, as long as tax law doesn't favor debt over equity, or vice versa.

12. The value of this tax shield varies from country to country. In the United States and Germany, provisions in their tax codes designed to reduce the double taxation of dividends have the effect of reducing the relative tax advantages of debt. In countries with tax laws that are somewhat more hostile to equity investors, such as the United Kingdom, the tax advantages of debt are greater.

13. "Investment grade" is defined as a rating of BBB – or better from S&P or Baa3 (or better) from Moody's. Bonds with lower ratings are considered "speculative grade." "Junk bond" is popular slang for speculative grade debt. The distinction between the two grades is important because many institutional investors are barred, by law or policy, from buying junk bonds. This helps to explain why a company's borrowing costs tend to spike upwards when its debt falls below investment grade.

14. EBITDA is earnings before interest, tax, depreciation, and amortization. It is a popular, though flawed, proxy for cash flow. Chapter 7, Business Valuation and Financial Statement Analysis, discusses this issue in detail.

15. Credit analysts view FOCF as a better indicator of a company's ability to repay debt than free cash flow measures that subtract all forms of investment from operating cash, including the purchase of financial securities. The idea is that other investments, including corporate acquisitions, are more discretionary in nature than capital investments. Because assets wear out and must be replaced, at least some capital investment is expected, even for companies that are no longer growing. (This is why FOCF is calculated net of capital expenditures.) But companies can always choose to avoid the takeover market and focus on organic growth (i.e., growth of existing businesses) instead. Corporate treasury movements (i.e., the purchase and sale of financial instruments, usually short-term, to manage the company's liquid resources) are also considered discretionary.

16. There is some debate over whether deferred tax liabilities and provisions should be included among total debts. If there is reason to doubt that a portion of either liability will not result in a future cash payment, that portion should be excluded. What this example shows is that the definition of total debt is not entirely straightforward.

17. E. Altman, "Financial ratios: discriminant analysis and the prediction of corporate bankruptcy," *Journal of Finance*, 1968, pp. 589–609; and J. Ohlson, "Financial ratios and the probabilistic prediction of bankruptcy," *Journal of Accounting Research*, 1980, pp. 109–131.

7

Business Valuation and Financial Statement Analysis

The final stage of financial statement analysis converts what has already been learned from the first three steps – industry and business analysis, accounting analysis, and ratio analysis – into forecasts of future benefits. This chapter shows how to convert such forecasts into estimates of value.

Valuation Principles

The key question to ask whenever we think of investing is how much the right to a future stream of benefits from the investment is worth to us today.[1] This value is a function of the *magnitude, timing*, and *uncertainty* of these future benefits.

By magnitude we mean that, all else being equal, the greater the benefit (whether we define it as "cash flow" or something else), the better. Timing means that we would rather have the benefit now than have to wait for it. For example, the earlier we expect to receive a cash flow, the more valuable that cash flow is to us today. Uncertainty refers to the possibility that the expected benefits might not materialize. Intuitively, the greater this uncertainty, the less valuable an expected benefit is to us now.

These insights are captured in the discounted cash flow (DCF) approach to valuation. With this approach, we project expected future cash flows (magnitude and timing), then discount them at an interest rate, or rate or return. The discount rate reflects both the time value of money (i.e., the idea that investors would rather have cash today than tomorrow and must therefore be paid to wait) and a risk premium that reflects the incremental return investors require to compensate them for the risk that the cash flow might not materialize (uncertainty). This approach is summarized in the formula:

$$\text{Value} = \sum_{t-1}^{t=n} \frac{\text{CF}_t}{(1+r)^t}$$

where n is the economic life of the investment (usually expressed in years)[2]; CF_t is the expected cash flow in period t; and r is the discount rate that reflects the perceived riskiness, or uncertainty, of the cash flows.

This equation tells us that the value of any asset, including a business enterprise, is equal to the sum of DCF. The discount rate is the opportunity cost of capital, which measures the return that investors would expect to receive if the cash were invested elsewhere in assets or companies of similar risk.[3]

Valuation: From Theory to Practice

The value of the firm equals the present value of its future cash flows, or more specifically, "free cash flows," plus the value of any existing cash balances. We define free cash flow as the amount of cash generated in any given year from the company's operations, net of the investment to be made in that year.

Recalling the cash flow statement, all cash flows are the result of operating, investing, or financing activities. Think of free cash flow as operating cash flows, net of investing cash flows, thus representing the amount of operating cash left over for distribution to the firm's capital providers. It's the prospect of receiving such cash in future that motivates investors to contribute cash now.

Free cash flow is calculated as follows:

$$
\begin{array}{ll}
 & \text{Operating income } (1-T) \\
+ & \text{Depreciation} \\
- & \text{Investment} \\
\hline
= & \text{Free Cash Flow}
\end{array}
$$

Operating income, sometimes known as EBIT, or Earnings before Interest and Tax, is the profit expected from the firm's normal, recurring business activities (sales – operating expenses). When operating income is multiplied by $(1 - T)$, where T is the corporate tax rate, the result is net operating profit after tax, or NOPAT. Depreciation (amortization too, if there is any) is added back because it is not a cash expense. Finally, investments in working capital and in property, plant and equipment (PP&E) are subtracted.[4]

Alternatively, free cash flow can be calculated as follows:

$$
\text{NOPAT} - \text{Change in Invested Capital}
$$

where the change in invested capital equals investment in working capital and PP&E, minus depreciation (and amortization).

To illustrate the equivalency of these alternative definitions of free cash flow, assume that:

$$
\begin{array}{l}
\text{Operating income} = \$1000 \\
T = 30\% \\
\text{Investment} = \$600 \\
\text{Depreciation} = \$350
\end{array}
$$

Free cash flow equals:

$$
\begin{array}{ll}
 & \$1000 \,(1-30\%) \\
+ & 350 \\
- & 600 \\
\hline
= & \$450
\end{array}
$$

Alternatively, free cash flow can be calculated by subtracting the change in net operating assets ($600 – $350) from NOPAT ($700). Here too, free cash flow is $450.

Value is simply the sum of future free cash flows, discounted at the opportunity cost of capital, as shown below:

$$\text{Value}_0 = \frac{\text{Free Cash Flow}_1}{(1+\text{OCC})} + \frac{\text{Free Cash Flow}_2}{(1+\text{OCC})^2} + \cdots$$

where OCC is the opportunity cost of capital.

One practical problem with this model is the theoretically indefinite life of the business. Obviously, annual cash flows cannot be estimated in perpetuity. This problem is usually solved by dividing the future cash flows into two separate elements, one that reflects the present value of cash flows during an explicit forecast period and the other that reflects the present value of cash flows after the forecast period. The latter value is commonly known as terminal, or continuing, value. The length of the explicit forecast period varies, but somewhere between three and seven years is typical.

Another complicating factor is that the above model measures only the value of operations. It must be extended to include the value of any nonoperating sources of value, such as cash and marketable securities. In effect, the value of the firm does not just include the present value of future cash flows, but also the value of any cash or near-cash resources that the company may already have. In fact, any resource that has a cash value, but which is not considered in the cash flow forecasts, can be viewed as a nonoperating asset. The value of such resources must also be considered in estimating the value of the firm.

Thus, a more complete picture of DCF valuation looks like this:

> Value = Nonoperating assets
>
>   + Present value of cash flows during the forecast period
>
>   + Terminal value

The Economic Profit Approach to Valuation

An alternative approach to valuation focuses on economic profit (EP), but yields results that are mathematically equivalent to DCF:

$$\text{Value}_0 = \text{IC}_0 + \frac{\text{NOPAT}_1 - (\text{OCC} \times \text{IC}_0)}{(1+\text{OCC})} + \frac{\text{NOPAT}_2 - (\text{OCC} \times \text{IC}_1)}{(1+\text{OCC})^2} + \cdots$$

where IC is invested capital. (Note that the comments on terminal value and nonoperating sources of value in the discussion of DCF valuation apply equally to the EP approach.)

EP is the numerator in the above formula, reflecting the difference between after-tax operating income (NOPAT) and the cost of the invested capital (OCC × IC) used to generate that income. The primary difference between EP and the traditional net income measure found in corporate income statements is that the former subtracts all capital costs from operating income; the latter considers only the cost of debt (i.e., interest). EP charges firms for the cost of equity while net income does not.

The logic of EP-based valuation is that if a firm is expected to earn just a normal rate of return (i.e., the OCC) on the book value of invested capital, investors should pay no more than book value to buy the firm. In other words, if future EPs are expected to be 0, the value of the firm equals the book value of the firm's invested capital. Investors are willing to pay more or less than book value depending on whether the company is expected to earn profits above or below this level. To put it another way, the willingness of investors to pay a price for the company that differs from the book value of the capital already invested in the business depends on the firm's ability to generate "abnormal" earnings. EP is just another term for abnormal earnings, as are "residual income" and "economic value added." All of these terms can be used interchangeably.

When the variables in an EP model are drawn from the same assumptions as those used for a DCF valuation, the resulting values should be the same. Given a certain set of assumptions regarding the future, the valuation will not be affected by whether the assumptions are fed into an EP or DCF model.

The DCF–EP equivalency can be seen in the following example:

> *A firm invests $600 in the expectation of receiving incremental operating income of $100 per year for the next four years. With a tax rate of 30%, NOPAT is expected to be $70 per year. At the end of the fourth year, the assets acquired with the initial investment will have no residual value. Therefore, assuming the straight-line method, annual depreciation charges are $150 ($600 ÷ 4). The opportunity cost of capital is 10%.*

This information is summarized in Table 7.1.

Under the DCF approach, the net present value of the investment equals the sum of the present values of the expected free cash flows in years 1 to 4, minus the initial investment of $600. The result is a net present value of $97. Alternatively, this result can be expressed as $97 of value creation.

When using the EP approach, net present value equals the sum of the present values of EP in years 1 to 4. EP equals NOPAT minus capital charges. Capital charges in any given year equal invested capital at the beginning of the year multiplied by the cost of capital. For year 1, capital charges equal the $600 initial investment, times 10%, or $60. Because invested capital declines by $150 over each of the next three years (as a result of depreciation), capital charges are reduced each year by $15 ($150 × 10%). When the present values of the EP figures are added, the result is a value of $97, exactly the same as under the DCF approach.

The primary difference between the DCF and EP approaches is in the treatment of the $600 initial investment. Under DCF the investment is charged immediately, while the EP approach spreads out the investment over the entire investment horizon. Instead of charging the $600 at time 0, it is charged gradually over the ensuing four years through depreciation and the capital

Table 7.1 Project Valuation Under the DCF and EP Methods

	Year 1	Year 2	Year 3	Year 4
NOPAT	$70	$70	$70	$70
Depreciation	150	150	150	150
Free cash flow	220	220	220	220
Present value of free cash flow	200	182	165	150
Net present value: $97				
NOPAT	70	70	70	70
Capital charges	60	45	30	15
Economic profit (EP)	10	25	40	55
Present value of economic profit	9	21	30	37
Sum of present values: $97				

charge. In fact, the cumulative present value for the four years of depreciation and capital charges, if discounted at the 10% cost of capital, is $600.

Although this example is based on a capital investment for a finite forecast horizon, the equivalency between DCF and EP equally holds for the valuation of a firm (where forecasts are made for benefits in perpetuity).

There are two important advantages to the use of EP over DCF, even if the valuations produced by the two approaches are identical. First, EP focuses on earnings instead of cash flow and, therefore, relates more easily to the sort of measures widely discussed and analyzed in the world's financial centers. Firms rarely hold press conferences to announce free cash flows, but they routinely announce earnings. The second advantage is that EP tends to be a better measure of year-on-year performance than free cash flow. Every business needs a system to track the performance of its managers. The principal flaw of free cash flow in this context is that any time a business or a division embarks on a major capital spending campaign, results will look poor because free cash flow calculations subtract all capital investment, in full, when investments are made. As we saw in the above example, EP spreads the cost of the investment gradually over the expected investment horizon. Thus, the cost of the investment is recognized in each year that is expected to benefit from it, instead of recognizing all of it in the year in which the investment is made.

A Case Study in Valuation: TSMC

In this section, we show how to value a company using the example of TSMC. Recent historical data are presented in Exhibits 1.1–1.3. The company will be valued based on forecasts for 2017 and beyond, applying both the DCF and EP approaches.

As discussed in Chapter 6, the first step in a business valuation is to perform an industry and competitive strategy analysis. Such an analysis for TSMC is shown in Appendix 6.1.

The analysis reveals that TSMC should continue to enjoy economies of scale as well as a premium price for superior technology. When combined with a generally favorable pricing environment, operating margins (NOPAT) are expected to remain stable, at least over the next five years. Competitive forces as well as the need to continually invest in R&D to maintain technological leadership will likely prevent increases in margins. Operating efficiency should also improve over the next five years, meaning that more sales will be generated for each NT$ of invested capital. From the breakdown of ROIC into the NOPAT margin and invested capital turnover components, we observed somewhat low asset efficiency of the company - hence the room for improvement. However, competitive forces will be an important constraining factor here too.

When this analysis is combined with the ratio analysis discussed in Chapter 6, the following forecasts result:

- annual growth rates in sales of 11% for the first five years of the forecast horizon (2017–2021), with 7% sales growth over the ensuing five years (2022–2026), and 6% in 2027;

- constant NOPAT margins over the first five years of 33%, which is roughly the historical average, with declines in 2022 and beyond in accordance with our predicted decline in returns on newly invested capital (see discussion below);

- improving invested capital efficiency in 2018 and 2019 from 0.60 to 0.65, and then again to 0.70 before leveling off.

We also assume that the opportunity cost of capital for TSMC is 9%, which analyst and academic surveys suggest is reasonable for the semiconductor industry.

The Financial Forecasts for TSMC

The forecasts are summarized in Exhibit 7.1. The sales forecast for 2017 of NT$1,052,211 million assumes 11% growth over the reported sales figure from the 2016 income statement, NT$947,938 million. NOPAT for 2017 equals 2017 sales, multiplied by the forecasted NOPAT margin of 33%, or NT$347,230 million. Beginning invested capital for 2017 is the same as the figure derived from the 2016 end-of-year balance sheet, which equals total assets of NT$1,886,298 million minus short-term, noninterest-bearing liabilities of NT$252,028 million, or NT$1,634,270 million. Invested capital at the end of 2017, or the beginning of 2018, equals forecasted sales for the following year, NT$1,167,954 million, an 11% increase over 2017, divided by the forecasted invested capital turnover of 0.65, or NT$1,796,853 million.

Free cash flow to the firm equals NOPAT minus the forecasted increase in invested capital, NT$347,230 million – (NT$1,796,853 million – NT$1,634,270 million), or NT$184,646 million.

Economic profit for 2017 equals the same NOPAT figure, NT$347,230 million, minus capital charges. Capital charges equal beginning invested capital, NT$1,634,270 million, times the OCC of 9%, or NT$147,084 million. Subtracting this amount from NOPAT yields a forecasted EP of NT$200,146 million.

Similar calculations are made for the next four years (2018–2021). At this point, we re-evaluate whether TSMC can continue to make such high returns on their investments. As of 2021, the ROIC equals 23.1%, as we multiply the forecasts of NOPAT margin (33%) and invested capital turnover (0.70). This level of return is far above the opportunity cost of capital of 9% and suggests that, despite significant barriers, competitors would observe such returns and act to erode some of TSMC's competitive advantage.

Therefore, from a modeling standpoint, we predict that TSMC's *past* investments continue to perform at the same level; yet, any *new* investments reflect a lower incremental return. We designate the return on newly invested capital as RONIC and predict that it hits the level of 15% in 2022. This is still above TMSC's opportunity cost of capital of 9%, but below the past ROIC of 23.1%.

To calculate NOPAT in 2022, we assume that the previous year's NOPAT of NT$527,119 million will persist. To be consistent with our view of competitive effects, we also forecast a lower sales growth of 7% in 2022. This yields forecasted sales of NT$1,709,144 in 2022. Given the invested capital turnover rate of 0.70, this suggests beginning invested capital of NT$2,441,634 million (i.e., NT$1,709,144 million divided by 0.70).

Thus, the newly invested capital must be NT$159,733 million (or NT$2,441,634 million – NT$2,281,901 million). If this newly invested capital yields 15%, then that amounts to additional NT$23,960 million of NOPAT. Thus, total NOPAT for 2022 become NT$551,079 million (or NT$527,119 million + NT$23,960 million).

Note that in our assumption table of Exhibit 7.1 NOPAT margin of 32.24% has fallen, reflecting the lower RONIC. Now NOPAT margin is an output of the model rather than an input. That is, the RONIC assumption of 15% on the newly invested capital along with the prediction that past NOPAT will persist yields the predicted value of NOPAT. The NOPAT margin then is derived by dividing this predicted NOPAT by the predicted revenue value, which will grow 7% from the previous year according to our estimates.

We use this RONIC assumption for the second half (2022–2026) of our 10-year forecast period.

Once the forecasts have been made, we can estimate the value of the free cash flows and EP for the entire 10-year horizon. This is done by calculating a present value for each of the future cash flows and economic profit estimates using the 9% OCC. Exhibit 7.2 shows the results. The present value of free cash flows through 2026 is NT$2,067,636 million. The present value of EP over the same period is NT$1,886,401 million.

Exhibit 7-1   Forecasts for TSMC: Free Cash Flows and Economic Profit (NT$ million)

	2017	2018	2019	2020	2021	2022	2023	2024	2025	2026	2027
Income statement											
Revenues	1,052,211	1,167,954	1,296,429	1,439,037	1,597,331	1,709,144	1,828,784	1,956,799	2,093,775	2,240,339	2,374,759
NOPAT	347,230	385,425	427,822	474,882	527,119	551,079	576,716	604,148	633,500	664,907	682,189
Balance sheet											
Beginning IC	1,634,270	1,796,853	1,994,507	2,055,767	2,281,901	2,441,634	2,612,548	2,795,427	2,991,107	3,200,484	3,392,513
Capital charges	147,084	161,717	179,506	185,019	205,371	219,747	235,129	251,588	269,200	288,044	305,326
Economic profit	200,146	223,708	248,316	289,863	321,748	331,332	341,587	352,560	364,300	376,863	376,863
Free cash flow	184,646	187,771	366,562	248,748	367,386	380,165	393,838	408,468	424,123	472,878	478,638
Assumptions											
Sales growth	11.00%	11.00%	11.00%	11.00%	11.00%	7.00%	7.00%	7.00%	7.00%	7.00%	6.00%
NOPAT margin	33.00%	33.00%	33.00%	33.00%	33.00%	32.24%	31.54%	30.87%	30.26%	29.68%	28.73%
IC Turnover	0.60	0.65	0.65	0.70	0.70	0.70	0.70	0.70	0.70	0.70	0.70
OCC	9.00%	9.00%	9.00%	9.00%	9.00%	9.00%	9.00%	9.00%	9.00%	9.00%	9.00%
RONIC	19.58%	23.49%	21.45%	76.82%	23.10%	15.00%	15.00%	15.00%	15.00%	15.00%	9.00%

NOPAT = net operating profit after tax; IC = invested capital; OCC = opportunity cost of capital; RONIC = return on newly invested capital.

Exhibit 7-2   Valuation Summary for TSMC (NT$ million)

	(1) Nonoperations value	(2) Beginning invested capital	(3) Value from forecasts 2017–26	(4) Terminal value	(5) Value of the firm
Discounted cash flow	541,254	N/A	2,067,636	3,201,823	5,810,713
Economic profit	541,254	1,634,269	1,866,401	1,768,789	5,810,713

Note: The value of the firm (column 5) equals the sum of columns 1, 3, and 4 for the DCF method, and the sum of columns 1 through 4 for the EP method.

These calculations are based on the assumption that cash flows and EP arrive at the end of the year. If we believe, quite reasonably, that returns are more likely to arrive throughout the year, the present value estimates can be adjusted upward if multiplied by:

$$1 + \frac{OCC}{2}$$

For example, consider the forecasted free cash flow for 2017, NT$184,646 million. If we assume that the cash flows arrive at the end of the year, the present value is NT$169,400 million.[5] All of the present value calculations shown in Exhibit 7.2 are based on this assumption. In contrast, if we assume that the cash flows arrive evenly throughout the year, the present value of the cash flows is NT$169,400 million × 1.045 or NT$177,023 million.

Terminal Value

Of course, TSMC is expected to survive far beyond 2026. Therefore, rather than make specific, year-by-year forecasts of performance for all future periods – a practical impossibility – we estimate a terminal value for the end of the forecast horizon. This estimate requires a forecast of future free cash flows, or EP, from 2027 onward.

There are a number of approaches to estimating this terminal value, but we believe that the best approach is one that assumes rapid convergence to a competitive equilibrium at the end of the forecast horizon. This means that value-creating investment is not likely to continue indefinitely. Instead, we expect that after the 10-year forecast horizon, any further investments made by TSMC will be value-neutral. Investments made beyond the horizon will generate enough NOPAT to cover the opportunity cost of capital, but no value-creating returns will be earned. This means that while the return on invested capital (ROIC) might remain well above the company's OCC for a long time, the return on any newly invested capital, or RONIC, is expected to equal the OCC.

In our approach with TSMC, we assumed there was an incremental decline in the ROIC by inputting a RONIC value in 2022 for the second half of the forecast period. Had we been more optimistic for the company, perhaps we would have let the ROIC stay constant up to the end of the forecast period and then predict the immediate convergence of RONIC to the OCC. That is a plausible modeling alternative, though in this case our choice was to have RONIC descend in "steps." Regardless of how one arrives there, we still believe that for the forecast into perpetuity the RONIC should equal the OCC.

Such an approach to terminal value assumes that TSMC will sustain any competitive advantage created before the end of 2026, but no further source of competitive advantage is expected. We believe this to be the most reasonable assumption one can make about terminal value because otherwise the valuation would implicitly assume that the company can create additional sources of competitive advantage in perpetuity. Competitive forces should prevent such a thing from happening. The practical effect of this assumption is that any growth achieved beyond the forecast horizon will be value-neutral.[6]

To calculate a terminal value for TSMC, NOPAT and free cash flow are estimated for 2027, the terminal year. We begin by estimating sales for 2027, based on the assumption that sales will grow by 6% from the previous year. The resulting sales forecast, NT$2,374,759 million, is used to infer the beginning invested capital of NT$3,392,513 million assuming the continued invested capital turnover of 0.70. The newly invested capital of NT$192,029 million (i.e., NT$3,392,513 million – NT$3,200,484) is expected to yield 9%, the OCC which is also expected to be the

RONIC, or NT$17,282. When this amount is added to the NOPAT of 2026, NT$664,907, we have the forecasted NOPAT for 2027 of NT$682,189. To estimate the terminal value, NOPAT is divided by the 9% OCC:

$$\frac{NT\$682,189 \text{ million}}{0.09} = NT\$7,579,878 \text{ million}$$

This figure reflects the value at the end of the investment horizon (end of 2026) for all free cash flows from 2027 onward. We then discount the terminal value (expected 10 years hence) by the 9% OCC, resulting in NT$3,201,823 million (Exhibit 7.2). When added to nonoperating sources of value (the cash balance of NT$541,254 million at the end of 2016) and the present value of the free cash flows over the 10-year forecast horizon, we get an estimated value for TSMC of NT$5,810.7 billion, or about NT$5.8 trillion.[7]

It should be noted that NT$5.8 trillion is our estimate for the value of the firm, also called "enterprise value," and not the value of TSMC's equity. It's the present value of current cash and future cash flows for all capital providers, including lenders. Given that lenders have priority of claim over shareholders, their claims must be subtracted from the value of the firm to arrive at equity value.[8]

If we assume that the market value of debt is equal to its book value,[9] the equity value for TSMC is calculated as follows:

Value of the firm:	NT$5,810.7 billion
Debt:	NT$329.1 billion
Value of equity:	NT$5,481.6 billion

This means that the shares of TSCM are worth approximately NT$5.5 trillion.

At the beginning of 2017, when the 2016 financial statements of NSCM were issued, the market value of TSMC's equity (otherwise known as its "market capitalization" or "market cap") was about NT$4.8 trillion, roughly NT$700 billion lower than the above figure. On the basis of this estimate, we would conclude that the shares of TSMC are somewhat undervalued, by about 12.7% of our valuation estimates. This may not be large enough to generate a "strong buy" recommendation, yet it does suggest a potential investing opportunity. However, remember that our valuation was based on a number of assumptions including sales growth, NOPAT margin, invested capital turnover, the time pattern over which excess profit erodes, as well as the opportunity cost of capital. An expanded approach would consider multiple future scenarios in order to conduct a sensitivity analysis of this valuation.

A Brief Word on Growth Rates

You may have noticed in the TSMC example that we assumed zero growth in NOPAT for the terminal value period. We could have made other growth assumptions, but they would have had no influence on the valuation. The reason is because our terminal value is based on the assumption that RONICs beyond the forecast horizon will equal the OCC. To borrow from the corporate finance lexicon, all investments in the terminal value period are expected to have zero *net present value* – no value is created or destroyed. This is the essence of the competitive equilibrium assumption, and the reason we assume zero growth for the terminal period.

Relative Valuation

A popular alternative to DCF and EP-based valuation is known as "relative valuation." Under this approach, the value of a company is determined in relation to how similar companies are priced in the market. The term "relative" means that value is defined relative to other, similar businesses, and not in any absolute sense (as with the DCF and EP approaches).

The idea is that the market pays for a certain attribute – earnings, sales, cash flow, or something else – that gives rise to value. Market price is then converted into a multiple of this attribute. For example, if the market is paying between €17 and €21 for every euro of net income reported by companies in a certain industry, an estimate of value can be derived simply by taking the product of this multiple (somewhere between 17 and 21) and earnings per share (EPS). If we deemed 20 to be a proper multiple for a given firm, and EPS was €4, the value of each share of stock is estimated to be €80 (€20 × €4). If shares were selling for less than €80, we would say that they trade at a discount. If, on the other hand, the shares were selling for more than €80, we would say that they trade at a premium.

From the above example it should be obvious that this method is much easier than the DCF/EP approaches. But as we will see below, there is a cost to this simplicity.

Performing a Relative Valuation

Here's how relative valuations are done:

1. **A list of comparable companies is created.** Usually these comparables are publicly traded (and therefore have easily observed market prices). The comparables may be industry peers, but it often pays to look beyond the industry for companies of similar size and with similar risk profiles.

2. **Market values are converted into trading multiples.** such as price–earnings (p/e), price-to-book (p/b), enterprise value-to-sales, and enterprise value-to-EBITDA ratios. The idea is to identify some attribute of a firm that gives rise to value and to define the market price with respect to this attribute. While some attributes apply to any business – examples include earnings, EBITDA, and sales – other attributes are industry specific. Examples of the latter type include number of rooms (hotel industry), kilowatt hours (power generation), and number of subscribers (cable television and mobile phone operators).

3. **Multiples are adjusted for differences between the comparables and the subject firm.** For example, if the comparables have an average p/e ratio of 15, but the subject company has an above-average growth rate, the p/e used for valuation purposes will probably be higher than 15.

The resulting multiples can then be used for a variety of purposes. For example, portfolio managers may use them to determine if a target company is underpriced (selling at a discount to its peers) or overpriced (selling at a premium).

One reason for the popularity of this approach is that key data – prices and multiples for comparable companies – are widely available. Reuters, Bloomberg, and other investor services provide such data via the Internet, either free of charge or for a small fee.

Until recently, most relative valuations focused on p/e ratios, and this approach continues to be popular. But in some investment circles, EBITDA multiples are now the most common relative valuation approach. EBITDA is thought to offer the following advantages:

- It can be calculated for firms with net losses because most such businesses at least show a positive EBITDA. (Obviously, p/e ratios cannot be used if earnings are negative.) Even firms with negative operating cash flow may have a positive EBITDA, because the latter measure does not subtract taxes or interest.

- It controls for differences among companies in their depreciation and amortization policies.

- EBITDA is popular for leveraged (i.e., high debt) transactions, such as management buyouts, because it is thought to represent cash generated by the firm before all discretionary expenditures, including asset replacement, and therefore represents the amount of operating cash available to support debt repayments.

- Because it ignores the costs of financial leverage, it allows for comparisons among firms with different capital structures.

Still, there are some important drawbacks and limitations to the use of EBITDA. For example, it ignores changes in working capital and thus overstates cash flow in periods of working capital growth. In profitable, fast-growing industries, EBITDA is a poor proxy for operating cash. Also, EBITDA does not consider the amount of required reinvestment, which can be a serious drawback in industries where the rate of technological change is high or in any business where assets are short-lived and must be frequently replaced.

Although EBITDA is useful in its simplicity, it is worth asking why so many analysts rely on it as a proxy for cash flow when other, more valid, measures are easily available.

Relative Valuation: The Verdict

Relative valuation may be easy, but it can easily go wrong. Perhaps the most serious deficiency is a direct consequence of its simplicity. One attractive aspect of multiples-based valuation is that it doesn't require the extensive range of assumptions required of a good DCF/EP model. For example, the pricing of companies using earnings or EBITDA multiples does not require explicit assumptions on reinvestment rates, returns on new invested capital, or terminal values. But contrary to popular wisdom, a multiples approach does incorporate these assumptions. The assumptions are buried in the multiple itself.

For example, any time you value a company using a p/e ratio or EBITDA multiple, you are making the same assumptions as users of sophisticated DCF models. The difference is that while they are forced to make the assumptions explicitly, your assumptions are embedded in the multiple. The problem with this approach is that you could be making wildly unrealistic assumptions regarding, say, RONIC, and not even know it. Your earnings multiple might assume a RONIC several percentage points greater than OCC, in perpetuity. Economic logic tells us that this is a practical impossibility in competitive markets. But you will never know this assumption is being made because you aren't forcing yourself to make it explicitly.

One could even argue that multiples-based valuations aren't really valuations at all, but merely ways of describing prices that have already been paid for similar assets. To our way of thinking, there is only one legitimate reason why you might resort to multiples: to communicate valuations, especially during negotiations with other investors. For example, many private equity firms value a target company using a rigorous DCF/EP model, and then translate the valuation into multiples. In effect, multiples constitute a language, a way for business people and investors to talk to each other in mutually understandable terms. But while multiples can be highly effective as communication tools, a proper valuation requires a DCF or EP approach.

KEY LESSONS FROM THE CHAPTER

- The value of any firm equals the present value of its expected future cash flows plus the value of existing cash balances and any nonoperating assets.

- Free cash flows are calculated as follows: net operating profit after tax (NOPAT) plus depreciation less investments in net operating assets. Free cash flows are the key to valuation because they equal the cash flows generated from recurring operations, net of investment, and therefore represent the amount of cash flow available in a given year for distribution to the firm's capital providers. In effect, shareholders and debt providers invest in companies because of the expectation of future free cash flows.

- An alternative approach to valuation focuses on EP, but yields results that are mathematically equivalent to the DCF model.

- EP, also known as economic value added, equals NOPAT, net of capital charges. Capital charges equal the product of invested capital and the opportunity cost of capital.

- Relative valuation, based on multiples of price/earnings, EBIT, EBITDA, and other accounting variables are more popular approaches to valuation than DCF. However, relative valuation suffers from several flaws. First, determining the appropriate multiples for a given company is always problematic. For a company to be truly "comparable" with other companies, it must be similar on a broad range of dimensions, including expected growth, accounting policy, physical asset endowment, and a host of other factors. Second, it can be argued that relative valuation isn't really valuation at all, but merely a way to describe the price recently paid for supposedly similar assets. It therefore ignores the fundamental truth that value and price are not the same. Our aim in valuation is to identify value, not price.

KEY TERMS AND CONCEPTS FROM THE CHAPTER

The time value of money

Free cash flows
Economic profit

Forecast period

Terminal value

Relative valuation

QUESTIONS

1. Compare and contrast the discount cash flow (DCF) approach to valuation with the economic profit approach. Which do you prefer, and why?

2. True or false: Using the economic profit approach for valuation yields identical results to the DCF approach.

3. EVA® is a well-known version of economic profit. Contrast and compare the two measures.

4. What factors influence the length of the explicit forecast horizon in a DCF valuation model? Why 5 years, or 10?

5. How are nonoperating assets (such as excess cash and real estate no longer used in current operations) handled in DCF models?

6. Numerous approaches are used to estimate terminal values for DCF models. Which approach do you prefer, and why?

7. What accounts for the popularity of relative valuation approaches (p/e ratios, EDITDA multiples, etc.)?

8. What are the drawbacks of relative valuation?

PROBLEMS

7.1 Estimating the Value of The Home Depot

Note: This problem is a continuation of the Home Depot exercise found at the back of Chapter 6.

Assume that your analysis of Home Depot's competitive strategy, industry economics, and previous financial performance led you to make the following forecasts:

- Sales will grow 12% per year in 2007 and 2008, and 10% per year in 2009, 2010, and 2011.

- NOPAT margins will equal 8% throughout the entire forecast horizon.

- The invested capital turnover (calculated on beginning IC) will equal 2.85 throughout the entire five-year forecast horizon except for 2007. In 2007, set beginning IC equal to Home Depot's ending IC from 2006 (a 2.77 invested capital turnover will exist in 2007).

- Terminal value will be estimated using the following approach that assumes a perpetuity:

$$\text{Terminal value} = (\text{NOPAT}_{2011} \div \text{OCC}).$$

- The opportunity cost of capital $\text{OCC} = 11\%$.

Required

a. Based on the above forecasts, estimate the expected economic profit for each year in the forecast horizon (2007–2011). Refer to the Home Depot question at the back of the previous chapter for any additional information that you need.

b. Assume that 2.124 billion shares of stock are outstanding, and the shares sell for $40 per share at the time of your investment decision. Assume that nonoperating assets are insignificant, all flows occur at the end of the period, and the market value of debt is $4 billion. Based on either an economic profit-based or discounted cash flow valuation model, is Home Depot Corporation a buy, hold, or sell?

The present value factors at 11% are as follows:

1 period	-	0.90090
2 periods	-	0.81162
3 periods	-	0.73119
4 periods	-	0.65873
5 periods	-	0.59345

7.2 Explaining Differences in P/E Ratios

The price/earnings ratios (from early 2012 prices and 2011 earnings) of several large companies are shown below:

Apple	23
Coca-Cola	13
Bank of China	9
Oracle	23
SABMiller	30
EDF (France)	56
Gazprom	6

Required

What factors might explain the differences in p/e ratios observed among these companies?

7.3 Explaining Differences in P/E Ratios

The price/earnings ratios (from early 2012 prices and 2011 earnings) of several large pharmaceutical companies are shown below:

Pfizer	20
Johnson & Johnson	12
GlaxoSmithKline	38
AstraZeneca	8
Eli Lilly	8
Bayer	37
Abbot Laboratories	17

Required

What factors might explain the differences in p/e ratios observed among these companies?

Case Study

7-1 Valuation Based on Discounted Cavsh Flows: The Case of Vardon Golf Ltd.

Vardon Golf Ltd. is a privately held maker of golf clubs. For decades, it produced a full range of clubs, but recently most of its sales have come from hybrids, clubs that combine the best attributes of fairway woods and long irons. The company also produces putters that are starting to find some traction among professionals and low-handicap amateurs. The company is profitable, but Cooper Palmer, a private equity firm based in London, believes that it has underperformed relative to its potential.

You are an analyst at Cooper Palmer and have been asked to perform a valuation of Vardon Golf. Financial data for 2012, the year just past, include the following:

Revenue	£10,000,000
Earnings before income and tax	2,000,000
Taxes on EBIT	600,000
Cash	£200,000

Working capital requirement (WCR)	1,500,000
Net fixed assets (NFAs)*	7,500,000
Total invested capital	£9,200,000

*Net fixed assets = Property, plant and equipment, net of depreciation.

If the company continues under current management, the following performance parameters are expected:

Annual revenue growth*	4%
EBIT margin	20%
Tax rate	30%
Cash as a % of revenue	2%
WCR as a % of revenue	15%
NFA as a % of revenue	75%
Continuing value growth rate for NOPAT	2%

*For the years 2013 through 2017.

However, the partners at Cooper Palmer are convinced that if they ran the company, Vardon could realize growth opportunities and operating efficiencies not expected under current ownership. For example, cost savings would boost EBIT margins, and improved asset utilization would reduce required investments in WCR and NFA. Based on your discussion with the partners, you reestimate the parameters as follows:

Annual revenue growth	6%
EBIT margin	22%
Tax rate	30%
Cash as a % of revenue	2%
WCR as a % of revenue	12%

NFA as a % of revenue	65%
Continuing value growth rate for NOPAT	3%

Required

a. Assuming a 5-year explicit forecast horizon and an opportunity cost of capital of 9%, estimate the value of Vardon Golf under current ownership.

b. Reestimate the value of Vardon Golf based on the partners' assessments of potential operating improvements. Vardon's current owners are willing to sell the company for £17.75 million. Is that an attractive price for Cooper Palmer?

NOTES

1. This section has been adapted from S.D. Young and S.F. O'Byrne, *EVA and Value Based Management: A Practical Guide to Implementation*, McGraw-Hill, 2001.

2. When valuing businesses, n is usually set to ∞.

3. A common error in valuation is to discount future cash flows at the cost of financing. To see the error in this practice, consider the following example. You have an investment opportunity that is expected to yield 10%. A bank is willing to lend the capital at 6%. Should you borrow the funds and invest them at 10%? The answer seems obvious, but imagine that other investments of similar risk are expected to yield 14%. Your original investment no longer seems like a good idea, does it? The moral of this story is that the relevant benchmark is not the cost of financing, but the rate of return one can expect from similar investments. Hence, the expected future cash flows must be discounted at the opportunity cost of capital.

4. PP&E is defined here as any form of capital expenditure, not just investment in tangible fixed assets.

5. NT$184,646 million × 0.91743 (the present value factor one period hence at 9%).

6. To clarify, TSMC may grow beyond 2027, but the growth will be neither value creating nor value destroying. One practical effect of this assumption is that whatever growth rate we choose for TSMC beyond 2027 will have no effect on value. Higher growth will translate into higher NOPAT, but the increase in NOPAT will be exactly offset by the required increase in capital investment. Therefore, higher growth assumptions have no effect on future free cash flows (nor, for that matter, do lower growth assumptions).

7. Including the full amount of the cash balance in the value of the firm assumes that the market values existing cash NT$ for NT$. In effect, it assumes that cash represents a zero NPV investment.

8. Debt is defined here as the sum of short-term financial liabilities, long-term financial liabilities, tax liabilities, and the net defined benefit liability (TSMC employees' pension plan). In addition, we include Noncontrolling Interest as debt, since these shareholders own stocks in subsidiaries where TSMC does not own 100% of the shares, but they do not have a claim on TSMC parent stock which is what we are valuing. TSMC's total debt at the end of 2016 is NT$329,074 million.

9. The assumption that book value of debt is equal to its market value is not entirely valid, but in a relatively stable interest-rate environment, we would expect the two figures to be roughly equal, especially for bluechip companies such as TSMC. Still, if we had an actual market value for the debt (i.e., what the debt claims were selling for at the time of the valuation), we would subtract that figure from the value of the firm to arrive at equity value.

8 Accounting for Receivables and Bad Debts

Introduction

Receivables are amounts owed to a business by outsiders. Most receivables arise from credit sales to customers and are called "accounts receivable" or "trade receivables." In this chapter, we discuss the accounting for customer-based receivables under US GAAP and IFRS. Both regimes require that accounts receivable appear in the balance sheet at net realizable value. In theory, this value should reflect the amount owed to the company by its customers. But not all receivables are collected (customers go bankrupt) and some merchandise might be returned. The accounting for receivables must incorporate both of these factors. The appendix to this chapter discusses the banking-industry analog to uncollectible accounts – loan loss reserves.

Estimating Bad Debts

Some credit sales never get collected. Most companies establish credit policies that balance the expected cost of credit sales (e.g., billing costs, collection costs, and the risk of bad debts) with the benefit of increased sales. Companies choose what they believe will be the profit-maximizing policy.

The challenge from an accounting point of view is that accounts receivable should reflect how much cash the company expects to collect from its customers, not how much cash is owed to it. Therefore, estimates of bad debts, otherwise known as "uncollectible accounts," must be made.

This estimate can be done in either of two ways:

- the sales revenue approach or
- the gross accounts receivable approach.

The Sales Revenue Approach

Under this approach, the company estimates bad debt expense based on a percentage of sales. For example, if a company has revenues of $5 million, and a review of customer accounts, current economic conditions, and historical experience suggests that 1% of these revenues will be uncollectible, the following entry would be made:

Bad debt expense	$50,000	
Allowance for doubtful accounts		$50,000

The bad debt expense appears as an operating expense on the income statement. The allowance for doubtful accounts is a "contra-asset" (as mentioned in Chapter 2) in that it offsets the gross receivables in determining the net receivables reported on the balance sheet. If half of the $5 million in sales remained uncollected at the end of the year, net accounts receivable would be $2.45 million ($2.5 million – $50,000).

The Gross Accounts Receivable Approach

This approach affects the same accounts but arrives at the estimate of bad debts by focusing on the receivables balance instead of sales revenues. For example, if historical experience and other factors suggest that 3% of receivables are uncollectible, and the balance in gross receivables is $2.5 million, the balance in the contra-account must be $75,000 ($2.5 million × 3%). The company then makes whatever entry is needed to bring the balance in the contra-account to this amount. If no previous entry has been made (i.e., the current balance is 0), the following entry is required:

Bad debt expense	$75,000	
Allowance for doubtful accounts		$75,000

If, on the other hand, the contra-asset already had a balance of $40,000, the entry would be:

Bad debt expense	$35,000	
Allowance for doubtful accounts		$35,000

Writing-off Accounts

Regardless of which method is chosen to estimate bad debts, accounts are written off using the following entry:

Allowance for doubtful accounts	XX	
Accounts receivable		XX

By writing off a specific account (i.e., the account of a specific customer), the company is conceding that the cash expected from the sale will never be collected. An important point to note from the above entry is that the income statement is unaffected. Writing off specific accounts, after they prove to be uncollectible, has no effect on earnings. The earnings impact is felt only when the allowance is taken (or adjusted).

The Direct Method: An Alternative Approach

Thus far, we have assumed that the company is using the "allowance method" in accounting for bad debts, the method required under US GAAP and IFRS. An alternative approach, sometimes allowed (or even required) for tax purposes, is called the "direct method." This method may even be used under US GAAP or IFRS, but only under those rare instances in which the allowance method is not practical. Under the direct method, bad debt expense is recognized only when individual accounts are written off. No estimates of bad debts are made, and there is no allowance account. When a specific account is deemed to be uncollectible, the following entry is made:

Bad debt expense	XX	
Accounts receivable		XX

Although this method offers the virtue of simplicity, it has been rejected for financial reporting purposes because

- Companies can easily manipulate bad debt expense by determining the precise timing that a specific account is written off. For example, if a company is having a mediocre year, it may choose to delay the recognition of a bad debt related to a specific account until the following accounting period. The result is higher reported income for the current period.

- The accounts receivable balance is misleading. Instead of reflecting what the company expects to collect in cash from its credit sales, it reflects the total amount owed by customers, even those amounts that are deemed to be uncollectible.

- It violates the matching principle. Instead of matching bad debt expense against the sales related to the expense, the expense is typically recognized in a later accounting period.

What Happens When Written-off Accounts Are Later Collected?

Occasionally, a company will recover at least a portion of what was owed by a customer whose account was written off. The accounting treatment for such recoveries depends on whether the allowance or direct method is used. Under the allowance method, the following entry is made:

Cash	XX	
Allowance for doubtful accounts		XX

In effect, the reduction to the contra-asset that occurred when the account was written off is restored. The income statement is unaffected; the recovery is treated as a balance sheet event only.

Recoveries under the direct method are different. Because the actual write-off of the customer's account had an income statement effect, the recovery too affects the income statement:

Cash	XX	
Other income		XX

The contra-asset account is not affected because there is no contra-asset account under the direct method.

The "Aging" of Accounts Receivable

Regardless of which approach is chosen to estimate bad debt expense under the allowance method (percentage of sales or percentage of gross receivables), the company must periodically determine whether or not the balance in the contra-asset is adequate. In other words, does the contra-asset reflect a good-faith estimate regarding the proportion of remaining receivables that will prove to be uncollectible? To make this judgment, an "aging of accounts receivable" is performed. This process is so fundamental to the accounting for receivables that even if the company does not perform the aging, you can be certain that the auditors will.

The aging is done by categorizing each receivable based on the number of days it is overdue. A bad-debt percentage is then assigned to each category, and a mathematical average is taken to determine the appropriate balance in the allowance account.

Table 8.1   **Distribution of Morris Inc.'s Outstanding Receivables**

(1) Number of days overdue	(2) Amount	(3) Probability of noncollection(%)	(2) × (3)
0	$6 million	0.3	$ 18,000
30–90	3 million	1.2	36,000
90–180	0.6 million	10.0	60,000
>180	0.4 million	50.0	200,000
			$ 314,000

To illustrate, assume that Morris Inc. has $10 million of outstanding receivables, as shown in Table 8.1. On the basis of this aging schedule, management would assume that the allowance account requires a balance of $314,000. If the existing balance is $200,000, the following entry would be required:

Bad debt expense   114,000
    Allowance for doubtful accounts   114,000

But notice that if the balance in the allowance account was far higher, say, $450,000, the following entry would be made:

Allowance for doubtful accounts   136,000
    Other income   136,000

This example shows that if Morris Inc. had overprovisioned for bad debts in previous years, it can reverse a portion of the balance in the allowance account and boost earnings. When companies overprovision in this way, "hidden" or "cookie-jar" reserves are created. US GAAP and IFRS prohibit this practice, but the doctrine of conservatism (which in this case means ensuring that the allowance account is never too low) gives companies some latitude in creating such reserves.

Sales Returns and Allowances

Sometimes the wrong goods are shipped to customers or the correct goods arrive damaged. In either case, the customer will return the item or request a discount. In such cases, accounts receivable must then be reduced and a charge made to the income statement. For example, if Morris, Inc. agrees to reduce by $15,000 the price of goods that arrived damaged at a customer, the following adjusting entry is required:

Sales returns and allowances   15,000
    Accounts receivable   15,000

The entry reflects that fact that the client owes $15,000 less than was previously billed, and that sales revenue is effectively reduced. Notice that sales revenues are not reduced directly. A contra-account (contra to sales revenues) is created instead, sales returns and allowances, which allows the company to keep a record of the frequency and amount of returns and price reductions. The sales figure reported on the income statement equals net sales (sales minus the sales returns and allowances).

In industries or sectors where product returns are common and significant in monetary terms, the company not only recognizes returns as they occur, but an estimate must also be made at the end of each accounting period for the amount of future returns and allowances arising from receivables already on the books. Otherwise, the matching principle would be violated. The following entry is made:

Sales returns and allowances	XX	
Allowances for sales returns		XX

The debit is the contra-account to sales revenues, while the credit is contra to accounts receivable. In practice, however, estimated sales returns and allowances are small enough in most industries to ignore the above entry. Consequently, no end-of-year adjustment is needed for these items. Also, when the actual returns and allowances change little from year to year, the above entry is not required because its effect on earnings will be minor.

Although less prone to manipulation than sales revenue, accounting games can be played with returns and allowances. These games fall into two basic categories:

1. Failure to record returns and

2. Deliberately misestimating the amount of returns for future periods.

In the former case, a company may deliberately ship the wrong product to customers near the end of the year, or ship the correct product in the wrong amount, without any adjustment. The effect is to overstate revenues and profits in the current period. In the second, a company can understate expected returns, boosting current sales and profits, or overstate expected returns, thereby creating hidden reserves that can boost profits in the following year.

Analyzing Receivables

Receivables are often the flip side to revenues. As companies recognize revenues, they often recognize accounts receivable at the same time. Therefore, the analysis of receivables plays an important role in the analysis of revenue recognition. Common sense suggests that as companies become increasingly aggressive in the recognition of revenue (for example, recognizing revenue too quickly), an increase in accounts receivable should be observed. For this reason, experienced analysts examine trends in the ratio of "receivables-to-sales." If the ratio is trending upward, it could indicate any combination of the following possibilities:

- The company has become more lenient in its credit terms, extending credit to riskier customers or extending more generous payment terms to existing customers.

- The company is encountering collection problems from several customers, perhaps because customers are in financial difficulty or they are retaliating for poor service or quality problems.

- Revenue-recognition policies are becoming more aggressive, as the company recognizes revenue earlier in its operating cycle than in previous periods or, in the most extreme cases, recognizes revenue for bogus sales.

One of the analyst's tasks in cases where the receivables-to-sales ratio is increasing is to determine which of the above explanations is relevant. An examination of the statement of cash flows is also helpful for this purpose. If receivables are growing more quickly than sales, the impact should be observed in the working capital requirement and in cash flows from operating activities. Analysts and investors will also calculate the receivables turnover ratio and receivables period (average collection period) when evaluating management's working capital policies. These measures are discussed, in detail, in Chapter 6.

KEY LESSONS FROM THE CHAPTER

- Receivables are amounts owed to a business by outsiders. Most receivables arise from credit sales to customers.

- Accounts receivables appear on the balance sheet at net realizable value. Net realizable value should reflect the amount of cash that the company expects to receive from its customers. This amount equals gross accounts receivable, minus an allowance for doubtful accounts.

- Most companies establish credit policies that balance the expected costs of credit sales with the benefit of increased sales.

- Estimates of bad debts can be done in either of two ways: the sales revenue approach or the gross accounts receivable approach.

- The aging of accounts receivable is done by categorizing each receivable based on the number of days it is overdue. A bad-debt percentage is then assigned to each category, and a weighted average is taken to determine the appropriate balance in the allowance account.

- Analyzing receivables plays an important role in the analysis of revenue recognition. If accounts receivable grow faster than revenues, it could indicate that the company has become more aggressive in its revenue-recognition policies, or that it is encountering problems in collecting cash from customers.

- Therefore, a growing receivables-to-sales ratio is a red flag that should be analyzed and explained.

KEY TERMS AND CONCEPTS FROM THE CHAPTER

Accounts receivable
Sales revenue approach
Gross accounts receivable
 approach

Aging of accounts
 receivable
Sales returns and
 allowances

Receivables-to-sales
 ratio
Net realizable
 value

Allowance for doubtful
 accounts
Contra-asset
 account

QUESTIONS

1. What are the major differences between the allowance method and the direct method in accounting for bad debts?

2. What are the advantages of the allowance method (relative to the direct method)?

3. Most tax authorities require use of the direct method. What reasoning would a tax official give for not permitting the allowance method?

4. Why might the allowance for doubtful accounts have a debit balance during the accounting period, but never at the end of the period?

5. Consider the following statement: "The fewer the uncollectible accounts, the better." Can you think of instances where this statement might be false?

6. What factors cause the balance in the allowance for doubtful accounts to increase or decrease from one year to the next?

7. How are recoveries of cash from previously written-off accounts treated under the allowance method? The direct method? Why is the accounting treatment for such events different under the two methods?

8. Many companies sell their receivables, either through a process known as "factoring" or through "securitization." Why do companies do this?

Appendix 8.1 Accounting for Loan Loss Reserves

Banks and other institutions in the financial services sector do not have accounts receivable in quite the manner discussed in this chapter. Instead, they have *loans* receivable. On the surface, the accounting for loan receivables is similar to that of accounts receivable, but there are differences.

Most national banking regulators require that banks include in their financial statements a contra-asset account called allowance for loan losses (also known as reserves for loan losses). This account absorbs losses both from loans that the bank has already identified as nonperforming (i.e., bad loans) and from some apparently good loans that will later prove to be nonperforming. In other words, banks establish reserves for both performing and nonperforming loans.[1] US GAAP's SFAS 5 and IASB's IFRS 9 share a number of features. Both are designed to provide financial statement users with more useful information about a company's Expected Credit Losses (ECLs) on financial instruments. Both standards require companies to base their measurements of ECL on reasonable and supportable information that includes historical, current, and – as of 2018 – forecast information. Thus, the effects of possible future credit loss events on ECL must be considered. Where the two standards differ is mainly in terms of the degree to which losses are recognized over an asset's lifetime. The FASB calls for a consideration of ECL over the life of a loan from the time of its origination, whereas the IASB favors a staged approach. A second key difference involves income recognition on problem loans. IFRS 9 continues to allow banks to book the accrual of interest income on nonperforming loans even if the bank is not receiving some or all of the cash income due on the loan. By contrast, the FASB standard allows a bank or other creditor to use existing accounting methods for recording payments received on nonaccrual assets, including a cash basis method, a cost recovery method or some combination of both. Since the accrued interest could be overstated and unreliable, the cash basis method and the cost recovery method are widely recognized as being more conservative approaches to interest income recognition for nonperforming loans.

The reserve for loan loss account is established and maintained by periodic charges against earnings. The charges (called loan loss provisions, or something similar) show up on the income statement as an expense. The loan loss provision is an expense that, when recognized, increases the contra-asset. The provision is determined after management reviews the bank's loan portfolio and determines the appropriate level of reserves.[2] The balance in the reserve account should be set by management's judgment and applied with consistency from one period to the next.

According to SFAS 5, the primary standard governing the accounting for bad loans under US GAAP, the evaluation and measurement should take into account environmental factors and document the following: delinquency and impaired loan trends, charge-off and recovery trends, volume and terms of loans, changing in lending practices, experience of lending personnel, national and local economies, industry conditions, among other factors.

When loan losses are recognized, that is, when a bank decides that some portion of a loan will not be collected and therefore must be charged off or written down, the amount of the loss is deducted from both the asset (loans, gross) and the contra-asset (reserves for loan losses). Net loans will be unaffected.

To recap, the contra-asset rises by the amount of the loan loss provision and is reduced by charge-offs.[3] It is then netted against gross loans to determine net loans, which is the amount that goes into the determination of total assets on the balance sheet.

Loan Loss Accounting Basics

To illustrate the accounting for bad loans, consider a bank with €5,000 in loans on the balance sheet and €100 in the loan loss reserve account as of the end of 2016. Net loans are therefore €4,900:

$$\text{Loans} (5,000) - \text{Loan Loss Reserve} (100) = \text{Net Loans} (4,900)$$

On May 25, 2017, a loan in the amount of 5 is judged to be uncollectible and is written off. The bank records the following journal entry:

Loan loss reserve	5	
Loans		5

The net loans remain at 4,900. Note that the accounting for writing-off loans largely parallels that of receivables. When receivables are written off, both the contra-asset and the receivables account are reduced, and net receivables are unchanged.

On August 10, 2017, a loan in the amount of 20 is deemed uncollectible and is written off. The journal entry will be similar to the one above:

Loan loss reserve	20	
Loans		20

The net loan value on the books is still 4,900 (4,975 – 75).

At the end of 2017, bank management estimates that the loan loss reserve should be 120. The contra-asset account must therefore be increased by 45 (120 – 75). The bank records the following entry:

Loan loss provision	45	
Loan loss reserve		45

Net loans are now 4,855 (4,975 – 120), a decrease of 45 from the beginning of 2017. The decrease results from the write-offs of (5 + 20), plus the net increase in the reserve (120 – 100, or 20).

PROBLEMS

8.1 Bad Debts on Loans Receivable

Excerpts from the 2008 Annual Report for J.P. Morgan Chase & Co. ("JPMC") are provided in Exhibit 8.1.

Note that the balance in the allowance for loan losses account at the end of JPMC's fiscal 2006 was $7,279 million, and the balance in their loan *asset* account was $483,127 million at the same date.

Required

a. Calculate JPMC's allowance for loan losses as a percentage of gross loans outstanding for each of the three years for which information has been provided.

b. What is the dollar value of JPMC's loan write-offs in 2007 and 2008?

c. Comment upon JPMC's loan loss provisioning over the periods shown. Do they appear to have used the provision to create hidden reserves? Are they sitting on a "cookie jar" reserve or are you expecting a big hit to the income statement in future periods as a result of past underprovisioning for bad loans?

8.2 Determining Bad Debt Expense from an Aging Schedule

Hilary Company's year-end accounts receivable show the following balances by age:

Age of accounts	Balance
Not due yet	€600,000
0–30 days	200,000
31–60 days	45,000
61–120 days	20,000
More than 120 days	10,000

The credit balance in the allowance for doubtful accounts is now €8,600. Hilary Company's prior collection experience suggests that Hilary should use the following percentages to compute the total uncollectible amount of receivables: 0–30 days, 0.5% 31–60 days, 1.0% 61–120, 10%, and more than 120 days, 70%.

Required

Prepare the journal entry to record Hilary's bad debt expense.

8.3 Analyzing Receivables and the Allowance for Doubtful Accounts

Vermeulen Company of Ghent, a producer of custom-made furniture, was founded in 2016. Revenues in its first year were €3.5 million, all on account. The balance in the receivables

Exhibit 8-1	Consolidated Balance Sheets

December 31 (in millions, except share data)	2008	2007
Assets		
Cash and due from banks	$26,895	$40,144
Deposits with banks	138,139	11,466
Federal funds sold and securities purchased under resale agreements (included $20,843 and $19,131 at fair value at December 31, 2008 and 2007, respectively)	203,115	170,897
Securities borrowed (included $3,381 and zero at fair value at December 31, 2008 and 2007, respectively)	124,000	84,184
Trading assets (included assets pledged of $75,063 and $79,229 at December 31, 2008 and 2007, respectively)	509,983	491,409
Securities (included $205,909 and $85,406 at fair value at December 31, 2008 and 2007, respectively, and assets pledged of $25,942 and $3,958 at December 31, 2008 and 2007, respectively)	205,943	85,450
Loans (included $7,696 and $8,739 at fair value at December 31, 2008 and 2007, respectively)	744,898	519,374
Allowance for loan losses	(23,164)	(9,234)
Loans, net of allowance for loan losses	721,734	510,140
Accrued interest and accounts receivable	60,987	24,823
Premises and equipment	10,045	9,319
Goodwill	48,027	45,270
Other intangible assets:		
Mortgage servicing rights	9,403	8,632
Purchased credit card relationships	1,649	2,303
All other intangibles	3,932	3,796
Other assets (included $29,199 and $22,151 at fair value at December 31, 2008 and 2007, respectively)	111,200	74,314
Total assets	**$2,175,052**	**$1,562,147**

Consolidated statements of cash flows

Year ended December 31 (in millions)	2008	2007	2006
Operating activities			
Net income	$5,605	$15,365	$14,444
Adjustments to reconcile net income to net cash (used in) provided by operating activities:			
Provision for credit losses	20,979	6,864	3,270
Depreciation and amortization	3,143	2,427	2,149
Amortization of intangibles	1,263	1,394	1,428
Deferred tax (benefit) expense	(2,637)	1,307	(1,810)
Investment securities (gains) losses	(1,560)	(164)	543
Proceeds on sale of investment	(1,540)	—	—
Gains on disposition of businesses	(199)	—	(1,136)
Stock-based compensation	2,637	2,025	2,368

| Exhibit 8-1 | (Continued) |

Year ended December 31 (in millions)	2008	2007	2006
Originations and purchases of loans held-for-sale	(34,902)	(116,471)	(178,355)
Proceeds from sales, securitizations, and paydowns of loans held-for-sale	38,036	107,350	173,448
Net change in:			
Trading assets	(12,787)	(121,240)	(61,664)
Securities borrowed	15,408	(10,496)	916
Accrued interest and accounts receivable	10,221	(1,932)	(1,170)
Other assets	(33,629)	(21,628)	(7,193)
Trading liabilities	24,061	12,681	(4,521)
Accounts payable and other liabilities	1,012	4,284	7,815
Other operating adjustments	(12,013)	7,674	(111)
Net cash provided by (used in) operating activities	23,098	(110,560)	(49,579)

Consolidated statements of income

Year ended December 31 (in millions, except per share data)	2008	2007	2006
Revenue			
Investment banking fees	$5,526	$6,635	$5,520
Principal transactions	(10,699)	9,015	10,778
Lending and deposit-related fees	5,088	3,938	3,468
Asset management, administration, and commissions	13,943	14,356	11,855
Securities gains (losses)	1,560	164	(543)
Mortgage fees and related income	3,467	2,118	591
Credit card income	7,419	6,911	6,913
Other income	2,169	1,829	2,175
Noninterest revenue	28,473	44,966	40,757
Interest income	73,018	71,387	59,107
Interest expense	34,239	44,981	37,865
Net interest income	38,779	26,406	21,242
Total net revenue	67,252	71,372	61,999
Provision for credit losses	20,979	6,864	3,270
Noninterest expense			
Compensation expense	22,746	22,689	21,191
Occupancy expense	3,038	2,608	2,335
Technology, communications, and equipment expense	4,315	3,779	3,653
Professional and outside services	6,053	5,140	4,450
Marketing	1,913	2,070	2,209

(Continued)

| Exhibit 8-1 | (Continued) |

Year ended December 31 (in millions, except per share data)	2008	2007	2006
Other expense	3,740	3,814	3,272
Amortization of intangibles	1,263	1,394	1,428
Merger costs	432	209	305
Total noninterest expense	43,500	41,703	38,843
Income from continuing operations before income tax expense (benefit)	2,773	22,805	19,886
Income tax expense (benefit)	(926)	7,440	6,237
Income from continuing operations	3,699	15,365	13,649
Income from discontinued operations	—	—	795
Income before extraordinary gain	3,699	15,365	14,444
Extraordinary gain	1,906	—	—
Net income	$5,605	$15,365	$14,444
Net income applicable to common stock	$4,931	$15,365	$14,440

| Exhibit 8-2 | Consolidated Balance Sheets |

	Reference to notes	end of	
		2009	2008
Assets (CHF million)			
Cash and due from banks		51,857	90,035
Interest-bearing deposits with banks		1,177	2,012
Central bank funds sold, securities purchased under resale agreements, and securities borrowing transactions	13	209,499	269,028
of which reported at fair value		128,303	164,743
Securities received as collateral, at fair value		37,516	29,454
of which encumbered		27,816	16,665
Trading assets, at fair value	14	332,238	342,778
of which encumbered		112,843	69,921
Investment securities	15	11,232	13,823
of which reported at fair value		10,793	13,019
Other investments	16	23,993	27,002
of which reported at fair value		21,126	24,866

Exhibit 8-2	(Continued)

	Reference to notes	end of	
		2009	2008
Net loans	17	237,180	235,797
of which reported at fair value		36,246	32,314
allowance for loan losses		(1,395)	(1,639)
Premises and equipment	18	6,436	6,350
Goodwill	19	9,267	9,330
Other intangible assets	19	328	423
of which reported at fair value		30	113
Brokerage receivables		41,960	57,498
Other assets	21	68,744	85,797
of which reported at fair value		29,125	34,086
of which encumbered		975	3,329
Assets of discontinued operations held-for-sale	4	0	1,023
Total assets		1,031,427	1,170,350

Consolidated statements of operations

	Reference to notes	2009	2008	2007
Consolidated statements of operations (CHF million)				
Interest and dividend income	6	25,288	47,939	62,550
Interest expense	6	(18,397)	(39,403)	(54,108)
Net interest income	6	6,891	8,536	8,442
Commissions and fees	7	13,750	14,812	18,929
Trading revenues	29	12,151	(9,880)	6,146
Other revenues	8	502	(4,200)	5,804
Net revenues		33,294	9,268	39,321
Provision for credit losses	9	506	813	240
Compensation and benefits	10	15,013	13,254	16,098
General and administrative expenses	11	7,701	7,809	6,833
Commission expenses		1,997	2,294	2,410
Total other operating expenses		9,698	10,103	9,243

(Continued)

Exhibit 8-2 **(Continued)**

	Reference to notes	2009	2008	2007
Total operating expenses		24,711	23,357	25,341
Income/(loss) from continuing operations before taxes		8,077	(14,902)	13,740
Income tax expense/(benefit)	25	1,835	(4,596)	1,248
Income/(loss) from continuing operations		6,242	(10,306)	12,492
Income/(loss) from discontinued operations, net of tax	4	169	(531)	6
Net income/(loss)		6,411	(10,837)	12,498
Less net income/(loss) attributable to noncontrolling interests		(313)	(2,619)	4,738
Net income/(loss) attributable to shareholders		6,724	(8,218)	7,760
of which from continuing operations		6,555	(7,687)	7,754
of which from discontinued operations		169	(531)	6
Basic earnings per share (CHF)				
Basic earnings/(loss) per share from continuing operations	12	5.14	(7.51)	7.06
Basic earnings/(loss) per share from discontinued operations	12	0.14	(0.50)	0.01
Basic earnings/(loss) per share	12	5.28	(8.01)	7.07
Diluted earnings per share (CHF)				
Diluted earnings/(loss) per share from continuing operations	12	5.01	(7.51)	6.77
Diluted earnings/(loss) per share from discontinued operations	12	0.13	(0.50)	0.01
Diluted earnings/(loss) per share	12	5.14	(8.01)	6.78

Consolidated statements of cash flows

in	2009	2008	2007
Operating activities of continuing operations (CHF million)			
Net income/(loss)	6,411	(10,837)	12,498
Less net income/(loss) attributable to noncontrolling interests	(313)	(2,619)	4,738
Net income/(loss) attributable to shareholders	6,724	(8,218)	7,760
(Income)/loss from discontinued operations attributable to shareholders, net of tax	(169)	531	(6)
Income/(loss) from continuing operations attributable to shareholders	6,555	(7,687)	7,754
Adjustments to reconcile net income/(loss) to net cash provided by/(used in) operating activities of continuing operations (CHF million)			
Impairment, depreciation, and amortization	1,114	1,174	893
Provision for credit losses	506	813	240

| Exhibit 8-2 | (Continued) |

in	2009	2008	2007
Deferred tax provision/(benefit)	875	(4,935)	(1,076)
Share of net income from equity method investments	(29)	17	(101)
Trading assets and liabilities, net	(11,471)	113,153	(65,739)
(Increase)/decrease in other assets	27,189	1,203	(64,540)
Increase/(decrease) in other liabilities	(40,993)	28,217	61,191
Other, net	2,068	(2,084)	3,503
Total adjustments	(20,741)	137,558	(65,629)
Net cash provided by/(used in) operating activities of continuing operations	(14,186)	129,871	(57,875)

account at the end of the year was €1 million. The company estimated uncollectible receivables at 2% of sales. Based on an aging schedule and other information about customer accounts, €40,000 of receivables were written off on December 31, 2016.

One year later, on December 31, 2017, the balances in selected accounts were as follows:

Sales	€4.0 million
Accounts receivable (gross)	€1.5 million
Allowance for doubtful accounts	€50,000

On December 31, 2017, Vermeulen Company estimated that its accounts receivable balance contained €55,000 of likely uncollectibles. An adjusting entry was made to the allowance account to reflect this estimate. As in the previous year, all sales were on account.

Required

1. What was the balance in accounts receivable (gross) at the end of 2016?
2. What was the balance in the allowance for doubtful accounts account at the end of 2017?
3. What was the bad debt expense for 2017?
4. What was the amount, in euro, of the specific accounts receivable written-off during 2017?
5. How much cash was collected in 2017 from customers?

6. What is the balance of accounts receivable (net) on the statement of financial position (i.e., balance sheet) dated December 31, 2017?

8.4 Provisions for Credit Losses

Credit Suisse is a Switzerland-based financial services company filing their financial statements under US GAAP. The balance in their allowance for loan losses at the end of 2007 was CHF 1,000 million, and their net loans outstanding were CFH 221,750 million. Financial statements are shown in Exhibit 8.2.

Required

a. Calculate Credit Suisse's allowance (i.e., reserves) for loan losses as a percentage of *gross loans* outstanding for each of the three years for which information has been provided.

b. What is the amount of Credit Suisse's loan write-offs for 2008 and 2009? *Hint:* You might want to reconstruct the T-account for the allowance for loan losses.

c. Comment upon Credit Suisse's loan loss provisioning over the periods shown. Do they appear to have used the provision for create hidden reserves? Are they sitting on a "cookie jar" reserve at the end of fiscal 2009 or are you expecting a hit to the income statement in future periods because of past under-provisioning for bad loans? Explain.

Case Study

8-1 Receivables and Bad Debts at Toyota

Toyota is one of the world's largest automobile manufacturers. Like all major players in the industry, the company provides credit to its customers, mainly in the form of installment sales on passenger cars and commercial vehicles. Toyota's ending balance sheet for fiscal year 2005 reveals accounts receivable (gross) of $15.05 billion.*

Accounting for Bad Debts

Toyota maintains an allowance for doubtful accounts representing management's estimate of the amount of asset impairment. According to the company's 2005 Annual Report:

> *The allowances are determined based on a systematic, ongoing review performed as part of the credit-risk evaluation process, historical loss experience, current economic conditions, and the estimated fair value and adequacy of collateral. This evaluation is inherently judgmental and requires material estimates, including the amounts and timing of future cash flows expected to be received, which may be susceptible to significant change. Although management considers the allowance for doubtful accounts . . . to be adequate based on information currently available, additional provisions may be necessary due to (i) changes in management estimates and assumptions about asset impairments, (ii) information that indicates changes in expected future cash flows, or (iii) changes in economic and other events and conditions.*

> Source: *Toyota 2005 Annual Report.*

Activity in the allowance for doubtful accounts relating to accounts receivable for the years ended March 31, 2003, 2004, and 2005 is summarized as follows:

*Toyota also has a dedicated financing arm for leasing transactions. Finance receivables (net) were $28.03 billion at the end of fiscal year 2005.

in millions of US dollars

For the years ended March 31,

	2003	2004	2005
Allowance for doubtful accounts at beginning of year..........................	$599	$532	$611
Provision for doubtful accounts	60	165	157
Write-offs	−60	−26	−129
Other...	−67	−60	−83
Allowance for doubtful accounts at end of year......................................	$532	$611	$556

The other amount includes the impact of consolidation and deconsolidation of certain entities due to changes in ownership interest and currency translation adjustments. A portion of the allowance for doubtful accounts balance at March 31, 2004 and 2005 totaling $322 million and $371 million, respectively, is attributed to certain noncurrent receivable balances which are reported as other assets in the consolidated balance sheets.

Required

a. Toyota prepares its accounts using US GAAP, which requires the use of the allowance method in accounting for bad debts. Why is this approach preferred to the direct method? What are the disadvantages of the direct method? Are there any drawbacks or limitations to the allowance method?

b. Give the summary journal entries to record the activity in the allowance for doubtful accounts for 2005. Be specific as to which accounts are affected.

c. What factors might explain the trends, from 2003 to 2005, in the provision for doubtful accounts?

d. Suppose Toyota writes off an account, but the customer subsequently pays. How would Toyota account for the recovery? How would recoveries be accounted for under the direct method?

Case Study

8-2 Johnson Perry

Johnson Perry is a major producer of pet foods and livestock feed. The company's primary customers are supermarket chains, discount retailers, pet shops, and feed wholesalers and distributors. The balance sheet and income statement from the 2016 Annual Report are shown in Exhibit 8.3, along with a schedule on changes in the allowance for doubtful accounts found in the notes.

Required

a. Considering the company's recent experience in estimating uncollectible accounts, project write-offs for 2017.

b. Suppose that the company had provided an amount for doubtful accounts in 2015 using the same percentage of net sales as the 2014 provision. Describe the effect on operating income in 2015 and 2016. What factors might cause bad debt expense as a percentage of sales to change from one year to the next?

c. Recast the relevant components of the 2016 balance sheet and income statement as if the company had been using the direct write-off method throughout its history instead of the allowance method.

Exhibit 8-3 Johnson Perry Company and Subsidiaries consolidated balance sheet

December 31 (dollars in millions)	2016	2015
Assets		
Current assets		
Cash	$11.1	$11.6
Marketable securities, at cost which approximates market	116.7	62.5
Receivables, less allowance for doubtful accounts	255.7	228.7
Inventories	382.8	412.3
Other current assets	72.2	60.0
Total current assets	838.5	775.1
Investments and other assets	182.1	250.7
Property at cost		
Land	88.8	91.4
Buildings	598.6	586.2
Machinery and equipment	1,047.3	991.8
Construction in progress	37.1	42.4
Accumulated depreciation	1,771.8	1711.8
	691.2	623.8
	1,080.6	1,088.0
Total	$2,101.2	$2,113.8
Liabilities and shareholders' equity		
Current liabilities		
Current maturities of long-term debt	$15.7	$16.5
Notes payable	25.2	47.7
Accounts payable and accrued liabilities	490.3	428.4
Dividends payable	20.0	19.8
Income taxes	9.7	18.7
Total current liabilities	560.9	531.1
Long-term debt	315.3	406.9
Deferred income taxes	115.0	70.6

(Continued)

December 31 (dollars in millions)	2016	2015
Minority shareholders' interest in consolidated subsidiaries	5.9	5.1
Shareholders' equity		
Preferred stock, $1 par value, authorized 6,000,000 shares – none outstanding		
Common stock, .41 2/3 par value, authorized 180,000,000 shares –		
Issued 112,015,371 shares in 2010 and 108,182,395 in 2015	46.7	45.1
Capital in excess of par value	144.3	87.8
Earnings invested in the business	1,251.6	1,077.9
Cumulative translation adjustment	(40.8)	(25.6)
Common stock in treasury, at cost – 16,903,420 shares in 2016 and 6,702,556 in 2015	(297.7)	(85.1)
Total Shareholders' equity	1,104.1	1,100.1
Total	$2,101.2	$2,113.8

consolidated statement of earnings

Year ended December 31 (Dollars in millions except per share data)	2016	2015	2014
Net sales	$4,872.4	$4,802.6	$5,146.4
Costs and expenses			
Cost of products sold	3,559.4	3,672.6	4,092.3
Selling, general and administrative	376.5	367.1	318.7
Advertising	438.0	384.1	343.0
Unusual or nonrecurring items		154.0	
Interest	35.2	47.5	53.9
	4,409.1	4,625.3	4,807.9
Earnings from continuing operations before income taxes	463.3	177.3	338.5
Income taxes	207.3	85.9	152.3
Earnings from continuing operations	256.0	91.4	186.2
Losses from discontinued operations		22.3	11.4
Earnings for the year	$256.0	$69.1	$174.8

Analysis of balance sheet changes: Allowance for doubtful accounts

	2016	2015	2014
Balance, beginning of year	$17.1	$11.8	$12.1
Provision charged to expense	4.0	8.1	2.7
Write-offs, less recoveries	(8.1)	(2.8)	(3.0)
Balance, end of year	$13.0	$17.1	$11.8

8-3 Citigroup Inc.: Accounting for Loan Loss Reserves*

Anne Yang, a buy-side[†] analyst working for a prominent asset management firm in Hong Kong, was considering whether or not to diversify her portfolio by taking a position in a financial institution such as Citigroup Inc., J.P. Morgan Chase & Co., or some other global bank.

Anne was impressed to learn that Citigroup's reported earnings for the fourth quarter of 2004 had once again surpassed the analysts' consensus estimates; this time by a penny. While she was encouraged by the earnings performance, she was confused by a comment in a recent *BusinessWeek* article which indicated that Citigroup achieved its numbers by some "cookie jar" accounting technique.[‡]

The technique discussed in the article referred to a bank's accounting for loan loss reserves. After carefully examining Citigroup's financial statements (see Exhibit 8.4) and reading the notes company's in the most recent annual report, she discovered that Citigroup reduced its loan loss reserve allowance in 2004 from $13.243 billion to $11.869 billion, and that this reduction helped boost the earnings figures. Unsure of what that meant, Anne decided to examine the issue further before making her investment decision.

Citigroup Inc.

Citigroup Inc. was formed in 1998 when Citicorp Inc. agreed to a $70 billion merger with Travelers Group Inc. At that time, Citicorp was both a consumer and commercial bank that spanned the globe, while Travelers was a large US-based financial services and insurance provider. The merged entity, Citigroup Inc., became a diversified global financial services holding company whose businesses provided a broad range of financial services to consumer and corporate customers. By the end of 2004, the company had more than 200 million customer accounts and was doing business in more than 100 countries. It employed approximately 148,000 employees in the United States and roughly 146,000 employees outside the United States.

Controversy

Loan loss reserves are reserves that banks record to cover bad debt, and they represent the amount of money that management believes the bank will not be able to collect from the currently outstanding loans it has made to borrowers. The allowance (or loan loss reserves) is established through a provision for loan losses which is charged to earnings.[§] Allowance for loan losses appears on a bank's balance sheet as a contra-asset, and the amount recorded is a deduction from the outstanding loans receivables. When bad loans are eventually written-off, they are charged against the loan loss reserves account.

When the economy slows down, the provision for loan losses of banks usually increases in anticipation of higher debt defaults. This results in a decrease in net income. As a result, the largest determinant of a bank's profit fluctuations is often its provision for loan losses. These higher reserves magnify the negative impact of the economic cycle on the income and capital of banks. As might be expected, the size and timing of loan loss provisions tend to improve with higher levels of economic activity.

Academic research has found that most banks around the world delayed provisioning for bad loans until it is too late – when the cyclical downturn had already set in – possibly exacerbating the negative impact of the economic cycle on the income and capital of banks.[¶]

Because loan loss provisions are based on managerial discretion, they are subject to income smoothing as management can overprovision when earnings are high and underprovision, or even release reserves, when earnings are low. Income smoothing goes against accounting regulations, as within these regulations, banks cannot shift funds around at will.

Thus, the controversy surrounding loan loss reserves revolved around whether banks with generous loan loss reserves were manipulating earnings or merely practicing conservative accounting.

Citigroup Loan Loss Reserves Footnotes

In its financial footnotes for 2004, Citigroup reported the following with regard to its loan loss reserves:

During the past two years, the worldwide credit environment has continuously improved, as evidenced by declining cash-basis loan balances and lower delinquency rates. Accordingly, the company has reduced its Allowance for Credit Losses.

---

*This case was written by Professors Jake Cohen (then at INSEAD), David Hawkins (Harvard Business School), and Gerald Lobo (University of Houston).
[†] Buy-side is the side of the financial industry comprising investing institutions such as the mutual funds, pension funds, and insurance firms that tend to buy securities for money-management purposes. In contrast, sell-side players offer recommendations for upgrades, downgrades, target prices, and opinions to the investing public.
[‡] Amey Stone, "How banks pretty up the profit picture." *BusinessWeek*, February 21, 2005.

[§] Citigroup Inc. refers to loan losses as credit losses.
[¶] Luc Laeven and Giovanni Majnoni, "Loan loss provisioning and economic slowdowns: too much, too late?" *Journal of Financial Intermediation*, 12(2), (2002): pp. 178–197.

(Continued)

During 2004, the company released $2.004 billion of reserves, consisting of $900 million from [Global Corporate Investment Bank's (GCIB)] reserves and $1.104 billion from Global Consumer's reserves . . . At December 31, 2004, the Company's total allowance for loans, leases, and commitments was $11.869 billion.

During 2003, the Company released $508 million of reserves, consisting of $300 million in GCIB and $208 million in Global Consumer. At December 31, 2003, the Company's total allowance for loans, leases and commitments was $13.243 billion.

Management evaluates the adequacy of loan loss reserves by analyzing probable loss scenarios and economic and geopolitical factors that impact the portfolios . . .

The allowance for credit losses represents management's estimate of probable losses inherent in the lending portfolio. This evaluation process is subject to numerous estimates and judgments. The frequency of default, risk ratings, and the loss recovery rates, among other things, are considered in making this evaluation, as are the size and diversity of individual large credits. Changes in these estimates could have a direct impact on the credit costs in any quarter and could result in a change in the allowance.

At December 31, 2004 and 2003, respectively, the total allowance for credit losses, which includes reserves for unfunded lending commitments and letters of credit, totalled $3.490 billion and $4.155 billion for the Corporate loan portfolio and $8.379 billion and $9.088 billion for the Consumer loan portfolio. Attribution of the allowance is made for analytic purposes only, and the entire allowance of $11.869 billion and $13.243 billion at December 31, 2004 and 2003, respectively, is available to absorb probable credit losses inherent in the portfolio, including letters of credit and unfunded commitments . . . **

In an interview with CNBC, Citigroup CFO Todd Thomson explained how loan loss reserves were used:

We put up reserves for the bad loans we think we're going to have. If it turns out [that] we were wrong, [and] things [get] much better than we expected, then we don't need those reserves. And in fact, according to the accounting rules, we have to release those reserves . . . We have an extremely analytical process internally. We don't have that much judgment around it. We have to release the reserves as credit continues to get better.[††]

He then said:

I think credit quality is going to continue to be very good. All of our forward-looking indicators continue to tell us that on the consumer side and the corporate side we're going to have a very benign credit environment for the foreseeable future. So that's good news. What we're not going to see in the future is the massive improvement we've seen in credit quality, which allowed us to release these reserves. I don't anticipate that going forward we're going to be releasing reserves to this extent, unless I'm wrong and things get much better than they are today.[‡‡]

Conclusion

By now, Anne Yang felt more confident in her understanding of loan loss reserves accounting and was considering her possible investment in Citigroup. For 2004, Citigroup beat the analysts' consensus EPS estimates of $4.03 by a penny, coming in at $4.04. The company had reduced its loan loss reserves during the year citing improved credit quality. Ms Yang understood that the problem with decreasing the reserves was that as banks issued new loans, they would have to replenish the reserves. Furthermore, if credit conditions worsened, banks would have to set aside even a larger amount to cover bad debts, which would further negatively impact profits.[§§]

For Anne, it was now time to weigh whether Citigroup's accounting for loan loss was truly capturing the economic reality of the credit markets or whether it was a technique used by the bank to beat the analysts' earnings per share numbers. She wondered, was it prudent for Citigroup to reduce its allowance? After all, many people predicted that the US economy could suffer a recession in 2007 owing to falling housing prices due to Federal Reserve Bank tightening of interest rates. If that was to happen, what would be the impact on banks' performance and their loan loss reserves? Lastly, Anne was curious, had Citigroup maintained the same ratio of allowance for credit losses to loans in 2004, as it had in 2003, by how much would it have missed the consensus analysts' earnings estimates?

Required

a. Based on the financial statements for Citibank, describe the primary differences between the financial statements of banks and those of companies not in financial services.

b. Banks are said to be in the business of "borrowing short and lending long." What does that mean?

** Citigroup Inc. SEC 10-K Filing, February 28, 2005, US Securities and Exchanges Commission, <www.sec.gov> (7 March 2006).

†† "Citigroup (C) CFO Todd Thomson and Private Bank Chief Global Investment Strategist Clark Winter – Thomson and Winter report on C's earnings and discuss the banking industry and the global markets," 14 October 2004, CNBC DowJones website <www.cnbcdowjones.com.>

‡‡ Ibid.

§§ Amey Stone, "How banks pretty up the profit picture." *BusinessWeek*, 21 February 2005.

c. How can banks create the "cookie jar reserves" referred to in the case?

d. What are loan loss reserves? Using journal entries, show how the reserves are (a) set up, (b) used, (c) written-off, and (d) reversed/released.

e. Do you agree with the following statement: "In the banking sector, conservative accounting is good accounting." Why or why not?

Exhibit 8.4 Citigroup Inc. Consolidated Income Statement

CONSOLIDATED STATEMENT OF INCOME	Citigroup Inc. and Subsidiaries		
	Year ended December 31		
In millions of dollars, except per share amounts	2004	2003	2002
Revenues			
Loan interest, including fees	$43,981	$38,110	$37,903
Other interest and dividends	22,728	18,937	21,036
Insurance premiums	3,993	3,749	3,410
Commissions and fees	16,772	16,314	15,258
Principal transactions	3,756	5,120	4,513
Asset management and administration fees	6,845	5,665	5,146
Realized gains (losses) from sales of investments	831	510	(485)
Other revenue	9,370	6,308	5,775
Total revenues	108,276	94,713	92,556
Interest expense	22,086	17,271	21,248
Total revenues, net of interest expense	86,190	77,442	71,308
Benefits, claims, and credit losses			
Policyholder benefits and claims	3,801	3,895	3,478
Provision for credit losses	6,233	8,046	9,995
Total benefits, claims, and credit losses	10,034	11,941	13,473
Operating expenses			
Non insurance compensation and benefits	23,707	21,288	18,650
Net occupancy expense	4,847	4,280	4,005
Technology/communications expense	3,586	3,414	3,139
Insurance underwriting, acquisition, and operating	1,234	1,063	992
Restructuring-related items	(5)	(46)	(15)
Other operating expenses	18,605	9,169	10,527
Total operating expenses	51,974	39,168	37,298
Income from continuing operations before income taxes, minority interest, and cumulative effect of accounting change	24,182	26,333	20,537
Provision for income taxes	6,909	8,195	6,998
Minority interest, net of income taxes	227	285	91
	17,046	17,853	13,448
Income from continuing operations before cumulative effect of accounting change			
Discontinued operations			
Income from discontinued operations	—	—	965
Gain on sale of stock by subsidiary	—	—	1,270
Provision for income taxes	—	—	360
Income from discontinued operations, net	—	—	1,875
Cumulative effect of accounting change, net	—	—	(47)
Net income	$17,046	$17,853	$15,276

(Continued)

CONSOLIDATED STATEMENT OF INCOME

| | Citigroup Inc. and Subsidiaries | | |
| | Year ended December 31 | | |
In millions of dollars, except per share amounts	2004	2003	2002
Basic earnings per share			
Income from continuing operations	$3.32	$3.49	$2.63
Income from discontinued operations, net	—	—	0.37
Cumulative effect of accounting change, net	—	—	(0.01)
Net income	$3.32	$3.49	$2.99
Weighted average common shares outstanding	5,107.2	5,093.3	5,078.0
Diluted earnings per share			
Income from continuing operations	$3.26	$3.42	$2.59
Income from discontinued operations, net	—	—	0.36
Cumulative effect of accounting change, net	—	—	(0.01)
Net income	$3.26	$3.42	$2.94
Adjusted weighted average common shares outstanding	5,207.4	5,193.6	5,166.2

CONSOLIDATED BALANCE SHEET

| | Citigroup Inc. and Subsidiaries | |
| | December 31 | |
In millions of dollars	2004	2003
Assets		
Cash and due from banks (including segregated cash and other deposits)	$23,556	$21,149
Deposits at interest with banks	23,889	19,777
Federal funds sold and securities borrowed or purchased under agreements to resell	200,739	172,174
Brokerage receivables	39,273	26,476
Trading account assets (including $102,573 and $65,352 pledged to creditors at December 31, 2004, and December 31, 2003, respectively)	280,167	235,319
Investments (including $15,587 and $12,066 pledged to creditors at December 31, 2004, and December 31, 2003, respectively)	213,243	182,892
Loans, net of unearned income		
Consumer	435,226	379,932
Corporate	113,603	98,074
Loans, net of unearned income	548,829	478,006
Allowance for credit losses	(11,269)	(12,643)
Total loans, net	537,560	465,363
Goodwill	31,992	27,581
Intangible assets	15,271	13,881
Reinsurance recoverable	4,783	4,577
Separate and variable accounts	32,264	27,473
Other assets	81,364	67,370
Total assets	$1,484,101	$1,264,032
Liabilities		
Non interest-bearing deposits in U.S. offices	$31,533	$30,074
Interest-bearing deposits in U.S. offices	161,113	146,675
Non interest-bearing deposits in offices outside the United States.	28,379	22,940
Interest-bearing deposits in offices outside the United States.	341,056	274,326
Total deposits	562,081	474,015

CONSOLIDATED BALANCE SHEET

Citigroup Inc. and Subsidiaries

	December 31	
In millions of dollars	**2004**	**2003**
Federal funds purchased and securities loaned or sold under agreements to repurchase	209,555	181,156
Brokerage payables	50,208	37,330
Trading account liabilities	135,487	121,869
Contractholder funds and separate and variable accounts	68,801	58,402
Insurance policy and claims reserves	19,177	17,478
Investment banking and brokerage borrowings	25,799	22,442
Short-term borrowings	30,968	36,187
Long-term debt	207,910	162,702
Other liabilities	64,824	48,380
Citigroup or subsidiary-obligated mandatorily redeemable securities of subsidiary trusts holding solely junior subordinated debt securities of—Parent	—	5,217
—Subsidiary	—	840
Total liabilities	**1,374,810**	**1,166,018**
Stockholders' equity		
Preferred stock ($1.00 par value; authorized shares: 30 million), at aggregate liquidation value	1,125	1,125
Common stock ($.01 par value; authorized shares: 15 billion), issued shares: 2004—5,477,416,086 shares and 2003—5,477,416,254 shares	55	55
Additional paid-in capital	18,851	17,531
Retained earnings	102,154	93,483
Treasury stock, at cost: 2004—282,773,501 shares and 2003—320,466,849 shares	(10,644)	(11,524)
Accumulated other changes in equity from nonowner sources	(304)	(806)
Unearned compensation	(1,946)	(1,850)
Total stockholders' equity	**109,291**	**98,014**
Total liabilities and stockholders' equity	**$1,484,101**	**$1,264,032**

CONSOLIDATED STATEMENT OF CASH FLOWS

Citigroup Inc. and Subsidiaries

	Year ended December 31		
In millions of dollars	**2004**	**2003**	**2002**
Cash flows from operating activities of continuing operations			
Net income	$17,046	$17,853	$15,276
Income from discontinued operations, net of tax	—	—	717
Gain on sale of stock by subsidiary, net of tax	—	—	1,158
Cumulative effect of accounting changes	—	—	(47)
Income from continuing operations	17,046	17,853	13,448
Adjustments to reconcile net income to net cash (used in) provided by operating activities of continuing operations			
Amortization of deferred policy acquisition costs and present value of future profits	687	547	405
Additions to deferred policy acquisition costs	(1,303)	(976)	(865)
Depreciation and amortization	2,060	1,574	1,521
Deferred tax (benefit) provision	(983)	861	(204)
Provision for credit losses	6,233	8,046	9,995
Change in trading account assets	(43,071)	(80,111)	(10,625)
Change in trading account liabilities	13,110	30,443	10,883
Change in federal funds sold and securities borrowed or purchased under agreements to resell	(28,131)	(32,228)	(2,127)

(Continued)

CONSOLIDATED STATEMENT OF CASH FLOWS *Citigroup Inc. and Subsidiaries*

In millions of dollars	Year ended December 31		
	2004	2003	2002
Change in federal funds purchased and securities loaned or sold under agreements to repurchase	22,966	19,468	7,176
Change in brokerage receivables, net of brokerage payables	81	14,188	(1,070)
Change in insurance policy and claims reserves	1,699	1,128	3,272
Net (gains)/losses from sales of investments	(831)	(510)	485
Venture capital activity	(201)	134	577
Restructuring-related items	(5)	(46)	(15)
Other, net	8,239	4,775	(6,827)
Total adjustments	(19,450)	(32,707)	12,581
Net cash (used in) provided by operating activities of continuing operations	(2,404)	(14,854)	26,029
Cash flows from investing activities of continuing operations			
Change in deposits at interest with banks	(2,175)	(3,395)	2,935
Change in loans	(68,451)	(30,012)	(40,780)
Proceeds from sales of loans	15,121	18,553	17,005
Purchases of investments	(195,903)	(208,040)	(393,344)
Proceeds from sales of investments	112,470	127,277	280,234
Proceeds from maturities of investments	63,318	71,730	78,505
Other investments, primarily short-term, net	(29)	130	(531)
Capital expenditures on premises and equipment	(3,011)	(2,354)	(1,377)
Proceeds from sales of premises and equipment, subsidiaries and affiliates, and repossessed assets	3,106	1,260	2,184
Business acquisitions	(3,677)	(21,456)	(3,953)
Net cash used in investing activities of continuing operations	(79,231)	(46,307)	(59,122)
Cash flows from financing activities of continuing operations			
Dividends paid	(8,375)	(5,773)	(3,676)
Issuance of common stock	912	686	483
Issuance of mandatorily redeemable securities of parent trusts	—	1,600	—
Redemption of mandatorily redeemable securities of parent trusts	—	(700)	—
Redemption of mandatorily redeemable securities of subsidiary trusts	—	(625)	(400)
Redemption of preferred stock, net	—	(275)	(125)
Treasury stock acquired	(779)	(2,416)	(5,483)
Stock tendered for payment of withholding taxes	(511)	(499)	(475)
Issuance of long-term debt	75,764	67,054	39,520
Payments and redemptions of long-term debt	(49,686)	(45,800)	(47,169)
Change in deposits	65,818	42,136	30,554
Change in short-term borrowings and investment banking and brokerage borrowings	(4,363)	6,647	11,988
Contractholder fund deposits	11,797	8,346	8,548
Contractholder fund withdrawals	(7,266)	(5,976)	(5,815)
Net cash provided by financing activities of continuing operations	83,311	64,405	27,950
Effect of exchange rate changes on cash and cash equivalents	731	579	98
Discontinued operations			
Net cash used in discontinued operations	—	—	(237)
Proceeds from sale of stock by subsidiary	—	—	4,093
Change in cash and due from banks	2,407	3,823	(1,189)
Cash and due from banks at beginning of period	21,149	17,326	18,515

CONSOLIDATED STATEMENT OF CASH FLOWS	Citigroup Inc. and Subsidiaries		
	Year ended December 31		
In millions of dollars	2004	2003	2002
Cash and due from banks at end of period	$23,556	$21,149	$17,326
Supplemental disclosure of cash flow information for continuing operations			
Cash paid during the period for income taxes	$6,808	$6,113	$6,834
Cash paid during the period for interest	$18,544	$15,732	$20,226
Non cash investing activities			
Transfers to repossessed assets	$1,046	$1,077	$1,180

Citigroup Inc. SEC 10-K Filing, February 28, 2005, US Securities and Exchanges Commission <www.sec.gov> (March 7, 2006).

NOTES

1. "Performing" means that payments are made on time. "Nonperforming" loans are those that are, say, at least three months past due or impaired in some other way.

2. The loan loss provision might actually be negative in some years, thereby increasing pretax income. This can happen if the bank overprovisioned for loan losses in previous years.

3. More specially, "net" charge-offs. If previously written-off loans are repaid, the amounts are restored to the contra-asset. Therefore, the account is reduced by total charge-offs, net of recoveries.

9 Accounting for Inventory

Introduction

Retail, distribution, and manufacturing companies purchase or produce goods and then try to sell them for a profit. These goods are referred to as "inventory" and are classified as a current asset, often the largest current asset on a company's balance sheet. Both US GAAP and International Financial Reporting Standards (IFRS) define inventories as assets that are held for sale in the ordinary course of business, in the process of production or for sale in the form of materials, or supplies to be consumed in the production process or in rendering services. Thus, inventory can take any of the following physical forms: raw materials and supplies, work-in-process, or finished goods. Most companies report an aggregate sum for all inventories on the balance sheet, with a more detailed description of the physical state of inventory provided in the notes.

By contrast, Procter & Gamble Co. (P&G), a global giant in personal care, household cleaning and pharmaceutical products, discloses each class of inventory directly on its balance sheet – see Table 9.1. We chose P&G as an example because its balance sheet allows us to see how costs flow through the inventory accounts as the operating cycle of the business turns. Here's how the process unfolds.

Table 9.1 **Current Assets of Procter & Gamble (Amounts in Millions)**

	June 3	
	2016	**2015**
Current assets		
Cash and cash equivalents	$7,102	$6,836
Accounts receivable	4,373	4,568
Available-for sales securities	6,246	4,767
Inventories		
Materials and supplies	1,188	1,266
Work-in-process	563	525
Finished goods	2,965	3,188
Total inventories	4,716	4,979
Deferred income taxes	1,507	1,356
Prepaid expenses and other current assets	2,653	2,708
Current assets held for sale	7,185	4,432
Total current assets	33,782	29,646

P&G reports raw materials and supplies of $1,188 billion at the end of fiscal year 2016. As materials and supplies are purchased, the company records the following journal entry:

Raw materials and supplies	XX	
Cash or accounts payable		XX

These raw materials are then moved into a work-in-process account as the manufacturing process begins:

Work in process inventory	XX	
Raw materials and supplies		XX

After materials are introduced to the assembly line or shop floor, they are gradually converted into finished goods. This conversion process also requires labor and the use of other resources (e.g., maintenance, public utilities, depreciation on machines and equipment, etc.). These resources are commonly known as "manufacturing overhead." Because labor and manufacturing overhead are required for the conversion process, the costs of these factors of production are capitalized (i.e., included on the balance sheet). The capitalization occurs through the work-in-process account. The costs will stay there until the manufacturing process is complete.

P&G explains this process in the note shown in Box 9.1.

The entries to record these costs include

Work-in-process inventory	XX	
Accrued labor costs or cash		XX
To record the costs of direct and indirect manufacturing labor[1]		

Work-in-process inventory	XX	
Accumulated depreciation		XX
To record the depreciation of equipment, buildings, and machines		

Work-in-process inventory	XX	
Freight-in payable or cash		XX
To record inbound freight costs		

Similar entries would be required for any other conversion costs incurred by P&G. The debit is always to the work-in-process account. The balancing credit is made to cash, a short-term liability, or a contra-asset, depending on the nature of the cost.

As individual units of product are completed, the costs associated with those units are transferred out of work-in-process and into finished goods inventory:

Finished goods inventory	XX	
Work-in-process inventory		XX

BOX 9.1 P&G Cost of Products Sold

Cost of products sold is primarily comprised of direct materials and supplies consumed in the manufacture of product, as well as manufacturing labor, depreciation expense, and direct overhead expense necessary to acquire and convert the purchased materials and supplies into finished product. Cost of products sold also includes the cost to distribute products to customers, inbound freight costs, internal transfer costs, warehousing costs, and other shipping and handling activity.

The inventory then remains on the balance sheet, in the finished goods account, until it is sold. According to the P&G balance sheet, most of the company's inventory at the end of fiscal year 2016, $2,965 billion, was in the form of finished goods and is awaiting sale.

When inventory is finally sold, the cost flows out of finished goods inventory and into the income statement through an expense called cost of goods sold:

Cost of goods sold	XX	
Finished goods inventory		XX

As an American company, P&G reports under US GAAP. According to US GAAP, inventory is reported on the balance sheet at the lower of cost or net realizable value (NRV). NRV equals the proceeds from disposing of inventory, net of any selling or disposal costs. A similar requirement exists under IFRS, although there are slight differences between the two regimes in the definition of NRV. This rule means that if a company's inventory is deemed to be worth less than its cost, the appropriate inventory account (usually materials or finished goods) must be written down to NRV. The amount of the write-down is recognized as a loss on the income statement. The journal entry would look like this:

Loss on write-down of inventory	XX	
Inventory		XX

If the company suffers a significant write-down of inventory during the year, you should expect to see some disclosure of it in the financial statement notes.

P&G's income statements for the years 2014–2016 are shown in Table 9.2. Cost of goods sold appears on the line immediately below revenues. This information reveals that in 2016 P&G earned $65.3 billion in revenues (net sales) and incurred $32.9 billion in cost of goods sold. This latter figure implies that the units of inventory sold in 2016 cost P&G $32.9 billion to produce, although several assumptions were required to calculate it. Some companies subtract cost of goods sold from revenues to show a gross profit or gross margin. P&G prefers to report operating income as the first profit figure on its income statement.

Table 9.2   Procter & Gamble's Income Statement for 2014–2016 (Amounts in Millions Except per Share Amounts)

	Years ended June 30		
	2016	**2015**	**2014**
Net sales	$65,299	$70,749	$74,401
Cost of goods sold	32,909	37,056	39,030
Selling, general, and administrative expense	18,949	20,616	21,461
Venezuela deconsolidation charge		2,028	
Operating income	13,441	11,049	13,910
Interest expense	579	626	709
Interest income	182	149	99
Other non-operating income, net	325	440	209
Earnings before income taxes	13,369	11,012	13,509
Provision for income taxes	3,342	2,725	2,851
Net earnings	$10,027	$8,287	$10,658

Inventory Valuation: LIFO, FIFO, and the Rest

As noted above, P&G reported $32.9 billion in cost of goods sold in 2016. The balance sheet, shown earlier, reported inventory of about $4.7 billion at the end of 2016. Most of this inventory, $2.965 billion, was in the form of finished goods. The challenge for P&G, given that so many millions of units of product flow through the company's manufacturing facilities each year, is to know how much cost should be assigned to each unit of product. Without such knowledge, the company cannot determine how much of its manufacturing costs for 2016 belong in cost of goods sold (i.e., the income statement) and how much in inventory (i.e., the balance sheet).

The problem arises because the costs incurred by P&G to produce inventory change constantly over the course of the year. In other words, from one day to the next, the costs of producing the same product can change. If different units of inventory, even for the same products, have different costs, how do we know which costs relate to units sold and which relate to units still in inventory? Answering this question is the essence of the inventory accounting problem.

One possible approach is a technique known as "specific identification." Here, a specific cost is attached to each individual unit. As a unit is sold, its cost enters cost of goods sold and is removed from the inventory account.[2] This method is allowed and sometimes used, but tends to be practical only in companies that sell a small number of items with very high unit costs. For example, an automobile dealer might use it. But for most other companies, such as P&G, specific identification is slow, cumbersome, and costly. Even bar coding and other computer-tracking systems fail to address all of these practical concerns. Also, specific identification creates an avenue for profit manipulation. If a company wants to boost earnings in any given year, it can simply choose to sell those units of product with the lowest unit costs.

Consequently, the overwhelming majority of retail, distribution, and manufacturing companies throughout the world account for inventory by making a cost-flow assumption. These assumptions allow the company to take a large number of interchangeable units of product, and determine which unit costs will be assigned to cost of goods sold and which to inventory. These assumptions include first-in-first-out (FIFO), last-in-first-out (LIFO), and average cost.

Before describing each of these alternatives in detail, we should first note that over the entire life of a company, cost of goods sold will be the same regardless of the cost-flow assumption employed. Over the life of a business, all the units of inventory will be sold or disposed of in some way. Consequently, all costs associated with inventory will be expensed. The choice of a cost-flow assumption affects only the allocation of inventory costs to particular accounting periods.

Simply put, the choice of inventory valuation method affects the amounts a company reports on its balance sheet for inventory and on its income statement for cost of goods sold (and, consequently, net income). Thus, in order to evaluate a company's financial position and performance, particularly in comparison with other companies, investors and creditors need to know which cost-flow assumption the company is using.

As shown in Box 9.2, P&G uses FIFO.

BOX 9.2   P&G's Note on its Inventory Valuation Method

Inventory Valuation

Inventories are valued at the lower of cost or market value. Product-related inventories are primarily maintained on the first-in, first-out method. Minor amounts of product inventories, including certain cosmetics and commodities, are maintained on the last-in, first-out method. The cost of spare part inventories is maintained using the average cost method.

On a global scale, FIFO is the most common method, because it is relatively easy to implement, and it offers a certain intuitive appeal (in most companies, the first units acquired or produced, are the first units sold).

The Lower of Cost or Net Realizable Value Rule

After inventories have been manufactured or acquired, their net realizable value (i.e., market price net of any selling costs) value will increase or decrease. The conservatism principle prevents the recognition of any increases until the item of inventory has been sold. However, if net realizable value declines below acquisition cost, a common occurrence for goods that carry high obsolescence risk, the inventory is judged to be impaired and must be written down. For example, if Galeries Lafayette, a large Paris-based retailer, has inventory costing €50,000 with a market value of only €20,000, the following entry would be required:

Unrealized holding loss on inventory	30,000	
Inventory		30,000

The loss would be reported in the period's income statement. If the market value of the inventory partly recovers before sale to, say, €34,000, the company makes the following entry:

Inventory	14,000	
Unrealized holding gain on inventory		14,000

The unrealized holding gain can be recognized up to the amount of the original write-off. For example, if market value increases to €55,000, higher than the acquisition cost, the gain is limited to €30,000.[3]

The Cost-flow Assumptions: An Example

To illustrate the differences among the three principal cost-flow assumptions, we draw on the example of Waller & Gamble, a retailer of toothpaste.

The inventory balance at the beginning of the year was $15,000 (15,000 units @ $1). Additional units were purchased during the year as shown in Table 9.3.

The inventory count at year-end indicates that 11,000 units were still on hand. Sales and expenses (excluding cost of goods sold) totaled $55,000 and $15,000, respectively. The rate of income tax is 30%.

To begin, let's consider the total costs that will eventually flow to the income statement from the purchase and sale of inventory. The cost of beginning inventory is $15,000. The cost of goods purchased during the year equals $32,500. Therefore, the *cost of goods available for sale* equals

Table 9.3 **Inventory Purchases for Waller & Gamble**

	Items purchased	Cost per item	Total cost
March 15	6,000	$1.30	$7,800
July 30	9,000	1.50	13,500
December 17	7,000	1.60	11,200
Total	22,000		$32,500

$47,500. The number of units available for sale equals 15,000 (from beginning inventory), plus 22,000 (purchases during the year), or 37,000.

The major task before us now is to determine how much of the $47,500 will be assigned to cost of goods sold and how much will be kept in the inventory account. We will now look at the following in more detail:

- FIFO

- LIFO

- average cost.

First in First Out or Last in Still Here

The FIFO method is based on the assumption that the units sold are the oldest units on hand. Therefore, the cost of the inventory still on hand is assumed to be the units acquired or produced most recently (last in, still here, or LISH).

Under FIFO, the ending inventory for Waller & Gamble is based on the 11,000 units acquired most recently:

$$\text{Ending Inventory} = (7,000 \text{ units} \times \$1.60) + (4,000 \text{ units} \times \$1.50) = \$17,200$$

We now assume that whatever is no longer in inventory must have been sold. Thus,

$$\text{Cost of Goods Sold} = \text{Cost of Goods Available for Sale} - \text{Ending Inventory}$$

which equals $47,500 − $17,200, or $30,300.

Cost of goods sold could also be calculated by focusing on the 26,000 units sold:

$$(15,000 \text{ units} \times \$1.00) + (6,000 \text{ units} \times \$1.30) + (5,000 \text{ units} \times \$1.50), \text{ or } \$30,300$$

It should be noted that this example assumes any units not found in inventory at the end of the year were sold. In other words, if 37,000 units were available for sale, and 11,000 are in ending inventory, 26,000 units must have been sold. The problem with this assumption is that it assumes no "inventory shrinkage." Shrinkage occurs whenever inventory declines for reasons other than a sale. For example, inventory might be lost, broken, or stolen. Therefore, actual sales may have been less than 26,000 units. But even if some units disappeared because of inventory shrinkage, the costs of those units were incurred and must be expensed. The normal practice is to recognize these expenses through cost of goods sold. Put another way, even if there is shrinkage, when calculating cost of goods sold we can still assume that 26,000 units were sold.

Last in First Out or First in Still Here

The LIFO method is based on the assumption that the newest units acquired or produced are the first units sold. The inventory still on hand is costed on the assumption that it was acquired in previous periods. In effect, inventory under LIFO is assumed to be first in still here, or FISH.

For Waller & Gamble, ending inventory under LIFO consists entirely of units already on hand at the beginning of the year, (11,000 units × $1.00), or $11,000.

$$\text{Cost of Goods Sold} = \text{Cost of Goods Available for Sale} - \text{Ending Inventory}$$
$$= \$47,500 - \$11,000, \text{ or } \$36,500.$$

Cost of goods sold under LIFO can also be calculated from the costs of inventory of the units acquired most recently:

$$(7,000 \text{ units @ } \$1.60) + (9,000 \text{ units @ } \$1.50) + (6,000 \text{ units @ } \$1.30)$$
$$+ (4,000 \text{ units @ } \$1.00), \text{ or } \$36,500.$$

In the United States, companies that use LIFO for tax must also use it for financial reporting. This requirement is known as the "LIFO conformity rule." Although most American companies do not use LIFO, it does offer one important advantage to those that do. At times of increasing prices, LIFO can lower a company's tax burden because it matches the most recent prices paid (which are higher than earlier prices) against revenues in calculating taxable income. A further advantage of LIFO is that because the most recent costs are subtracted from current revenues, it can result in a better matching of revenues and expenses. However, few companies choose LIFO for this reason. The use of LIFO is driven almost entirely by tax considerations.

Because LIFO does a poor job of tracking the actual physical flow of inventory in most companies,[4] and because governments are usually loath to provide a tax benefit that contributes little or nothing to productivity or job growth, LIFO is explicitly banned in most countries, and also is banned under IFRS. Apart from the United States, no country allows LIFO for tax purposes. Even the US has considered legislation to eliminate the practice, although powerful interests have made it clear that they will vigorously oppose any changes to LIFO rules. That said, there are plenty of non-US firms that use LIFO accounting, but only for their US-based operations.

For those companies that use LIFO for financial reporting purposes, a "LIFO reserve" must be disclosed in the notes to the financial statements. This reserve measures the difference between the inventory balance under LIFO and what it would be under FIFO. Therefore,

LIFO Inventory + LIFO Reserve = FIFO Inventory

This disclosure is important because it allows the financial-statement reader to convert a LIFO company's accounts into a FIFO equivalent, thus facilitating comparison between companies that use different inventory methods. Also, changes in the reserve can be used to adjust cost of goods sold. For example, if the reserve increases, the implication is that cost of goods sold in that year was higher under LIFO. Subtracting the change in the reserve can convert a LIFO-based cost of goods sold into its FIFO equivalent.

LIFO presents two fundamental problems for companies that use it:

- First, it is more complicated, and therefore more costly to administer, than other cost-flow assumptions.

- Second, LIFO gives rise to a "LIFO layer problem."

In any year in which inventory grows (i.e., the number of units acquired or produced exceeds the number sold), a layer of inventory from that year remains in the inventory account. To illustrate, imagine a company that increases its inventory for 10 consecutive years. For each of those 10 years, a LIFO layer of inventory costs is left behind. As long as inventory grows, or at least remains constant, these layers present no real problem for the company or the financial statement reader. But if inventory costs have been steadily increasing over this 10-year period, a problem emerges when the company starts to reduce inventory levels. When inventory levels are reduced, the company is forced to dig into LIFO layers from previous years. The result: current selling prices are matched with older inventory costs.

The LIFO liquidation process begins with the layer created in the previous year, then goes on to the layer created in the year before that, and so on. At some point, especially if the company undergoes a major restructuring effort and liquidates the entire inventory, it could be forced to match very old costs against current revenues. Artificially high profits then result and, unfortunately for the reporting entity, so too does a large tax bill.

The LIFO liquidation problem helps to explain why LIFO systems are more costly to administer than those of the other inventory methods. Tax authorities require companies to maintain meticulous records on each layer for every product or material accounted for under LIFO, which typically demands additional software and personnel support. This fact implies that the expected tax savings need to be substantial; otherwise, LIFO is not worth the effort.

Average Cost

This method calculates cost of goods sold as an average of the cost to purchase or manufacture all of the inventories available for sale during the year. The first step is to compute the average cost per unit:

Cost per Unit = Cost of Goods Available for Sale ÷ Number of Units Available for Sale

For Waller & Gamble, the average cost per unit equals $47,500 ÷ 37,000 units, or $1.284. Ending inventory therefore equals the number of units in ending inventory, 11,000, multiplied by the average cost of $1.284 per unit, or $14,124.

Cost of Goods Sold equals Cost of Goods Available for Sale, minus Ending Inventory,

$47,500 − $14,124, or $33,376

Alternatively, cost of goods sold (COGS) can be calculated from the product of the number of units sold, 26,000, and the unit cost, $1.284, or $33,376.

Inventory Cost-flow Assumptions: A Summary

As the above example demonstrates, the choice of inventory method can have a significant impact on the income statement and balance sheet. For Waller & Gamble, the figures are summarized as shown in Table 9.4.

Table 9.4 **Waller & Gamble's Income Statement and Balance Sheet**

Income statement	FIFO	LIFO	Average
Revenues	$55,000	$55,000	$55,000
Cost of goods sold	30,300	36,500	33,376
Expenses	15,000	15,000	15,000
Earnings before taxes	9,700	3,500	6,624
Taxes @ 30%	2,910	1,050	1,987
Net income	6,790	2,450	4,637
Balance sheet	**LISH**	**FISH**	**Average**
Beginning inventory	$15,000	$15,000	$15,000
Ending inventory	17,200	11,000	14,124

Notice that net income is far higher under FIFO than under LIFO, with average cost somewhere in between. In a period of rising prices for inventory, these differences are expected. Eventually the differences between profits under FIFO and LIFO will reverse, with the liquidation of low-cost LIFO layers.

KEY LESSONS FROM THE CHAPTER

- Retail, distribution, and manufacturing companies purchase or produce goods and try to sell them for a profit. These goods are referred to as "inventory" and are classified as current assets.

- For manufacturing companies, inventory goes through three stages: raw material, work-in-process, and finished goods.

- Inventory is carried on the balance sheet at the lower of cost or net realizable value.

- The most direct approach to costing inventory is the specific identification method. However, most companies find it impractical. Instead, they make a cost-flow assumption.

- In the absence of specific identification, cost-flow assumptions allow a company to decide which unit costs will be assigned to cost of goods sold and to inventory. These assumptions include FIFO, LIFO, and average cost.

- Any company that uses LIFO for financial reporting purposes is required to disclose a "LIFO reserve" in the notes to the financial statements. This reserve measures the difference between the inventory balance under LIFO and what it would be under FIFO.

- LIFO presents two fundamental problems for companies that use it: first, it is more complicated, and therefore more costly to administer, than other cost-flow assumptions. Second, LIFO gives rise to a "LIFO layer problem."

- Partly because of the LIFO layer problem, LIFO is not permitted under IFRS. Essentially, LIFO has become a US-only phenomenon. However, non-US companies can use LIFO for their US-based subsidiaries, and sometimes do.

- The choice of inventory method can have a significant impact on the income statement and balance sheet, especially if input prices (e.g., for raw materials) are trending up or down. When input prices are stable, the choice of cost-flow assumption has little effect on the financial statements.

KEY TERMS AND CONCEPTS FROM THE CHAPTER

Work-in-process	Lower of cost or net realizable	First in first out (FIFO)	LIFO reserve
Finished goods	value	Last in first out (LIFO)	Liquidation of LIFO
inventory	Specific identification	Average cost method	layers

QUESTIONS

1. How would the inventory accounts in a retailer or distribution business differ from those in a manufacturing company?

2. Which cost-flow assumption is most common, and why?

3. Why is the LIFO cost-flow assumption not allowed under IFRS?

4. What are the advantages of LIFO accounting?

5. What are the disadvantages of LIFO accounting?

6. Can you think of why rapid economic growth and expanding industrial power in China has resulted in LIFO accounting becoming more attractive (in the few countries that allow it, of course)?

7. True or false: Inventory accounting should follow from the actual physical flow of the inventory.

8. What is the meaning of "lower of cost or market" and how does it apply to inventory accounting? What is the logic behind this rule?

9. How can a company create hidden reserves from inventory accounts?

10. What is the difference between a perpetual and a periodic inventory system? Which system would you expect a large supermarket chain or discount retailer to use, and why?

11. What is a major advantage and disadvantage of the specific identification method?

12. Do you expect the use of specific identification accounting to become more common or less common in the future? Why?

13. True or false: Inventory cost-flow assumptions don't matter much in periods of stable prices.

PROBLEMS

9.1 Calculating Inventory Under the FIFO and Average-cost Methods

Enterprise Renaud, a distributor of ski equipment, sells a snowboard known as the RemyGlide. Information relating to Renaud's purchases of RemyGlide snowboards during October is shown below. During the same month, 242 RemyGlide snowboards were sold. Renaud uses a periodic inventory system.

Date	Transaction	Units	Unit cost	Total cost
1 Oct	Inventory	52	€194	€10,088
10 Oct	Purchase	90	204	18,360
18 Oct	Purchase	40	208	8,320
25 Oct	Purchase	100	210	21,000
Totals		282		€57,768

Required

a. Compute the ending inventory at October 31 and the cost of goods sold for the month of October using the FIFO and average cost methods.

b. For both FIFO and average cost, calculate the sum of ending inventory and cost of goods sold. What do you notice about the answers you found for each method?

9.2 Inventories and Ratio Analysis

The following information is available for Romaine Corporation, a wholesaler, for 2010, 2011, and 2012:

	2010	2011	2012
Beginning inventory	€ 50,000	€ 150,000	€ 200,000
Ending inventory	150,000	200,000	240,000
Cost of goods sold	450,000	560,000	650,000
Sales	600,000	800,000	950,000

Required

Calculate inventory turnover, the inventory period, and the gross profit percentage for Romaine Corporation for each of the three years. Comment on any trends.

9.3 Correcting Inventory Errors

An internal audit at Parker Corporation discovered the following inventory valuation errors:

- The 2010 year-end inventory was overstated by $34 000.

- The 2011 year-end inventory was understated by $70 000.

- The 2012 year-end inventory was understated by $23 000.

The reported income before tax for Parker was:

2010	$142,000
2011	$273,000
2012	$170,000

Required

Determine what income before taxes for 2010, 2011, and 2012 should have been after correcting for the errors.

9.4 The Lower of Cost or Net Realizable Value Rule

Segal Company, a retailer of Nokia mobile phones, uses FIFO for costing its inventory. A physical count of inventory at the end of the year revealed the following:

Model 3720	60 units at a per unit cost of €90
Model 6700	150 units at a per unit cost of €85
Model 6303	100 units at a per unit cost of €75

The net realizable value per unit at year-end was €72, €130, and €105 for the Models 3720, 6700, and 6303, respectively.

Required

Determine the amount of ending inventory that should appear on the balance sheet.

9.5 Calculating Cost of Goods Sold Under FIFO and Specific Identification

It is December 10 and Fraser Home Goods has four high-end microwave ovens in stock. All are identical, and each is priced at £200. The four ovens were purchased on different dates and at different cost: Oven #1 was purchased on June 15 at a cost of £80; oven #2 on 3 August for £75; oven #3 on September 5 for £70; and oven #4 on 2 October for £65.

Required

a. Calculate the cost of goods sold using FIFO, assuming that three of the four ovens were sold before the end of the year.

b. If Fraser uses the specific identification method instead, how could it maximize earnings from the sale of the three ovens? How could it minimize earnings?

c. Which of these two methods is better, and why?

Case Study

9-1 LIFO Accounting at Tamar Chemicals

Purchasing Policy Under LIFO

Tamar Chemicals sells chemical compounds made from a material known as Rtu330. The company has used LIFO as its inventory cost-flow assumption since it was founded 25 years ago.

The inventory of Rtu330 on December 31, 2017 comprised 4,000 kg, costing $161,200. Most of the cost comes from inventory acquired in previous years, as shown in the following table:

Year acquired	Purchase price per kg	2017 Year-end inventory	
		kg	Cost
2008	$30	2,000	$60,000
2013	46	200	9,200
2014	48	400	19,200
2017	52	1,400	72,800
		4,000	$161,200

Rtu330 cost $62 per kg throughout most of 2018. It is now late 2018, and prices are not expected to change before the end of the year. But Tamar's purchasing agent expects the price to fall back to $57 early in 2019. Sales for 2018 require 7000 kg of Rtu330. Current policy is to maintain a stock of 4000 kg. Because of the pending price drop, the purchasing agent suggests that the company should decrease inventory to 600 kg by the end of 2018 and replenish it to the desired level of 4,000 kg early next year.

The chief accountant disagrees. If inventory falls to 600 kg at the end of 2018, the consumption of old, low-cost LIFO layers will cause cost of goods sold to be unusually low. As a result, the company will face a high income tax liability. The chief accountant suggests that Tamar plan 2018 purchases to maintain an end-of-year inventory of 4,000 kg.

Required

1. Assuming that sales for 2018 require 7,000 kg of Rtu330, calculate the cost of goods sold and the end-of-year inventory for 2018 if Tamar Chemicals follows the advice of the chief accountant.

2. Recalculate cost of goods sold and the end-of-year inventory if the company follows the purchasing agent's advice.

3. The CEO wants to know what discretion the company has to vary income in 2018 by planning its purchases of Rtu330. If the firm follows the chief accountant's policy, net income for 2018 will be $60,000. What is the range of net income that the company can report by managing purchases of Rtu330? Assume a tax rate of 30%.

Case Study

9-2 Deere and CNH Global: Performance Effects of Inventory Accounting Choice

Deere and CNH Global compete against each other as manufacturers in the global market for agricultural and construction equipment. Both companies operate finance subsidiaries in order to extend credit to their dealer networks and end-customers. Deere is the larger of the two companies (1.6X greater in sales, 1.4X in assets, and 1.9X in employees). CNH is headquartered in the Netherlands, but like Deere it follows US GAAP and is traded on the New York Stock Exchange.

Despite the obvious similarities between the two companies, they have chosen different cost-flow assumptions for inventory, as revealed in the disclosures shown below.

Required

a. What is CNH's policy regarding inventory valuation and cost-flow assumptions?

b. What is the balance in CNH's inventory account at the end of 2010, both in dollars and as a percentage of total assets?

c. What is Deere's policy regarding inventory valuation and cost-flow assumptions?

d. What is the balance in Deere's inventory account at the end of 2010, both in dollars and as a percentage of total assets?

e. What would the year-end inventory amounts be for Deere if they used the FIFO cost assumption for 100% of its inventories?

f. Calculate inventory turnover for CNH.

g. Calculate inventory turnover for Deere using the financial data as reported.

h. Calculate inventory turnover for Deere, *assuming that it used FIFO on 100% of its inventories.*

i. Review the figures above. How does Deere compare to CNH on this measure when you use the data as originally reported? How do they compare when you recast Deere's financial data on the basis of FIFO?

Excerpts from Deere's financial statements

DEERE & COMPANY

STATEMENT OF CONSOLIDATED INCOME

For the Years Ended October 31, 2010, 2009, and 2008

(In millions of dollars and shares except per share amounts)

	2010	2009	2008
Net sales and revenues			
Net sales	$23,573.2	$20,756.1	$25,803.5
Finance and interest income	1,825.3	1,842.1	2,068.4
Other income	606.1	514.2	565.7
Total	26,004.6	23,112.4	28,437.6
Costs and expenses			
Cost of sales	17,398.8	16,255.2	19,574.8
Research and development expenses	1,052.4	977.0	943.1
Selling, administrative, and general expenses	2,968.7	2,780.6	2,960.2
Interest expense	811.4	1,042.4	1,137.0
Other operating expenses	748.1	718.0	697.8
Total	22,979.4	21,773.2	25,312.9
Income of consolidated group before income taxes	3,025.2	1,339.2	3,124.7
Provision for income taxes	1,161.6	460.0	1,111.2
Income of consolidated group	1,863.6	879.2	2,013.5
Equity in income (loss) of unconsolidated affiliates	10.7	(6.3)	40.2
Net income	1,874.3	872.9	2,053.7
Less: Net income (loss) attributable to noncontrolling interests	9.3	(.6)	.9
Net income attributable to Deere & Company	$1,865.0	$873.5	$2,052.8
Per share data			
Basic	$4.40	$2.07	$4.76
Diluted	$4.35	$2.06	$4.70
Dividends declared	$1.16	$1.12	$1.06
Average shares outstanding			
Basic	424.0	422.8	431.1
Diluted	428.6	424.4	436.3

The notes to consolidated financial statements are an integral part of this statement.

(Continued)

DEERE & COMPANY
CONSOLIDATED BALANCE SHEET
As of October 31, 2010 and 2009
(In millions of dollars except per share amounts)

	2010	2009
Assets		
Cash and cash equivalents	$3,790.6	$4,651.7
Marketable securities	227.9	192.0
Receivables from unconsolidated affiliates	38.8	38.4
Trade accounts and notes receivable – net	3,464.2	2,616.9
Financing receivables – net	17,682.2	15,254.7
Restricted financing receivables – net	2,238.3	3,108.4
Other receivables	925.6	864.5
Equipment on operating leases – net	1,936.2	1,733.3
Inventories	3,063.0	2,397.3
Property and equipment – net	3,790.7	4,532.2
Investments in unconsolidated affiliates	244.5	212.8
Goodwill	998.6	1,036.5
Other intangible assets – net	117.0	136.3
Retirement benefits	146.7	94.4
Deferred income taxes	2,477.1	2,804.8
Other assets	1,194.0	1,458.4
Assets held for sale	931.4	
Total assets	$43,266.8	$41,132.6
Liabilities and stockholders' equity		
Liabilities		
Short-term borrowings	$7,534.5	$7,158.9
Payables to unconsolidated affiliates	203.5	55.0
Accounts payable and accrued expenses	6,481.7	5,371.4
Deferred income taxes	144.3	167.3
Long-term borrowings	16,814.5	17,391.7
Retirement benefits and other liabilities	5,784.9	6,165.5
Total liabilities	36,963.4	36,309.8
Commitments and contingencies (Note 22)		
Stockholders' equity		
Common stock, $1 par value (authorized – 1,200,000,000 shares; issued – 536,431,204 shares in 2010 and 2009), at paid-in amount	3,106.3	2,996.2
Common stock in treasury, 114,250,815 shares in 2010 and 113,188,823 shares in 2009, at cost	(5,789.5)	(5,564.7)
Retained earnings	12,353.1	10,980.5

	2010	2009
Accumulated other comprehensive income (loss):		
Retirement benefits adjustment..........................	(3,797.0)	(3,955.0)
Cumulative translation adjustment.......................	436.0	400.2
Unrealized loss on derivatives..........................	(29.2)	(44.1)
Unrealized gain on investments.........................	10.6	5.6
Accumulated other comprehensive income (loss)............	(3,379.6)	(3,593.3)
Total Deere & Company stockholders' equity...............	6,290.3	4,818.7
Noncontrolling interests...............................	13.1	4.1
Total stockholders' equity.............................	6,303.4	4,822.8
Total liabilities and stockholders' equity	$43,266.8	$41,132.6

The notes to consolidated financial statements are an integral part of this statement.

15. Inventories

Most inventories owned by Deere & Company and its U.S. equipment subsidiaries are valued at cost, on the "last-in, first-out" (LIFO) basis. Remaining inventories are generally valued at the lower of cost, on the "first-in, first-out" (FIFO) basis, or market. The value of gross inventories on the LIFO basis represented 59% of worldwide gross inventories at FIFO value on October 31, 2010 and 2009. The pretax favorable income effect from the liquidation of LIFO inventory during 2009 was approximately $37 million. If all inventories had been valued on a FIFO basis, estimated inventories by major classification at October 31 in millions of dollars would have been as follows:

	2010	2009
Raw materials and supplies	$1,201	$940
Work-in-process..	483	387
Finished goods and parts	2,777	2,437
Total FIFO value	4,461	3,764
Less adjustment to LIFO value.............................	1,398	1,367
Inventories..	$3,063	$2,397

Excerpts from CNH'S financial statements: CNH Global N.V. Consolidated statements of operations for the years ended December 31, 2010, 2009, and 2008

	Consolidated		
	2010	2009	2008
	(in millions, except per share data)		
Revenues			
Net sales	$14,474	$12,783	$17,366
Finance and interest income	1,134	977	1,110
	15,608	13,760	18,476
Costs and expenses			
Cost of goods sold	11,891	10,862	14,054
Selling, general and administrative	1,698	1,486	1,698

(Continued)

| | Consolidated | | |
	2010	2009	2008
	(in millions, except per share data)		
Research, development, and engineering	451	398	422
Restructuring	16	102	39
Interest expense – Fiat subsidiaries	112	189	308
Interest expense – other	718	482	457
Other, net	306	334	342
	15,192	13,853	17,320
Income (loss) before income taxes and equity in income (loss) of unconsolidated subsidiaries and affiliates	416	(93)	1156
Income tax provision	77	92	385
Equity in income (loss) of unconsolidated subsidiaries and affiliates:			
Financial services	11	9	13
Equipment operations	88	(46)	40
Net income (loss)	438	(222)	824
Net loss attributable to noncontrolling interests	(14)	(32)	(1)
Net income (loss) attributable to CNH Global N.V.	$452	$(190)	$825
Earnings (loss) per share attributable to CNH Global N.V. common shareholders			
Basic	$1.90	$(0.80)	$3.48
Diluted	$1.89	$(0.80)	$3.47

CNH Global N.V. Consolidated balance sheets as of December 31, 2010 and 2009

| | Consolidated | |
	2010	2009
	(in millions, except share data)	
Assets		
Current assets		
Cash and cash equivalents	$3,618	$1,263
Restricted cash	914	128
Deposits in Fiat subsidiaries' cash management pools	1,760	2,251
Accounts and notes receivable, net	8,621	5,190
Inventories, net	2,937	3,297
Deferred income taxes	633	517
Prepayments and other	822	462
Total current assets	19,305	13,108

	Consolidated	
	2010	**2009**
	(in millions, except share data)	
Long-term receivables	5,407	3,236
Property, plant and equipment, net	1,786	1,764
Investments in unconsolidated subsidiaries and affiliates	490	415
Equipment on operating leases, net	622	646
Goodwill	2,385	2,374
Other intangible assets, net	679	717
Other assets	915	948
Total	$31,589	$23,208
Liabilities and equity		
Current liabilities		
Current maturities of long-term debt – Fiat subsidiaries	$253	$836
Current maturities of long-term debt – other	3,641	1,550
Short-term debt – Fiat subsidiaries	194	537
Short-term debt – other	3,669	1,435
Accounts payable	2,367	1,915
Other accrued liabilities	3,345	2,678
Total current liabilities	13,469	8,951
Long-term debt – Fiat subsidiaries	331	1,516
Long-term debt – other	8,209	3,534
Pension, postretirement, and other postemployment benefits	1,770	1,871
Other liabilities	426	526
Redeemable noncontrolling interest	4	—
Equity		
Common shares, €2.25 par value; authorized 400,000,000 shares in 2010 and 2009, issued 238,588,630 shares in 2010, 237,553,331 shares in 2009	599	595
Paid-in capital	6,198	6,188
Treasury stock, 154,813 shares in 2010 and 2009, at cost	(8)	(8)
Retained earnings	658	210
Accumulated other comprehensive loss	(142)	(267)
Noncontrolling interests	75	92
Total equity	7,380	6,810
Total	$31,589	$23,208

Inventories
Inventories are stated at the lower of cost or net realizable value. Cost is determined by the first-in, first-out method.
The cost of finished goods and work-in-progress includes the cost of raw materials, other direct costs, and production overheads. Net realizable value is the estimate of the selling price in the ordinary course of business, less the cost of completion and selling. Provisions are made for obsolete and slow-moving inventories.

NOTES

1. For P&G, indirect labor refers to any personnel in a factory setting who are not directly involved in producing the company's products. Examples include maintenance, security, engineering, accounting, and computer services staff.

2. When a firm records the cost of goods sold each time an inventory item is sold, it uses a "perpetual" inventory system. In this chapter, however, we assume the use of a "periodic" inventory system. Here, a firm determines the cost of goods sold at the end of each period by taking a physical inventory; any units acquired that are not in ending inventory are assumed to have been sold.

3. US GAAP does not allow for any recovery from written-off inventory. If market value increases subsequent to a write-off, the company must wait until the inventory is sold before recognizing a gain.

4. An obvious exception would be a business where inventory is stored in piles, with the items on top sold first.

Accounting for Property, Plant, and Equipment

10

Introduction

Property, plant, and equipment (PP&E) is defined as tangible assets that are held for use in the production or supply of goods or services, for rental to others, or for administrative purposes. They are expected to be used for more than one year. In this chapter, we look at the accounting for PP&E by examining the financials of McDonald's Corporation. The following discussion applies to both US GAAP and IFRS, unless otherwise noted. This chapter also discusses intangible assets.

PP&E is usually reported on the balance sheet at historical cost (in the case of land) or at historical cost less accumulated depreciation (for depreciable assets such as buildings and machinery). At the end of 2016, McDonald's reported PP&E with an historical cost of $34.4 billion and $13.2 billion of accumulated depreciation – see Table 10.1. The resulting net book value, $21.2 billion, represents 68.5% of total assets. Such a high figure is common in capital intensive businesses such as McDonald's.

Table 10.1   McDonald's Corporation – Assets (in Millions, US$)

	2016/12/31	2015/12/31
Current assets		
Cash and equivalents	$1,223.4	$7.685.5
Accounts and notes receivable	1,474.1	1,298.7
Inventories, at cost, not in excess of market	58.9	100.1
Prepaid expenses and other current assets	565.2	558.7
Assets of businesses held for sale	1,527.0	—
Total current assets	4,848.6	9,643.0
Other assets		
Investments in and advances to affiliates	725.9	792.7
Goodwill	2,336.5	2,516.3
Miscellaneous	1,855.3	1,869.1
Total other assets	4,917.7	5,178.1
Property and equipment		
Property and equipment, at cost	34,443.4	37,692.4
Accumulated depreciation and amortization	(13,185.8)	(14,574.8)
Net property and equipment	21,257.6	23,117.6
Total assets	$31,023.9	$37,938.7

Table 10.2   **Disclosure from McDonald's Notes Regarding Breakdown of PP&E (in Millions, US$)**

	2016/12/31	2015/12/31
Land	$5,465.0	$5,582.5
Buildings and improvements on owned land	13,695.2	14,011.7
Buildings and improvements on leased land	11,511.9	12,892.9
Equipment, signs, and seating	3,270.9	4,658.5
Other	500.4	546.8
	34,443.4	37,692.4
Accumulated depreciation and amortization	(13,185.8)	(14,574.8)
Net property and equipment	$21,257.6	$23,117.6

Table 10.3   **Capital Expenditures (in Millions, US$)**

	2016/12/31	2015/12/31	2014/12/31
New restaurants	$ 674	$ 892	$ 1,435
Existing restaurants	1,108	842	1.044
Other properties[a]	39	80	104
Total	$ 1,821	$ 1,814	$ 2,583

[a]Primarily corporate equipment and other office-related expenditures.

The above disclosure from the company's notes provides a breakdown of PP&E, or "Net property and equipment" (see Table 10.2) as McDonald's calls it. The overwhelming majority of the company's assets are held in the form of land and buildings used for the many thousands of restaurants owned around the world. Information on the company's capital expenditures is shown in Table 10.3.

The capital investments made in 2016 (see Table 10.3) can be summarized as follows (in millions, US$):

PP&E	$1,821	
Cash/Liabilities		$1,821

Initial Recognition of PP&E

The initial measurement of PP&E includes not just the costs directly incurred to acquire the asset (e.g. the price paid to a manufacturer for a piece of equipment), but also those costs directly attributable to bringing the asset to the location and working condition necessary for it to operate in the way management intends. Examples include the costs of site preparation, initial delivery and handling, installation and assembly, and employee benefits arising from construction or acquisition of the asset. Even borrowing costs incurred during the period of acquiring, constructing, or producing the asset are sometimes included in historical cost.

Some assets, especially those with considerable environmental consequences, may lead to significant costs upon retirement of the asset. The asset cannot simply be thrown away when its useful life is over, but rather must be carefully disposed of. This means that when such assets are acquired, an asset-retirement obligation (i.e., a liability) is incurred. The fair value of this liability must be recognized when the asset is acquired if a reasonable estimate of it can be made. These costs are added to the asset's carrying amount. The journal entry would look like this:

```
PP&E              XX
    Liability             XX
```

Subsequent Expenditures: Repair or Improvement?

The costs of maintenance and repairs incurred after the asset has been put into service are expensed as incurred. Replacement parts can be capitalized when certain criteria are met, but parts that are used for routine maintenance are usually expensed. The journal entry is

```
Repair expense    XX
    Cash                 XX
```

In contrast, major overhauls of an asset are capitalized when deemed to be an "improvement." In this case, the journal entry would be

```
PP&E              XX
    Cash                 XX
```

The line separating one type of cost from the other (i.e., routine repair and maintenance vs. improvement) is not always obvious. Often, judgment is required. However, US GAAP and IFRS do provide some guidance on how to determine the appropriate accounting treatment. To be considered an improvement, the expenditure must

1. increase the asset's useful life,

2. increase the quality of the asset's output,

3. increase the quantity of the asset's output, or

4. reduce the cost associated with operating the asset.

If the expenditure meets one of these criteria, the expenditure should be capitalized. Otherwise, it should be expensed.

Accounting for Depreciation

Apart from land, assets categorized as PP&E tend to wear out over time, and therefore must be depreciated. To depreciate an asset, the following must be determined:

1. **The depreciable basis of the asset.** For many assets, if not most, the depreciable basis and acquisition cost are the same. To illustrate, if a machine costs $100,000, the total amount to be depreciated over the asset's life is also $100,000. However, many other assets are expected to have significant residual, or salvage, values at the end of their useful lives. For example, trucks and airplanes typically have residual values substantially greater than zero. In such cases, the depreciable basis of the asset equals the acquisition cost minus the residual value. For example, if a truck costs $60,000, and is expected to be worth $10,000 at the end of its useful life for the company, only $50,000 is to be depreciated.

2. **The estimated useful life.**   The estimated life is normally defined as the period of time, usually expressed in years, that the company is expected to derive economic benefits from the use of the asset. For some assets, however, useful life is expressed in units other than time. A common example is any transportation vehicle – such as automobiles, vans, or trucks. In such cases, useful life may be defined as miles or kilometers driven. Other examples where useful life is defined in terms other than calendar time include some classes of machinery, in which useful life is defined as number of units produced; oil wells, where life is usually defined as number of barrels to be extracted; and coal mines, where life is defined as numbers of tons of coal to be mined.

3. **Depreciation method.**   The depreciation method is the pattern by which the depreciable basis of an asset will be allocated to the future accounting periods that will benefit from the use of an asset. The most common method, and the one used by McDonald's (see Box 10.1), is straight-line, in which each year of the asset's use receives an identical amount of depreciation expense. However, other, more accelerated approaches may be used. Accelerated methods are popular for tax purposes because they allow companies to enjoy the tax benefits provided by depreciation charges more quickly than they would under the straight-line method. In effect, accelerating depreciation increases the present value of the tax shield, thereby reducing the effective cost of the asset.

Every depreciation method yields an identical amount of total depreciation expense over an asset's useful life. The only difference is in the pattern, that is, the amount of depreciation expense recognized in each year of the asset's life. For example, the straight-line method allocates depreciation evenly across time, while the accelerated methods, such as double-declining-balance (see below), allocate the depreciable basis more rapidly in the early years and more slowly in the later years.

To illustrate the different allocation patterns that arise from the use of different depreciation methods, let's assume that McDonald's buys a machine for $300,000. Management estimates that it will use the machine for four years. At the end of the fourth year, the machine is expected to have a salvage value of $60,000. If the company chooses the straight-line depreciation method,

$$\text{Depreciation per year} = (\text{Cost} - \text{Salvage Value}) \div \text{Useful Life}$$
$$= (\$300,000 - \$60,000) \div 4 \text{ years} = \$60,000/\text{year}$$

McDonald's will make the following entry each year, for the next four years:

Depreciation expense	$60,000	
Accumulated depreciation		$60,000

A common alternative to straight-line depreciation is the accelerated method known as "declining balance." Under this approach, the annual depreciation charge is based on the straight-line

BOX 10.1   McDonald's Note on Depreciation Method Used McDonald's – Property and Equipment

Property and equipment are stated at cost, with depreciation and amortization provided using the straight-line method over the following estimated useful lives: buildings – up to 40 years; leasehold improvements – the lesser of useful lives of assets or lease terms, which generally include option periods; and equipment – 3 to 12 years.

Table 10.4   **Double-declining-balance Depreciation**

Date	Depreciation factor(%)	Depreciation expense	Cost	Accumulated depreciation	Book value
1/1/17			$300,000	$ 0	$300,000
12/31/17	50	$150,000[a]	300,000	150,000	150,000
12/31/18	50	75,000	300,000	225,000	75,000
12/31/19	50	15,000[b]	300,000	240,000	60,000
12/31/20	50	0	300,000	240,000	60,000

[a]Depreciation Expense = (Book Value at Beginning of the Period) × (Depreciation Factor).
[b]Book Value × Depreciation Factor = $75,000 × 50% = $37,500. If McDonald's depreciated $37,500 in 2019, the asset's book value would drop below salvage value. To prevent this from happening, depreciation expense for 2019 is limited to $15,000.

depreciation rate (in this case 25% per year), multiplied by a number greater than 1 but usually not greater than 2. Because the annual depreciation rate exceeds the straight-line rate, the higher rate must be applied to a declining balance, to ensure that total depreciation charges do not exceed the asset's depreciable basis.

In this example, we assume that McDonald's chooses double-declining-balance, which means that the annual depreciation charge is twice the straight line rate (i.e., 50%). See Table 10.4 for details of double-declining-balance depreciation.

Notice that the 50% depreciation rate is applied to a smaller balance each year. Notice also that the asset is fully depreciated by the end of the third year. If there had been no salvage value, and the depreciable basis of the asset was $300,000 (instead of $240,000), the company would recognize $37,500 of depreciation expense for both 2019 and 2020.

Unlike the straight-line method, salvage value (or residual) is not taken into account up front. The annual depreciation rate of 50% is applied to the total cost of the asset, not the cost less salvage value. This explains why the depreciation charge for the first year, $150,000, is more than double the charge under straight-line. However, the company must ensure that accumulated depreciation does not allow net book value to fall below salvage value.

Changes in Depreciation Estimates or Methods

Changes in depreciation policy are common. Depreciation methods can change, while changes in estimates of useful life or salvage value are even more common. McDonald's explains this in its annual report – see Box 10.2.

Changes in depreciation policy are treated on a prospective basis. This means that when a company changes depreciation method, or changes estimates of useful lives or residual value, no adjustments are made to financial statements from previous years.

BOX 10.2   McDonald's Explanation of Changes in Depreciation Methods
McDonald's – Property and Equipment

Property and equipment are depreciated or amortized on a straight-line basis over their useful lives . . . The Company periodically reviews these lives relative to physical factors, economic factors and industry trends. If there are changes in the planned use of property and equipment, or if technological changes occur more rapidly than anticipated, the useful lives assigned to these assets may need to be shortened, resulting in the accelerated recognition of depreciation and amortization expense or write-offs in future periods.

To illustrate, assume that a $6 million asset is depreciated over six years using the straight-line method. Depreciation expense is $1 million each year over the asset's life. Now assume that after the second year, when the net book value is $4 million ($6 million, minus $2 million of depreciation), the company decides that the asset will last another five years, instead of four. In other words, the company is changing the estimated useful life from six years to seven. With $4 million of depreciable cost, and five years of remaining useful life, the annual depreciation charge is $800,000, instead of $1 million, as it was in the previous two years. No correction is made to the depreciation expense recognized in the previous two years. Instead, the adjustment is made going forward. This approach is also required for changes in depreciation method too – for example, when an accelerated method is replaced with straight-line.

Asset Impairment

Apart from an exception reported later in this chapter, PP&E is carried at cost less accumulated depreciation, unless the value of an asset has been "impaired." Impairment means that the fair value of the asset (i.e., usually defined as the future cash flow benefits an owner can expect if the asset is held in use; otherwise, the price a company can expect from selling the asset) is significantly and permanently below that of net book value. The disclosure shown in Box 10.3 reveals how McDonald's deals with impairments of PP&E. Loss on impairment is an income statement account, which means that impairment is a profit-reducing (or loss-increasing) event.

US GAAP and IFRS are broadly similar in how impairment is defined. Under both regimes, intangible assets with indefinite lives (e.g., trademarks, brand names, etc.) must be reviewed at least annually for impairment and more frequently if impairment indicators are present. Impairment of PP&E is not tested annually, but rather when there are indicators of impairment. Indicators that assets have been impaired, and therefore should be written down, may arise from external events such as a significant decline in market value for the asset or changes in the technological, market, economic, or legal environment. Despite these similarities, however, differences exist between the two regimes in the way in which impairment is reviewed, recognized, and measured.

According to IAS 36 (the main standard under IFRS), an asset is considered impaired to the extent that the carrying value on the balance sheet exceeds its recoverable amount. The recoverable amount is the greater of: (1) fair value less selling costs and (2) value in use (the present value of future cash flows in use, including disposal value). IFRS defines fair value as "the amount for which an asset could be exchanged or a liability settled between knowledgeable, willing parties in an arm's length transaction." This fair value definition is essentially market value, assuming

BOX 10.3   McDonald's – Long-lived Assets Impairment Review

Long-lived assets (including goodwill) are reviewed for impairment annually in the fourth quarter and whenever events or changes in circumstances indicate that the carrying amount of an asset may not be recoverable. In assessing the recoverability of the Company's long-lived assets, the Company considers changes in economic conditions and makes assumptions regarding estimated future cash flows and other factors. Estimates of future cash flows are highly subjective judgments based on the Company's experience and knowledge of its operations. These estimates can be significantly impacted by many factors including changes in global and local business and economic conditions, operating costs, inflation, competition, and consumer and demographic trends. A key assumption impacting estimated future cash flows is the estimated change in comparable sales. If the Company's estimates or underlying assumptions change in the future, the Company may be required to record impairment charges.

the existence of an active market for the asset. Value in use refers to the discounted present value of cash generated by the asset in question. This concept recognizes that sometimes (indeed, most times) an asset is more valuable as used in the business (value in use) than it would be if used by others (fair value). Otherwise, why would a business retain the asset?

To illustrate, suppose a taxi company owns a vehicle with a carrying value of €12,000 (cost of €30,000 less accumulated depreciation of €18,000). The asset has a fair value of €10,000 (market price, net of selling costs) and a discounted cash flow (value in use) of €14,000. The recoverable value is €14,000 and, thus, there is no impairment. Alternatively, imagine the same facts except that the value in use is €11,000. Thus, the recoverable value is €11,000 (the higher of fair value and value in use). In this case, the carrying value (€12,000) is higher than the recoverable value and there is an impairment of €1,000. The journal entry would be:

Impairment loss	€1,000	
Accumulated impairment loss		€1,000

Accumulated impairment loss is a contra-asset account and is deducted from the impaired asset account on the balance sheet.

On the other hand, the US GAAP method for impairment testing is a two-step approach that requires a recoverability test be performed first – the carrying amount of the asset is compared to the sum of future *undiscounted* cash flows generated through use and eventual disposal. If the carrying value of the asset is greater than the total undiscounted cash flows, the present (i.e., discount) value of the future cash flows must be determined. The impairment loss equals the difference between the carrying value and the discounted cash flows.

Returning to the example above, assume that the sum of the *undiscounted* cash flows from the future use of the taxi equals €13,500. Under US GAAP, no impairment would be recorded because the carrying value is €12,000. However, because the *discounted* cash flow is €11,000, an impairment loss is recorded under IFRS. If, on the other hand, the sum of the undiscounted cash flows was €11,900, the asset would be deemed "unrecoverable" (the carrying value of €12,000 is greater than €11,900) and thus subject to impairment. The impairment loss would be calculated as the difference between the €12,000 carrying value and the sum of the discounted cash flows of €11,000. The journal entry would be:

Impairment loss	€1,000	
Asset		€1,000

Note that the credit entry under IFRS was to "accumulated impairment loss," a contra-asset account, but under US GAAP the credit is made directly to the asset account. This difference stems from another difference between the two reporting regimes: if an asset's value recovers, the previous impairment loss can be reversed under IFRS, but not under US GAAP. Any future recovery in value under IFRS is recognized by reducing the balance in the contra-asset. If recovery is complete, the contra-asset is brought to zero.

Fair Value vs. Historical Cost

The most important difference between US GAAP and IFRS in the accounting for PP&E is that the latter gives companies the option of reporting PP&E at fair value, even if fair value is greater than acquisition cost. When assets are written up, the entry looks like this:

PP&E	XX	
Revaluation surplus		XX

where revaluation surplus is a shareholders' equity account. The income statement is not affected at the moment that the asset is revalued.

However, the overwhelming majority of companies reporting under IFRS have chosen not to exercise this option. The primary reason for this reluctance is that once fair value is used, frequent updates are required, unless the company chooses to revert to historical cost. Also, the company must subject all assets of the same class to revaluation. For example, it cannot choose to revalue some of its real estate, while using historical cost for the rest. Because this process is costly, most companies reporting under IFRS use historical cost for PP&E, just like companies reporting under US GAAP. But remember that fair value must be used under both regimes in the case of impaired assets.

If an IFRS company elects to use fair value for nonimpaired assets, meaning that the carrying (balance sheet) value is increased above acquisition cost, any subsequent impairment can be offset against increases recognized in previous years. In other words, the impairment loss is offset against previous revaluations for the same asset. The income statement is unaffected. But any uncovered loss (i.e., a loss greater than previous revaluations) must be recognized as a loss on the income statement.

Divestitures and Asset Sales

Gains and losses resulting from the disposal of PP&E are based on the difference between the proceeds received from the disposal and the asset's book value. Therefore, one would have to know the book value of each individual property in order to be able to determine the gain or loss from selling it. Book value equals the original cost of the asset less any accumulated depreciation associated with it.

If the asset is sold for a price greater than net book value, the company records the following entry:

Cash	XX	
Accumulated depreciation	XX	
Asset (at cost)		XX
Gain on disposal of asset		XX

The gain on disposal is an income statement account. Therefore, the gain increases net income for the period. If the asset is sold for a price lower than net book value, the company records a loss (also an income statement account):

Cash	XX	
Accumulated depreciation	XX	
Loss on disposal of asset	XX	
Asset (at cost)		XX

Intangible Assets

Intangible assets are nonfinancial assets that lack the physical substance of land, building, equipment, and machinery. Common examples include patents, copyrights, customer lists, and brand names. The accounting for intangible assets is roughly the same under US GAAP and IFRS. The initial recording of the acquired intangible asset is at cost.

To illustrate, in April 2012 Microsoft paid AOL $1 billion for 800 patents. Most of these patents relate to instant messaging and e-mail as well as browser and search engine technologies. The journal entry to record the acquisition of the patents would have been:

Patents	$1bn	
Cash		$1bn

with patents being classified as a long-term asset.

Finite-lived intangible assets (i.e., assets that have a limited legal or economic life) are amortized using the straight-line method over their estimated useful lives and are tested for impairment annually. In the case of patents, the useful life is the legal life or the economic life (i.e., the period over which the asset is expected to provide economic benefits to the owner), whichever is shorter. For example, if the legal life of a patent is 20 years, but the rate of technology in the industry results in nearly all patents becoming obsolete before their legal expiration, a shorter time period is used for amortization purposes. Assuming the average useful life of the patents acquired by Microsoft is 10 years, the following journal entry would be recorded each year for the next 10 years:

Amortization expense	$100m	
Patent		$100m

Indefinite-lived intangible assets – intangibles with no legal limits on their useful lives, such as brand names and trademarks – are carried at cost with annual impairment testing.

With a few exceptions – notably costs from the development phase of R&D under IFRS and software development under both regimes – internally generated intangible assets are not recorded on the balance sheet. Here's how Microsoft disclosed its R&D spending in the 2011 Annual Report:

> *During fiscal years 2011, 2010, and 2009, research and development expense was $9.0 billion, $8.7 billion, and $9.0 billion, respectively. These amounts represented 13%, 14%, and 15%, respectively, of revenue in each of those years. We plan to continue to make significant investments in a broad range of research and product development efforts.*

The journal entries recorded in 2011 for these activities sum up to:

Research and development expense	$9bn	
Cash		$9bn

There is one important difference in the accounting for intangible assets under US GAAP and IFRS. In a practice that mirrors the accounting for tangible PP&E, intangible assets previously written down may be revalued upward under IFRS if the annual impairment test indicates an increase in fair value. Under US GAAP, once an intangible asset is written down because of impairment, it may never be written up.

We leave the subject of goodwill, perhaps the most important of all intangible assets, to Chapter 18.

Key Lessons from the Chapter

- Property, plant, and equipment (PP&E) is defined as tangible assets that are held for use in the production or supply of goods or services.

- PP&E is usually reported on the balance sheet at historical cost, or historical cost less accumulated depreciation.

- The initial measurement of PP&E includes all costs to get the asset ready for its intended use.

- Maintenance costs are expensed as incurred. Improvements are capitalized and depreciated over the useful life. The boundary that separates maintenance from improvements is not always obvious, which means that some judgment may be required in determining whether to expense or capitalize.

- The useful life is the period of time, usually (but not always) expressed in years, that the company is expected to derive economic benefit from use of the asset.

- The depreciation method is the pattern by which the depreciable basis of an asset will be allocated to the future accounting periods that will benefit from the use of an asset.

- The most common depreciation method, by far, is straight-line. However, other, more accelerated approaches may be used. These accelerated approaches are popular for tax purposes because they increase the present value of the tax shields offered by depreciation.

- Depreciation methods for given assets can change, although changes in estimates of useful life or salvage value are more common.

- PP&E should be carried at cost less accumulated depreciation, unless the fair value of an asset has been "impaired." Impairment means that the fair value of an asset is significantly and permanently below that of net book value.

- Gains and losses resulting from the disposal of PP&E are based on the difference between the proceeds received from disposal and the asset's net book value.

KEY TERMS AND CONCEPTS FROM THE CHAPTER

Intangible assets	Net book value	Accelerated method	Asset Impairment	Double-declining
Historical cost	Useful life	Straight-line method	Depletion	balance method
Depreciation	Residual/salvage value	Amortization		

QUESTIONS

1. Describe each of the following terms: depreciation, amortization, and depletion.

2. Why do tax laws permit accelerated depreciation methods?

3. IFRS permits the use of fair value accounting for property and plant assets. Why, then, do most companies prefer to use historical (or acquisition) cost?

4. Why are transport, installation, and training costs added to the asset account, and not expensed immediately?

5. What is goodwill? What is the proper accounting treatment for it?

6. Why does the accounting treatment for repairs and maintenance differ from that of improvements?

7. Why are research costs expensed under IFRS, but development costs are capitalized? What's the difference between "research" and "development"?

8. True or false: the amortization period for an intangible asset is equal to its legal life.

9. How should a company account for an asset, such as a building or piece of equipment, that has been fully depreciated?

10. Why are brand names and trademarks not amortized?

11. True or false: most large, publicly traded companies use straight-line depreciation for book purposes but accelerated methods for tax.

12. How is a gain or loss determined on an asset sale?

PROBLEMS

10.1 Comparing the Effects of Depreciation Choice on Financial Ratios

Dieter Loch AG is about to purchase two new assets – a machine for €75,000 and a state-of-the art forklift truck for €40,000. The assets would be acquired at the beginning of 2013. The company's 2012 income statement and other information are shown below:

Sales	€550,000
Cost of goods sold	310,000
Gross profit	240,000
SG&A expenses	140,000
Income before tax	100,000
Income taxes	30,000
NOPAT	€70,000

Additional information:

- Dieter Loch management expects the addition of the two assets to generate a 20% annual growth rate in sales.

- Depreciation on the new machine will be included as part of cost of goods sold. Depreciation on the new forklift will be classified under other operating expenses.

- Excluding the new machine's depreciation, cost of goods sold is expected to increase at an annual rate of 7%.

- Excluding the new forklift's depreciation, selling, general, and administrative (SG&A) expenses are expected to grow at an annual rate of 5%.

- Dieter Loch's invested capital, not counting the new machine and forklift, is expected to increase at a rate of 15% per year. Average invested capital at the end of 2012 was €500,000.

- Both the machine and the forklift have an estimated useful life of five years, and zero residual value.

- The tax rate is 30%.

Required

a. Can you explain why depreciation charges on the two assets are classified differently – COGS for the machine and SG&A for the forklift?

b. Prepare forecasted income statements for 2013 and 2014, assuming that Dieter Loch AG elects to use straight-line depreciation for both assets.

c. Calculate the firm's gross profit percentage, NOPAT margin, and return on invested capital.

d. Repeat (b), assuming that the company elects to use the double-declining balance method instead for both assets.

e. Repeat (c). How does the choice of different depreciation methods affect the behavior of the ratios in 2013 and 2014?

10.2 Analyzing Depreciation on PP&E

The following note is taken from the 2004 Annual Report of ExxonMobil Corporation:

	December 31, 2004		December 31, 2003	
	Historical cost	Accumulated depreciation	Historical cost	Accumulated depreciation
(millions of dollars)				
Upstream	$148,024	$62,013	$138,701	$58,727
Downstream	62,014	29,810	59,939	29,566
Chemical	21,777	10,049	20,623	10,115
Other	10,607	6,767	10,052	6,557
Total	$242,422	$108,639	$229,315	$104,965

In the upstream segment, depreciation is on a unit-of-production basis, so depreciable life will vary by field. In the downstream segment, investments in refinery and . . . manufacturing facilities are generally depreciated on a straight-line basis over a 25-year life and service station buildings and fixed improvements over a 20-year life. In the chemical segment, investments in process equipment are depreciated on a straight-line basis over a 20-year life. Accumulated depreciation and depletion totaled $133,783 million at the end of 2004 and $124,350 million at the end of 2003.

Required

Based on the above note, answer the following:

a. By 2004, what percentage of the upstream segment costs have been depreciated? Assume no salvage value and assume that in 2005, no upstream acquisitions or divestitures take place. If the upstream PP&E are used to produce 10% of their capabilities, what would be the depreciation expense and net book value at the end of 2005?

b. By December 31, 2003, assuming a 20% salvage (residual) value, on average, what is the age of the chemical PP&E?

c. Assuming no divestiture or retirement of assets, what was the depreciation expense for all PP&E in 2004?

10.3 Calculating and Analyzing Amortization Expense

The 2003 Annual Report for Microsoft reports the acquisition of Navision:

In fiscal 2003, Microsoft acquired all of the outstanding equity interests of Navision a/s, Rare Ltd., and Placeware, Inc. Navision, headquartered in Vedbaek, Denmark, is a provider

of integrated business solutions software for small and mid-sized businesses in the European market that is part of the Microsoft Business Solutions segment. Navision, Rare, and Placeware have been consolidated into our financial statements since their respective acquisition dates. The estimated fair values of the assets acquired and liabilities assumed at the date of the acquisitions for fiscal 2003 are as follows:

(In millions)	Navision a/s at July 12, 2002	Rare Ltd. at September 24, 2002	Placeware, Inc. at April 30, 2003
Current assets	$240	$25	$30
Property, plant, and equipment	8	8	7
Intangible assets	169	75	30
Goodwill	1,197	281	180
Total assets acquired	1,614	389	247
Current liabilities	(148)	(12)	(32)
Long-term liabilities	(1)	(13)	
Total liabilities assumed	(149)	(12)	(45)
Net assets acquired	$1,465	$377	$202

The note provides supplemental information on the intangible assets acquired by Microsoft:

The components of intangible assets acquired in the acquisitions above are as follows (no significant residual value is estimated for these assets):

	Navision a/s	Weighted average life	Rare Ltd.	Weighted average life	Placeware, Inc.	Weighted average life
Contract-based	$115	6 years	$16	5 years	$1	6 years
Technology-based	48	4 years	36	5 years	4	4 years
Marketing-related	4	3 years	10	5 years	2	1 year
Customer-related					23	10 years
Research and development	2[a]		13[a]			
Total	$169	5 years	$75	5 years	$30	8 years

[a]Amounts assigned to research and development assets were written off in accordance with FIN 4. Those write-offs were included in research and development expenses.

Required

a. How much amortization expense would you expect Microsoft to record in 2004 for the intangible assets purchased in 2003?

b. What impact would the amortization expense have on each of the company's three principal financial statements?

10.4 Calculating Depreciation Expense

On January 1, 2013, Double Happiness Delivery Company acquired a new truck for $90,000. The truck is estimated to have a useful life of five years and no residual value.

Required

Indicate the amount of the depreciation charge for each year of the asset's life under the following methods:

a. The straight-line method.

b. The declining balance method at twice the straight-line rate, with a switch to straight-line in 2016. Why would the company switch to straight-line after using the declining balance method for the same asset?

10.5 Effects of Changes in Estimates on Depreciation Expense

At the end of each year, Patty Chu, the chief accountant at Rex Lin Enterprises, a Singapore-based trading company, reviews long-term assets at the end of each year to determine whether changes are called for in how these assets are depreciated. In December 2017, her attention focused on two assets in particular:

	Date acquired	Cost	Accumulated depreciation end of 2017	Useful life	Residual value
Warehouse	1/1/13	$200,000	$50,000	25 years	$10,000
Building	1/1/12	1,600,000	228,000	40 years	100,000

Patty is proposing the following changes:

For the warehouse: a decrease in the useful life to 20 years and a decrease in residual value to $6,000.

For the building: an increase in the useful life to 50 years and a decrease in the residual value to $55,000.

Before agreeing to the changes, Patty's bosses would like to know what the depreciation charges will be for each asset if the changes are adopted. All assets are depreciated using the straight-line method.

Required

Calculate the revised annual depreciation expenses for each asset in 2018 and compare them to what the expenses would be if the changes were not made.

10.6 Interpreting Disclosures for Property, Plant, and Equipment

Petrobras, which operates in the energy sector, is Brazil's largest company. Its shares trade on several of the world's leading stock exchanges. A portion of Petrobras' balance sheet, its income statement, and extracts from a note on PP&E are presented in Exhibit 10.1.

Required

Based on the information provided, answer the following questions:

a. What portion of Petrobras' "Equipment and other assets" had been "used up" by the end of fiscal 2008?

Exhibit 10-1   Petrobras Disclosures

Statements of Income

December 31, 2008 and 2007

(In thousands of reais, except net income per share)

		Consolidated	
Statements of Income	Note	2008	2007
Gross operating revenues			
Selling expenses			
Products		266,217,208	218,050,202
Services, mainly freight		276,872	203,972
		266,494,080	218,254,174
Sales charges		(51,375,544)	(47,676,449)
Net operating revenues		215,118,536	170,577,725
Cost of products and services sold		(141,623,359)	(104,398,043)
Gross profit		73,495,177	66,179,682
Operating income (expenses)			
Selling expenses		(7,162,264)	(6,059,734)
Financial			
Expenses	18	(4,193,135)	(3,292,002)
			(Continued)

Statements of Income	Note	Consolidated 2008	Consolidated 2007
Revenues	18	3,494,430	2,417,659
Exchange and monetary variations, net	18	3,827,489	(3,146,547)
Administrative and general expenses			
Management and board of directors remuneration		(35,792)	(29,259)
Administrative		(7,211,566)	(6,398,633)
Taxes		(862,766)	(1,255,511)
Cost of research and technological development		(1,705,572)	(1,712,338)
Loss of recovery of assets		(933,088)	(446,129)
Exploratory costs for the extraction of crude oil and gas		(3,494,258)	(2,569,724)
Healthcare and pension plans	21	(1,427,395)	(2,494,510)
Other operating income and expenses, net	18	(4,712,243)	(5,188,393)
		(24,416,160)	(30,175,121)
Equity in income of subsidiaries and associated companies			
Equity in earnings (losses) of investments	13	(874,218)	(465,274)
Income from operations before income and social contribution taxes, employee and management profit sharing and minority interest		48,204,799	35,539,287
Social contribution	20,5	(4,169,529)	(2,876,775)
Income tax	20,5	(11,792,449)	(8,395,983)
Income before employees' and directors' profit-sharing and minority interest		32,242,821	24,266,529
Employees' and directors' profit-sharing	22	(1,344,526)	(1,011,914)
Income before minority interest		30,898,295	23,254,615
Minority interest		2,089,497	(1,742,826)
Net income for the year		32,987,792	21,511,789
Net income per share at the end of the year – R$		3,76	4,90

See the accompanying notes to the financial statements.

Balance Sheets

December 31, 2008 and 2007

(In thousands of reais)

Assets	Note	Consolidated 2008	Consolidated 2007
Current assets			
Cash and cash equivalents	5	15,888,596	13,070,849
Marketable securities	10	288,751	589,788
Trade accounts receivable, net	6	14,903,732	11,328,967
Dividends receivable	7.1	20,101	80,596
Inventories	8	19,977,171	17,599,001

Taxes and contributions	20.1	9,641,247	7,781,536
Prepaid expenses		1,393,879	1,429,829
Other current assets		1,461,801	1,493,200
		63,575,278	**53,373,766**
Noncurrent assets			
Long-term receivables			
Trade accounts receivable, net	6	1,326,522	2,901,902
Petroleum and alcohol account – STN	9	809,673	797,851
Marketable securities	10	4,066,280	3,922,370
Project financing	11.2		
Deposits in court	12	1,853,092	1,693,495
Prepaid expenses		1,400,072	1,514,301
Advance for pension plan	21		1,296,810
Deferred income and social contribution taxes	20.3	10,238,308	8,333,490
Inventories	8	303,929	236,753
Other long-term receivables		1,256,96	1,325,865
		21,254,843	**22,022,837**
Investments	13	5,106,495	7,822,074
Property, plant, and equipment	14	190,754,167	139,940,726
Intangible assets	15	8,003,213	5,532,053
Deferred charges		3,469,846	2,536,344
		228,588,564	**177,854,034**
		292,163,842	**231,227,800**

See the accompanying notes to the financial statements.

Property, Plant, and Equipment By Type of Asset

		Consolidated			
		2008			**2007**
	Estimated Useful Life in Years	**Cost**	**Accumulated Depreciation**	**Net**	**Net**
Buildings and improvements	25 to 40	9,382,619	(3,115,564)	6,267,055	3,800,350
Equipment and other assets	3 to 30	119,999,208	(55,854,051)	64,145,157	49,414,524
Land		1,138,720		1,138,720	854,848
Material		6,034,143		6,034,143	4,247,098
Advances to suppliers		5,189,735		5,189,735	2,624,093
Expansion projects		59,238,898		59,238,898	39,964,366
Oil and gas exploration and production development costs (E&P)		83,883,258	(35,142,799)	48,740,459	39,035,447
		284,866,581	**(94,112,414)**	**190,754,167**	**139,940,726**

b. How many years are left in the lives of Petrobras' "Equipment and other assets," on average? State clearly any assumptions that you make in arriving at your estimate.

c. Suppose that Petrobras assumes a zero salvage value for their "Equipment and other assets." For each $100 in new asset investments, what is the annual amount of depreciation expense charged to the income statement?

d. Suppose that other leading energy companies charge $12 in depreciation expense for each $100 invested in new equipment. Are Petrobras' depreciation policy assumptions materially different from those of their competitors? Support your answer.

e. What line item on Petrobras' income statement is most affected by their depreciation policy? Explain why.

f. Aside from comparing Petrobras' depreciation policy assumptions to those of their competitors, what other "red flags" might one look for in order to assess whether Petrobras is overly conservative or overly aggressive in taking depreciation expenses? Is there any evidence of these issues on Petrobras' financial statements?

10.7 Capitalizing or Expensing Costs

Air France, a subsidiary of the Air France-KLM Group, is one of the world's largest airlines. It operates a mixed fleet of Airbus and Boeing wide-bodied jets on long-haul routes and relies mainly on the Airbus A320 family of aircraft for shorter flights. Assume that Air France made the following expenditures related to these aircraft in the current year:

a. Routine maintenance and repairs on various aircraft costing €1.1 billion.

b. The jet engines on several of the airline's A321s received a major overhaul at a cost of €18 million. The intent of the overhaul was to improve fuel efficiency and reduce carbon emissions.

c. The avionics were replaced on the fleet of Boeing 747s. This is expected to extend the useful life of the planes by 3 years.

d. Noise abatement kits were installed on some of the older A320s in accordance with EU regulations on maximum allowable noise levels on takeoff. The equipment and installation cost €14 million.

e. The airline painted several of its aircraft as part of a campaign to promote new routes to Asia. The painting cost €1.2 million.

f. The existing seats on several A320s were replaced with more comfortable seats costing €3.5 million.

g. New jet engines were installed on several A318s. The total cost was €42 million.

Required

Which of the above expenditures should be capitalized and which should be expensed? Explain your answers.

10.8 Journal Entries for Depreciation and Amortization Expense

Prepare journal entries for each of the following transactions or events for Liu Cybersystems:

a. Acquired computers costing $800,000 and software costing $80,000 on January 1, 2016. Liu expects the computers to have a service life of 10 years and $80,000 residual value. The software is expected to have a service life of four years and zero residual value.

b. Paid $40,000 to install the computers at Liu's office. Paid $20,000 to test the software.

c. Liu records depreciation and amortization expense for the computers and the computer software using the straight-line method for 2016 and 2017.

d. On January 1, 2018, new software on the market makes the software acquired in 2011 obsolete.

e. On January 2, 2018, Liu revised the depreciable life of the computers to a total of 14 years and the salvage value to $112,000. Give the entry to record depreciation expense for 2018.

f. On December 31, 2019, Liu sells the computers for $520,000. Give the required journal entries for 2019.

Leases and Off-Balance-Sheet Debt

11

Introduction

A lease is an agreement between two parties for the rent of an asset. The lessor is the legal owner of the asset who then rents out the asset to the lessee. At the end of the lease period, the asset is usually, but not always, returned to the lessor. The lessee pays a periodic (monthly, quarterly, yearly) rental fee to the lessor in return for use of the asset. In this chapter, we address the accounting treatment for leases and off-balance-sheet debt. The discussion is limited to the lessee's perspective. Leasing is a critically important topic for the financial statement reader because in many industries it is the most common form of asset financing. The economic rationale for such a large industry is complex, and beyond the scope of this book, but accounting practice has certainly played an important role in the pervasive use of leasing.

Lease accounting is in the midst of a profound transformation. To put that transformation into context, we begin with an examination of lease accounting before 2019 (when the new accounting standard is scheduled to come into effect). Several of these elements will be retained, while others will no longer apply. After we have presented the pre-2019 treatment, we will discuss the recent changes.

Leasing Accounting Before 2018: Capital vs. Operating Leases

US GAAP and IFRS distinguished between two types of leases: capital and operating. In the case of the former, future lease payments were capitalized at an appropriate borrowing rate, with the present value appearing as both an asset and a liability on the balance sheet. Operating leases were treated as rental contracts, with the periodic lease payments recorded as operating expenses. The present value of the lease does not appear on the balance sheet as either an asset or a liability. In fact, operating leases were the most common form of off-balance-sheet (OBS) financing. OBS financing refers to a debt or future obligation, which, for whatever reason, did not appear on the balance sheet as a liability.

In contrast, a capital lease was viewed as a purchase agreement. This implied that the company had, in substance, acquired an asset and that the lease was simply a note payable for the acquisition of that asset. Thus, the present value of the future cash outflows specified in the lease agreement was reported as a liability.

The most important controversy in pre-2018 lease accounting was determining the demarcation point that separates the two types of leases. In other words, how did we know whether a lease should be capitalized or accounted for as a rental contract?

Under US GAAP, four "bright line" rules were used for determining whether a lease was to be classified as a capital or operating lease. If the lease met at least one of the rules, it was classified as a capital lease. Otherwise, it was classified as an operating lease. The four tests were:

1. Transfer of ownership of the property to the lessee by the end of the lease term.

2. The lease contains a bargain purchase option, meaning that lessee can acquire the asset at a price significantly below fair value.

3. The lease term is equal to 75% or more of the economic life of the leased property.

4. The present value of the minimum lease payments (at the beginning of the lease) equals or exceeds 90% of the fair value of the leased property.

IFRS was more principles-oriented in drawing the capital/operating lease distinction. This meant that rather than providing detailed operating guidance, as US GAAP did with its bright line rules (75% of economic life, 90% of fair value, etc.), IFRS guidance was more general. The idea was that the accountants preparing the financial statements, and the ones who audit them, should rely more on professional judgment than on detailed rules.

According to IFRS (IAS 17), a lease was to capitalized under any of the following conditions:

- The lease transfers ownership of the asset to the lessee by the end of the lease term;

- The lessee has the option to purchase the asset at a price that is expected to be sufficiently lower than fair value at the date the option becomes exercisable and, that, at the inception of the lease, it is reasonably certain that the option will be exercised;

- The lease term is for the major part of the economic life of the asset, even if title is not transferred;

- At the inception of the lease, the present value of the minimum lease payments amounts to at least substantially all of the fair value of the leased asset;

- The leased asset is of a specialized nature such that only the lessee can use it without major modifications being made.

Notice the absence of any specific percentages, as was the case under US GAAP.

However, while the standards for determining the classification of a lease were somewhat different under US GAAP and IFRS, once the classification decision had been made, the accounting treatments were nearly the same. The following discussion shows, in detail, how each of the two types of leases were accounted for. We will then discuss which aspects of the accounting for leases are still relevant.

Accounting for Capital Leases

Under a capital lease, the company records an asset and an obligation (short-term for the portion that must be paid within 12 months and long-term for the rest). The amount is based on the present value of the minimum lease payments:

Capitalized lease asset	XX	
Capitalized lease liability		XX

After the asset has been capitalized, the company amortizes it just as it would depreciate the asset if it had been purchased outright. The amortization is done using the straight-line method. The resulting journal entry looks like this:

Amortization expense	XX	
Accumulated amortization		XX

Similar to a mortgage payment on a purchased asset, the periodic (monthly, quarterly, etc.) capital lease payment is comprised of an interest cost and a loan principal repayment amount:

Interest expense	XX	
Capital lease liability	XX	
Cash		XX

The interest expense equals the interest rate on the lease, multiplied by the balance of the capital lease liability at the beginning of the accounting period.

Under US GAAP, the interest expense appears as a reduction in earnings and as a reduction in operating cash flows. The principal repayment portion of the capital lease payment is shown as a financing cash outflow (repayment of debt). IFRS is more flexible on this point. While the repayment of principal is always classified as a financing cash flow, preparers have the choice of classifying the interest portion of the payment as either operating or financing.

Accounting for Operating Leases

In contrast to an asset purchase or capital lease, no asset or liability is recorded on the balance sheet in the case of an operating lease. The company leasing the asset pays a predefined periodic lease payment during the term of the lease. This payment is usually classified as a rent or lease expense:

Rent expense	XX	
Cash		XX

Lease Accounting: An Example

Bankers Group Inc., a financial consulting firm, signs a five-year lease for a computer system that requires annual payments of $10,000 at the end of each year, starting in 2013. The effective interest rate on the lease is 8%.

If Bankers Group records the contract as an operating lease, the following journal entries are required:

Lease expense	10,000	
Cash		10,000

Incurred and paid lease expense for 2013.

The same entry would be repeated for each of the following four years.

However, if Bankers Group chose to capitalize the lease, the following entries would be needed:

Capital lease asset[a]	39,927	
Lease liability		39,927

Record the capitalized lease ($10,000 × 3.9927).[b]

Depreciation expense	7,985.40	
Accumulated depreciation		7,985.40

Record depreciation of the capitalized asset for 2013 ($39 927 ÷ 5).

Lease liability	6,805.84	
Interest expense	3,194.16[c]	
Cash		10,000

Lease payment for 2013. The interest portion equals the balance in the liability at the beginning of the period. The remaining portion reduces the loan principal.

[a] Or the company could refer to the asset as "computer equipment."
[b] 3.9927 is the present value factor of an ordinary annuity over five years at 8%.
[c] $39,927 × 8%.

Depreciation expense	7,985.40	
Accumulated depreciation		7,985.40

Record depreciation for 2014.

Lease liability	7,350.32	
Interest expense	2,649.68	
Cash		10,000

Lease payment for 2014.

Depreciation expense	7,985.40	
Accumulated depreciation		7,985.40

Record depreciation for 2015.

Lease liability	7,938.32	
Interest expense	2,061.68	
Cash		10,000

Lease payment for 2015.

Depreciation expense	7,985.40	
Accumulated depreciation		7,985.40

Record depreciation for 2016.

Lease liability	8,573.36	
Interest expense	1,426.64	
Cash		10,000

Lease payment for 2016.

Depreciation expense	7,985.40	
Accumulated depreciation		7,985.40

Record depreciation for 2017.

Lease liability	9,260.00	
Interest expense	740.00	
Cash		10,000

Lease payment for 2017.

In the first year of the lease, 2013, classifying the contract as an operating lease leads to both higher net income and a lower debt/equity ratio. Ignoring tax effects, net income is reduced by $10,000 each year because of the rent expense. On the other hand, if the lease is capitalized, total expenses in 2013 would be $11,179.56 (interest expense of $3,194.16 + depreciation expense of $7,985.40). But notice that by 2017, the operating lease treatment leads to lower net income. By the final year of the lease's term, most of the principal has been paid, meaning that the interest portion of the annual lease payment is small ($740.00). When added to the annual depreciation expense, the total comes to just $8,725.40. Therefore, operating lease treatment results in lower total expenses and higher net income in the early years of the lease, while the reverse is true in the latter years of the lease term. The total (pretax) expense over the five years is the same under either approach, in this case, $50,000. However, the timing of the expense is different, as well as the effect on the Bankers Group balance sheet.

Note also that as long as a portion of the loan principal has not been paid, capital lease treatment will always result in higher reported debt. Debt/equity ratios will also be higher, not just because of the higher debt, but because the lower net income reported in the early years under capital lease treatment leads to lower retained earnings (and, therefore, lower shareholders' equity).

Interpreting Lease Disclosures

All companies reporting under US GAAP and IFRS are required to provide supplemental disclosures on lease commitments in the notes to their financial statements. These disclosures should include the minimum, noncancelable payments required under both capital and, in the case of US GAAP, operating leases for each of the ensuing five years, and a total amount for all years thereafter. To illustrate, we use the example of AMR, Inc., the holding company for American Airlines. The note in Box 11.1 comes from AMR's 2009 Annual Report.

This note reveals that the present value of lease payments under capital leases is $689 million at the end of 2009. This means that the AMR balance sheet dated 31 December 2009 included $689 million of liabilities related to those leases. The total minimum payments required by AMR are $1,152 million, of which $463 million represents the interest component. One way to interpret these figures is that AMR has future mortgage payments of $1,152 million on 80 jet aircraft (see description in the note), of which $689 million is the principal amount of the loan.

The note also reveals the minimum payments required under operating leases. Assuming no additional leases, AMR can be expected to report rent expense of $1,057 million in 2010 for the 181 jet aircraft and 39 turboprop aircraft accounted for as operating leases. The total amount of $9,327 million is not a present value, but is rather the total nominal payments AMR is expected to make under these leases.

Many analysts would attempt to convert this stream of future cash flows into a present value, and include the resulting amount as part of the company's debt. One approach is to take the

BOX 11.1   AMR's note on leases from their 2009 Annual Report

AMR's Footnote No. 5 – Leases

AMR's subsidiaries lease various types of equipment and property, primarily aircraft and airport facilities. The future minimum lease payments required under capital leases, together with the present value of such payments, and future minimum lease payments required under operating leases that have initial or remaining noncancelable lease terms in excess of one year as of December 31, 2009, were (in millions):

At 31 December 2009, the Company was operating 181 jet aircraft and 39 turboprop aircraft under operating leases and 80 jet aircraft under capital leases. The aircraft leases can generally be renewed at rates based on fair market value at the end of the lease term for one to five years. Some aircraft leases have purchase options at or near the end of the lease term at fair market value.

Year Ending December 31,	Capital Leases	Operating Leases
2010	$181	$1,057
2011	184	1,032
2012	134	848
2013	119	755
2014	98	614
2015 and thereafter	436	5,021
	1,152	$9,327
Less amount representing interest	463	
Present value of net minimum lease payments	$689	

payments from 2015 and thereafter, $5,021 million, and divide by the minimum payments from the previous year, $614 million. This amount, slightly greater than eight, implies that AMR can expect minimum annual payments of $614 million for about eight years beyond 2015. Based on an implied borrowing rate, the analyst can then convert the assumed cash-flow stream, plus the minimum payments from the first five years, into a present value. This figure would then reflect the value of the debt represented by the operating leases.

Off-Balance-Sheet Debt

The operating lease is a prototypical example of what has come to be known as off-balance-sheet (OBS) debt. More generally, OBS debt describes the acquisition of cash, goods, or services without the borrowing arrangements being formally acknowledged as a liability on the balance sheet. Operating leases fall into a broader category of OBS debt known as executory contracts. Here, firms sign contracts promising to pay specified amounts in the future in exchange for future benefits. These benefits can take on many forms, such as the take-or-pay contracts signed by petroleum refiners to ensure access to adequate supplies of petroleum. What all such contracts have in common is that they give the company access to a vitally needed resource without having to formally acquire it or to acknowledge the corresponding obligation in the accounts. The financial statements are usually unaffected by such arrangements until cash payments are made, although some form of disclosure should appear in the notes if the amounts are material. The payments will either be accumulated in inventory accounts, as in the case of petroleum refiners, or sent directly to cost of goods sold.

Another type of OBS finance, introduced in Chapter 5, is the securitization of receivables.[1] Here, a firm transfers its receivables to a separate legal entity, which then packages the receivables as securities and sells them to investors. The cash paid by investors is then passed back to the company. In effect, it constitutes a form of borrowing in which the receivables act as collateral. However, if the transfer occurs in a certain way, the company may be able to "derecognize" the receivables and remove them, and any corresponding debt, from the balance sheet.

Why companies engage in OBS debt is a complicated subject, and beyond the scope of this book. But we will say that there are positive aspects to the practice (that is, actions that are potentially value enhancing for the firm) and negative aspects (actions that are value destroying). For example, OBS financing arrangements may allow a company to avoid violating debt covenants that restrict the amount of debt that appear in the financial statements. In such case, OBS financing allows the company to avoid costly loan renegotiations with its bankers. The problem, however, is that for such practices to work bankers and other lenders have to be strikingly naïve. From our experience, the lenders who survive over the long term are anything but naïve and will build protections against OBS debt into their lending contracts.

It is also worth noting that the trend under US GAAP and IFRS is to force companies to bring many financing arrangements that traditionally have been OBS into the balance sheet. The recent change in lease accounting, discussed below is the most obvious example.

Recent developments in lease accounting

In 2008, the FASB and IASB initiated a joint project to develop a new standard for leases. The IASB released its standard, known as IFRS 16, in January 2016. The following month, the FASB released its Accounting Standards Update (ASU) 2016-02. Although the project began as a joint effort, the boards diverged in some key areas. The most important difference is that the IASB chose to apply a single model to all leases, while the FASB chose to retain the dual model. In short, the IFRS requires that all long-term leases (>12 months) be treated as finance (or "capital") leases. The FASB, by contrast, requires all leases to be capitalized, but continues to use the operating lease designation for income statement purposes.

Under the FASB model, a lessee should classify a lease based on whether the arrangement is effectively a purchase of the underlying asset. Leases that transfer control of the underlying asset to a lessee are classified as finance leases; all others will be classified as operating leases. To put it another way, in an operating lease, a lessee obtains control of only the use of the underlying asset, but not the underlying asset itself. Under the IFRS model, this distinction is not relevant. All leases that come under the scope of the new standard will be accounted for as finance leases. However, there are some types of leases that fall outside the scope of the new standards. Examples include leases of intangible assets, leases to explore for or use natural resources, and leases of biological assets.

To illustrate how the accounting will work from now on for an operating lease under US GAAP, let's assume that a company leases an automobile from the leasing arm of a global car maker. The terms of the lease are as follows:

Lease term: 3 years

Economic life of the automobile: 6 years

Monthly lease payments: $1,000

Payment date: beginning of the month

The lessee's incremental borrowing rate: 6% (this is the rate used for discounting purposes if the rate the lessor charges the lessee is not readily determinable).

Title to the automobile remains with the lessor upon expiration of the lease.

Fair value of the automobile: $60,000

The lessee covers all maintenance costs over the period of the lease.

The lessee determines that the contract is an operating lease. The lessee records the following journal entry upon the commencement date of the lease:

Right-of-use asset	$33,036	
Lease liability		$33,036

The amount, $33,036, represents the present value of the monthly payments ($1,000 for 36 months, discounted at 6%). The very same entry would be made if the contract had been judged to be a financial lease. The right-of-use asset is a lessee's right *to* use the asset over the life of a lease. The asset here is the right to use the asset for a specific period of time and not the physical asset.

Once the lease has begun, the lessee then calculates the straight-line expense to be recorded each month. This is done by dividing the total lease payments ($36,000) by the total number of periods (36 months). Therefore, the monthly expense will be $1,000. The important point here is that the monthly expense is exactly the same as it would be under the old accounting rules for operating leases.

To illustrate, the following entry is made on the date of the first monthly payment:

Interest expense	$ 165.18	
Amortization expense	$ 834.82	
Cash		$1,000

Interest expense for the month equals the present value of the future leases payments (which is $33,036 at the beginning of the first month), multiplied by the 6% annual discount rate, divided by 12 (for the number of months in a year). The amortization of the right-of-use asset is calculated as the difference between the straight-line expense ($1,000) and the interest expense on the lease liability ($165.18). This approach forces the sum of the two debits to equal the straight-line expense.

Over the 36-month term of the lease, the sum of the monthly amortization charges will equal the present value of the lease, $33,036, and the interest expense will sum to the difference between this figure and the 36 monthly payments ($36,000), or $2,964.

Note that both of the debits in the above journal entry are to income-statement accounts. Therefore, the effect of the first monthly lease payment is to reduce pretax income by $1,000, exactly the same as if the old accounting method for operating leases had been used.

To summarize, although the lease has been capitalized in the same way as a finance lease, the income-statement effect is like that of an old operating lease. The difference between the new method and the old method is that under the former, only the amortization portion of the expense goes into the operating-income section of the income statement. The interest expense appears with other financing costs below operating income. Under the old method, all of the expense was included in operating income.

KEY LESSONS FROM THE CHAPTER

- A lease is an agreement between two parties for the rental of an asset.

- Accounting rules distinguish between two types of leases: capital and operating.

- Before 2018, operating leases were treated as rental contracts, with periodic lease payments recorded as an operating expense. Operating leases were the most common form of off-balance-sheet financing.

- Capital leases are viewed as a purchase agreement. This implies that the company has, in substance, acquired an asset and that the lease is simply a note payable for the acquisition of the asset.

- Under US GAAP four "bright line" rules were used for determining whether a lease is classified as a capital lease. If a lease met at least one of the rules, the lease was classified as a capital lease. Otherwise, it was classified as an operating lease. These rules will largely disappear when the new accounting standard for leases goes into effect.

- The FASB and the IASB have issues standards that now require all long-term leases (>12 months) to be capitalized, appearing as both a right-of-use asset and a debt. Under IFRS, the operating-lease designation has disappeared, meaning that all leases are treated as capital leases. Under US GAAP, all leases are capitalized, just like under IFRS, but the operating lease distinction still applies for income-statement purposes.

KEY TERMS AND CONCEPTS FROM THE CHAPTER

Operating lease

Off-balance-sheet financing

The criteria for capitalizing leases

Capital or finance lease

Right-of-use asset

QUESTIONS

1. This issue wasn't discussed in the chapter, but why do you think so many assets are leased instead of bought? What are the advantages of leasing relative to buying?

2. Why are managers so often averse to capitalizing leases?

3. True or false: Leasing reduces a firm's lending capacity.

4. True or false: All else being equal, a profitable company is more likely to rely on leasing to finance its assets than an unprofitable company.

5. In what ways is the economic substance of a lessee's capital lease similar to, and different from, that of purchasing the asset using proceeds from a secured (i.e., collateralized) loan?

6. How is cash flow from operations affected by the capitalization of a lease that had previously been recognized as an operating lease?

7. Lease accounting is likely to undergo important changes in the near future. What are these changes likely to be, and do you agree with them?

PROBLEM

11.1 The Financial Reporting Effects of Selling Receivables

The following note appears in Daimler's 2011 Annual Report:

> *Based on market conditions and liquidity needs, Daimler may sell portfolios of retail and wholesale receivables to third parties. At the time of the sale, Daimler determines whether the legally transferred receivables meet the criteria for derecognition in conformity with the appropriate provisions. If the criteria are not met, the receivables continue to be recognized in the Group's statement of financial position.*

As of 31 December 2011, the carrying amount of receivables from financial services sold but not derecognized for accounting purposes amounted to €3496 million (2010: €1254 million). The associated risk and rewards are similar to those with respect to receivables from financial services that have not been transferred.

Required

a. Why does Daimler sell receivables from its financial services arm?

b. What does Daimler mean by "derecognition" from the sale of receivables? What entry does the company make to record the sale of receivables when the sales are derecognized?

c. What is meant by receivables "sold but not derecognized"? What entry is made in this case?

11-1   Lease Accounting at Metro AG

Metro AG is one of the world's largest discount retailers. Headquartered in Germany, its activities are segmented as follows:

- Cash and carry (47%): Food and nonfood products at wholesale prices, primarily to business customers, under the Metro and Makro store brands.

- Hypermarkets and supermarkets (21%): Food products under the Extra store brand and, in hypermarkets, food and nonfood products under the Real store brand.

- Specialty stores (25%): Two chains in this group, Media Markt and Saturn, offer electronic products, and the other, Praktiker, specializes in the home improvement market.

- Department stores (7%): A variety of household and clothing products in more upscale shopping environments under the Kauflof store brand.

Metro generates about 53% of its sales within Germany, 45% from the rest of Europe, and 2% from elsewhere. Revenues were €53.5 billion in 2004.

Most of its nearly 4,000 stores worldwide are leased. Some of these leases are capitalized (i.e., the present value of future lease payments appear on the balance sheet), but most are not.

Metro's 2004 annual report reveals the following information:

- Capital leases at the end of 2004 had a present value of €2,090 million. Minimum payments required in 2005 are €280 million. The weighted-average interest rate for these leases was 6.1%.

- As of the end of 2004, minimum payments required under operating leases were €1182 million for 2005, €4,234 million in total payments over the next four years (2006–2009), and €5,548 million in total payments for 2010 and beyond.

- Shareholders' equity at the end of 2004 was €4,739 million, debt was €9,506 million, and invested capital was €14 245 million.

Metro reported the following results in 2005:

- Revenues were €55.7 billion.

- Net operating profit after tax (NOPAT) was €1,368 million, based on a tax rate of 30%.

- Net income was €649 million.

- Cash flow from operations was €2.2 billion in 2005, down from €2.9 billion in 2004 and €3.1 billion in 2003.

Required

Note: Round all euro amounts to the nearest million.

a. What reasons can you give for why Metro relies so extensively on leasing?

b. Prepare the journal entry to record cash payments under capital leases for 2005.

c. Prepare the journal entry to record cash payments under operating leases for 2005.

d. Using the year-end 2004 figure for invested capital, estimate ROIC for 2005.

e. Calculate the present value of Metro's operating leases as of the end of 2004. For your calculations, assume that (1) the lease payments are made at the end of each year, (2) the implicit weighted-average interest rate for the leases is 6%, (3) payments for 2006 through 2009 are made evenly throughout the period (i.e., lease payments are the same in each year), and (4) payments in 2010 and beyond are made evenly over the next 10 years.

f. Give the journal entries to convert the operating leases into capital leases as of the end of 2004, and account for them as capital leases in 2005. Assume an amortization period of 15 years.

g. Reestimate NOPAT for 2005 after accounting for the operating leases as capital leases.

h. Reestimate ROIC, after accounting for the operating leases as capital leases.

i. What effect will capitalization of the operating leases have on cash flow from operations?

Case Study

11-2 Pennzoil-Quaker State and the Sale of Receivables

Pennzoil-Quaker State (PQS) is one of the world's leading producers of motor oil. The company sells some of its receivables through a special purpose entity. The receivables sold under this facility totaled $153 million at the end of Year 9 and $115 million at the end of Year 8. None of these receivables, or the related financing, appears on PQS's balance sheet.

Additional information (all amounts in millions of $)

Sales (Year 9)	$2,951
Receivables (end of Year 9)	312
Receivables (end of Year 8)	546
Total debt (end of Year 9)	1,096

Shareholders' equity (end of Year 9)	950
Cash flow from operations (Year 9)	58

Required

a. Calculate PQS's days of receivables based on (1) end-of-year receivables, and (2) average receivables for the year.

b. Calculate PQS's debt–equity ratio.

c. Recalculate your answers to (a) after restoring the receivables that were removed from the balance sheet. Do the same for (b). Restate cash flow from operations, if necessary. What insights can you draw from these adjustments?

Case Study

11-3 Executory Contracts

Alcoa is one of the world's leading producers of aluminum and related products. According to the company's Year 6 Annual Report, Alcoa's Australian subsidiary is party to a number of natural gas and electricity contracts that expire at various times over the next 20 years.

Under these take-or-pay contracts, Alcoa of Australia is obligated to pay for a minimum amount of natural gas or electricity even if these commodities are not required for operations. Commitments related to these contracts total (in millions):

Year 7	$176
Year 8	180
Year 9	185
Year 10	178
Year 11	154
Thereafter	2,243

Required

a. Using a discount rate of 6%, calculate the present value of Alcoa's take-or-pay contracts. Assume payments are made at the beginning of each year. Make whatever assumptions you think are appropriate regarding the $2243 million of commitments after Year 11. Assume that your analysis takes place early in Year 7.

b. Alcoa reports the following data in its Year 6 Annual Report:

Total debt	$6,633 million
Shareholders' equity	$10,614 million

Calculate Alcoa's debt-to-equity ratio. Recalculate the ratio after adjusting for the take-or-pay contracts. Comment on the results.

c. Should Alcoa's take-or-pay contracts appear on its balance sheet? Why or why not?

NOTE

1. The theme of the discussion in Chapter 5 is when securitization is used to remove receivables from the balance sheet, it can artificially boost cash flow from operations.

12 Accounting for Bonds

Introduction

To finance the purchase of assets, corporations can raise investment capital in one of two ways: debt or equity. If a company's management decides to raise debt capital, they can borrow from either a financial institution, such as HSBC or Citigroup, or by issuing bonds through the capital markets.

Bonds are normally sold to the public through a third party ("underwriter"), for example, an investment bank. Bonds are interest-bearing notes that involve contractual commitments requiring the issuing company to make cash interest payments to the bondholder and a principal payment when the bond matures. The maturity date is usually between 1 and 30 years from the date of the issuance. After issuance, bonds are freely negotiable; that is, they can be purchased and sold in the open market.

In this chapter, we focus on corporate bonds, drawing on the example of Oracle Corporation and a fictional competitor, BriteSoft Ltd. (The topic of convertible bonds – bonds that are convertible into shares of common stock – will be covered in the chapter on shareholders' equity.)

In November 2017, Oracle issued bonds (or what the company calls "notes") in the capital markets. To accomplish this sale, it hired a consortium of investment banks and produced a prospectus that describes the terms of the notes.

In addition, a pricing notice (Table 12.1) was published, dated 7 November 2017.

The notice reveals that Oracle issued notes with a face value (or "par value") of $10 billion. The offering comprised five distinct parts, each with a face value of $2,000. The bonds were sold at a discount to par, ranging from 99.934% of par for the notes expiring in 2023, down to 99.531% for the notes expiring in 2047.

For example, the 2023 notes were issued at an initial selling price of $1,998.68 (or $2,000 × 99.934%). In total, the amount of cash raised by Oracle was $9.97583 billion. Oracle had to share some of the proceeds with its underwriters. More specifically, it is paid commissions of 0.2990% of the aggregate principle amount ($10 billion), or $29.9 million. Therefore, the net proceeds were $9.94593 billion.

Although the accounting for bonds is broadly the same under US GAAP and IFRS, one difference is worth noting. Under the former, fees paid to underwriters, investment bankers, lawyers, and accountants involved in the bond issue are recorded separately as an asset and amortized over the life of the bond. The carrying value of the bond is therefore unaffected by the fees. Under IFRS, however, the fees are treated as a reduction in the proceeds from issuance. The contractual obligations of the bond are the same in either case, but the recorded debt is lower under IFRS. This means that the effective interest rate is higher than it would be under US GAAP. Because Oracle is a US GAAP company, it recorded the liability at the full amount of the cash proceeds (before the underwriting commissions of nearly $30 million). The underwriting commissions were then capitalized as assets, to be amortized gradually over the lives of the bonds. If Oracle

Table 12.1   Oracle Corp (A stock corporation incorporated under the laws of the United States of America, having its corporate seat in Delaware): USD 10,000,000,000 five-part US dollar Notes

Characteristics of the notes

Aggregate principal amount:	$1,250,000,000 principal amount of 2.625% Notes due 2023 $2,000,000,000 principal amount of 2.950% Notes due 2024 $2,750,000,000 principal amount of 3.250% Notes due 2027 $1,750,000,000 principal amount of 3.800% Notes due 2037 $2,250,000,000 principal amount of 4.000% Notes due 2047
Form and denomination:	The Notes of each series will be issued in denominations of $2,000 in principal amount and multiples of $1,000 in excess thereafter
Issue price:	2023 Notes 99.934% 2024 Notes 99.842% 2027 Notes 99.889% 2037 Notes 99.624% 2047 Notes 99.531%
Interest rate:	2.625% per year for the 2023 Notes 2.950% per year for the 2024 Notes 3.250% per year for the 2027 Notes 3.800% per year for the 2037 Notes 4.000% per year for the 2047 Notes
Net proceeds before deduction of total expenses:	USD 9,975,830,000
Underwriting commission:	0.2990% of the aggregate principal amount
Yield:	2.637% for the 2023 Notes 2.975% for the 2024 Notes 3.263% for the 2027 notes 3.827% for the 2037 Notes 4.027% for the 2047 notes

were an IFRS company, the total bond liability would be the cash proceeds net of commissions. Because the commissions would be subtracted in calculating the net proceeds, there would be no need for a corresponding asset account.

Accounting for Bond Issuance

The price at which a firm issues bonds depends on two factors: the future cash payments that the bond contract requires the firm to make; and the rate of return demanded by investors. The required return is driven by the perceived the risk of the borrower, the general level of interest rates, and potential other factors. The issuing price equals the required cash flows, discounted at the appropriate market interest rate.

When bonds are sold in the market they can sell at face (par) value, at a premium to par, or at a discount to par. To understand when each scenario will play out we need to compare the stated coupon interest rate that the bond promises to pay with the interest rate required by the market:

Coupon Rate	=	Market-required rate	Bonds will sell at face (par) value
Coupon Rate	>	Market-required rate	Bonds will sell at premium to face value
Coupon Rate	<	Market-required rate	Bonds will sell at discount to face value

The following equation can be used to determine the value of a bond that makes coupon payments annually, where C represents the coupon payment, F the face value or principal, and r the market-required interest rate:

$$B_0 = C\left[\frac{1-(1+r)^{-t}}{r}\right] + \frac{F}{(1+r)^t}$$

Most bonds make interest payments semiannually. The equation to determine the value of such bonds is shown below. Note that the coupon payment and market-required interest rate are divided by two and the number of payments is multiplied by two.

$$B_0 = \frac{C}{2}\left[\frac{1-(1+r/2)^{-2t}}{r/2}\right] + \frac{F}{(1+r/2)^{2t}}$$

Accounting for Bonds Sold at Par

Let's assume that a five-year bond is issued by BriteSoft Ltd., with a coupon of 9% paying interest semiannually and a market interest rate of 9%. Because the coupon rate and market interest rate are the same, the bond is issued at face value.

The accounting entry to record the issue of a €100,000 on 1 January 2018 would be:

Cash	100,000	
Bonds payable		100,000

The company will later record the semiannual coupon payments as follows:

Interest expense	4,500	
Cash or accrued interest		4,500

When bonds are redeemed at the maturity date, BriteSoft would simply pay cash to the bondholders in the amount of the face value and remove the bonds payable from the balance sheet. The journal entry will be:

Bonds payable	100,000	
Cash		100,000

Table 12.2 summarizes the transactions that would occur over the life of the bond.

Accounting for Bonds Sold at a Premium

If the coupon rate exceeds the market interest rate, the bonds will sell at a premium to face value. This result occurs because, if the bonds were sold at par, the rate of return would exceed that demanded by investors. The bonds can sell at a premium and still offer a competitive return to investors.

Table 12.2   The Transactions and Accounting for a Bond Sold at Par.

Issue date:	1 January 2018	
Maturity face:	€100,000	
Coupon rate:	9%	Market interest rate: 9%
Coupon payment:	Semiannually	

Semiannual interest date	Coupon payment	Interest expense	Bond carrying amount
1 January 2018			€100,000
1 July	€4,500	€4,500	100,000
1 January 2019	4,500	4,500	100,000
1 July	4,500	4,500	100,000
1 January 2020	4,500	4,500	100,000
1 July	4,500	4,500	100,000
1 January 2021	4,500	4,500	100,000
1 July	4,500	4,500	100,000
1 January 2022	4,500	4,500	100,000
1 July	4,500	4,500	100,000
1 January 2023	4,500	4,500	100,000

To illustrate, if BriteSoft issues a bond with a 9% coupon when the market interest rate is only 8%, the issuance price is €104,100. This figure is determined by discounting, at the market rate of interest on the issuance date, the expected future cash flows (€4,500 every six months and €100,000 when the bond matures). The entry would be:

```
Cash                   104,100
   Bonds payable                100,000
   Bond premium                   4,100
```

The carrying value on the balance sheet equals the credit to bonds payable, plus the bond premium or, in this case, €104,100.

As for the income statement, the premium needs to be offset against future interest expense, a process called bond premium amortization. Two methods of amortization are possible: effective interest method and straight line method.

Effective Interest Method

Under the effective interest method, the periodic interest expense is determined by multiplying the amount to be amortized (book value at the beginning of each period), by the "effective" (market) interest rate at the time the bonds were issued (8% in our example). As the issuing entity pays the coupon (€4,500), which is higher than the effective interest expense (4% × €104,100, or €4,164, for the first six months in year 1), the "excess" interest paid partly amortizes the premium. Put another way, the premium amortization for each (interest) period is the difference between the interest calculated at the stated coupon rate (9%) and the interest calculated at the effective rate (8%).

The virtue of this approach is that interest expense equals a fixed interest rate (the rate that prevailed in the market when the bonds were issued), multiplied by the balance in the bonds payable account at the beginning of each period. In other words, interest expense will be 8% of the outstanding balance in the bonds payable account in every period throughout the bond's life.

The journal entry on the date of the first payment will be:

Interest expense	4,164	
Amortization of bond premium	336	
Cash or accrued interest		4,500

The balance sheet total for bonds will equal €104,100 the proceeds from the bond issue, minus the amortization of the bond premium of €336, or €103,764.

The journal entry on the date of the second payment will be the following:

Interest expense	4,151	
Amortization of bond premium	349	
Cash or accrued interest		4,500

where interest expense equals the carrying value of the bond at the beginning of the period ($103,764), times the semiannual interest rate of 4%:

$$103,764 \times 4\% = 4,151$$

The carrying value on the balance sheet will now equal €103,764, minus the amortized portion of the bond premium for the second six months (€349), or €103,415. Over time, the carrying value will converge to the par value of €100,000, reaching this value just as the bond is about to mature.

Straight-Line Method

Here, interest expense is a constant amount each payment period. The bond premium of €4,100 is divided by 10 (the number of six-month periods over the bond's life), or €410. The interest expense in each of those 10 periods is therefore €4,500, minus €410, or €4,090. The resulting journal entry is:

Interest expense	4,090	
Amortization of bond premium	410	
Cash or accrued interest		4,500

Because the carrying value of the bonds decreases after each interest payment, while the interest expense is the same in each period, interest expense will gradually increase as a percentage of the carrying value.

The effective interest method is preferred because interest expense is a constant percentage of the carrying value, and that percentage is exactly equal to the market interest rate that prevailed when the bonds were issued. For this reason, the method is required under both US GAAP and IFRS. For tax purposes, however, many countries permit the straight-line approach.

In either case, by the time BriteSoft's bonds reach maturity, any premium on the bonds will have been completely amortized.

The journal entry for the payment of the principal (i.e., maturity value) will be:

Bonds payable	100,000	
Cash		100,000

The above example, for both the effective interest and straight-line methods, is summarized in Table 12.3.

Table 12.3   Bond Issued at a Premium: Effective Interest and Straight-Line Methods (in Box) Amortization

Issue date:	1 January 2018				
Maturity face:	€100,000				
Coupon rate:	**9%**		Market interest rate: **8%**		
Coupon payment:	Semiannually				

Semiannual interest date	Coupon payment	Interest expense	Premium amortization	Premium balance	Bond carrying amount
1 January 2018				−€4,100	€104,100
1 July	€4,500	€4,164	−€336	−3,764	103,764
1 January 2019	4,500	4,151	−349	−3,415	103,415
1 July	4,500	4,137	−363	−3,051	103,051
1 January 2020	4,500	4,122	−378	−2,673	102,673
1 July	4,500	4,107	−393	−2,280	102,280
1 January 2021	4,500	4,091	−409	−1,871	101,871
1 July	4,500	4,075	−425	−1,446	101,446
1 January 2022	4,500	4,058	−442	−1,004	101,004
1 July	4,500	4,040	−460	−544	100,544
1 January 2023	4,500	3,956	−544	0	100,000

Semiannual interest date	Coupon payment	Interest expense	Premium amortization	Premium balance	Bond carrying amount
1 January 2018				−€4,100	€104,100
1 July	€4,500	€4,090	−€410	−3,690	103,690
1 January 2019	4,500	4,090	−410	−3,280	103,280
1 July	4,500	4,090	−410	−2,870	102,870
1 January 2020	4,500	4,090	−410	−2,460	102,460
1 July	4,500	4,090	−410	−2,050	102,050
1 January 2021	4,500	4,090	−410	−1,640	101,640
1 July	4,500	4,090	−410	−1,230	101,230
1 January 2022	4,500	4,090	−410	−820	100,820
1 July	4,500	4,090	−410	−410	100,410
1 January 2023	4,500	4,090	−410	0	100,000

Bond Redemption Before Maturity

Corporate bonds often come with a provision that gives the issuing company the option to retire all or part of the bond issue before maturity. In effect, the bond grants a call option to the issuer, granting it the right to buy back the bonds at a stipulated price. The bonds are therefore said to be "callable bonds." Normally, the call provision does not kick in right away. The company will have to wait some period of time, say, two to five years, before it can buy them back.

The call feature tends to be exercised in periods of declining interest rates. As interest rates fall, the value of the bond may rise above the call price, giving the company a strong incentive to repurchase the bonds. Such provisions give rise to reinvestment risk for the bondholders because, if the call is exercised, the cash proceeds will be reinvested in other financial instruments at presumably lower rates of interest. For this reason, investors demand a higher return on bonds having call features.

To illustrate the accounting, imagine bonds with a €100,000 face value and a €3,000 unamortized premium are redeemed for €102,000. The following journal entry is recorded:

Bonds payable	100,000	
Premium on bonds payable	3,000	
Cash		102,000
Gain on redemption		1,000

When a firm retires a bond for cash, it reports the cash paid in the financing section of the cash flow statement. In most cases, the amount of cash needed to retire the liability differs from the book value of the liability at the time of retirement. The retirement therefore generates a gain (when the book value exceeds cash paid), as in the above example, or a loss (when the cash paid exceeds book value). In calculating cash flow from operations under the indirect method, gains are subtracted from net income, while losses are added back.

Accounting for Bonds Issued at a Discount

If the market-required rate exceeds the coupon rate, the bonds will sell at a discount to par. Investors are unwilling to pay the par value for a bond that offers a coupon rate lower than the prevailing interest rate for bonds in that class.

As you may recall, in the case in the Oracle offering, the price of the bond was 99.755% of par. The expected capital gain for investors (the difference between par and the issuance price) compensates them for the discrepancy between the cash return promised by the bond and the market interest rate.

Returning to our example for BriteSoft Ltd., if the market rate is 10% and the coupon rate remains at 9%, the €100,000 bonds will be issued at a discount, selling at a price of 96.149. The proceeds are based on 10 payments of €4,500 and the maturity value of €100,000, discounted at 10%. The journal entry would be:

Cash	96,149	
Bond discount	3,851	
Bonds payable		100,000

Although the bond's maturity value is €100,000, the carrying value on the balance sheet on the date of issuance is €96,149. Just like the bond premium example, the discount (€3,851) will have to be amortized over the life of the bond. The amortization process will gradually cause the bond's balance sheet value to converge to the maturity value, such that the carrying value will be exactly €100,000 just as the bond is ready to mature.

Below, we show the entries for the first six-month period under both the effective interest and straight-line methods. The payments and interest expense under both methods are summarized in Table 12.4.

Table 12.4   Bond Issued at a Discount: Effective Interest and Straight-Line Methods (in Box) Amortization

Issue date:	1 January 2018				
Maturity face:	€100,000				
Coupon rate:	**9%**		Market interest rate: **10%**		
Coupon payment:	Semiannually				

Semiannual interest date	Coupon payment	Interest expense	Discount amortization	Discount balance	Bond carrying amount
1 January 2018				€3,851	€96,149
1 July	€4,500	€4,807	€307	3,544	96,456
1 January 2019	4,500	4,823	323	3,221	96,779
1 July	4,500	4,839	339	2,882	97,118
1 January 2020	4,500	4,856	356	2,526	97,474
1 July	4,500	4,874	374	2,152	97,848
1 January 2021	4,500	4,892	392	1,760	98,240
1 July	4,500	4,912	412	1,348	98,652
1 January 2022	4,500	4,933	433	915	99,085
1 July	4,500	4,954	454	461	99,539
1 January 2023	4,500	4,961	461	0	100,000

Semiannual interest date	Coupon payment	Interest expense	Discount amortization	Discount balance	Bond carrying amount
1 January 2018				€3,851	€96,149
1 July	€4,500	€4,885	€385	3,466	96,534
1 January 2019	4,500	4,885	385	3,081	96,919
1 July	4,500	4,885	385	2,696	97,304
1 January 2020	4,500	4,885	385	2,311	97,689
1 July	4,500	4,885	385	1,926	98,075
1 January 2021	4,500	4,885	385	1,540	98,460
1 July	4,500	4,885	385	1,155	98,845
1 January 2022	4,500	4,885	385	770	99,230
1 July	4,500	4,885	385	385	99,615
1 January 2023	4,500	4,885	385	0	100,000

Effective Interest Method

Interest expense for the first six months is set equal to the semiannual market interest rate (5%), times the carrying of the debt at the moment of issuance (€96,149), or €4,807. The semiannual coupon payment is €4,500, as it was in the bond premium example. The resulting journal entry on the day of the first payment (6 months after the bond is issued) will be:

Interest expense	4,807	
Amortization of bond discount		307
Cash or accrued interest		4,500

Straight-Line Method

Under this method, an equal portion of the bond's discount is amortized for each six-month period over the bond's five-year life. This means that every six months, the bond will be amortized by €3,851 (the total discount), divided by 10 (the number of six-month periods over the bond's life), or $385:

Interest expense	4,885	
Amortization of bond discount		385
Cash or accrued interest		4,500

Zero-Coupon Bonds

A special class of long-term debt, known as "zero-coupon bonds," does not offer regular interest payments. Instead, the investor receives all the interest in one lump sum when the bond matures. The bond is therefore sold at a deep discount and redeemed at full face (i.e., par) value when it matures. The difference between face value and the issuance price is the interest that accumulates over the bond's life.

The issuing price is based on the present value of the principal amount to be received by the bondholder at maturity, with the discount rate equal to the market interest rate on date of issuance. It is calculated using the equation for the present value of a single sum:

$$PV = \frac{CF_t}{(1+r)^t}$$

Assuming BriteSoft Ltd. issues a five-year €100,000 par value zero-coupon bond when the market interest rate is 10% and the interest compounds semi-annually, the selling price would be €61,391 [€100,000 ÷ (1 + 5%)^{10}]. The transaction would be recorded as follows:

Cash	61,391	
Bond discount	38,609	
Bonds payable		100,000

As with coupon-paying bonds, the discount is amortized using either the effective interest method or the straight-line method. Just as in the previous examples, the bond's carrying value, which begins at €61,391, will gradually increase over the bond's life, reaching €100,000 just prior to maturity.

Table 12.5   Zero-Coupon Bonds: Effective Interest and Straight-Line Methods (in Box) Amortization

Issue date: 1 January 2018

Maturity face: €100,000

Coupon rate: **0%**   Market interest rate: **10%**

Coupon payment: Semiannually

Semiannual interest date	Coupon payment	Interest expense	Discount amortization	Discount balance	Bond carrying amount
1 January 2018				€38,609	€61,391
1 July	€0	€3,070	€3,070	35,539	64,461
1 January 2019	0	3,223	3,223	32,316	67,684
1 July	0	3,384	3,384	28,932	71,068
1 January 2020	0	3,553	3,553	25,379	74,621
1 July	0	3,731	3,731	21,648	78,352
1 January 2021	0	3,918	3,918	17,730	82,270
1 July	0	4,113	4,113	13,617	86,383
1 January 2022	0	4,319	4,319	9,298	90,702
1 July	0	4,535	4,535	4,762	95,238
1 January 2023	0	4,762	4,762	0	100,000

Semiannual interest date	Coupon payment	Interest expense	Discount amortization	Discount balance	Bond carrying amount
1 January 2018				€38,609.0	€61,391.0
1 July	€0	€3,860.9	€3,860.9	34,748.1	65,251.9
1 January 2019	0	3,860.9	3,860.9	30,887.2	69,112.8
1 July	0	3,860.9	3,860.9	27,026.3	72,973.7
1 January 2020	0	3,860.9	3,860.9	23,165.4	76,834.6
1 July	0	3,860.9	3,860.9	19,304.5	80,695.5
1 January 2021	0	3,860.9	3,860.9	15,443.6	84,556.4
1 July	0	3,860.9	3,860.9	11,582.7	88,417.3
1 January 2022	0	3,860.9	3,860.9	7,721.8	92,278.2
1 July	0	3,860.9	3,860.9	3,860.9	96,139.1
1 January 2023	0	3,860.9	3,860.9	0.0	100,000.0

Below, we show the entries for the first six-month period under both methods. The figures are summarized in Table 12.5.

Effective Interest Method

The journal entry to record interest expense is:

Interest expense	3,070	
Amortization of bond discount		3,070

where interest expense equals the bond's carrying value at the beginning of the period (€61,391), times the semiannual interest rate of 5%. Notice that because there is no coupon payment, the full amount of the interest expense is used to amortize the bond discount.

The balance sheet value at the end of the first six-month period would equal the beginning amount (€61,391), plus the accumulated bond discount (€3,070), or €64,461.

Because the bond is issued at a steep discount, and the carrying value rises over the bond's life, the interest expense noticeably increases over time.

Straight-Line Method

Here, the interest expense is a constant amount in each period, resulting in the following entry for each of the 10 periods over the bond's life:

Interest expense	3,860.90	
Amortization of bond discount		3,860.90

where the amount of the bond discount to be amortized, and therefore the interest expense, is equal to the total discount (€38,609), divided by 10, or €3,860.90.

KEY LESSONS FROM THE CHAPTER

- Bonds are normally sold to the public through a third party (called an underwriter).

- Bonds are interest-bearing notes that involve contractual commitments requiring the issuing company to make cash interest payments to the bondholder and a principal payment when the bond matures.

- The price at which a firm issues bonds in the capital market depends on two factors: the future cash payments that the bond contract requires the firm to make; and the discount rate that the market deems appropriate given the risk of the borrower, and the general level of interest rates in the economy.

- If the coupon rate equals the market rate, the bond will sell at par. If the coupon rate is higher than the market rate, the bond will sell at a premium. If the coupon rate is less than the market rate, the bond will sell at a discount. If the coupon rate is zero

(a so-called "zero-coupon" bond), the bond will sell at a deep discount to face value.

- Under US GAAP and IFRS bond premiums and discounts are amortized using the effective interest rate method. In some countries, the straight-line approach is used for tax purposes. The former method is preferred because interest expense will be a constant percentage of the bond's carrying value throughout the life of the bond. The percentage will equal the market interest rate that prevailed when the bonds were issued. (US GAAP does allow the straight-line method, but only if it yields results similar to those under the effective rate method.)

- In most cases, the amount of cash used to retire a bond differs from the book value of the bond at the time of retirement. Thus, the retirement generates a gain (when the book value exceeds the cash payment) or a loss (when the cash payment exceeds book value).

KEY TERMS AND CONCEPTS FROM THE CHAPTER

Face value	Straight-line method	Market rate	Sell at premium
Coupon rate	Maturity	Zero-coupon bond	Sell at discount
Effective interest method	Callable bonds	Sell at par	zero-coupon

QUESTIONS

1. What are the advantages to companies of issuing bonds instead of borrowing from commercial banks?

2. Describe the relationship between interest rates and bond prices.

3. True or false: The yield on a bond is independent of the coupon rate.

4. What happens to the carrying (i.e., balance-sheet) value of a bond after issuance, both for bonds issued at a premium and those issued at a discount?

5. What are the relative advantages and disadvantages of the effective interest method and straight-line amortization for bond discounts and premiums?

6. True or false: The effective interest method gives a constant amount of interest expense on bonds each period.

7. Firm A issues €10 million face value, 8% semiannual coupon bonds at a price to yield 7% compounded semiannually. Firm B issues €10 million face value, 6% semiannual coupon bonds at a price to yield 7%. Will these firms receive the same initial issue price for these bonds? Explain.

PROBLEMS

12.1 Journal Entries and Balance Sheet Presentation for Bonds

On 1 May 2016, Société LePoint issued €2,400,000, 9%, five-year bonds at face value. The bonds pay interest semiannually on 1 May and 1 November. Financial statements are prepared each year on 31 December.

Required

a. Prepare the journal entry to record the issuance of the bonds.

b. Prepare the adjusting entry to record the accrual of interest on 31 December 2016.

c. Show the balance sheet presentation for bonds on 31 December 2016.

d. Prepare the journal entry to record the payment of interest on 1 May 2017.

e. Prepare the journal entry to record the payment of interest on 1 November 2017.

f. Assume that on 1 November 2017, LePoint calls the bonds (i.e., buys them back) at 102. Record the redemption of the bonds.

12.2 Amortization of Bond Discount and Premium

Carmon Trading and Distribution Company issued $30 million, 10% coupon bonds on 1 January 2014, due on 31 December 2018. The market interest rate on the issuance date was 12%, and the bonds pay interest on 30 June and 31 December of each year.

On January 1, 2015, Carmon issues another tranche of $30 million, 10% coupon bonds, due on 31 December 2019. However, the market interest rate had declined to 8% on the date of issuance. The bonds pay interest on 30 June and 31 December of each year.

At the end of 2016, the carrying value for the first tranche of bonds was $28,960,650 and $31,572,150 for the second tranche. At the end of 2017, the carrying value for the first tranche was $29,450,100 and $31,088,850 for the second tranche.

Required

a. How much interest expense did Carmon record in 2017 for the first tranche?

b. How much interest expense did Carmon record in 2017 for the second tranche?

12.3 Journal Entries for Bond Issuance and Subsequent Interest Payments

On 1 July 2016, Rosenhurst Corporation issued £6 million face value, 10%, 10-year bonds for £6,815,439. The proceeds resulted in an effective interest rate of 8%. Rosenhurst uses the effective-interest method to amortize a bond discount or premium. The bonds pay interest semiannually on 1 July and 1 January.

Required

a. Prepare the journal entry to record the issuance of the bonds on 1 July 2016.

b. Prepare an amortization table through 31 December 2017.

c. Prepare the journal entry to record the accrual of interest and the amortization of the premium on 31 December 2016.

d. Prepare the journal entry to record the payment of interest and amortization of the premium on 1 July 2017.

e. Prepare the journal entry to record the accrual of interest and the amortization of the premium on 31 December 2017.

13 Provisions and Contingencies

Introduction

The purpose of this chapter is to address the accounting treatment for provisions and contingencies. The chapter draws on the examples of L'Oréal and Merck to illustrate the key concepts. Sources of provisioning include corporate restructuring, warranties, environmental clean-up, litigation, and onerous contracts.[1] Contingencies can arise for several reasons, but litigation-related costs are the most common.

To begin, let's imagine a vacuum-cleaner manufacturer offering a two-year warranty for its products. If something goes wrong within the warranty period, the company either repairs the machine or replaces it. This means that every time a vacuum cleaner is sold, a potential liability is assumed. For accounting purposes, the company could, in theory, report a warranty-related expense only when resources are paid out to service a warranty (e.g., when a faulty machine is brought in by a customer for repair). But this approach would violate both the matching principle and conservatism. The matching principle says that any costs incurred to generate revenue must be "matched" against the revenue in the period in which the revenue is recognized, even if cash payments will not be made until a future period, and the amount is not known with certainty. Conservatism says that companies should not understate liabilities or expenses. If we have reason to believe that the company has incurred obligations as a result of past transactions (e.g., the sale of vacuum cleaners), the related liability and the warranty expense that go with it should be recognized immediately.

Simply put, both matching and conservatism require the recognition of the liability and expense in the period of sale, even if cash payments will not happen until later. Of course, this requirement gives rise to a problem: how do we know what the warranty cost is likely to be? In fact, we cannot know (at least not with precision), but estimates must be made anyway.

Because all provisions are estimates, and estimates are a function of a set of assumptions made by management, companies have some latitude in the figures they report in the financial statements. In short, they can underprovision or overprovision. The effect of the former is to understate expenses or losses in the current period, thereby boosting profits. Of course, underprovisioning must eventually be corrected, as actual expenditures related to the provision will, at some point, exceed the recognized provision. This means that future accounting periods will be burdened with higher expenses or losses, and thus lower profits. Overprovisioning has the opposite effect, overstating expenses in the current period (and understating profits), while understating expenses in future periods. Overprovisioning is especially important for the financial statement reader to understand because of the tendency of some companies to use it as a means of creating "hidden" or "cookie-jar" reserves. The risk of overprovisioning is highest when companies enjoy highly profitable years or, conversely, when they take huge write-offs to acknowledge underperforming assets bought in previous years. The temptation in such cases is to deliberately overstate the amount of the write-off, allowing reversals (and higher profits) in future years. This practice is widely known as "big bath accounting."

Defining Provisions

IFRS has one specific standard that deals generally with how companies should account for provisions, while US GAAP has several standards addressing specific types of provisions – for example, environmental liabilities or restructuring costs.[2]

According to IFRS, a company should recognize a provision only when:

- the entity has a present obligation to transfer economic benefits as a result of past events;

- it is probable that such a transfer will be required to settle the obligation; and

- a reliable estimate of the amount of the obligation can be made.

A present obligation arises from an obligating event and may take the form of either a legal obligation or a constructive obligation. A legal obligation may arise, for example, from minimum payments a company must make to laid-off employees. A constructive obligation may arise from the same event if the company has a practice of paying workers above the legal minimum. Even if the company is not legally obligated to make supplemental payments, but corporate history and policy suggest that they will, a constructive obligation exists. The key point is that without some obligation on the company's part, whether legal or constructive, a provision cannot be recognized. Also, if the company can avoid the expenditure by its future actions, it has no present obligation, and a provision is not recognized.

To illustrate, consider the case of restructuring events. According to IFRS, a present obligation exists only when the entity is "demonstrably committed" to the restructuring. This criterion is met when there is a binding agreement to sell or dispose of assets (legal obligation), or when the company has a detailed plan for the restructuring and is unable to withdraw because implementation has already started or the main features have been announced to those affected by the plan (constructive obligation).

The term "past events" implies that provisions cannot be taken for events that might happen in the future. In other words, a company is not permitted to recognize a provision as a sort of contingency in case some loss is incurred.

Under IFRS, "probable" means "more likely than not" (i.e., any probability greater than 50%). The meaning of probable under US GAAP normally conveys a higher probability threshold, perhaps as high as 80%.[3]

Finally, a provision should not be recognized unless a reliable estimate can be made of it. In cases where the other criteria are met but this one is not, disclosure is made in the form of a note.

Measuring the Provision

According to IFRS, the amount recognized as a provision must be the best estimate of the minimum expenditure required to settle the present obligation at the balance sheet date. The entity must discount the anticipated cash flows using a discount rate that reflects current market assessments of the time value of money and those risks specific to the liability. If a range of estimates is predicted and no amount in the range is more likely than any other, the "midpoint" of the range must be used to measure the liability.

US GAAP is similar to IFRS, however, if a range of estimates is present and no amount in the range is more likely than any other amount in the range, the "minimum" (rather than the midpoint) must be used. Also, a provision is discounted only when the timing of the cash flows is fixed.

Disclosure of Provisions: Interpreting the Notes

This section focuses on how to interpret corporate disclosures of provisions. The material in Box 13.1 comes from the 2016 annual report of L'Oréal, the Paris-based cosmetics giant.

The first panel in the note (part (a)) reports total provisions of €1,144.0 million as of the end of 2016 (2015 = €950.4 million), of which €810.7 million are current (i.e., payment of the liability is expected within 12 months) and €333.3 million are noncurrent. Nearly all of these provisions

BOX 13.1   Example of Corporate Disclosures for Provisions

13.1.1 Closing Balances

€ millions	12.31.2016	12.31.2015	12.31.2014
Non-current provisions for liabilities and charges	333.3	195.9	193.6
Other non-current provisions[1]	333.3	195.9	193.6
Current provisions for liabilities and charges	810.7	754.6	722.0
Provisions for restructuring	47.5	50.9	65.5
Provisions for product returns	323.4	309.3	244.4
Other current provisions[1]	439.8	394.4	412.1
TOTAL	1,144.0	950.4	915.6

(1) This item includes provisions for tax risks and litigation, industrial, environmental and commercial risks relating to operations (breach of contract), personnel-related costs and risks relating to investigations carried out by competition authorities.
The provisions relating to investigations carried out by competition authorities amount to €214.4 million at December 31st, 2016 compared with €212.5 million at December 31st, 2015 and €239.4 million at December 31st, 2014 (note 12.2.2.a and b).
The provisions relating to the dispute on IPI with the tax administration in Brazil amount to €91.4 million and €20.8 million respectively at December 31st, 2016 and December 31st, 2015 (note 12.2.1.).
This caption also includes investments in associates when the Group's share in net assets is negative (note 8).

13.1.2 Changes in Provisions for Liabilities and Charges During the Period

€ millions	12.31.2014	12.31.2015	Charges[2]	Reversals (used)[2]	Reversals (not used)[2]	Other[1]	12.31.2016
Provisions for restructuring	65.5	50.9	48.5	−40.4	−6.1	−5.4	47.5
Provisions for product returns	244.4	309.3	303.1	−216.8	−79.3	7.2	323.4
Other provisions for liabilities and charges	605.7	590.2	219.7	−115.2	−51.8	130.1	773.1
TOTAL	915.6	950.4	571.3	−372.4	−137.2	131.9	1,144.0

1 Mainly resulting from translation differences and €58.4 million relating to the dispute on IPI with the tax administration in Brazil (note 12.2.1.).
2 These figures can be analysed as follows:

€ millions	Charges	Reversals (used)	Reversals (not used)
◆ Other income and expenses	50.6	−40.5	−7.8
◆ Operating profit	480.2	−322.2	−107.1
◆ Income tax	40.5	−9.7	−22.3

relate to tax risks (including, for example, disputes with fiscal authorities over the amount of tax owed), litigation, restructuring costs, and a variety of commercial risks such as potential losses from breaches of contract and product returns.

The second panel (part (b)) reports on variations in provisions from the end of the previous year. In effect, it tells us the debits and credits made by L'Oréal in 2016 to the provisions account and why those entries were made. For example, "charges" indicates the additional provisions taken by the company during the year. Although numerous entries were probably made as a result of the charges, they can be summarized as follows:

Expenses and losses	571.3	
Provisions		571.3

For tax risks, litigation, breaches of contract, product returns, and restructuring.

"Reversals" indicate the reductions taken to the provisions account during the year. These reductions, recorded as debits to provisions, occur for either of two reasons:

1. The company pays off at least a portion of the liabilities incorporated in the account (e.g., redundancy payments are actually made to laid-off employees) or

2. The company is correcting an overestimation of provisions from previous years.

In L'Oréal's case, €372.4 of reversals were "used," which implies that they fall into the former category. Assuming that all of the payments were made in cash, the summary entry looks like this:

Provisions	372.4	
Cash		372.4

The reversals "not used" have a very different interpretation. In effect, L'Oréal is telling us that €137.2 million of provisions recognized in previous years will not have to be paid and, therefore, should be reversed. Put another way, provisions taken before 2016 were overstated by €137.2 million. Based on the final section of panel (b), the summary entry to record the unused provisions would be (in millions of €):

Provisions	137.2	
Other income and expenses		7.8
Income tax expense		22.3
Operating profit		107.1

Readers of financial statements should be especially wary of such reversals because their effect is to boost earnings. Note that all three credits are to income statement accounts, which means that the reversal allowed L'Oréal to increase reported pretax income by €137.2 million. And none of that increase in profit had anything to do with L'Oréal's activities in 2016. It simply reflected accounting adjustments. In effect, pre-2016 overprovisioning created a "hidden reserve" of profits that L'Oréal could draw on in 2016 to report higher profits. Judging whether the overprovisioning was deliberate or a good-faith reflection of conservative accounting policy is beyond the scope of this book.

Contingent Liabilities

IFRS defines a contingent liability as a possible obligation whose outcome will be confirmed only on the occurrence or nonoccurrence of uncertain future events outside the entity's control. It can also be a present obligation that is not recognized because it is not probable that an outflow of economic benefits (e.g., cash) is required, or the amount of the outflow cannot be reliably measured. Contingent liabilities are disclosed in the notes unless the probability of outflows is remote (in which case no disclosure is required). The most common type of contingent liability arises from litigation, where payment by the entity will depend on a future verdict or settlement.

When a contingency is both probable and the amount can be reasonably estimated, the contingency is accounted for in the same manner as a provision. Accounting for contingencies under US GAAP and IFRS is roughly the same, with the exception (noted earlier) that the bar for determining whether or not a liability is probable is set higher under US GAAP. To illustrate how contingencies work, and to contrast contingencies with provisions, we draw on the example of Merck, the US-based pharmaceutical company. The following example focuses on Merck's problems with Vioxx, an anti-inflammatory pain medication that had to be withdrawn after the drug was linked in scientific studies to heart disease.

Three basic issues arise. How does Merck account for (1) the drug's withdrawal, (2) current and future litigation costs (mainly the fees paid to legal counsel), and (3) any losses Merck suffers because of adverse court decisions or out-of-court settlements?

The note in Box 13.2 addresses the first issue.[4]

Ignoring tax effects, the summary entries to record these estimates include:

Sales	491.6	
Payables		491.6

To record the return of Vioxx after the recall.

If the customer had not yet paid for the product, the balancing credit is to accounts receivable. If the customer had already paid, the balancing credit is to a payable (i.e., a current liability).

Materials and production expense	93.2	
Inventories		93.2

To record the write-off of Vioxx inventory.

Marketing and admin expense	141.4	
Provision		141.4

To record the provision for the costs of the withdrawal.

This provision covers all of the costs of the product recall, apart from the write-off of inventories.

As for legal costs, those expected to be incurred before the end of 2007 were accrued, but later costs were not, as the note shown in Box 13.3 explains.

BOX 13.2   Merck's Note on the Accounting for the Withdrawal of Vioxx

On 30 September, 2004, the Company announced a voluntary worldwide withdrawal of *Vioxx*, its arthritis and acute pain medication. . . . In connection with the withdrawal, in 2004 the Company recorded an unfavorable adjustment to net income of $552.6 million. . . . The adjustment to pre-tax income was $726.2 million. Of this amount, $491.6 million related to estimated customer returns of product previously sold and was recorded as a reduction of Sales, $93.2 million related to write-offs of inventory held by the Company and was recorded in Materials and production expense, and $141.4 million related to estimated costs to undertake the withdrawal of the product and was recorded in Marketing and administrative expense. The tax benefit of this adjustment was $173.6 million. . . . The adjustment did not include charges for future legal defense costs.

BOX 13.3 Merck's Note on Legal Costs

Legal defense costs . . . are accrued when probable and reasonably estimable. As of December 31, 2004, the Company had established a reserve of $675 million solely for its future legal defense costs related to the *Vioxx* Litigation. During 2005, the Company spent $285 million in the aggregate in legal defense costs worldwide related to *Vioxx*. . . . In the fourth quarter, the Company recorded a charge of $295 million to increase the reserve . . . to $685 million at December 21, 2005. This reserve is based on certain assumptions and is the best estimate of the amount that the Company believes, at this time, it can reasonably estimate will be spent through 2007. . . . Events such as scheduled trials, that are expected to occur throughout 2006 and 2007, and the inherent inability to predict the ultimate outcomes of such trials, limit the Company's ability to reasonably estimate its legal costs beyond the end of 2007.

In 2004, the following entry was made:

Litigation expense	675.0	
Provisions		675.0

To record the establishment of the provision for litigation costs.

During 2005, the company disbursed $285 million to cover litigation needs:

Provisions	285.0	
Cash		285.0

To record litigation-related expenditures.

At the end of 2005, Merck management estimated that additional litigation costs, through the end of 2007, are expected to be $685 million. To bring the liability account up to the required amount, the following entry was needed:

Litigation expense	295.0	
Provisions		295.0

To record the increase in provisions.

Note that because no reliable estimate can be made for litigation costs beyond 2007, no liability is recognized.

Finally, the excerpt shown in Box 13.4 explains why the actual losses from adverse court decisions have not yet been accrued.

BOX 13.4 Merck's Explanation of Their Treatment of Losses from Adverse Court Decisions

. . . on August 19, 2005, in a trial in state court in Texas, the jury in Ernst vs. Merck reached a verdict in favor of the plaintiff and purported to award her a total of $253 million in compensatory and punitive damages. Under Texas law, the maximum amount that could be awarded to the plaintiff is capped at approximately $26 million. The Company intends to appeal this verdict after the completion of post-trial proceedings in the trial court. The Company believes that it has strong points to raise on appeal and is hopeful that the appeals process will correct the verdict. Since the Company believes that the potential for an unfavorable outcome is not probable, it has not established a reserve with respect to the verdict.

Although an analyst would rightly assume that Merck is likely to incur significant liabilities related to the thousands of cases pursued against it (losses may eventually run in the many billions of dollars), no reliable estimate of the amount could be made by the time the 2005 annual report was published. In addition, Merck could claim that losses from specific lawsuits, like the one cited above, might not result in any losses at all. As a result, no potential losses from court judgments of settlements had been acknowledged as of the end of 2005. As Merck's losses come into sharper focus, provisioning for those losses can be expected.

Contingent Assets

A contingent asset is a possible asset arising from past events whose existence will only be confirmed by future events not wholly within the entity's control. Possible cash receipts from the favorable settlement of a lawsuit is one common example. Contingent assets may require disclosure but should not be recognized in the accounts. In practice, the recognition of contingent assets is rare. However, such contingencies should be disclosed in the notes if an inflow of economic benefits is probable. When the realization of benefits is virtually certain, the related asset is no longer a contingency. At this point the asset should be recognized on the balance sheet. The asymmetric treatment of contingent liabilities (which often are recognized) and contingent assets (which almost never are) is a consequence of conservatism.

KEY LESSONS FROM THE CHAPTER

- Contingencies can arise for several reasons, but litigation-related costs are the most common source. Contingent liabilities are accrued (i.e., lead to an accounting entry affecting the income statement and balance sheet) only if the likelihood of the liability is greater than 50% under IFRS, rising to 80% under US GAAP, and it can be reasonably estimated. Otherwise, the contingency is disclosed in the notes (assuming it is material).

- Contingent assets are almost never recognized, unless the receipt of economic benefits is virtually certain. The asymmetric treatment between contingent liabilities and contingent assets is driven by the conservatism doctrine.

- Because all provisions are estimates, and estimates are a function of a set of assumptions made by management, companies have some latitude in the figures they report in the financial statements.

- Analysts should recognize that companies often create "cookie jar" (or "hidden") reserves in good years and reverse them in bad years. The effect is to smooth the time series of earnings.

- The creation of hidden reserves ranks among the most common forms of financial statement manipulation.

- A company should recognize a provision only when the entity has a present obligation to transfer economic benefits as a result of a past event, it is probable that such a transfer will be required, and a reliable estimate of the amount can be made.

- The amount recognized as a provision must be the best estimate of the minimum expenditure required to settle the present obligation as of the balance sheet date.

KEY TERMS AND CONCEPTS FROM THE CHAPTER

Provisions   Legal obligation   Constructive obligation   Contingent liabilities   Contingent assets

QUESTIONS

1. Why are contingent liabilities often recognized on the balance sheet, but contingent assets are not?

2. What requirements must be met before a provision can be recognized?

3. How are provisions used to "smooth" earnings?

4. Companies should neither over- nor underprovision for losses and routine expenses such as bad debts. And yet both forms of misstatement are common. Why?

5. True or false: The widespread adoption of IFRS has led to an increase in reported provisions.

6. What criteria determine whether a contingent liability should be accrued?

7. What is meant by the term "provisions reversal," and what effect does it have on the balance sheet and income statement?

PROBLEMS

13.1 Accounting for Warranties

The following note comes from a recent annual report for Sony Corporation:

> *Sony provides for the estimated cost of product warranties at the time revenue is recognized by either product category group or individual product. The product warranty is calculated based upon product sales, estimated probability of failure and estimated cost per claim. The variables used in the calculation of the provision are reviewed on a periodic basis.*
>
> *Certain subsidiaries in the Electronics business offer extended warranty programs. The consideration received through extended warranty service is deferred and amortized on a straight-line basis over the term of the extended warranty.*

Required

Based on this note, answer the following:

a. How does Sony account for the product warranties? What would be the impact of the estimated cost of product warranties on each of the three principal financial statements?

b. If Sony underestimates product warranties expense, how would it correct the error?

c. How does Sony treat the extended warranty program at (a) time of sale, and (b) in subsequent periods? How would the accounting affect each of the three principal financial statements?

8. True or false: When companies recognize a provision, for whatever purpose, it is highly unlikely that they will be able to deduct the loss or expense on their tax returns.

13.2 Analyzing and Interpreting Disclosures on the Provision for Warranties

Creative Technology, Ltd., a Singapore-based consumer electronics company, disclosed the following information regarding warranty provisions in its 2011 Annual Report.

The warranty period for the bulk of the products typically ranges between 1 to 2 years. The product warranty provision reflects management's best estimate of probable liability under its product warranties. Management determines the warranty provision based on known product failures (if any), historical experience, and other currently available evidence. Movements in provision for warranty are as follows:

($000)	2011	2010
Beginning of financial year	2,784	2,899
Provision (written back) made	(606)	1,915
Provision utilized	(711)	(2,030)
End of financial year	1,467	2,784

Required

a. Make the necessary journal entries to record the movements in the provisions for warranties account for 2010 and 2011.

b. What is meant by "provision made" and "provision written back"?

c. What does "provision utilized" mean?

d. Describe what happened in 2011 regarding Creative's provisions.

Case Study

13-1 Accounting for Contingent Assets: The Case of Cardinal Health

In a complaint dated 26 July 2007, and after a four-year investigation, the US Securities and Exchange Commission (SEC) accused Cardinal Health, the world's second largest distributor of pharmaceutical products, of violating generally accepted accounting principles (GAAP) by prematurely recognizing gains from a provisional settlement of a lawsuit filed against several vitamin manufacturers. Weeks earlier, the company agreed to pay $600 million to settle a lawsuit filed by shareholders who bought stock between 2000 and 2004, accusing Cardinal of accounting irregularities and inflated earnings.[*] The recovery from the vitamin companies should have been an unqualified positive for Cardinal Health. What happened?

[*]"Cardinal Health Settles Shareholders' Suit," The Associated Press, 1 June 2007.

(Continued)

Background

The story begins in 1999 when Cardinal Health joined a class action to recover overcharges from vitamin manufacturers. The vitamin makers had just pled guilty to charges of price-fixing from 1988 to 1998. In March 2000, the defendants in that action reached a provisional settlement with the plaintiffs under which Cardinal could have received $22 million. But Cardinal opted out of the settlement, choosing instead to file its own claims in the hopes of getting a bigger payout.

The accounting troubles started in October 2000 when senior managers at Cardinal began to consider recording a portion of the expected proceeds from a future settlement as a litigation gain. The purpose was to close a gap in Cardinal's budgeted earnings for the second quarter of FY 2001, which ended 31 December 2000. According to the SEC, in a November 2000 e-mail a senior executive at Cardinal Health explained why Cardinal should use the vitamin gain, rather than other earnings initiatives, to report the desired level of earnings: "We do not need much to get over the hump, although the preference would be the vitamin case so that we do not steal from Q3."

On 31 December 2000, the last day of the second quarter of FY 2001, Cardinal recorded a $10 million contingent vitamin litigation gain as a reduction to cost of sales. In its complaint, the SEC alleged that Cardinal's classification of the gain as a reduction to cost of sales violated GAAP. It is worth noting that had the gain not been recognized, Cardinal would have missed analysts' average consensus EPS estimate for the quarter by $.02.

Later in FY 2001, Cardinal considered recording a similar gain, but its auditor at the time, PricewaterhouseCoopers (hereafter PwC), was opposed to the idea. Accordingly, no litigation gains were recorded in the third or fourth quarters of FY 2001. Moreover, PwC advised Cardinal that the $10 million recognized in the second quarter of FY 2001 as a reduction to cost of sales should be reclassified "below the line" as nonoperating income. Cardinal management ignored the auditor's advice, and the $10 million gain was not reclassified.

The urge to report an additional gain resurfaced during the first quarter of FY 2002, and for the same reason as in the prior year: to cover an expected shortfall in earnings. On 30 September 2001, the last day of the first quarter of FY 2002, Cardinal recorded a $12 million gain, bringing the total gains from litigation to $22 million. As in the previous year, Cardinal classified the gain as a reduction to cost of sales, allowing the company to boost operating earnings. However, PwC disagreed with Cardinal's classification. The auditor advised Cardinal that the amount should have been recorded as nonoperating income on the grounds that the estimated vitamin recovery arose from litigation, was nonrecurring, and stemmed from claims against third parties that originated nearly 13 years earlier.

By May 2002, PwC had been replaced as Cardinal's auditor by Arthur Andersen.[†] Andersen was responsible for auditing Cardinal's financial statements for the whole of FY 2002, ended 30 June 2002, and thus, it reviewed Cardinal's classification of the $12 million vitamin gain. The Andersen auditors agreed with PwC that Cardinal had misclassified the gain. After Cardinal's persistent refusal to reclassify the gains, Andersen advised the company that it disagreed but would treat the $12 million as a "passed adjustment" and include the issue in its Summary of Audit Differences.[‡]

In spring 2002 Cardinal Health reached a $35.3 million settlement with several vitamin manufacturers. The $13.3 million not yet recognized was recorded as a gain in the final quarter of FY 2002. But while management thought its accounting policies had been vindicated by the settlement, the issue wouldn't go away.

On 2 April 2003, an article in the "Heard on the Street" column in *The Wall Street Journal* sharply criticized Cardinal Health for its handling of the litigation gains.[§] "It's a CARDINAL rule of accounting:" the article begins, pun intended. "Don't count your chickens before they hatch. Yet new disclosures in Cardinal Health Inc.'s latest annual report suggests that is what the drug wholesaler has done not just once, but twice." Nevertheless, management continued to defend its accounting practices, partly on the grounds that the amounts later received from the vitamin companies exceeded the amount of the contingent gains recognized in FY 2001 and FY 2002. Moreover, after the initial settlement, Cardinal Health received an additional $92.8 million in vitamin related litigation settlements, bringing the total proceeds to over $128 million.

The Outcome

Cardinal management finally succumbed to reality in the following year, and in the Form 10-K (annual report) filed with the SEC for FY 2004, Cardinal restated its financial results to reverse both gains, restating operating income from the two

---

[†] Arthur Andersen ceased operating months later in the aftermath of the Enron scandal. The Cardinal Health audit was then taken over by Ernst & Young.

[‡] A Summary of Audit Differences is a nonpublic document that lists the errors and adjustments identified by the auditor. It serves as the basis for the audit opinion. If the net effect of the errors exceeds the materiality threshold established for the client, the auditor will require an adjustment to the financial statements. "Passed adjustment" means that the error in question was waived; that is, no adjustment was demanded by the auditor.

[§] "Cardinal Health's Accounting Raises Some Questions," by Jonathan Weil, *The Wall Street Journal*, 2 April 2003, p. C1.

affected quarters. But the damage had already been done. The article in *The Wall Street Journal* triggered the SEC investigation alluded to earlier. A broad range of issues, going far beyond the treatment of the litigation gains, were brought under the agency's scrutiny, culminating in the SEC complaint. Two weeks after the complaint was filed, Cardinal Health settled with the SEC, agreeing to pay a $35 million fine.

Required

a. What justification could be given for deducting the expected litigation gain from cost of goods sold? Why did Cardinal Health choose this alternative instead of reporting it as a nonoperating item?

b. What did the senior Cardinal executive mean when he said, "We do not need much to get over the hump, although the preference would be the vitamin case so that we do not steal from Q3"? And more specifically, what is meant by the phrase, "not steal from Q3"?

c. What specifically did Cardinal Health do wrong that got it into trouble with the SEC?

d. What might Cardinal Health's senior managers say in their own defense? How might they justify the timing of the $10 million and the $12 million gains?

e. Cardinal Health ended up receiving a lot more than $22 million from the litigation settlement. Were their actions so wrong as to justify the actions of the SEC? On a scale of 1 to 10, with 1 being "relatively harmless" and 10 being "downright fraudulent," where would you classify Cardinal's behavior, and why?

Case Study

13-2 Firestone Tire and Rubber Company (A)

Throughout most of the twentieth century, Firestone Tire and Rubber Company was one of the world's leading manufacturers of tires for passenger cars and trucks. In 1978 the company was forced to recall some of its radial tires for alleged defects. The following pages provide excerpts from Firestone's 1979 annual report, detailing the provisions and contingencies involved in the tire recall and related issues. The report of the company's auditors is also provided.

Required

a. Reconstruct summary journal entries for all of the activity in the "accrued liability for tire recall" account since it was established in 1978 (see Note 15). Assume that settlements with customers take the form of both cash refunds and tire replacements. Ignore tax effects.

b. Explain why the company has provided for potential losses on the tire recall, but not for the lawsuits relating to the defective tires.

c. What key messages are the auditors trying to convey in their report?

15. Provision for tire recall and related costs

In October 1978, a provision for tire recall of $234.0 million ($147.4 million after income taxes) was charged against income. The provision represented management's estimate of the cost of fulfilling the company's obligations under the agreement with the National Highway Traffic Safety Administration and the Company's program of cash refunds to those customers who had received an adjustment on tires that would otherwise have been subject to recall and free replacement.

In October 1979, based on experience to date and anticipated future charges, the 1978 provision was reduced. Management also determined that the provision should be broadened to include $30.8 million of other related costs which were not considered for inclusion in the original provision. The net effect of the above was to reduce the provision by $46.9 million, for which no provision for income taxes was required because of the use of 1978 foreign tax credits of $20.8 million.

It should be recognized that the number of tires still to be returned and the other costs yet to be incurred may vary from management's estimates. Any additional adjustments required by such variance will be reflected in income in the future.

The activity in the accrued liability for tire recall and related costs for 1979 and 1978 follows:

	1979	1978
Accrued liability at beginning of year	$227.2	$ —
Amount accrued (reversed) during the year	(46.9)	234.0
Amounts charged thereto	(123.9)	(6.8)
Accrued liability at end of year	$ 56.4	$227.2

(Continued)

16. Contingent liabilities

Twelve purported consumer commercial class actions (one of which consolidates five previous actions) are presently pending against the Company in various state and federal courts . . . In the purported class actions, the named plaintiffs are requesting . . . various forms of monetary relief, including punitive damages, as a result of the Company's having manufactured and sold allegedly defective Steel Belted Radial 500 and other steel belted radial passenger tires.

. . . In addition to the class actions, there are several thousand individual claims pending against the Company for damages allegedly connected with steel belted radial passenger tires . . .

. . . The Company is a defendant in a purported class action which seeks, among other things, recovery for losses by stockholders who purchased the Company's common stock between December 1975 and July 1978 by reason of the decline in market price for such stock alleged to result from the Company's alleged failure to make proper disclosure of, among other things, the steel belted radial passenger tire situation.

In March 1979, the United States brought an action seeking recovery against the Company in the amount of approximately $62 million by reason of alleged illegal gold trading activity in Switzerland.

Following a federal grand jury investigation into the Company's incomes taxes, the Company entered into a plea agreement in July 1979 under which the Company pleaded guilty to two counts charging the inclusion in its taxable income for 1972 and 1973 amounts that had been generated in prior years: the courts imposed a total fine of ten thousand dollars on the Company by reason of its plea. A civil tax audit by the Internal Revenue Service is currently in progress covering some of the same matters investigated by the grand jury as well as other matters. The government may assess substantial tax, interest and penalties in connection with the matters under investigation.

The Securities and Exchange Commission is conducting an investigation of the adequacy of the Company's disclosures in earlier years concerning the Steel Belted Radial 500 tire . . .

. . . The Company has various other contingent liabilities, some of which are for substantial amounts, arising out of suits, investigations and claims related to other aspects of the conduct of its business . . .

. . . Increased uncertainties have developed during the past year with regard to some of the contingencies identified in this note. Because of the existing uncertainties, the eventual outcome of these contingencies cannot be predicted, and the ultimate liability with respect to them cannot be reasonably estimated. Since the minimum potential liability for a substantial portion of the claims and suits described in this note cannot be reasonably estimated, no liability for them has been recorded in the financial statements. Management believes, however, that the disposition of these contingencies could well be very costly. Although the Company's management, including its General Counsel, believes it is unlikely that the ultimate outcome of these contingencies will have a material adverse effect on the Company's consolidated financial position, such a consequence is possible if substantial punitive or other damages are awarded in one or more of the cases involved.

Report of independent certified public accountants

To the Stockholders and Board of Directors,
The Firestone Tire & Rubber Company:

We have examined the balance sheets of The Firestone Tire & Rubber Company and consolidated subsidiaries at October 31, 1979 and 1978, and the related statements of income, stockholders' equity, and changes in financial position for the years then ended. Our examinations were made in accordance with generally accepted auditing standards and, accordingly, included such tests of the accounting records and such other auditing procedures as we considered necessary in the circumstances.

As set forth in Note 16 to the financial statements, the Company is a party to various legal and other actions. These actions claim substantial amounts as a result of alleged tire defects and other matters. The ultimate liability resulting from these matters cannot be reasonably estimated. In our report dated December 18, 1978, our opinion on the financial statements for the year ended October 31, 1978, was unqualified. However, due to the increased uncertainties that developed during the year ended October 31, 1979, with respect to these matters, our present opinion on the financial statements for the year ended October 31, 1978, as presented herein, is different from that expressed in our previous report.

In our opinion, subject to the effects on the financial statements of adjustments that might have been required had the outcome of the matters referred to in the preceding paragraph been known, the financial statements referred to above present fairly the financial position of The Firestone Tire & Rubber Company and consolidated subsidiaries at October 31, 1979 and 1978, and the results of their operations and the changes in their financial position for the years then ended, in conformity with generally accepted accounting principles applied on a consistent basis.

Coopers & Lybrand
Cleveland, Ohio
December 12, 1979

Case Study

13-3 Firestone Tire and Rubber Company (B)

Late in 1979, to save the company from pending collapse, Firestone brought in John Nevin as CEO. He closed several of the company's manufacturing plants, and spun off nontire-related businesses, including the famous Firestone Country Club. In 1988, after the company had been restored to some measure of profitability, Nevin negotiated the sale of Firestone to the Japanese company Bridgestone. The North American division, headquartered in Nashville, became known as Bridgestone-Firestone (BFS).

It's déjà vu All over Again

But just as memories were fading of the tire recall from the late 1970s, rumours began to circulate regarding new quality concerns at BFS. The trouble started in 1996 as customers began to allege that Firestone tires on their Ford Explorers were faulty. As the complaints grew louder, BFS decided to conduct an internal investigation. The conclusion: the tires had either been misused or underinflated.

But the problem wouldn't go away. The tires were linked to several road deaths in Venezuela, and a nasty argument ensued between BFS and Ford, with each blaming the other for the fiasco.

In May 2000, the National Highway Traffic Safety Administration in the US began an investigation of several brands of tires produced by BFS. In August 2000, BFS responded by announcing a "voluntary" recall of the Firestone Radial ATX, ATX II, and Wilderness AT tires produced at their factory in Decatur, Illinois. The recall was substantially complete by August of the following year. Meanwhile, BFS became the target of many lawsuits.

Financial Statement Effects

The financial statement consequences of the recall were documented in the notes to Bridgestone's financial statements. According to Bridgestone's 2001 Annual Report,

For the fiscal years 2001 and 2000, BFS has recorded $661 million and $754 million provisions, respectively, presented as loss on voluntary tire recall in the . . . statements of income, for the direct costs of voluntary tire recall and for product liability suits and claims . . . , net of anticipated proceeds from product liability insurance recoveries, and BFS has paid $479 million and $406 million, respectively.

From the 2002 Annual Report,

In fiscal years 2002 and 2001, [Bridgestone] has paid $245 million and $479 million, respectively, for the direct costs of voluntary tire recall and for product liability suits and claims . . . As a result of the payments, as of December 31, 2002 and 2001, [Bridgestone] has recorded liabilities for matters related to the voluntary tire recall and resulting litigation amounting to $285 million and $530 million, respectively.

And from the 2003 Annual Report,

In fiscal years 2003 and 2002, [Bridgestone] has paid $96 million and $245 million, respectively, for the direct cost of voluntary tire recall and for product liability suits and claims, class actions . . . As a result of the payments, as of December 31, 2003 and 2002, [Bridgestone] has recorded liabilities for matters related to the voluntary tires recall and resulting litigation amounting to $140 million and $285 million, respectively.

Bridgestone reported net income of $132 million in 2001, $378 million in 2002, and $828 million in 2003.

Required

a. Based on the notes from the 2001, 2002, and 2003 annual reports, make whatever summary journals are needed to reconcile the ending balances in the liability account ($530 million in 2001, $285 million in 2002, and $140 million in 2003).

b. Did Bridgestone create hidden reserves from the provision for voluntary tire recall? How would you know?

NOTES

1. An onerous contract is one in which the unavoidable costs of meeting the obligations under the contract exceed the benefits to be received from the contract. In other words, the terms of the contract effectively condemn the reporting entity to future losses.

2. The IFRS standard addressing provisions is IAS 37. US GAAP provides the commentary on provision and reserves in the following: SFAS 5, EITF 88–0, FAS 143, FAS 146, SOP 96–1.

3. See http://wiki.ifrs.com/Provisions-and-Contingencies

4. All of the notes shown in this chapter are excerpted from Merck's 2005 Annual Report.

14 Accounting for Pensions

Introduction

A pension is a contractual benefit promised by an employer to provide an employee with a source of income during his or her retirement years. In the corporate world, there are two primary retirement schemes: defined benefit plans and defined contribution plans. In this chapter, we focus mainly on the accounting challenges posed by the former.

Under IFRS and US GAAP, the primary principle underlying all of the detailed requirements in pension accounting is that the cost of providing retirement benefits should be recognized in the period in which the benefit is earned by the employee, not when it is paid or payable.

A Brief Word on Defined Contribution Plans

In a defined contribution plan, the employer promises to contribute a certain amount to a pension plan each period for each employee. The amount of the contribution is usually a specified percentage of the employee's salary. The term "defined contribution" implies that while the amount contributed by the employer is specified, the retirement benefits received by the employee are not. The amounts eventually received by the employee depend on the investment performance of the pension plan. In short, the risk of ensuring adequate pension fund returns to fund the employee's retirement needs is borne entirely by the employee.

The accounting for defined contribution plans is straightforward. As pension benefits are earned in a given period, the employer makes the following entry:

Pension expense	XX	
Pension liability		XX

When the cash contributions are then made to the pension fund:

Pension liability	XX	
Cash		XX

As long as the company has made all required contributions, there are no further financial statement effects.

Defined Benefit Plans

In a defined benefit plan, the employer specifies the benefit that employees will receive during retirement.[1] Employers must therefore ensure that cash contributions and subsequent returns on pension fund assets are sufficient to cover the promises made to their employees. The risk of pension fund performance therefore falls entirely on the employer.

Typically, the amount of periodic benefit received in retirement is based on the employee's length of service and level of pay. This guaranteed benefit is difficult to estimate and manage given that there are so many uncertainties that can affect it, including employee life expectancy, future salaries, the possibility of early retirement, and turnover rates. To gain an appreciation for the difficulties of managing these plans, we first need to distinguish between funded and unfunded plans.

According to IAS 19 (the IFRS standard that deals with pensions), the amount recognized in the balance sheet should be the present value of the defined benefit obligation (that is, the present value of expected future payments required to settle the obligation resulting from employee service in the current and prior periods), adjusted for unrecognized actuarial gains and losses and unrecognized past service cost, and reduced by the fair value of plan assets at the balance sheet date. (We will define these terms shortly.)

Similarly, but not exactly, SFAS 158 (the US GAAP equivalent to IAS 19) requires an employer to recognize the overfunded or underfunded status of a defined benefit postretirement plan as an asset or liability in its balance sheet and to recognize, through comprehensive income, changes in that funded status in the year in which the changes occur.

Unfunded Defined Benefit Plans

Accounting for unfunded plans requires fewer estimates than a funded plan. In accordance with the matching principle, pension expense and the associated liability are accrued each period as employees earn their right to future benefits. The journal entry is:

Pension expense	XX	
Pension liability		XX

This entry is recorded for every period during the employee's working life. The primary complication stems from the need to estimate the number of years an employee will survive postretirement. That is, for how long will the company have to pay the retirement benefits? The actual pension cost cannot be known for certain until the employee's death as well as the death of any survivors who might also be covered under the pension plan and are therefore entitled to benefits. Other variables such as employee turnover rates, and future salary and wage rates, also have an impact on this calculation.

Once the employee retires and the company starts to make payments, the following journal entry is recorded:

Pension liability	XX	
Cash		XX

This entry is recorded every time a pension payment is made to the employee from the time of retirement until death.

Funded Defined Benefit Plans

In a funded or partially funded defined benefit plan, the company makes regular contributions to a separate legal entity. The contributions are then invested with the hope of earning positive returns and growing the total asset pool. Thus, the pension fund assets are the sum of the company contributions and the returns earned through investments. The journal entry to record the contributions made by the employer to the pension fund is:

```
Pension expense          XX
    Cash                        XX
```

However, it is unusual for the pension expense and the cash contributions to equal in any given year, meaning that an overfunding or underfunding situation will exist.

When the cash contributions in a given year are greater than the pension expense, the residual amount is recorded as a debit either increasing the net *over*funded situation or decreasing net *under*funding:

```
Pension plan expense       XX
Pension asset or liability XX
    Cash                        XX
```

When the cash contributions are smaller than the pension expense, the difference is recorded as a credit either decreasing the net overfunded situation or increasing the net underfunding:

```
Pension plan expense     XX
    Cash                      XX
    Pension asset/liability   XX
```

Determining the pension expense for the period is somewhat more complicated. Until 2017, the pension plan expense is calculated by aggregating several components:

a. Service cost, which is the present value of benefits earned by employees during the accounting period. The discount rate is usually the current market interest rate for high quality, fixed-income investments.

b. Interest costs, which is the increase in present value from benefits earned in previous years. It arises because as each year passes, earned pension benefits are one year closer to being paid, and therefore the present value of those benefits has increased.

c. Plan asset returns, which includes the interest, dividends, and other revenue derived from the plan assets, together with realized and unrealized gains or losses on the assets, less any costs of administering the plan. This component *reduces* the pension expense by the assumed investment income from the plan assets based on assumed rates of return. Technically, this is an actuarial calculation and is not based on the plan's actual returns. The expected return on plan assets is determined based on the expected long-term rate of return on plan assets and the market-related value of the plan assets, and is used to reduce the volatility which would come about from using actual returns.

d. Amortization of unrecognized gains or losses. Actual returns on plan assets in excess of or less than assumed returns above are treated as gains or losses. These gains or losses are then amortized over a period equal to the average remaining service time of employees (the average number of years to retirement). However, for the sake of simplicity, we will lump both assumed returns and the gain or loss together as one component called "plan asset returns." Similarly, gains and losses will be recognized from changes in actuarial assumptions. For example, if an actuarial investigation concludes that covered employees will live longer than previously expected, a loss must be recognized for the increase in the present value of future benefits caused by the increase in longevity. Other examples of potential gains and losses include changes in expected salary growth and employee turnover. As with the differences between assumed returns and actual returns on plan assets, the gains and losses on actuarial changes are amortized over the average remaining service life of employees.

e. Prior service costs, which is the term used to describe the change in the obligation for employee service in prior periods, arising from changes to plan arrangements in the current period. Past service cost may be either positive (where benefits are introduced or improved) or negative (where existing benefits are reduced). Past service cost should be recognized immediately to the extent that it relates to former employees or to active employees already vested. Otherwise, it should be amortized on a straight-line basis over the average period until the amended benefits become vested.

f. The effect of any plan curtailments or settlements. Gains or losses resulting from the curtailment or settlement of a plan are recognized when the event curtailments are reductions in either the scope of employees covered or in benefits.

Under U.S. GAAP, the defined benefit pension cost (net benefit cost) included the above components that reflected various aspects of an employer's financial arrangements, along with the cost of the benefits given to employees. Those components were supposed to be aggregated when they were reported on the financial statements.

However, members of the FASB learned that the presentation of defined benefit cost on a net basis combines elements that are quite different in nature. Important stakeholders argued that the presentation requirement was not as transparent as it should be.

As of 2018, FASB requires a reporting organization to separate the service cost component from the other parts of the net benefit cost for presentation purposes. The standard update included specific guidance on how to present the service cost component and other parts of the net benefit cost within the income statement. Specifically, the amendment requires that an employer report the service cost component in the same line item or items as other compensation costs arising from services rendered by the relevant employees during the period. The other components of net benefit cost are required to be presented in the income statement separately from the service cost component and outside a subtotal of income from operations, if one is presented. The amendment to the standard also allows only the service cost component to be eligible for capitalization when applicable (for example, as a cost of internally manufactured inventory or a self-constructed asset).

Moody's Investors Service issued a statement praising the new standard. According to one of Moody's accounting analysts, "The change to pension expense classification on the income statement provides a more authentic view of the operating income. Pension expense includes many components, but only the service cost component is a true period expense. Historically, Moody's and many other financial analysts manually adjusted the non service cost components of pension expense out of operating income in line with the FASB's change to presentation. After adoption of the new accounting standard, companies reporting will require less manipulation and be more useful for financial analysis."

In general, the amount that an employer reports on its balance sheet is the net of the pension benefit obligations and the pension plan assets on the balance sheet date.

Net Pension Asset (or Liability)

Pension Plan Assets (at Market Value)
− <u>Projected Benifit Obligation (PBO)</u>
= Funded Status

If the pension plan assets are greater than the pension plan obligations, the plan is said to be over-funded. Pension plans tend to become overfunded as a result of a stock market boom (provided the pension plan is invested in stocks, as many are). In such cases, a pension fund asset appears on the balance sheet. For most companies, however, pension plan assets are less than the pension plan obligations and, thus, the pension plan is underfunded. The amount of the underfunding appears on the balance sheet as a liability.

Under US GAAP and IFRS, a firm having multiple plans for different groups of employees, with some of the plans underfunded while others are overfunded, must show both a liability (for the former) and an asset (for the latter). The company is not permitted to net underfunded plans against overfunded plans, or vice versa, and report the net amount on the balance sheet.

Pension Plan Assets

Pension Plan Assets, Beginning Balance

+ Actual Returns on Investments (Interest, Dividends, Gains, and Losses)

+ Company Contributions to Pension Plan

− Benefits Paid to Retirees

= Pension Plan Assets, Ending Balance

Pension Obligation

Projected Benefit Obligation, Beginning Balance

+ Service Cost

+ Interest Cost

+ / − Actuarial Losses (Gains)

− Benefits Paid to Retirees

= Projected Benefit Obligation, Ending Balance

To better understand the accounting for defined benefit plans, we turn now to a simple case study. Europa Inc. begins operations with one employee we will call Hector. Management offers Hector a suitable compensation plan, including a defined benefit pension package. The firm estimates that Hector will work for five years, retire, and then live another five years (see Figure 14.1). Projections like this have to be made so that the company can estimate how much it will owe Hector for the promised pension.

For each year of work, Hector will receive $1,800 at the end of each year during retirement. Further, Europa estimates an interest rate on pension obligations of 5% and that it can earn 8%

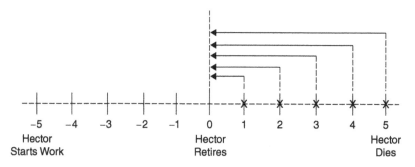

FIGURE 14.1 A graphical overview of Hector's pension plan.

on its pension assets. The funding policy of Europa is to contribute $2,500 at the end of each year that Hector works for the company.

The service cost is the cost to the employer incurred as the result of the employee's working for the firm and earning pension benefits upon retirement. In the case of Europa, for each year that Hector works, the company must pay him $1,800 per year during retirement, which we assume lasts five years. These cash flows are diagrammed below. This diagram runs from time $t = -5$ (read "five years until retirement"), when the employee begins working for the firm, until time $t = 5$ ("five years after retirement"), when the employee will die.

By agreement, for each year of work Europa's pension plan pays Hector $1,800 at the end of each year during retirement. This forms an ordinary annuity with a payment of $1,800. At an interest rate of 5%, the present value of this ordinary annuity at retirement, $t = 0$, is $7,792.

As shown in the graph in Figure 14.1, there are five cash flows, one for each year during retirement. These cash flows constitute an ordinary annuity. With an interest rate of 5%, Europa would compute this present value as $7,792. But this present value is as of the date Hector retires, when time $t = 0$. When Europa prepares its income statement for the year ending at $t = -4$, it will need to discount this amount back another four years. Treat the $7,792 as a single sum and discount it back four years at 5%, and the present value is $6,411; this is the service cost for that year.

When Hector works a second year, he will earn another pension benefit of a second $1,800 payment each year during retirement. To obtain the service cost for the next year, Europa will discount the $7,792 back to the year ending at $t = -3$, so the present value is $6,731. In like manner, Europa establishes that the service cost for Hector's third, fourth, and fifth years of work is $7,068, $7,421, and $7,792.

After first year of work (t = −5):	$6,411
After second year of work (t = −4):	$6,731
After third year of work (t = −3):	$7,068
After fourth year of work (t = −2):	$7,421
After fifth year of work (t = −1):	$7,792

The projected benefit obligation measures how much the employer will have to pay out for the employee's pension in today's terms. The projected benefit obligation differs from the service cost because service cost quantifies the effects of a given year's impact on the pension commitments, while the projected obligation assesses the cumulative effect from all the years worked by the employees.

Consider Hector's second year of work. The service cost measures the present value of the incremental $1,800 per year he will receive during retirement, and this service cost is $6,731. To measure the projected benefit obligation, we must realize that Hector will get $3,600 per year during retirement since he has worked two years for Europa, each year earning him $1,800 per year during retirement. The projected benefit obligation is a present value of $3,600 per year for five years, and this present value is $15,584 at time $t = 0$. Discounting this back for the financial statements ending time $t = -3$, the projected benefit obligation is $13,462. An easy shortcut for computing this is to multiply the numbers of years worked by the current year's service cost (2 times $6,731 equals $13,462). Similarly, the projected benefit obligation for the next three years is $21,204, $29,684, and $38,960, respectively.

To complete this basic pension example, we need to analyze the other components of the pension expense calculation. We have already computed the service costs and the projected benefit obligations, and we copy them to the service cost column and to the projected benefit obligation column in this exhibit. The interest cost is the interest rate multiplied by the projected benefit obligation at the beginning of the year. In this case, it is 5% times these amounts. For example, for the second year, the interest cost is $6,411 times 5% or $321. The expected return on plan assets is 8% times the plan assets at the beginning of the year. For Europa's second year, the amount is 8% of $2,500, or $200. The net pension cost is the service cost for the year plus the interest cost

Table 14.1   **Basic Defined Benefit Pension Example**

End of year	Service cost	Interest cost	Expected return on plan assets	Net pension cost or pension expense	Funding	Accrued pension cost	Prepaid cost pension cost/accrued pension cost	Projected benefit obligation	Plan assets
t – 5	6,411	0	0	6,411	2,500	(3,911)	(3,911)	6,411	2,500
t – 4	6,731	321	200	6,852	2,500	(4,352)	(8,263)	13,462	5,200
t – 3	7,068	673	416	7,325	2,500	(4,825)	(13,088)	21,204	8,116
t – 2	7,421	1,060	649	7,832	2,500	(5,332)	(18,420)	29,684	11,265
t – 1	7,792	1,484	901	8,375	2,500	(5,875)	(24,295)	38,960	14,667

minus the expected return on plan assets. For example, in the second year, the net pension cost is $6,731 plus $321 minus $200, or $6,852. This amount is shown on the income statement.

The funding is $2,500 in this example by assumption. In practice, managers can contribute to funded pension plans any amount they want as long as it meets regulatory requirements imposed by local regulations, such as the Employee Retirement Income Security Act (ERISA) in the United States.

The prepaid pension cost (an asset account) or accrued pension cost (a liability account) is the previous year's balance minus the net pension expense plus the funding. It is prepaid pension cost if this amount is positive but accrued pension cost if the amount is negative. We obtain $(8,263) in the second year as the previous balance of $(3,911) minus the net pension cost of $6,731 plus the funding of $2,500. Since this amount is shown on the balance sheet as an asset when positive and as a liability when negative, Europa has a liability of $8,263 for the underfunding of the defined benefit pension plan.

In Table 14.1, the plan assets equal the previous balance plus the expected return on plan assets plus any additional funding. For the second year, we have the previous balance of $2,500 plus the return of $200 plus additional funding of $2,500, for a new balance of $5,200. At this point, there is an internal check on our computations. The prepaid pension cost or accrued pension cost should equal the plan assets minus the projected benefit obligation.

While these items are important to comprehend pension accounting, only two of them go on the financial statements. The net pension cost or pension expense goes on the income statement, although its components are disclosed in the footnotes. If there is a prepaid pension cost, it goes on the asset section of the balance sheet; if there is an accrued pension cost, it reaches the liability section of the balance sheet. The constituents of this asset or liability are also revealed in the footnotes.

Europa would record the following journal entries over the five years of Hector's employment and carry the following balances on its balance sheet:

End of t – 5:   Pension expense   €6,411
                          Accrued pension   €3,911
                          Cash   €2,500

Balance sheet: net liability for underfunding: €3,911

End of t – 4:   Pension expense   €6,852
                          Accrued pension   €4,352
                          Cash   €2,500

Balance sheet: net liability for underfunding: €8,263

End of t – 3:   Pension expense   €7,325
                          Accrued pension   €4,825
                          Cash   €2,500

Balance sheet: net liability for underfunding: €13,088

End of *t* − 2:   Pension expense   €7,832
        Accrued pension   €5,332
        Cash   €2,500

Balance sheet: net liability for underfunding: €18,420

End of *t* − 1:   Pension expense   €8,375
        Accrued pension   €5,875
        Cash   €2,500

Balance sheet: net liability for underfunding: €24,295

End of *t* + 1 through *t* + 5:
        Projected pension obligation €9,000
        Pension plan assets/cash   €9,000

Assumptions:

- Service cost computation is given in Table 14.1.

- Interest cost is 5% of the projected benefit obligation at the end of the previous year.

- Expected return on plan assets is 8% of the plan assets at the end of the previous year.

- Net pension cost equals the service cost plus the interest cost minus the expected return on the plan assets.

- The prepaid or accrued pension cost equals the previous balance plus the net pension cost minus the funding. Projected benefit obligation is the present value of all pension cash flows.

- The plan assets equal the previous balance plus the expected return on plan assets plus the funding.

One of the most important developments in the retirement landscape over the past years is the global trend away from defined benefit plans and toward defined contribution plans. The attraction to companies is that, under defined contribution plans, the risk of future pension fund asset returns is borne entirely by employees. As long as defined contributions are paid, the corporate sponsor bears no further liability.

American Airlines: An Example of Defined Benefit Plan Disclosure

American Airlines pension footnote below indicates that the funded status of its pension plan is $(7,180) million on December 31, 2016. This means American's plan is underfunded. In Box 14.1 are the disclosures American Airlines makes in its pension footnote, in $millions.

American Airlines pension benefit obligation (PBO), also known as the pension liability, began the year with a balance of $16,310 million. It increased by the accrual of $2 million in service cost and $746 million in interest cost. During the year, American also realized an actuarial loss of $725 million, which increased the pension liability. Finally, the PBO decreased as a result of $635 million in benefits paid to retirees, leaving a balance of $17,148 million at year-end.

BOX 14.1   American Airlines: Defined Benefit Plan Disclosure

Pension obligation on at January 1, 2016	$16,310
Service cost	2
Interest cost	746
Actuarial loss (gain)	725
Benefit payments	(635)
Obligation at December 31, 2016	$17,148
Fair value of plan assets at January 1, 2016	$9,660
Actual return on plan assets	911
Employer contributions	32
Benefit payments	(635)
Fair value of plan assets at December 31, 2016	$9,968
Funded status at December 31, 2016	$(7,180)

Pension plan assets began the year with a fair market value of $9,660 million, which increased by $911 million from investment returns and by $32 million from company contributions. The company drew down its investments to make pension payments of $635 million to retirees. The $635 million payment reduced the PBO by the same amount, as discussed above, leaving the pension plan assets with a year-end balance of $9,968 million. The funded status of American Airlines pension plan at year-end is $(7,180) million, computed as $17,148 million – $9,968 million. The negative balance indicates that its pension plan is underfunded. Most analysts treat the funded status as an operating item (either asset or liability).

American Airlines incurred $154 million of pension expense in 2016 and an additional $761 million of expense relating to defined contribution plans (companies typically maintain different types of retirement plans). The combined expense of $915 million is not broken out separately in the income statement. Instead, it is included in SG&A expense. Details of this expense are found in its 2016 pension footnote, shown in Box 14.2 (in $ millions).

BOX 14.2   Pension Expense Relating to Defined Contribution Plans

Components of net periodic benefit cost

Defined benefit plans:	
Service cost	$2
Interest cost	746
Expected return on assets	(747)
Amortization of:	
Prior service cost	28
Unrecognized net loss	125
Net periodic benefit cost for defined benefit plans	154
Defined contribution plans	761
Total	$915

Table 14.2 **Basic Defined Contribution Pension Example**

	t − 5	t − 4	t − 3	t − 2	t − 1	t	t + 1	t + 2	t + 3	t + 4	t + 5
Salary	€100,000	€103,000	€106,090	€109,273	€112,551		0	0	0	0	0
Contribution	**5,000**	**5,150**	**5,305**	**5,464**	**5,628**		0	0	0	0	0
Return (8%)	—	400	844	1,336	1,880		2,481	1,984	1,488	992	496
Total assets	5,000	10,550	16,699	23,499	31,007		24,805	18,604	12,403	6,201	0
Withdrawals	0	0	0	0	0		8,682	8,186	7,690	7,194	6,697

Let's return to the example of Europa Inc. and Hector, except this time, imagine that management offers Hector €100,000 in compensation plus a defined contribution pension scheme equal to 5% of salary (see Table 14.2). As before, the firm estimates that Hector will work for five years, retire, and then live another five years. Assume that Hector's annual salary is expected to grow at 3% per year. We will make an assumption that the return on Hector's individual pension account is 8% per year and that he will withdraw the balance in the account at retirement over the five years in equal amounts in addition to taking the returns earned every year. Europa would record the following journal entries over the five years of Hector's employment:

End of $t − 5$:	Pension expense	€5,000	
	Cash		€5,000
End of $t − 4$:	Pension expense	€5,150	
	Cash		€5,150
End of $t − 3$:	Pension expense	€5,305	
	Cash		€5,305
End of $t − 2$:	Pension expense	€5,464	
	Cash		€5,464
End of $t − 1$:	Pension expense	€5,628	
	Cash		€5,628

Assumptions:

- annual salary growth of 3% per year;
- 5% of annual compensation contributed;
- 8% return on total assets;
- annual withdrawal (total assets at time of retirement/assumed retirement period) + annual return.

KEY LESSONS FROM THE CHAPTER

- A pension is a contractual benefit promised by an employer to provide an employee with a source of income during his or her retirement years.

- There are two primary types of retirement schemes: *defined benefit plans* and *defined contribution plans*.

- Defined contribution plans specify amounts to be invested for the employee during the employee's career. The employee's retirement benefits will be based on the value of these investments at retirement. Therefore, the risk of pension plan investment performance falls entirely on the employee.

- The accounting for defined contribution plans is straightforward.

- Defined benefit plans specify amounts to be received during retirement. The effect is to place the risk of future investment performance on the employer.

- The accounting for defined benefit plans is highly complex, influenced not only by investment returns (which have no effect on the accounting for defined contribution plans) but also by interest rates, employee longevity, turnover, and future salary increases.

- Pension expense for defined benefit pension plans consists of service cost, interest cost, expected return on plan assets, and amortization of past service costs and changes in actuarial assumptions.

- Overfunded defined benefit plans are reported as assets on the employer's balance sheet. Underfunded plans are reported as liabilities.

- There has been a pronounced trend in recent years toward the adoption of defined contribution plans.

KEY TERMS AND CONCEPTS FROM THE CHAPTER

Defined benefit plans
Defined contribution plan

Underfunded/ overfunded plan
Service cost

Amortization of unrecognized gain or losses

Plan asset returns
Prior service costs

Interest cost

QUESTIONS

1. Describe the differences between defined benefit and defined contribution plans.

2. Many companies are closing down their defined benefit plans and replacing them with defined contribution plans. Why?

3. Interest rates have sharply declined in most economies over the past 10 years. What effects would you expect this trend to have had on pension liabilities and pension expenses?

4. As a prospective employee, which type of plan (defined benefit or defined contribution) do you prefer, and why?

5. Define "underfunded" and "overfunded."

6. What is the difference between "service cost" and "interest cost?"

Case Study

14-1 Comprehensive Pension Review Problem: Cathay Pacific

Headquartered in Hong Kong, Cathay Pacific is one of the world's leading airlines. The disclosures shown below are taken from Note 19 in the Company's 2010 annual report.

Required

a. Describe what is meant by service cost and interest cost.

b. How much pension expense does Cathay Pacific report in 2009 and 2010 for its defined benefit plans?

c. Cathay Pacific reports a HK$518 million expected return on plan assets as an offset to 2010 pension expense. How was this amount determined? What is the actual gain or loss realized on its 2010 plan assets? What is the purpose of using this estimated amount instead of the actual gain or loss?

d. What factors affected Cathay Pacific's 2010 pension liability? What factors affected its 2010 plan assets?

e. What does the term "funded status" mean? What is the funded status of the pension plans over the previous 5 years, from 2006 until 2010?

f. The company reduced its discount rate from 4.8% in 2009 to 4.4% in 2010. What effect(s) did this change have on the balance sheet and the income statement?

g. Assume that Cathay Pacific decreased its estimate of expected annual wage increases used to determine its defined benefit obligations in 2010. What effect(s) does this decrease have on its financial statements? In general, how does such a decrease affect income?

h. What journal entry was needed to record pension plan expense in 2010 for Cathay's defined contribution plans?

Retirement benefits

The Group operates various defined benefit and defined contribution retirement schemes for its employees in Hong Kong and in certain overseas locations. The assets of these schemes are held in funds administered by independent trustees. The retirement schemes in Hong Kong are registered under and comply with the Occupational Retirement Schemes Ordinance and the Mandatory Provident Fund Schemes Ordinance ("MPFSO"). Most of the employees engaged outside Hong Kong are covered by appropriate local arrangements.

The Group operates the following principal schemes:

a. Defined benefit retirement schemes

The Swire Group Retirement Benefit Scheme ("SGRBS") in Hong Kong, in which the Company and Cathay Pacific Catering Services (H.K.) Limited ("CPCS") are participating employers, provides resignation and retirement benefits to its members, which include the Company's cabin attendants who joined before September 1996 and other locally engaged employees who joined before June 1997, upon their cessation of service. The Company and CPCS meet the full cost of all benefits due by SGRBS to their employee members who are not required to contribute to the scheme.

Staff employed by the Company in Hong Kong on expatriate terms before April 1993 were eligible to join another scheme, the Cathay Pacific Airways Limited Retirement Scheme ("CPALRS"). Both members and the Company contribute to CPALRS.

The latest actuarial valuation of CPALRS and the portion of SGRBS funds specifically designated for the Company's employees were completed by a qualified actuary, Watson Wyatt Hong Kong Limited, as at December 31, 2009, using the projected unit credit method. The figures for SGRBS and CPALRS disclosed as at December 31, 2010, were provided by Cannon Trustees Limited, the administration manager.

	2010		2009	
	SGRBS(%)	CPALS(%)	SGRBS(%)	CPALS(%)
The principal actuarial assumptions are:				
Discount rate used	4.40	4.40	4.80	4.80
Expected return on plan assets	8.00	6.50	8.00	6.50
Future salary increases	2–5	1–5	2–5	1–5

The Group's obligations are 106% (2009: 97%) covered by the plan assets held by the trustees as at December 31, 2010.

	2010 HK$M	2009 HK$M
Net expenses recognized in the Group profit and loss:		
Current service cost	324	316
Interest on obligations	311	342
Expected return on plan assets	(518)	(371)
Actuarial loss recognized	1	30
Total included in staff costs	118	317
Actual return on plan assets	820	1,578

	Group	
	2010 HK$M	2009 HK$M
Net (asset)/liability recognized in the statement of financial position:		
Present value of funded obligations	7,615	7,460
Fair value of plan assets	(8,077)	(7,217)
	(462)	243

(Continued)

	Group	
	2010 HK$M	2009 HK$M
Movements in present value of funded obligations comprise:		
At January 1	7,460	7,108
Movements for the year		
– current service cost	324	316
– interest cost	311	342
– employee contributions	12	14
– benefits paid	(524)	(681)
– actuarial losses	32	361
At December 31	7,615	7,460

	Group	
	2010 HK$M	2009 HK$M
Movements in fair value of plan assets comprise:		
At January 1	7,217	5,924
Movements for the year		
– expected return on plan assets	518	371
– employee contributions	12	14
– employer contributions	552	382
– benefits paid	(524)	(681)
– actuarial gain	302	1,207
At December 31	8,077	7,217

	Group	
	2010 HK$M	2009 HK$M
Fair value of plan assets comprises:		
Equities	5,318	4,297
Debt instruments	1,919	1,725
Deposits and cash	840	526
Others	—	669
	8,077	7,217

The overall expected rate of return on plan assets is determined based on the average rate of return of major categories of assets that constitute the total plan assets.

	Group				
	2010 HK$M	2009 HK$M	2008 HK$M	2007 HK$M	2006 HK$M
Present value of funded obligations	7,615	7,460	7,108	8,223	7,844
Fair value of plan assets	(8,077)	(7,217)	(5,924)	(9,131)	(8,065)
(Surplus)/deficit	(462)	243	1,184	(908)	(221)

The difference between the fair value of the schemes' assets and the present value of the accrued past services liabilities at the date of an actuarial valuation is taken into consideration when determining future funding levels in order to ensure that the schemes will be able to meet liabilities as they become due. The contributions are calculated based upon funding recommendations arising from actuarial valuations. The Group expects to make contributions of HK$378 million to the schemes in 2011.

b. Defined contribution retirement schemes

Staff employed by the company in Hong Kong are eligible to join a defined contribution retirement scheme, the CPA Provident Fund.

Under the terms of the schemes, other than the Company contribution, staff may elect to contribute from 0% to 10% of their monthly salary. During the year, the benefits forfeited in accordance with the schemes' rules amounted to HK$18 million (2009: HK$ 19 million), which have been applied toward the contributions payable by the Company.

A mandatory provident fund ("MPF") scheme was established under the MPFSO in December 2000. Where staff elect to join the MPF scheme, the Company and staff are required to contribute 5% of the employee's relevant income (capped at HK$20 000). Staff may elect to contribute more than the minimum as a voluntary contribution.

Contributions to defined contribution retirement schemes charged to the Group profit and loss are HK$756 million (2009: HK$677 million).

NOTE

1. In some countries, such as the United Kingdom, defined benefit plans are often described as "final salary plans," because benefits are driven, in part, by salaries in the final years of an employee's career.

15

Accounting for Income Tax

Introduction

In this chapter, we explore how companies account for income tax under US GAAP and IFRS. Key concepts are illustrated using the financial statements and notes of Intel Corporation.

The single most important fact to know about the accounting for income tax is that the rules for calculating profits under GAAP or IFRS – known as "book income" – do not correspond to the rules for calculating profits under tax law ("tax income"). This divergence is seen in every rich country, and, increasingly, in the developing world. While some people may be disturbed by the idea that a company can report one profit number to its shareholders and a very different (often smaller) number on its tax returns, the practice is a logical outcome of the different objectives underlying book and tax accounting.

Financial accounting exists, first and foremost, to provide relevant financial information to lenders and equity investors. To advance this aim, GAAP and IFRS rely on the matching principle and accrual accounting. For example, if a company sells products under warranty, a provision is taken in the year of sale even if the cash costs of the warranty are not incurred until future periods. But while financial accounting principles require the recognition of such expenses, tax authorities will demand that cash actually be spent to service the warranty before a tax deduction is allowed. The result is a timing difference between the recognition of warranty expense in the calculation of book and tax income.

In addition, tax law is designed to serve purposes separate and apart from the goal of promoting efficient capital allocation. Governments use taxes not just to collect revenues from businesses, but to do so in ways that advance public policy priorities. One such priority may be the promotion of capital investment. For this reason, tax law offers companies the right to accelerate depreciation charges. This practice can dramatically increase the value of the resulting tax shield, and the more valuable the tax shield, the lower the net cost of an asset to the investing firm. But actual usage or industry practice may suggest the straight-line method for book purposes. As a result, the company uses two depreciation methods – an accelerated approach for tax income and straight-line for book income.

Or consider the fines that companies pay for violating environmental or worker-safety regulations. While GAAP/IFRS recognizes these payments as expenses, the public interest demands that such expenses are not recognized for tax purposes. As a result, a permanent difference arises between expenses for book income and expenses for tax income.

As we will show in the next section, differences between book and tax income can arise in a broad range of accounting issues. Much of tax accounting deals with how companies reconcile these differences.

Temporary and Permanent Differences

As the above discussion suggests, the differences between the determination of tax income and book income fall into two broad categories:

- temporary differences
- permanent differences.

Temporary Differences

Temporary differences result when a revenue, gain, expense, or loss enters in the calculation of book income in one period but affects tax income in a different (earlier or later) period. In the previous section, the warranty and depreciation examples fall into this category. Such differences are considered temporary because they eventually reverse. For example, if an asset is purchased for $1 million, the total amount to be depreciated over the asset's life must be $1 million (assuming no residual value). This is true under GAAP/IFRS and under tax law. In other words, net book value must be 0 in either case by the end of the asset's life. Therefore, if tax law permits accelerated depreciation (i.e., higher expense than under the straight-line method in the early years of the asset's life), charges must be lower in later years. As the end of the asset's life approaches, total book depreciation converges to total tax depreciation.

A similar argument applies to warranty expense. The only difference is that the expense for tax purposes lags the book expense instead of leading it, as it does for depreciation.

Other common sources of temporary differences include the following:

- **Deferred revenue.** When customers make advanced payments for goods or services, GAAP/IFRS requires the payment to be treated as a liability. Revenue is recognized later when it is deemed to have been earned. Many tax jurisdictions require such payments to be taxed when received.

- **Long-term contracts.** Book income is usually calculated using "percentage-of-completion." However, some tax authorities permit other methods.

- **Bad debts expense.** For book purposes, firms estimate uncollectible accounts in the year of sale using the allowance method. However, in most countries, bad debt expense cannot be recognized for tax purposes until a specific customer account is deemed to be uncollectible.

- **Prepaid expenses.** Under GAAP/IFRS, prepayments for rent and insurance are reported as current assets. Expenses are recognized gradually over time as the benefits from the related contracts are consumed. Tax law, on the other hand, may permit companies to deduct the full amount when the payments are made.

- **Equity income.** The equity method requires firms to recognize their proportionate share of any profits or losses reported by affiliates (investments with 20–50% ownership). Most tax codes, on the other hand, require recognition of income only when dividends are received.

- **Installment sales.** Under GAAP/IFRS, sales are generally recognized for book purposes when goods are delivered to the customer regardless of when the payments are made. If customers make payments over an extended period, tax rules may allow revenues to be recognized only as cash is received.

Temporary differences that cause tax income to be *higher* than book income in future periods, as in the case of depreciation, give rise to a "deferred tax liability." Differences that cause tax income to be *lower* in future periods, e.g., the treatment of warranties expense, give rise to a "deferred tax asset." In all cases, deferred tax accounts are reported on an undiscounted basis.

Under IFRS, deferred tax assets and liabilities are classified as noncurrent on the balance sheet, with supplemental disclosures in the notes for (a) the components of the temporary differences and (b) amounts expected to be recovered within 12 months and beyond 12 months of the balance sheet date. US GAAP also requires a detailed breakdown of deferred tax components, but the classification rules are different. Deferred tax assets and liabilities can appear as current or noncurrent, depending on the classification of the related asset or liability responsible for the temporary difference. For example, a deferred tax liability resulting from the excess of tax depreciation over book depreciation is reported as a noncurrent liability, because the temporary difference relates to noncurrent assets. A deferred tax asset resulting from prepaid expenses might be classified as current, given that prepaid expenses are current assets.

Permanent Differences

Permanent differences between tax and book income are caused by either of the following:

- An item that affects book income but which will never affect tax income. The nondeductible fine cited in the previous section is one such example. Bribes and excessively lavish entertainment expenses are others. Any income source that is exempt from income tax also falls in this category. For example, interest income on municipal bonds in the United States is exempt from federal income tax. If such income is earned, it is recognized for book purposes, not for tax purposes.

- An item that affects taxable income but which will never affect book income. For example, many tax jurisdictions allow companies to deduct a portion of the dividends received from another company. Only taxable income is affected by such laws. Book income is not.

What both categories have in common is that the differences between book and tax income do not reverse. That is, any such differences are not offset by corresponding differences in subsequent periods. Therefore, they do not give rise to deferred tax liabilities or assets.

Deferred Taxes and the Balance Sheet Approach

US GAAP and IFRS require a balance sheet approach in calculating the impact of timing differences between book and tax accounting.[1] The process begins by calculating the book basis and the tax basis for each balance sheet item with a timing difference. The difference between these two values is then multiplied by the relevant tax rate to determine the deferred tax asset/liability. This balance is compared with the prior year's deferred tax balance. The process can be summarized as follows:

$$\text{Temporary Differences} = \text{GAAP/IFRS Basis of Assets or Liabilities}$$
$$-\text{Tax Basis of Assets or Liabilities}$$
$$\text{Deferred Tax Liabilities or Assets} = \text{Temporary Differences} \times \text{Tax Rate}$$

The tax rate used here is the rate expected to apply to the period when the asset is realized or the liability is settled. Therefore, if tax rates are expected to change, the balances in the deferred tax accounts will change too.

Also, as we discuss later, deferred tax assets can arise from unused tax losses that are carried forward. The deferred tax asset equals the unused tax losses, multiplied by the relevant tax rate.

Changes in any of these deferred tax accounts will then impact the income tax expense reported on the income statement:

$$\text{Tax Expense} = \text{Taxes Paid} \pm \text{Changes in Deferred Tax Assets and Liabilities}$$

The Balance Sheet Approach: An Example

Assume that on June 30, 2018, a company pays $100,000 for a new machine. At the time of purchase, the book basis and tax basis are both $100,000. For book purposes, the machine is depreciated over a three-year period using the straight-line method. For tax purposes, the company selects the double-declining-balance method. No residual value is expected, which means that both book and tax depreciation must equal $100,000 over the three-year life of the asset.

For book purposes, 2018 depreciation is $16,667, equal to $100,000 divided by 3 (three-year expected life), divided by 2 (because the asset was put in service on July 1, 2018, the middle of the year). Tax depreciation is $33,333, or double the amount under straight-line. Assuming no other expenses, a tax rate of 40%, and revenues of $100,000, the income statements under both book and tax accounting look like Table 15.1. The net book value under both methods is shown in Table 15.2.

The balance sheet perspective measures the asset basis under the two methods. Calculating the change in the deferred tax liability account begins with the excess of the asset's book basis over the tax basis, multiplied by the tax rate: ($83,333 – $66,667) × 40%, or $6,666. This figure is then subtracted from any existing deferred tax liability already recorded for the asset. Given that this is the first year of the asset's life, there is no previous liability. Therefore, the deferred tax liability is the entire $6,666 and the journal entry is reported as follows:

Tax expense	33,333	
Tax payable		26,667
Deferred tax liability		6,666

Table 15.1 **Income Statements under Book and Tax Accounting**

Tax year 2018	Book reporting		Tax reporting
Revenues	$100,000	Revenues	$100,000
Depreciation expense	16,667	Depreciation deduction	33,333
Income before tax	83,333	Taxable income	66,667
Tax expense @ 40%	**33,333**	Tax payable @ 40%	**26,667**
Net income	50,000		

Table 15.2 **Measuring the Asset Basis**

Asset basis	Book reporting	Tax reporting
Beginning June 30, 2018	$100,000	$100,000
Less: 2018 depreciation	16,667	33,333
Ending December 31, 2018	**$83,333**	**$66,667**

The $33,333 figure represents the expense on the income statement; the company owes $26,667 in tax to the government for that year.

Consistent with the equation shown above:

$$\text{Tax Expense} = \text{Taxes Paid} \pm \text{Changes in Deferred Tax Assets and Liabilities}$$
$$\$33,333 = \$26,667 + \$6,666$$

In 2019, the company recognizes a full year of straight-line depreciation ($33,333 = $100,000/ 3 years) for book purposes and $44,444 using double-declining balance (net book value of $66,667 at the beginning of 2019, divided by 3 years and multiplied by 2, to reflect double the straight-line rate). The results are summarized in Table 15.3.

The deferred tax liability at the end of 2019 equals the excess of the book basis over the tax basis, multiplied by the tax rate of 40%: ($50,000 – $22,223) × 40%, or $11,111. This means that the liability account needs to be increased by $4,445, the difference between the required ending balance of $11,111 and the beginning balance of $6,666. Tax expense therefore equals the taxes payable of $22,223 plus the change in the deferred tax liability of $4,445. The required journal entry is:

Tax expense	26,667	
Tax payable		22,222
Deferred tax liability		4,445

In 2020 the company recognizes another full year of straight-line depreciation for book purposes, $33,333 (the same as in 2019), while depreciation expense for tax purposes is $14,815 (beginning net book value of $22,223, divided by 3 years and multiplied by 2) – see Table 15.4.

Table 15.3   **Measuring the Asset Basis Through 2019**

Asset basis	Book reporting	Tax reporting
Beginning 30 June 2018	$100,000	$100,000
Less: 2018 depreciation	16,667	33,333
Ending 31 December 2018	83,333	66,667
Less: 2019 depreciation	33,333	44,444
Ending: 31 December 2019	**$50,000**	**$22,223**

Table 15.4   **Measuring the Asset Basis Through 2020**

Asset basis	Book reporting	Tax reporting
Beginning June 30, 2018	$100,000	$100,000
Less: 2018 depreciation	16,667	33,333
Ending December 31, 2018	83,333	66,667
Less: 2019 depreciation	33,333	44,444
Ending: December 31, 2019	50,000	22,223
Less: 2020 depreciation	33,333	14,815
Ending: December 31, 2020	**$16,667**	**$7,408**

Table 15.5 **Measuring the Asset Basis Through 2021**

Asset basis	Book reporting	Tax reporting
Beginning June 30, 2018	$100,000	$100,000
Less: 2018 depreciation	16,667	33,333
Ending December 31, 2018	83,333	66,667
Less: 2019 depreciation	33,333	44,444
Ending: December 31, 2019	50,000	22,223
Less: 2020 depreciation	33,333	14,815
Ending: December 31, 2020	16,667	7,408
Less: 2021 depreciation	16,667	7,408
Ending: December 31, 2021	**0**	**0**

The ending balance for the deferred tax liability equals ($16,667 − $7,408) × 40%, or $3,704. Because the beginning balance is $11,111, the following journal entry is required:

Tax expense	26,667	
Deferred tax liability	7,407	
Tax payable		34,074

where $7,407 is the difference between the beginning balance and the required ending balance for the deferred tax liability. Because the required balance has declined, the account is debited.

Finally, for 2021, see Table 15.5.

By the end of 2021, the asset has been fully depreciated for both book and tax purposes, meaning that the asset basis is 0 under both measurement systems. Any remaining balance in the deferred tax liability account must therefore be reversed:

Tax expense	33,333	
Deferred tax liability	3,704	
Tax payable		37,037

Note that a similar approach is taken for any items that give rise to temporary differences between book and tax income, including differences that lead to deferred tax *assets*. In principle, deferred tax assets are recognized in the same way as deferred tax liabilities. However, as with all assets, the question of recoverability arises. Deferred tax assets are regarded as recoverable if, on the basis of available evidence, it is more likely than not that there will be enough taxable profit from which the future reversal of the underlying timing differences can be deducted. We discuss this issue in more detail in the following section.

Interpreting Income Tax Disclosures: The Case of Intel Corporation

In this section, we examine the income tax disclosures of Intel based on its 2016 Annual Report. We begin with the income statement, as shown in Table 15.6. Intel reports income before taxes for 2016 of $12.936 billion. The "provision for taxes," or the "income tax expense," is $2.620 billion. The tax expense is based on the tax owed under tax law for that year, plus or minus changes in deferred tax assets and liabilities.

Table 15.6   Intel Corporation's Consolidated Statements of Income

Years Ended (In Millions, Except Per Share Amounts)	Dec 31, 2016	Dec 26, 2015	Dec 27, 2014
Net revenue	$ 59,387	$ 55,355	$ 55,870
Cost of sales	23,196	20,676	20,261
Gross margin	36,191	34,679	35,609
Research and development	12,740	12,128	11,537
Marketing, general, and administrative	8,397	7,930	8,136
Restructuring and other charges	1,886	354	295
Amortization of acquisition-related intangibles	294	265	294
Operating expenses	23,317	20,677	20,262
Operating income	12,874	14,002	15,347
Gains (losses) on equity investments, net	506	315	411
Interest and other, net	(444)	(105)	43
Income before taxes	12,936	14,212	15,801
Provision for taxes	2,620	2,792	4,097
Net income	$ 10,316	$ 11,420	$ 11,704
Basic earnings per share of common stock	$ 2.18	$ 2.41	$ 2.39
Diluted earnings per share of common stock	$ 2.12	$ 2.33	$ 2.31
Weighted average shares of common stock outstanding:			
Basic	4,730	4,742	4,901
Diluted	4,875	4,894	5,056

See accompanying notes.

Tax Rates

By comparing income tax expense with income before taxes, we can calculate Intel's effective tax rate. For 2016, this rate equals $2.620 ÷ $12.936, or 20.3%. The statutory tax rate in the US (that is, the rate set by law) was recently lowered from 35% to 21%. However, in 2016 the statutory rate was still 35%, which means that Intel's effective tax rate was significantly lower. Whenever a company's effective and statutory tax rates differ, and they nearly always do for large publicly traded companies such as Intel, a reconciliation must be provided in the notes. Intel's appears in Table 15.7.

Table 15.7 reveals that the single biggest source for the difference is foreign taxation. Because so much of Intel's business is outside the United States, the company can take advantage of preferential tax regimes in other countries. For example, Intel can use transfer pricing policies to ensure that when one of its business units sells to another, the costs are high (or the revenues low) in the high-tax jurisdiction. Such practices shift profits to countries with relatively low tax rates. As a result, the effective tax rate is significantly lower than the statutory rate.

Deferred vs. Current Taxes

Table 15.8 breaks down the Income before taxes into US income of $6.957 billion and non-US income of $5.979 billion. As shown in the table, foreign earned income has increased year-on-year since 2014. However, US-based income has decreased significantly year-on-year from a

Table 15.7 Intel's Effective Tax Rate

Years Ended	Dec 31, 2016	Dec 26, 2015	Dec 27, 2014
Statutory federal income tax rate	35.0%	35.0%	35.0%
Increase (reduction) in rate resulting from:			
Non-U.S. income taxed at different rates	(11.7)	(7.9)	(6.1)
Research and development tax credits	(2.3)	(1.7)	(1.7)
Domestic manufacturing deduction benefit	(1.4)	(2.0)	(2.1)
Settlements, effective settlements, and related remeasurements	(0.1)	(2.9)	—
Other	0.8	(0.9)	0.8
Effective tax rate	20.3%	19.6%	25.9%

Table 15.8 Intel's Disaggregation of Provision for Taxes

Income Tax Provision

Income before taxes and the provision for taxes consisted of the following:

Years Ended (In Millions)	Dec 31, 2016	Dec 26, 2015	Dec 27, 2014
Income before taxes:			
U.S.	$ 6,957	$ 8,800	$ 11,565
Non-U.S.	5,979	5,412	4,236
Total income before taxes	12,936	14,212	15,801
Provision for taxes:			
Current:			
Federal	1,319	2,828	3,374
State	13	40	38
Non-U.S.	756	842	969
Total current provision for taxes	2,088	3,710	4,381
Deferred:			
Federal	658	(862)	(263)
Other	(126)	(56)	(21)
Total deferred provision for taxes	532	(918)	(284)
Total provision for taxes	$ 2,620	$ 2,792	$ 4,097
Effective tax rate	20.3%	19.6%	25.9%

high of $11.565 billion in 2014 to $6.957 billion in 2016. Table 15.8 also disaggregates the provision for taxes (i.e., the income tax expense) into its current and deferred components:

The term "current" refers to the amount that Intel owed to governments for 2016 – $2.088 billion. The table also reveals a total provision of $2.620 billion, or $532 million higher than current taxes. The implication is that Intel's tax income in 2016 was significantly lower than its book income. As shown in the deferred tax liabilities disclosure in Table 15.9, most of this difference can be explained by the depreciation component (which increased from $505 in 2015 million to

Table 15.9 **Intel's Deferred Tax Liabilities**

Deferred tax liabilities for 2016 and 2015

Deferred tax liabilities:

Property, plant, and equipment...	(1,574)	(505)
Licenses and intangibles...	(1,036)	(563)
Convertible debt...	(1,098)	(1,042)
Unrealized gains on investments and derivatives.............................	(940)	(717)
Investment in non-U.S. subsidiaries...	—	(37)
Other, net...	(450)	(358)
Total deferred tax liabilities	**(5,098)**	**(3,222)**
Net deferred tax assets (liabilities)..	**(823)**	**97**
Reported as:		
Deferred tax assets	907	1,051
Deferred tax liabilities	(1,730)	(954)
Net deferred tax assets (liabilities)..	**$ (823)**	**$ 97**

$1,574 million in 2016). What likely happened is that significantly more temporary differences from depreciation methods were created in 2016. Consequently, Intel reported lower taxable income than book income, thereby incurring a tax liability lower than the amount of tax expense recognized on the income statement.

Deferred Tax Liabilities

As with most large companies, the single biggest source of deferred tax liabilities, by far, is depreciation. Intel uses accelerated depreciation methods for tax purposes and the straight-line method for GAAP-based earnings – see Table 15.9.

Unrealized gains on investments are another important source of deferred tax liabilities. These items reflect expected tax for holding gains on investments that are marked to market (i.e., reported at fair value) as of the balance sheet date. The figures reported for Intel imply that if marked-to-market investments were sold at their end-of-2016 balance sheet values, the company would have to pay $940 million in taxes on the capital gains. Of course, the amount of this liability will change over time because the investments are held and not sold, and fair values will change. If the fair value of the investments declines, the deferred tax liability does too. In fact, if values fall far enough, the liability will be replaced by a deferred tax *asset*.

Deferred tax is not recognized for revaluations of fixed assets (property, plant, and equipment) unless the assets are continually marked to fair value with changes recognized in the income statement, or the company has entered into a binding commitment to dispose of an asset and expects to pay tax on the sale.

Deferred Tax Assets

As of the end of 2016, Intel reports net deferred tax assets of $4.275 billion – see Table 15.10.

These assets come from a variety of sources, but they all share one attribute: they represent expenses or losses that have already been recognized in GAAP-based earnings, with the relevant tax benefits expected to arise in the future. For example, Table 15.10 suggests that $1.182 billion of accrued compensation expense was recognized in book income, but tax law does not allow Intel to deduct the expense until cash is paid to employees.

Table 15.10   Intel's Deferred Tax Assets

(In Millions)	Dec 31, 2016	Dec 26, 2015
Deferred tax assets:		
Accrued compensation and other benefits..	$ 1,182	$ 931
Share-based compensation...	373	424
Deferred income..	596	694
Inventory...	1,044	598
State credits and net operating losses..	846	613
Other, net..	1,187	760
Gross deferred tax assets..	**5,228**	**4,020**
Valuation allowance..	(953)	(701)
Total deferred tax assets..	**4,275**	**3,319**

Intel also reports future tax benefits from net operating losses. Such losses are a common source of deferred tax assets. Because firms pay taxes during profitable years, it would be unfair to deny them some form of tax relief in loss-making years. For this reason, most tax codes provide the opportunity for firms to offset operating losses against either past or future tax payments. In other words, when an operating loss occurs (deductible expenses exceed taxable revenues), the business can apply the loss to tax income already reported and receive a refund for taxes paid or a reduction of taxes due in the current period. However, restrictions are imposed on how far back the company can go to capture the tax benefit, and sometimes on how far forward it can be carried. In the United States, for example, firms can carry back losses for up to two years. To the extent that losses cannot be used (because the company did not have enough taxable income in the previous two years), they can be carried forward for up to 20 years to offset future taxable income.[2] After that period, the losses expire and can no longer be used to reduce taxes.

When the future realization of any deferred tax asset is uncertain – because there might not be enough taxable income for the deduction to be offset against when the reversal occurs, or tax losses might expire unused – the company must establish a "deferred tax valuation allowance." The allowance reduces the net carrying value of the deferred tax asset on the balance sheet, and therefore functions in much the same way as other contra-asset accounts, such as accumulated depreciation and the allowance for bad debts. Establishing the allowance also has the effect of increasing income tax expense and reducing shareholders' equity. These effects are reversed in the future when realization of the tax benefits becomes more likely.

In determining whether such an allowance is needed, companies should consider all available evidence, both negative and positive. Negative evidence (i.e., the tax benefits are unlikely to be realized) includes the following:

- cumulative losses in recent years

- a history of operating loss carryforward expiring unused, or

- losses expected in early future years.

    Positive evidence includes the following:

- a strong earnings history

- existing contracts that will produce taxable income in the period of the asset reversal, or

- property having market values significantly greater than their tax basis.

BOX 15.1   Intel Corporation – Valuation Allowance Disclosure

The valuation allowance as of December 31, 2016, included allowances related to unrealized state credit carryforward of $839 million and matters related to our non-U.S. subsidiaries of $114 million.

Despite being a profitable company, Intel recognizes a valuation allowance, as discussed in the note in Box 15.1.

Taken together, Intel's disclosures reveal that while the company has deferred tax assets of $5.228 billion as of the end of 2016, some portion of those tax benefits ($953 million) is expected to expire without ever being used. Apparently, Intel does not expect to earn enough profits in the jurisdictions where the losses were recognized to take advantage of the tax breaks. As a result, future cash savings from the deferred tax assets are expected to be $4.275 billion.

Why Deferred Income Tax is Important

The analysis of deferred taxes can often yield interesting and important insights. Remember that when deferred tax liabilities increase, book income for the year is greater than tax income. One possible reason for such an outcome is that the company acquired a lot of depreciable assets during the year. But a growing gap between book income and tax income, as reflected in rapidly increasing deferred tax liabilities, could result from increasingly aggressive revenue recognition practices. In fact, there were disturbing signs throughout the dot-com boom in the late-1990s that such practices were becoming commonplace.

Data from the US Internal Revenue Service show that the gap between book income and taxable income for American companies was close to zero in the early 1990s. But by 1996, as the boom began to gain momentum, a gap of over $92 billion had appeared (i.e., the amount by which book income exceeded taxable income). Two years later, the gap had increased to $159 billion, a fourth of the total taxable income reported.[3] The troubling conclusion is that much of the GAAP-based income reported in the years leading up to the dot-com meltdown was illusory. Investors learned this lesson the hard way when the crash arrived in early 2000.

The key lesson for financial statement readers is to continuously monitor deferred tax positions. Be wary of rapid growth in deferred tax liabilities, especially if the increase cannot be explained by capital expenditures on depreciable assets. Such growth implies a widening gap between book and tax income.

Deferred tax assets should be monitored too. For deferred assets to have value, the company must be profitable enough in future years to capture the implied tax savings. For example, in spring 2011 Sony was compelled to write off ¥360 billion ($4.5 billion) of deferred tax assets. The company had incurred large operating losses as a result of the earthquake and tsunami that hit Japan in March of that year. The company admitted that the disruptions to its supply chain and the devastating effect of the natural disasters on Japan's economy meant that Sony would be unable to earn enough taxable profits in Japan in the foreseeable future to take advantage of its earlier operating losses.[4]

Indeed, anytime a company's auditors have reason to doubt its future profitability, a large valuation allowance appears or write-offs are required. The key point here is that the firm is signaling to the financial statement reader that future cash savings on income tax will be lower than previously expected. In addition, the reader can take the reduction in deferred tax assets as a signal that future profitability will likely be impaired.

KEY LESSONS FROM THE CHAPTER

- The rules for calculating profit under financial accounting principles, known as book income, are not the same as the rules used under tax law.

- Governments use taxes not just to collect revenues from businesses but also to promote public policy priorities. The result is that tax law creates financial statements that are highly unlikely to be "true and fair." This problem explains why different rules are needed for investors.

- The differences between the determination of tax income and book income can be temporary or permanent.

- Temporary differences result when a revenue, gain, expense, or loss enters in the calculation of book income in one period but affects tax income in a different period.

- Common sources of temporary differences include depreciation methods, deferred revenue, long-term contracts, bad debt expense, prepaid expenses, equity income, and installment sales.

- Permanent differences between tax and book income are caused by items that affect book income but will never affect tax income, or vice versa.

- Accounting principles require a balance sheet approach in calculating the impact of timing differences between book and tax accounting.

- Temporary differences result in either a deferred tax asset or a deferred tax liability.

- When the future realization of a deferred tax asset is uncertain – because there might not be enough taxable income for the deduction to be offset against when the reversal occurs, or tax losses might expire unused – the company must establish a deferred tax valuation allowance. This allowance serves as a contra-account to the deferred tax asset.

- The analysis of deferred taxes can often yield interesting and important insights. For example, a high deferred tax liability (compared to industry competitors) may indicate a tendency to overstate book income.

KEY TERMS AND CONCEPTS FROM THE CHAPTER

Temporary differences
Deferred tax liability

Deferred tax asset
Permanent differences

The balance sheet approach
Valuation allowance

QUESTIONS

1. What are deferred income taxes and why do they exist?

2. Define temporary differences. Give some examples.

3. Define permanent differences. Give some examples.

4. What is the difference between a deferred tax asset and a deferred tax liability?

5. What is the biggest source of deferred tax liabilities?

6. What is the biggest source of deferred tax assets?

7. What purpose is served by the deferred tax valuation allowance?

8. Why might a company have to write down a deferred tax asset?

9. True or false: The larger the gap between book income (i.e., income under GAAP or IFRS) and taxable income, the more confidence we have in the quality of the accounting numbers.

10. True or false: Analysts tend to be more concerned about deferred tax *assets* than deferred tax *liabilities*.

PROBLEMS

15.1 Calculating Temporary and Permanent Differences

Hernan Company reports the following information for the year:

Book income before income taxes	€636,000
Income tax expense	€312,000
Income taxes payable for the year	€96,000
Income tax rate on taxable income	40%

The company has both permanent and temporary differences between book income and taxable income.

Required

a. What is the amount of temporary differences for the year? Indicate whether the effect is to make book income larger or smaller than taxable income.

b. What is the amount of permanent differences for the year? Indicate whether the effect is to make book income larger or smaller than taxable income.

15.2 Interpreting Income Tax Disclosures

The following note was taken from the 2011 Annual Report of Tesco, a global UK-based grocery and discount retailing chain.

Required

a. Based on this disclosure, which figure do you think was higher: taxable income reported under tax law, or pretax income reported under IFRS? How would you know? Does the magnitude and direction of this difference imply "conservative" accounting or "aggressive" accounting on the part of Tesco?

b. What is meant by the term "origination and reversal of temporary differences?" What effect did the change in the UK corporate tax rate have on deferred income tax, and why?

c. What would you expect to be the largest source of Tesco's deferred income tax liability?

Recognized in the Group income statement

	2011 £m	2010 £m
Current tax expense		
UK corporation tax	694	566
Foreign tax	181	128
Adjustments in respect of prior years	(114)	(91)
	761	603
Deferred income tax		
Origination and reversal of temporary differences	148	110
Adjustments in respect of prior years	12	124
Change in tax rate	(57)	3
	103	237
Total income tax expense	864	840

A number of changes to the UK corporation tax system were announced in the June 2010 Budget Statement. The Finance (No.2) Act 2010 included legislation to reduce the main rate of corporation tax from 28 to 27% from April 1, 2011. The proposed reduction from 28 to 27% was substantively enacted at the balance sheet date and has therefore been reflected in these Group financial statements.

In addition to the changes in rates of corporation tax disclosed above, a number of further changes to the UK corporation tax system were announced in the March 2011 UK Budget Statement. A resolution passed by Parliament on March 29, 2011, reduced the main rate of corporation tax to 26% from April 1, 2011. Legislation to reduce the main rate of corporation tax from 26 to 25% from April 1, 2012, is expected to be included in the Finance Act 2011. Further reductions to the main rate are proposed to reduce the rate by 1% per annum to 23% by April 1, 2014. None of these expected rate reductions had been substantively enacted at the balance sheet date and, therefore, are not reflected in these Group financial statements.

The effect of the changes enacted by Parliament on March 29, 2011, to reduce the corporation tax rate to 26%, with effect from April 1, 2011, is to reduce the deferred tax liability provided at the balance sheet date by £32m (£46m increase in profit and £14m decrease in the Group Statement of Comprehensive Income).

The effect of the changes expected to be enacted in the Finance Act 2011 to reduce the corporation tax rate from 26 to 25%, with effect from April 1, 2012, would be to reduce the deferred tax liability provided at the balance sheet date by a further £32m (£46m increase in profit and £14m decrease in the Group Statement of Comprehensive Income).

The proposed reductions of the main rate of corporation tax by 1% per year to 23% by April 1, 2014, are expected to be enacted separately each year. The overall effect of the further changes from 25 to 23%, if these applied to the deferred tax balance at the balance sheet date, would be to reduce the deferred tax liability by £66m (being £33m recognized in 2013 and £33m recognized in 2014).

15.3 Deferred Income Taxes and the Statement of Cash Flows

The operating activities section from recent statements of cash flows for Group Air France-KLM is shown below. A note from the Group's fiscal year 2011 Annual Report is also provided.

Required

a. Deferred taxes are a negative adjustment to net income in both years. What do these adjustments signify?

b. What events or circumstances gave rise to the adjustments?

in ε million, period from April 1 to March 31	2011	2010
Net income for the period – equity holders for Air France-KLM	613	(1 559)
Noncontrolling interests	(1)	(1)
Amortization, depreciation, and operating provisions	1,676	1,675
Financial provisions	(3)	7
Gain on disposals of tangible and intangible assets	(11)	61
Loss/(gain) on disposals of subsidiaries and associates	(13)	—
Gain on WAM (ex Amadeus) operation	(1,030)	—
Derivatives – nonmonetary result	(25)	(8)
Unrealized foreign exchange gains and losses, net	33	13
Share of (profits)/losses of associates	21	17
Deferred taxes	(215)	(591)
Other nonmonetary items	(209)	143
Subtotal	**836**	**(243)**
(Increase)/decrease in inventories	(10)	(28)
(Increase)/decrease in trade receivables	171	(89)
Increase/(decrease) in trade payables	245	126
Change in other receivables and payables	108	(564)
Net cash flow from operating activities	**1,350**	**(798)**

12.5 Deferred tax recorded on the balance sheet

(in € millions)	April 1, 2010	Amounts recorded in income	Amounts recorded in equity	Currency translation adjustment	Reclassification	March 31, 2011
Flight equipment	(1,039)	(78)	—	—	26	(1,091)
Pension assets	(683)	(50)	—	—	1	(732)
Financial debt	453	36	(236)	—	(3)	486
Other liabilities	387	(31)	—	—	(109)	11
Deferred revenue on ticket sales	206	—	(80)	—	(1)	205
Others	(252)	(41)	—	—	90	(283)
Deferred tax corresponding to fiscal losses	1,452	379	—	—	(5)	1,826
Deferred tax asset/(liability)	524	215	(316)	—	(1)	422

(in € millions)	April 1, 2009	Amounts recorded in income	Amounts recorded in equity	Currency translation adjustment	Reclassification	March 31, 2010
Flight equipment	(812)	(174)	(1)	1	(53)	(1,039)
Pension assets	(623)	(59)	—	(1)	—	(683)
Financial debt	442	47	(36)	—	—	453
Other liabilities	911	24	(579)	(2)	33	387
Deferred revenue on ticket sales	209	(3)	—	—	—	206
Others	(254)	(70)	62	—	10	(252)
Deferred tax corresponding to fiscal losses	599	826	—	1	26	1,452
Deferred tax asset/(liability)	472	591	(554)	(1)	16	524

15-1 Deferred Tax Assets and the Valuation
      Allowance: The Case of Ford Motor Company

Exhibit 15.1 provides the income statements and balance sheets from Ford's 2011 Annual Report. Excerpts from the note on deferred income taxes are provided in Exhibit 15.2. The statements of cash flow for Ford reveal cash flows provided

by operations of $9.784 billion, $11.477 billion, and $15.477 billion in 2011, 2010, and 2009, respectively. In 2011, Ford reported its highest net income ever (over $20 billion), an improvement of nearly $14 billion from the previous year. But did Ford's profitability really improve that much?

Exhibit 15.1   Ford Motor Company and Subsidiaries: Income Statements for the Years Ended December 31, 2011, 2010, and 2009 (in millions, Except per Share Amounts)

	2011	2010	2009
Automotive			
Revenues	$128,168	$119,280	$103,868
Costs and expenses			
Cost of sales	113,345	104,451	98,866
Selling, administrative and other expenses	9,060	9,040	8,354
Total costs and expenses	122,405	113,491	107,220
Operating income/(loss)	5,763	5,789	(3,352)
Interest expense	817	1,807	1,477
Interest income and other nonoperating income/(expense), net (Note 19)	825	(362)	5,284
Equity in net income/(loss) of affiliated companies	479	526	330
Income/(loss) before income taxes – Automotive	6,250	4,146	785
Financial Services			
Revenues	8,096	9,674	12,415
Costs and expenses			
Interest expense	3,614	4,345	5,313
Depreciation	1,843	2,024	3,937
Operating and other expenses	675	845	738
Provision for credit and insurance losses	(33)	(216)	1,030
Total costs and expenses	6,099	6,998	11,018
Other income/(loss), net (Note 19)	413	315	552
Equity in net income/(loss) of affiliated companies	21	12	(135)
Income/(loss) before income taxes – Financial Services	2,431	3,003	1,814
Total Company			
Income/(loss) before income taxes	8,681	7,149	2,599
Provision for/(Benefit from) income taxes (Note 22)	(11,541)	592	(113)
Income/(loss) from continuing operations	20,222	6,557	2,712
Income/(loss) from discontinued operations	—	—	5
Net income/(loss)	20,222	6,557	2,717
Less: Income/(loss) attributable to noncontrolling interests	9	(4)	—
Net income/(loss) attributable to Ford Motor Company	$20,213	$6,561	$2,717

	2011	2010	2009
Net Income/(Loss) Attributable to Ford Motor Company			
Income/(loss) from continuing operations	$20,213	$6,561	$2,712
Income/(loss) from discontinued operations	—	—	5
Net income/(loss) attributable to Ford Motor Company	$20,213	$6,561	$2,717

Balance sheets (in millions)

	December 31, 2011	December 31, 2010
Assets		
Cash and cash equivalents	$17,148	S14,805
Marketable securities (Note 6)	18,618	20,765
Finance receivables, net (Note 7)	69,976	70,070
Other receivables, net	8,565	8,381
Net investment in operating leases (Note 8)	12,838	11,675
Inventories (Note 10)	5,901	5,917
Equity in net assets of affiliated companies (Note 11)	2,936	2,569
Net property (Note 14)	22,371	23,179
Deferred income taxes (Note 22)	15,125	2,003
Net intangible assets (Note 15)	100	102
Other assets	4,770	5,221
Total assets	$178,348	$164,687
Liabilities		
Payables	$17,724	$16,362
Accrued liabilities and deferred revenue (Note 16)	45,369	43,844
Debt (Note 18)	99,488	103,988
Deferred income taxes (Note 22)	696	1,135
Total liabilities	163,277	165,329
Equity		
Capital stock (Note 24)		
Common stock, par value $.01 per share (3745 million shares issued)	37	37
Class B stock, par value $.01 per share (71 million shares issued)	1	1
Capital in excess of par value of stock	20,905	20,803
Retained earnings/(accumulated deficit)	12,985	(7,038)
Accumulated other comprehensive income/(loss)	(18,734)	(14,313)
Treasury stock	(166)	(163)
Total equity/(deficit) attributable to Ford Motor Company	15,028	(673)
Equity/(deficit) attributable to noncontrolling interests	43	31
Total equity/(deficit)	15,071	(642)
Total liabilities and equity	$178,348	$164,687

(Continued)

Exhibit 15.2   Ford Motor Company and Subsidiaries

Excerpts from Note 22
2011 Annual Report

Valuation of deferred tax assets and liabilities

Deferred tax assets and liabilities are recognized based on the future tax consequences attributable to temporary differences that exist between the financial statement carrying value of assets and liabilities and their respective tax bases, and operating loss and tax credit carryforward on a taxing jurisdiction basis. We measure deferred tax assets and liabilities using enacted tax rates that will apply in the years in which we expect the temporary differences to be recovered or paid.

Our accounting for deferred tax consequences represents our best estimate of the likely future tax consequences of events that have been recognized in our financial statements or tax returns and their future probability. In assessing the need for a valuation allowance, we consider both positive and negative evidence related to the likelihood of realization of the deferred tax assets. If, based on the weight of available evidence, it is more likely than not that the deferred tax assets will not be realized, we record a valuation allowance.

	2011	2010	2009
Reconciliation of effective tax rate			
US statutory rate	35.0%	35.0%	35.0%
Non-US tax rates under US rates	(1.5)	(0.1)	(0.6)
State and local income taxes	1.1	1.5	(1.9)
General business credits	(1.9)	(1.8)	(6.2)
Dispositions and restructurings	6.8	(9.5)	(4.3)
US tax on non-US earnings	(0.8)	0.1	0.6
Prior year settlements and claims	(0.2)	(10.0)	10.4
Tax-related interest	(0.9)	(0.7)	(1.5)
Tax-exempt income	(3.9)	(4.7)	(10.4)
Other	(2.5)	0.2	0.2
Valuation allowances	(172.3)	(1.0)	(26.0)
Effective rate	(141.1)%	9.0%	(4.7)%

At the end of 2011, our US operations had returned to a position of cumulative profits for the most recent three-year period. We concluded that this record of cumulative profitability in recent years, our 10 consecutive quarters of pretax operating profits, our successful completion of labor negotiations with the UAW, and our business plan showing continued profitability, provide assurance that our future tax benefits more likely than not will be realized. Accordingly, at year-end 2011, we released almost all of our valuation allowance against net deferred tax assets for entities in the United States, Canada, and Spain.

At December 31, 2011, we have retained a valuation allowance against approximately $500 million in North America related to various state and local operating loss carryforward that are subject to restrictive rules for future utilization, and a valuation allowance totaling $1 billion primarily against deferred tax assets for our South American operations.

Components of deferred tax assets and liabilities

The components of deferred tax assets and liabilities at December 31 were as follows (in millions):

	2011	2010
Deferred tax assets		
Employee benefit plans	$8,189	$6,332
Net operating loss carryforward	3,163	4,124
Tax credit carryforward	4,534	4,546
Research expenditures	2,297	2,336
Dealer and customer allowances and claims	1,731	1,428
Other foreign deferred tax assets	694	1,513
Allowance for credit losses	194	252
All other	1,483	2,839
Total gross deferred tax assets	22,285	23,370
Less: valuation allowances	(1,545)	(15,664)
Total net deferred tax assets	20,740	7,706
Deferred tax liabilities		
Leasing transactions	932	928
Deferred income	2,098	2,101
Depreciation and amortization (excluding leasing transactions)	1,659	1,146
Finance receivables	551	716
Other foreign deferred tax liabilities	360	334
All other	711	1,613
Total deferred tax liabilities	6,311	6,838
Net deferred tax assets/(liabilities)	$14,429	$868

Operating loss carryforward for tax purposes was $8.5 billion at December 31, 2011, resulting in a deferred tax asset of $3.2 billion. A substantial portion of these losses begin to expire in 2029; the remaining losses will begin to expire in 2018. Tax credits available to offset future tax liabilities are $4.5 billion. A substantial portion of these credits have a remaining carryforward period of 10 years or more. Tax benefits of operating loss and tax credit carryforward are evaluated on an ongoing basis, including a review of historical and projected future operating results, the eligible carryforward period, and other circumstances.

Required

a. What are "net operating loss carryforward," and why did they give rise to deferred tax assets? Answer the same question for "tax credit carryforward."

b. Why do depreciation and amortization give rise to deferred tax liabilities?

c. What are the "valuation allowances" referred to in the financial statements and the notes?

d. What happened to the valuation allowances in 2011? Give the appropriate summary journal entry. What was the effect on earnings for the year?

e. What would Ford have reported as net income for 2011 if there had been no change in the valuation allowance?

f. Describe, in detail, what happened in 2011 to allow Ford Motor Company to sharply reduce the allowance account.

NOTES

1. There is also an income statement approach to determine deferred taxes, but we do not discuss it here because the method is no longer allowed.

2. While nearly all countries allow carryforward, some do not allow carrybacks. Examples include Australia, Italy, Spain, and Switzerland. The US policy of allowing tax loss carryforward for up to 20 years is unique. Other major market-based economies use either shorter periods or allow tax losses to be carried forward indefinitely. For example, France, Japan, and Korea allow only five years, while Australia, Germany, Ireland, the Netherlands, and the United Kingdom impose no time limits.

3. "Align the Books," by Tim Reason, *CFO Magazine*, November 2002.

4. "Full-year loss of Y260bn forces preliminary filing from Sony," by Jonathan Soble, *The Financial Times*, May 24, 2011.

Accounting for Shareholders' Equity

16

Introduction

This chapter examines the financial reporting consequences of the most common transactions and events that impact shareholders' equity, including:

- the issuance of common and preferred shares
- the declaration and payment of cash dividends
- share repurchases
- stock dividends and stock splits
- convertible securities.

Relevant concepts and practices will be illustrated using the balance sheets and statements of shareholders' equity for The Coca-Cola Company (see Exhibits 16.1 and 16.2). Unless otherwise noted, the following discussion applies equally to financial statements prepared under US GAAP or IFRS.

Shareholders' Equity: An Introduction

Shareholders' equity consists of two parts:

- contributed capital and
- earned capital.

Contributed capital (sometimes called "paid-in" or "share" capital) represents the cumulative cash inflow that a company has received from the sale of various classes of stock, less the cash paid out to repurchase stock. For Coca-Cola, contributed capital equals

Common Stock + Capital Surplus − Treasury Stock

Common stock is the par value of issued shares, capital surplus is the additional capital raised above par value from the issuance of those shares, and treasury stock is the price paid for shares that were repurchased and still held in corporate treasury (i.e., have not yet been reissued or canceled). Each of these accounts will be examined in more detail as follows.

As presented on Coca-Cola's balance sheet (Exhibit 16.1), at the end of 2016, contributed capital was $1,760 million + $14,993 million −$47,988 million, or −$31,235 million. The negative figure resulted from Coca-Cola paying more for the shares it bought back than what the company received when the shares were issued.

Exhibit 16.1	The Coca-Cola Company and Subsidiaries Consolidated Balance Sheets

December 31,	2016	2015
(In millions except par value)		
ASSETS		
CURRENT ASSETS		
Cash and cash equivalents	$ 8,555	$ 7,309
Short-term investments	9,595	8,322
TOTAL CASH, CASH EQUIVALENTS AND SHORT-TERM INVESTMENTS	18,150	15,631
Marketable securities	4,051	4,269
Trade accounts receivable, less allowances of $466 and $352, respectively	3,856	3,941
Inventories	2,675	2,902
Prepaid expenses and other assets	2,481	2,752
Assets held for sale	2,797	3,900
TOTAL CURRENT ASSETS	34,010	33,395
EQUITY METHOD INVESTMENTS	16,260	12,318
OTHER INVESTMENTS	989	3,470
OTHER ASSETS	4,248	4,110
PROPERTY, PLANT AND EQUIPMENT — net	10,635	12,571
TRADEMARKS WITH INDEFINITE LIVES	6,097	5,989
BOTTLERS' FRANCHISE RIGHTS WITH INDEFINITE LIVES	3,676	6,000
GOODWILL	10,629	11,289
OTHER INTANGIBLE ASSETS	726	854
TOTAL ASSETS	$ 87,270	$ 89,996
LIABILITIES AND EQUITY		
CURRENT LIABILITIES		
Accounts payable and accrued expenses	$ 9,490	$ 9,660
Loans and notes payable	12,498	13,129
Current maturities of long-term debt	3,527	2,676
Accrued income taxes	307	331
Liabilities held for sale	710	1,133
TOTAL CURRENT LIABILITIES	26,532	26,929
LONG-TERM DEBT	29,684	28,311
OTHER LIABILITIES	4,081	4,301
DEFERRED INCOME TAXES	3,753	4,691
THE COCA-COLA COMPANY SHAREOWNERS' EQUITY		
Common stock, $0.25 par value; Authorized — 11,200 shares; Issued — 7,040 and 7,040 shares, respectively	1,760	1,760

(Continued)

Exhibit 16.1 (Continued)

December 31,	2016	2015
Capital surplus	14,993	14,016
Reinvested earnings	65,502	65,018
Accumulated other comprehensive income (loss)	(11,205)	(10,174)
Treasury stock, at cost — 2,752 and 2,716 shares, respectively	(47,988)	(45,066)
EQUITY ATTRIBUTABLE TO SHAREOWNERS OF THE COCA-COLA COMPANY	23,062	25,554
EQUITY ATTRIBUTABLE TO NONCONTROLLING INTERESTS	158	210
TOTAL EQUITY	23,220	25,764
TOTAL LIABILITIES AND EQUITY	$ 87,270	$ 89,996

Refer to Notes to Consolidated Financial Statements.

Exhibit 16.2 The Coca-Cola Company and Subsidiaries Consolidated Statements of Shareowners' Equity

Year Ended December 31,	2016	2015	2014
(In millions except per share data)			
EQUITY ATTRIBUTABLE TO SHAREOWNERS OF THE COCA-COLA COMPANY			
NUMBER OF COMMON SHARES OUTSTANDING			
Balance at beginning of year	4,324	4,366	4,402
Treasury stock issued to employees related to stock compensation plans	50	44	62
Purchases of stock for treasury	(86)	(86)	(98)
Balance at end of year	4,288	4,324	4,366
COMMON STOCK	$ 1,760	$ 1,760	$ 1,760
CAPITAL SURPLUS			
Balance at beginning of year	14,016	13,154	12,276
Stock issued to employees related to stock compensation plans	589	532	526
Tax benefit (charge) from stock compensation plans	130	94	169
Stock-based compensation expense	258	236	209
Other activities	—	—	(26)
Balance at end of year	14,993	14,016	13,154
REINVESTED EARNINGS			
Balance at beginning of year	65,018	63,408	61,660
Net income attributable to shareowners of The Coca-Cola Company	6,527	7,351	7,098

(Continued)

Exhibit 16.2	(Continued)

Year Ended December 31,	2016	2015	2014
Dividends (per share — $1.40, $1.32 and $1.22 in 2016, 2015 and 2014, respectively)	(6,043)	(5,741)	(5,350)
Balance at end of year	65,502	65,018	63,408
ACCUMULATED OTHER COMPREHENSIVE INCOME (LOSS)			
Balance at beginning of year	(10,174)	(5,777)	(3,432)
Net other comprehensive income (loss)	(1,031)	(4,397)	(2,345)
Balance at end of year	(11,205)	(10,174)	(5,777)
TREASURY STOCK			
Balance at beginning of year	(45,066)	(42,225)	(39,091)
Treasury stock issued to employees related to stock compensation plans	811	696	891
Purchases of stock for treasury	(3,733)	(3,537)	(4,025)
Balance at end of year	(47,988)	(45,066)	(42,225)
TOTAL EQUITY ATTRIBUTABLE TO SHAREOWNERS OF THE COCA-COLA COMPANY	$ 23,062	$ 25,554	$ 30,320
EQUITY ATTRIBUTABLE TO NONCONTROLLING INTERESTS			
Balance at beginning of year	$ 210	$ 241	$ 267
Net income attributable to noncontrolling interests	23	15	26
Net foreign currency translation adjustment	(13)	(18)	(5)
Dividends paid to noncontrolling interests	(25)	(31)	(25)
Contributions by noncontrolling interests	1	—	—
Business combinations	—	(3)	(22)
Deconsolidation of certain entities	(34)	—	—
Other activities	(4)	6	—
TOTAL EQUITY ATTRIBUTABLE TO NONCONTROLLING INTERESTS	$ 158	$ 210	$ 241

However, Coca-Cola's total shareholders' equity is strongly positive because of its earned capital. Earned capital represents the cumulative profit that has been retained by the company. For Coca-Cola, earned capital equals

Reinvested Earnings + Accumulated Other Comprehensive Loss

Reinvested earnings, also known as retained earnings, are the cumulative profits of the company that have been retained in the business (i.e., not paid out as dividends). Accumulated other comprehensive loss includes gains and losses that have not yet found their way onto the income statement. Earned capital is increased by profits and decreased by losses and dividend payments.

One way to view shareholders' equity is that it represents the investment made in the firm by its shareholders. That investment is both direct (contributed capital) and indirect (earned capital). Indirect capital arises from the company earning profits that are not distributed as dividends, and are therefore reinvested in the firm on the shareholders' behalf.

Alternatively, shareholders' equity is known as book value. The term "value" is potentially misleading because the book value of equity is different than its market value. The market value of shares, otherwise known as "market capitalization," is computed by multiplying the number of common shares outstanding by the share price. In the case of Coca-Cola, the difference between its market capitalization and book value is enormous. While book value was $23,220 million at the end of 2016, the market capitalization of the company's shares was $190 billion.

Although the notion of book value might seem to be of no practical use to the financial statement reader, when combined with market value (i.e., stock price) it can offer a profitable stock-picking tool. The idea is that stocks selling for high price-to-book ratios, relative to competitors and other firms, are pricey, and therefore likely to underperform relative to stock market benchmarks in the future. Companies with low ratios, according to this practice, are relative bargains and should therefore outperform market averages. Academic evidence supports this idea. Large portfolios that comprise low price-to-book stocks tend to beat the market, while those that comprise high price-to-book tend to underperform. Coca-Cola's price-to-book ratio was about 8X at the end of 2016, well above the market average. The high ratio value can be accounted for mainly by the absence of the company's powerful brands from book value.

More on Contributed Capital

Companies issue two types of stock: preferred and common. The difference between the two lies in the legal rights and claims conferred upon each class.

Preferred Stock

As the term implies, preferred stock has some preference, or priority, over common shares. Specifically, preferred shareholders have priority over common shareholders in the receipt of dividends, and are entitled to receive payment in full if the company liquidates before common shareholders are entitled to any payout. Preferred shares are less risky to the investor than common shares, and therefore carry lower expected returns.

One common feature of preferred stock is a fixed dividend rate. For example, "6% preferred stock, par value $10 per share" pays an annual dividend equal to 6% of par, or $0.60 per share. The fixed dividend is attractive to those who seek stable income from their investments.

"Cumulative dividend preference," another common feature, requires that any dividends on preferred stock not paid in full accumulate over time. In other words, any unpaid dividends accumulated from previous years must be paid in full before any common dividends are paid.

Also, many issues of preferred stock are "convertible." This feature gives the stockholder the right to convert their stock into common shares at a predetermined exchange ratio. The benefit to investors is that they can participate in common-stock price appreciation. If the share price increase is high enough, preferred shareholders profit by converting their preferred shares into common shares.[1]

Common Stock

Common shares are the basic voting stock issued by a corporation. Because they carry the company's voting power, it's the common shareholders who we think of when we use the term "owners." Common shareholders are the residual claimants on the firm, a term that means that, in the event of liquidation, all other claimants on the firm must be paid in full (i.e., creditors and preferred shareholders) before common shareholders are entitled to any payment. In fact, one way to define ownership is that it represents a residual claim on the firm's assets.

When discussing share ownership, confusion sometimes arises in distinguishing among authorized, issued, and outstanding shares.

Authorized Shares

These are the maximum number of shares in any given class, common or preferred, that a company can issue. This amount is specified in the corporate charter, and is usually shown on the balance sheet. For Coca-Cola, 11.2 billion shares of common stock have been authorized. (The company does not have any preferred stock.) The corporate charter can be amended to increase the authorized share amount; however, shareholder approval is required.

Issued Shares

These represent the total number of shares of stock that have been sold or distributed, and not yet retired. As shown on the balance sheet Exhibit 16.1, 7.0 billion of shares of Coca-Cola common stock were issued as of the end of 2016. This figure means that another 4.2 billion shares of common stock could be issued without amending the corporate charter.

Outstanding Shares

These refer to the total number of shares owned by shareholders on any particular date. It equals the number of shares issued, less the number of shares in treasury. Treasury shares are those shares that were issued, later purchased by the company, and retained in corporate treasury.[2] (In countries that do not allow for treasury stock, **outstanding shares** will always equal the number of issued shares.) Coca-Cola discloses on its income statement that the average number of shares outstanding for 2016 was 4.317 billion shares. This figure is important because earnings per share calculations are based on it. The number of shares outstanding at the end of 2016 is easily calculated from information on the balance sheet: 7.040 billion shares issued, less 2.752 billion shares in treasury, or 4.288 billion.

Accounting for Stock Transactions

In this section we cover the accounting for stock transactions, including stock issuances and stock repurchases.

Issuing Stock

The issuance of stock increases both assets and shareholders' equity. But to understand which accounts are affected, the concept of "par value" must be addressed.

Par value is the nominal, or stated, value per share of stock. This amount is specified in the corporate charter, but has little economic meaning. Think of it as a legal figure that appears on a stock certificate, but has no bearing on what the shares are worth, even at the moment of issuance.

The par value of Coca Cola shares, according to the 2016 balance sheet, was $0.25. We'll have more to say about this figure later in the chapter.

Contributed capital also consists of capital surplus. A more common term for this account is "additional paid-in capital (APIC)." APIC is the difference between the price paid by investors when the shares were issued and the par value. For example, if Coca-Cola issues a share of stock for $50, the journal entry would be:

Cash	50.00	
Common stock (par value)		0.25
Additional paid-in capital		49.75

A standard practice in many countries is to combine common stock and additional paid-in capital into a single account, known variously as "share capital," "contributed capital," or "paid-in capital." In such cases, the above example leads to the following entry:

Cash	50.00	
Share capital		50.00

Share Repurchases

Companies repurchase their own shares for many reasons. Perhaps the company has surplus cash that cannot be profitably invested. The cash could be returned to investors as dividends, but dividends are often subject to high marginal tax rates. Returning cash to shareholders through buybacks may be more tax efficient.

Another common reason for buybacks is that the repurchased shares can be used for an employee bonus or stock ownership plan. Using share buybacks instead of issuing new shares allows the company to control dilution. If new shares are issued instead, the percentage ownership held by existing owners declines. Shareholders with large blocks might resist such an approach because over time their influence or control over the business may decline. Microsoft is one such example. As employees exercised stock options throughout the 1980s and 1990s, the dilution effect was reduced by granting shares bought in the open market and kept as treasury stock. Although some dilution occurred anyway, this practice has allowed Bill Gates, Steve Ballmer, and other large shareholders to maintain control over the company.

Share buybacks can also be used to adjust a company's capital structure. Because buybacks reduce shareholders' equity, debt/equity ratios increase. In other words, buybacks allow companies to increase their financial leverage without additional borrowing. This approach may be attractive to companies that have surplus cash, but are viewed as underlevered, thus benefiting from a higher debt/equity ratio.

Under US GAAP, when shares are acquired with the intent of retiring or cancelling the shares, the following options are available:

- charge the excess of the cost of treasury stock over its par value entirely to retained earnings;

- allocate the excess between retained earnings and additional paid-in capital (APIC); or

- charge the excess entirely to APIC.

The last of these alternatives is the most common, and is broadly in line with practice under IFRS.

When treasury stock is acquired for purposes other than retirement (i.e., the intent is to hold the shares for an unspecified period), the cost of the acquired stock may be shown separately as a deduction from equity (i.e., as the contra-equity account, treasury stock) or it may be treated in exactly the same way as the retirement of stock (a reduction in par value and APIC). IFRS requires the first of these approaches. The journal entry looks like this:

Treasury stock	XX	
Cash		XX

In effect, a share repurchase has the opposite financial statement effects from a share issuance. Cash is reduced by the price paid for the shares, and shareholders' equity is reduced by the same amount.

Reissuing Treasury Stock

By keeping repurchased shares in treasury, the company is signaling its intent to reissue the shares in the future. Otherwise, the shares would be retired. When repurchased shares are subsequently reissued, no gain or loss is recognized. Instead, the difference between the proceeds received from the sale and the purchase price of the treasury stock is shown as an increase or decrease to additional paid-in capital.

To illustrate, assume that Coca-Cola repurchases 10,000 shares of its stock at $40 per share. It then reissues the shares on the open market for $45 per share. The journal entry would be:

Cash	450,000	
Treasury stock		400,000
APIC		50,000

Notice that no profit is acknowledged from the transaction, despite reissuance at a price exceeding the cost of the treasury shares. The logic of this treatment is that because profit or gain effectively belongs to shareholders, no profit should be recognized from a company trading stock with its own shareholders. In addition, if gains or losses could be recognized from a company trading in its own shares, managers would possess a powerful tool for profit manipulation. Prohibiting any income statement effects from such transactions removes this avenue for earnings management.

Notice also that the increase in shareholders' equity that arises from the resale of the treasury stock depends entirely on the price paid for the reissued shares. For example, if treasury stock had cost Coca-Cola only $300,000, shareholders' equity would still increase by $450,000. To make up the difference, APIC is now credited for $150,000.

Similarly, if the shares are resold at a price below the cost of the treasury stock, no loss is recognized. Again, the balancing entry is made to APIC. For example, if the shares are resold for $325,000, the journal entry becomes:

Cash	325,000	
APIC	75,000	
Treasury stock		400,000

Earned Capital

We now examine the earned capital portion of shareholders' equity. Earned capital represents the cumulative profit that has been retained by the company. For Coca-Cola, it equals the sum

Table 16.1 **Retained Earnings Equation**

Beginning retained earnings
  + Earnings (net income)
  − Distributed earnings (dividends)
  = Ending retained earnings
	Coca-Cola Company reinvested earnings, 2016	

	In millions	
	Beginning balance	$65,018
	Net income	6,527
	Dividends	(6,043)
	Ending balance	65,502

of reinvested earnings and accumulated other comprehensive loss. Earned capital is therefore a function of any transaction or circumstance that affects either of those accounts, including:

- net income or loss

- cash dividends

- stock dividends

- any gains or losses that bypass the income statement.

Reinvested earnings, or more commonly "retained earnings," encompasses the first three items on the above list; the final item is captured by accumulated other comprehensive income (or loss).

Retained Earnings

Retained earnings are the link between the income statement and the balance sheet. As seen in Table 16.1, the ending retained earnings balance equals the beginning balance, plus the current year's net income (or minus net loss), minus dividends. Coca-Cola pays only cash dividends, but if stock dividends were paid, these too would have to be deducted in order to arrive at the ending balance.

Dividends on Common Stock

Investors purchase common stock on the expectation of a competitive return. This return can come in two forms: stock price appreciation and dividends.

Some investors prefer to buy stocks that pay little or no dividends because companies that reinvest the majority of their earnings tend to increase their future earnings potential, along with their stock price. Wealthy investors in high tax brackets prefer to receive their return in the form of higher stock prices because capital gains may be taxed at a lower rate than dividend income. Other investors, such as retirees who need a steady income, prefer to receive their return in the form of dividends. Such investors tend to seek out stocks that pay high dividends, such as public utilities (electricity companies, etc.).

One way to determine a company's dividend policy – i.e. is it a "high" or "low" dividend stock? – is to observe its "dividend yield." This ratio measures annual dividend payments as a percentage of the share price:

$$= \frac{\text{Annual Dividends per Share}}{\text{Price per Share}}$$

Coca-Cola's 2016 dividend yield equals dividends ($6.043 billion according to the Statement of Cash Flows, or $1.40 on a per-share basis) divided by the end-of-year share price ($41.46), or 3.4%.

Coca-Cola's dividend is high compared to the average yield on the S&P 500 (a stock market index based on the market capitalizations of 500 large American companies with common stock listed on the New York Stock Exchange or the NASDAQ). The average yield for the S&P 500 was about 2.0% for 2016.

Another way to describe dividend policy is the dividend payout ratio. This measure expresses dividends as a percentage of net income. 1 – (the dividend payout ratio) measures the portion of net income retained in the business. Another way to look at this ratio is that is shows how well dividend payments are supported by earnings. The higher the payout ratio, the greater the risk that a downturn in profits might force the company to cut its dividend. The ratio is calculated as follows:

$$= \frac{\text{Yearly Dividend per Share}}{\text{Earnings per Share}}$$

or equivalently:

$$= \frac{\text{Dividends}}{\text{Net Income}}$$

Coca-Cola's dividend payout ratio for 2016 was 92.6%, or $6.043bn divided by $6.527bn. This figure is high compared to other large publicly traded companies, suggesting that unless Coca-Cola's profitability improves, the company might have to reduce dividends.

In some countries, such as the US, dividends are usually paid on a quarterly basis. In other countries, semiannual payments are more common. In either case, the common stock investor needs to be aware of three distinct dates: The declaration date, the record date, and the payment date. To illustrate, we will refer to the final quarterly dividend payment made by Coca-Cola in 2009.

Declaration date: 20 October 2016.   This is the date on which the board of directors officially approves the dividend. Because the declaration commits the company to transfer assets, a liability (dividends payable) is recognized. Therefore, the following entry is made:

Retained earnings	XX	
Dividends payable		XX

Because dividends represent a distribution of earnings, the retained earnings account is charged when the dividends are declared.

Record date: 1 December 2016.   This is the date on which the corporation prepares the list of current stockholders as shown on its records; dividends can be paid only to the shareholders who own stock on that date. No journal entry is required.

Payment date: 15 December 2016.   The payment date is the date on which a cash dividend is paid to the shareholders of record. The journal entry is:

Dividends payable	XX	
Cash		XX

Why companies pay dividends is something of a mystery to financial economists, especially when there may be more tax-efficient ways of returning cash to shareholders, such as share buybacks. One popular argument is that dividend policy can be used by managers, in possession of superior information about their businesses, to signal their beliefs about the company's underlying profitability to the investing community.

Also, some companies face "clientele effects" among their shareholders. For example, because public utilities (such as electricity providers and water companies) have steady cash flows and pay high dividends, they tend to attract investors who seek high dividends. Such investors include tax-exempt institutions (which can avoid the high marginal tax rates associated with dividend income) and retirees who rely on dividends to supplement their income.

On the other hand, companies in high-growth industries are less likely to pay dividends and, when they do, the dividend yields are likely to be far lower than those of public utilities. The primary reason for this difference is that high-growth industries, by their nature, yield an abundance of value-creating investment opportunities. Companies will therefore use whatever cash they generate from the business for capital investment, leaving little or no cash available for shareholders. Paying high dividends in high-growth industries may be interpreted by the capital markets as a signal that the company expects growth to significantly decline in the future.

Stock Dividends and Stock Splits

Not all dividends are paid in cash. Some companies pay dividends in the form of additional shares of stock. Additional shares can be distributed in either of two ways: stock dividends and stock splits.

Stock Dividends

Stock dividends are treated as a reduction in retained earnings and an increase in contributed capital. The amount by which the relevant accounts are affected depends on the proportion of shares distributed to the total outstanding shares on the issue date. If the proportion is less than 20–25%, the distribution is deemed to be a small stock dividend. Retained earnings are reduced by the market value of the shares distributed, common stock is increased by the number of shares × par value per share, and APIC is increased for the balance. For example, if a company issues a 10% stock dividend when its share price is $30 and 50 million shares of stock are outstanding (par value = $5), the following entry is made:

Retained earnings	150 million	
Common stock		25 million
APIC		125 million

Retained earnings are charged for the market value of the distributed shares (5 million shares, or 10% of the total, × $30); common stock is credited for the par value of the shares 5 million × $5); and APIC is credited for the balance. In effect, the stock dividend gives each shareholder 1 additional share for every 10 shares already owned. Proportional ownership is unchanged.

As the above journal entry shows, one important difference between a stock dividend and a cash dividend is that the former never reduces assets. The balancing entries for the reduction of retained earnings are always other shareholders' equity accounts. For this reason, declaration of a stock dividend does not give rise to a liability. To put it another way, stock dividends merely shift amounts among different shareholders' equity accounts. Assets and liabilities are unaffected.

For large stock dividends, where the proportion of shares distributed is greater than 20–25%, retained earnings are decreased by the par value of the distributed shares. Common stock is increased by the same amount. Because the reduction in retained earnings is based on par value, no entry to APIC is needed. Returning to the above example, if the dividend was 30%, the entry becomes:

| Retained earnings | 75 million | |
| Common stock | | 75 million |

The amount is based on the distribution of 15 million shares (30% × 50 million) × the par value of $5.

For both small and large stock dividends, companies are required to adjust shares outstanding for all prior periods for which earnings per share (EPS) are reported in the financial statements. The reasoning is that a stock dividend has no effect on the ownership percentage of each shareholder. To show a dilution, or reduction, in EPS would wrongly suggest a decline in profitability when the decline in EPS is due entirely to an increase in shares outstanding.

In any case, because the aggregate value of outstanding shares does not change, but the number of shares increases, a stock dividend should, in theory, result in a lower share price proportionate to the size of the dividend.

Stock Splits

Stock splits are proportionate distributions of shares and, therefore, similar in substance to stock dividends. But unlike stock dividends, there are no financial statement effects. Retained earnings and contributed capital accounts, such as common stock and APIC, are unaffected. Confusion arises, however, because most stock splits can be viewed as large stock dividends. The distinction that separates a large stock dividend and a stock split is a subtle one, depending largely on local corporate law for the precise treatment.

The most common stock split is 2-for-1, meaning that the number of shares held by every shareholder is automatically and instantaneously doubled. For example, if a shareholder held 100 shares before the split, that investor now holds 200 shares.

Although stock splits are not considered monetary transactions, and therefore no accounting entries are expected, some jurisdictions require a proportionate adjustment to par value. For example, if par value is $5 before a 2-for-1 split, par value becomes $2.50 after the split. This rule explains why Coca-Cola's par value is only $0.25. Many years ago, its par value was far higher. But a series of stock splits over the course of many years has gradually reduced par value. For example, in the early 1990s, par value was $1, but since then Coca-Cola has had two 2-for-1 stock splits. The first of these splits reduced par value to $0.50, the second to $0.25.

Just as companies can use stock splits to reduce their share price, a reverse stock split can be used to increase it. For example, instead of, say, a 2-for-1 stock split, a company might implement a 1-for-2 reserve split. In this case, the number of shares is halved. Share price should increase proportionately, although it may not because reverse splits are often stigmatized. For example, many investors, including large mutual funds, have rules against purchasing a stock whose price is below some minimum, perhaps $5. If a company's stock is selling for $3 per share, a 1-for-2 split should lift the price above the minimum. In extreme cases, a company's share price may have dropped so low that it is in danger of being delisted from its stock exchange. This fate befell many dot-com start-ups after the boom of the late 1990s. In short, reverse stocks splits should have the short-term effect of boosting share price, but investors are rarely fooled by the gesture, especially when undertaken as an act of desperation.

However, a reverse stock split can be useful as a tactic to reduce the number of shareholders. For example, in a 1-for-100 reverse split any investor holding fewer than 100 shares receives a cash payment and no shares of stock. These investors are no longer shareholders of record. Why would a company be interested in reducing the number of shareholders on its rolls? In most jurisdictions, if the resulting number of shareholders drops below a specific threshold, the company is placed into a different, less costly, regulatory category.

Accumulated Other Comprehensive Income

Comprehensive income is a measure of profit, but more inclusive than that of net income. It includes all changes in shareholders' equity that occur during a period except those resulting from contributions by, and distributions to, owners. Comprehensive income includes net income, but also gains and losses that net income excludes, such as:

Unrealized gains and losses on available-for-sale (AFS) securities;

Changes in fair value for certain derivative instruments;

Foreign currency translation adjustments;

Gains and losses on actuarial adjustments for defined benefit pension plans

Notice that the above items result from changes in market prices and foreign currency exchange rates, factors normally viewed as beyond the control of management. For this reason, some analysts consider net income to be a measure of management's performance, while comprehensive income is a measure of company performance.

"Other comprehensive income" is the term given to the above gains and losses; that is, the elements of comprehensive income that bypass net income and are therefore not included in retained earnings. The term "accumulated" implies that these gains and losses are carried forward from one year to the next, until they are realized (and thus become part of net income and ultimately, retained earnings).

As of the end of 2016, Coca-Cola reported accumulated other comprehensive income of negative $11,205 million. The consolidated statements of shareowners' equity (Exhibit 16.2) shows:

- a beginning balance of −$10,174 million (which means that Coca-Cola had an accumulated other comprehensive *loss*);

- and $1,031 million of net other comprehensive loss for the year 2016;

- The ending balance (−$11,205 million) equals the beginning balance (−$10,174 million) plus the other comprehensive loss for the year ($1,031 million).

Convertible Bonds

Convertible bonds allow their owner either to hold the security as a bond or to convert the security into shares of common stock. Under IFRS "split accounting" is used, whereby the proceeds of issuing debt are allocated between the two components:

- the equity conversion rights (recognized in equity); and

- the liability, recognized at fair value calculated by discounting at a market rate for nonconvertible debt (recognized in liabilities).

On the other hand, under US GAAP, most forms of convertible debt are treated as a single unit and recorded as a liability; no recognition is given to the equity component. However, complex convertibles may require the recognition of the equity component as a derivative.

To illustrate the accounting for convertible bonds, assume that a company plans to issue $100,000 in bonds (in increments of $1,000), paying a coupon rate of 10% (5% paid semi-annually) over a 10-year period. The prevailing interest rate for bonds of that risk is 14%. Assume that the company wants to issue the bonds at par (i.e., $100,000), but without having to pay more than a 10% coupon rate. To lower the coupon rate and still satisfy the investor seeking an expected return of 14%, the firm can issue convertible bonds. Assume that each bond ($1,000 par value) grants the holder the right to convert the bond into 50 shares of the company's common stock. (Holders in aggregate can convert the entire bond issue into 5,000 shares.) Assuming a par value of $0.25, US GAAP accounting requires the following entry:

Cash	100,000	
Bonds payable		100,000

This entry effectively treats convertible bonds just like ordinary, nonconvertible bonds, ignoring the value of the conversion feature.

In contrast, IFRS allocates a portion of the issue price to the conversion feature. Assume that 10%, 10-year semiannual nonconvertible coupon bonds are sold for 79% of par when the market borrowing rate is 14%. Thus, if the firm can issue 10% convertible bonds at par, the conversion feature must be worth 21% of par. In effect, investors have paid 21% of the proceeds from the bond issue as a capital contribution, that is, for the right to acquire common stock later. The entry would be as follows:

Cash	100,000	
Bonds payable		79,000
Additional paid-in capital		21,000

The above entry requires a credible estimate of the proceeds of an issue of nonconvertible bonds with other features similar to the convertible bonds. Because auditors often believe that they are unable to estimate this information with reasonable objectivity, US GAAP does not allow it.

The usual entry to record the conversion of bonds into shares ignores current market prices in the interest of simplicity and merely shows the swap of shares for bonds at their book value. For example, assume that the common stock of the above company increases to $30 a share, so that the holder of one $1,000 bond, convertible into 50 shares, can convert it into shares with a market value of $1,500. If holders convert the entire bond issue into common shares at this time, the following journal entry is made:

Convertible bonds payable	100,000	
Common shares ($0.25 par)		1,250
Additional paid-in capital		98,750

An allowable alternative treatment recognizes that market prices provide information useful in quantifying the value of the shares issued. Under this alternative, with a $30 per share market price and $150,000 of fair value for the 5,000 shares issued on conversion, the journal entry would be:

Convertible bonds payable	100,000	
Loss on conversion of bonds	50,000	
Common shares ($0.25 par)		1,250
Additional paid-in capital		148,750

The loss on conversion is an income statement account. However, despite the loss, the alternative approach results in the same total shareholders' equity as the previous approach. Lower retained earnings from the loss on conversion are offset by higher contributed capital.

The Statement of Shareholders' Equity

All changes to equity accounts are summarized in the consolidated statements of shareholders' equity (Exhibit 16.2). Officially, this statement is given the same status as the other principal financial statements: the balance sheet, the income statement, and the statement of cash flows. However, most analysts view it more like a supporting schedule that helps the reader to understand the changes that have occurred in equity accounts over the past three years.

A review of Coca-Cola's statements of shareowners' equity reveals the following for 2016:

- Shareholders' equity increased by $130 million from the tax benefits earned when the employee stock options were exercised. Many countries, the US among them, grant companies a deduction equal to the difference between the market price of the stock on the exercise date and the strike price of the options. In other words, the extent to which the options are "in-the-money" when exercised is considered a tax-deductible compensation expense. But treating the tax benefit as a reduction in tax expense increases net income. Such treatment was thought to violate the principle that companies should not recognize gains or losses from trading (i.e., issuing or buying back) their own shares. Therefore, the tax benefits were added to contributed capital instead (usually additional paid-in capital). However, given a recent change in U.S. GAAP, any tax savings from 2017 onward will be shown on the income statement. Therefore, the savings will find their way into shareholders' equity via retained earnings instead of capital surplus.

- Stock-based compensation, mainly in the form of additional option grants, increased shareholders' equity by $258 million. When companies issue options to employees, the fair value of those options is recognized as an expense as the options vest.[3] The balancing entry is to an equity account (usually additional paid-in capital, as it was in Coca-Cola's case).

- Net income increased shareholders' equity by $6,527 million.

- Dividend payments decreased shareholders' equity by $6,043 million.

- Other comprehensive loss (gains and losses not included in net income) decreased shareholders' equity by $11,205 million.

- Purchases of treasury stock during 2016 decreased shareholders' equity by $3,733 million.

When these (and several other) changes are aggregated, the beginning and ending balances in shareholders' equity ($25,764 million and $23,220 million, respectively) are reconciled.

IFRS companies have the option of providing an alternative to the statement of shareholders' equity. Called the "statement of recognized gains and losses," it includes many of the same items, but excludes transactions with owners (such as new share issues and share buybacks). Any items excluded from the statement must be described in the notes to the financial statements.

KEY LESSONS FROM THE CHAPTER

- The shareholders' equity section of the balance sheet consists of two parts: contributed capital and retained earnings.

- Contributed capital represents the cumulative investment that a company has received from the sale of various classes of shares, less the cash paid for share buybacks.

- Retained earnings are the cumulative profits of the company that have been retained in the business rather than paid out in dividends.

- Shareholders' equity is also called the "book value of equity."

- Companies issue two broad classes of shares: preferred and common. The difference between the two lies in the legal rights and claims conferred upon each class.

- Common shareholders are the residual claimants of the firm, which means that, in the event of liquidation, all other claimants on the firm must be paid in full before common shareholders are entitled to any payment.

- Common stock investors need to be aware of three distinct dividend dates: the declaration date, the record date, and the payment date.

- Comprehensive income includes net income, but also items excluded from net income but which affect shareholders' equity, such as unrealized gains and losses on available-for-sale securities, changes in the fair value of certain derivative instruments, and some foreign currency translation adjustments. The concept emerged, in part, to highlight gains and losses that, for whatever reason, bypass the income statement and therefore are not included in net income.

- Convertible bonds allow their owners to either hold the security as a bond or convert the security into shares of common stock. Under IFRS "split accounting" is used, whereby the proceeds from the issuance of convertible debt are allocated between the equity conversion rights (recognized in equity) and the liability.

KEY TERMS AND CONCEPTS FROM THE CHAPTER

Contributed capital	Treasury stock	Authorized shares	Accumulated other	Dividend payout ratio
Common stock	Earned capital	Outstanding shares	comprehensive income	Stock splits
Issued shares	Preferred stock			

QUESTIONS

1. What is a convertible bond?

2. What are the advantages of a convertible bond from the standpoint of the bondholders and the issuing corporation?

3. Describe the accounting for share buybacks.

4. How is the reissuance of repurchased shares accounted for? What if the price paid for repurchased shares exceeds their cost? What if the price paid is below cost?

5. What is a stock split, and what motive might a company have for doing it?

6. What effect does a stock split have on the balance sheet?

7. What is a stock dividend and what effect does it have on the balance sheet and income statement?

8. A company issues equity for $15 a share. The stated, or par, value of those shares is $1. Give the required journal entry for a typical American company and for a typical European company.

PROBLEMS

16.1 Effect of Selected Transactions on Net Income and Shareholders' Equity

	Net Income	Retained earnings	Total shareholders' equity
a. A stock dividend is declared and paid			
b. Merchandise is purchased on credit			
c. Marketable securities are sold above cost			
d. Accounts receivable are collected			
e. A cash dividend is declared and paid			
f. Treasury stock is purchased and recorded at cost			
g. Treasury stock is sold above cost			
h. Common stock is sold			
i. A machine is sold for less than book value			
j. Bonds are converted into common stock			

Required

Indicate the effects of the above transactions on net income, retained earnings, and total shareholders' equity. Use + to indicate an increase and − to indicate a decrease, and 0 to indicate no effect.

16.2 Share Buybacks

The following note comes from the 2007 annual report for The Walt Disney Company:

> *As of the filing date of this report, the Board of Directors had not yet declared a dividend related to fiscal 2007. The Company paid a $637 million dividend ($0.31 per share) during the second quarter of fiscal 2007 related to fiscal 2006.*
>
> *During fiscal 2007, the Company repurchased 202 million shares of Disney common stock for $6.9 billion. During fiscal 2006, the Company repurchased 243 million shares of Disney common stock for $6.9 billion. On May 1, 2007, the Board of Directors of the Company increased the share repurchase authorization to a total of 400 million shares. As of September 29, 2007, the Company had remaining authorization in place to repurchase approximately 323 million additional shares. The repurchase program does not have an expiration date.*
>
> *The par value of the Company's outstanding common stock totaled approximately $26 million.*

Required

a. What reasons can you give for why Disney bought back so many of its shares (a total of nearly $14 billion in 2006 and 2007 combined)?

b. Disney's normal policy regarding buybacks is to retain the shares in treasury (instead of cancelling them). Why is treasury stock a contra-equity account and not an asset?

c. Based on the above note, what do you think must have happened to Disney's share price from 2006 to 2007? Did it go up, go down, or stay the same?

16.3 The Financial Statement Effects of Dividend Payments and Buybacks

The following note is taken from The Walt Disney Company's 2004 Annual Report:

> *The Company declared an annual dividend of $0.24 per share on December 1, 2004 related to fiscal 2004. The dividend is payable on January 6, 2005 to shareholders of record on December 10, 2004. The Company paid a $430 million dividend ($0.21 per share) during the first quarter of fiscal 2004.*
>
> *During the fourth quarter of fiscal 2004, the Company repurchased 14.9 million shares of Disney common stock for approximately $335 million. As of September 30, 2004, the Company had authorization in place to repurchase approximately 315 million additional shares.*

Based on the above note, answer the following:

a. Explain what would be recorded on each of the dates relating to the $0.24/share dividend (i.e., provide the necessary journal entries).

b. How would the $430 million dividend payment affect each of the three principal financial statements?

c. How would the $335 million repurchase of Disney common stock affect each of the three principal financial statements?

16.4 The Accounting and Economic Consequences of Stock Splits and Stock Dividends

The following note is taken from the 2005 Annual Report of eBay:

> *In January 2005, our Board of Directors approved a two-for-one split of our shares of common stock to be issued in the form of a stock dividend. As a result of the stock split, our stockholders received one additional share of our common stock for each share of common stock held of record on January 31, 2005. The additional shares of our common stock were distributed on February 16, 2005. All share and per share amounts in these consolidated financial statements and related notes have been retroactively adjusted to reflect this and all prior stock splits for all periods presented.*

Required

a. What was the impact of the stock split on each of the three principal financial statements?

b. What reasons can you give for eBay to split its stock?

c. The note says that the stock split was issued in the form of a stock dividend. The implication is that stock splits and stock dividends are equivalent. Is this true?

Case study

16-1 Stock Options, Stock Dividends, and Stock Splits

Diodes Inc. is a manufacturer and supplier of semiconductor products, primarily to the communications, computing, industrial, consumer electronics, and automotive markets. The company is headquartered in southern California, but most of its production facilities are in Asia (China, Taiwan, and Hong Kong). Revenues and net income in 2004 were $185.7 million and $25.6 million, respectively.

In 2004, employees exercised stock options on 1,135,982 shares, with a par value of 66⅔ cents per share. The average exercise price was $5. In addition, Diodes received a tax benefit from the exercise of the stock options of $8,514,000. The tax benefit resulted from a US tax law that gives companies a tax deduction equal to the difference between the market price of their stock and the exercise price of the stock options on the date the options are exercised. The tax benefit reflects this difference, multiplied by the company's marginal tax rate. Diodes' accounting policy, in accordance with US GAAP, is to lump together the tax benefit and the cash proceeds received from the employees who exercise their options.

In November 2005, Diodes declared a 50% stock dividend, payable on 30 November 2005, to stockholders of record on 18 November 2005. Under the terms of the stock dividend, Diodes' stockholders received one additional share for every two shares held on the record date. The company expected the number of outstanding shares of common stock after the dividend to increase from 16.8 million to 25.2 million shares. The par value of the company's stock was not affected by the dividend and remained at 66⅔ cents per share. At the end of November 2005, Diodes' share price was $38.40.

Required

a. Why do companies issue stock options to employees? What are the potential drawbacks? Why not just issue shares of stock instead of stock options?

b. Why is the average exercise price of the stock options so low relative to the current share price?

c. Give the summary journal entry to record the exercise of stock options in 2004.

d. What's the difference between a stock dividend and a stock split? Why do companies issue stock dividends? What motive might they have for a stock split?

e. Given the journal entry to record Diodes' stock dividends, how would the accounting change if the transaction was considered a stock split?

Case study

16-2 Share Buybacks: Economic Rationale and Financial Reporting Effects

Groupe Danone is the world's #1 producer of fresh dairy products. The company is also among the world leaders in bottled water and several other food and beverage categories. Based in France, its net revenues in 2004 were €13.7 billion.

In 2004, the following transactions affecting shareholders' equity took place:

- Dividends of €308 million were declared and paid.

- 2.6 million shares of common stock were bought back at an average price of €60.40. The shares were cancelled immediately after purchase.

- 750,000 shares of common stock (par value = €0.50) were reissued from corporate treasury at an average price of €51. The average price paid by Danone for the reissued shares was €74.67.

Required

a. Why do companies buy back their own shares?

b. Why does Danone keep some of the repurchased shares in corporate treasury, and not cancel them?

c. Give the summary journal entries to record all of the above events.

Case study

16-3 The Accounting for Convertible Bonds

Milacron Inc. is a leading supplier of plastics-processing technologies and industrial fluids. Headquartered in Cincinnati, Ohio, the company employs 3,500 people and operates major manufacturing facilities in North America, Europe, and Asia. Milacron's financial performance has been poor in recent years, including net losses of $191.1 million in 2003 (on sales of $740 million).

In March 2004, Milacron announced the issuance of bonds to Glencore Finance AG and Mizuho International. The proceeds were used to repay outstanding notes that were about to come due. Glencore and Mizuho purchased $100 million of debt in total, $30 million of which would be convertible into Milacron common stock (par value = $1) at the option of the holders.

Required

a. Why would Milacron use a "hybrid" instrument like convertible bonds, instead of issuing debt and equity securities separately?

b. Milacron raised $30 million from the issuance of the convertible bonds. Assume that a similar straight bond (a nonconvertible bond with the same coupon payments and maturity value) would have raised $26 million. Prepare the journal entry to record the issuance of the convertible bonds in accordance with IFRS.

c. Assume that early in 2005, Glencore and Mizuho exercised their option and converted the bonds into 9 million shares of Milacron common stock. The stock price on the date of the conversion was $3.75, and the net book value of bonds payable was $24 million. Prepare the journal entry to record the conversion of Milacron bonds into common stock, assuming that no gain or loss is recognized on the transaction.

Case study

16-4 Why Do Companies Buy Back Their Own Shares? The Case of the Scomi Group

The Scomi Group is an investment holding company, based in Malaysia, with three principal subsidiaries involved in oil and natural gas support services. The group's products and services include:

- drilling fluids and related engineering services for drilling operations;

- drilling waste management equipment;

- production and industrial chemicals;

- marine vessel transportation;

- machine shops; and

- distribution.

    Revenues and net income for 2004 were RM 590 million and RM 69 million, respectively.* The group's shares are traded on the Kuala Lumpur stock exchange (KLSE).

    In May 2005, the Board of Directors proposed a share buyback program to the group's shareholders. The board sought permission to repurchase shares representing up to 10% of the Scomi Group's issued and paid-up capital from the open market. At the discretion of the board, any repurchased shares would either be cancelled or retained in treasury for later distribution.

    In the formal proposal submitted to shareholders, the board cited the following reasons for the share buyback program:

1. It would enable the company to utilize surplus financial resources to purchase Scomi shares at prices that are viewed as favorable as well as help stabilize the supply and demand of Scomi shares traded on the KLSE, thereby supporting its fundamental value.

*RM = Malaysian ringgit; RM 3.80 = 1 US$.

2. If the purchased shares are held in corporate treasury, the shares may potentially be resold on the KLSE at a higher price, enabling Scomi to realize a potential gain without affecting its total share capital.

3. Purchased shares retained in treasury may also be distributed to shareholders as dividends, which would serve to reward the shareholders of Scomi.

4. Shareholders may enjoy an increase in the value of their investment in Scomi due to the increase in net earnings per share resulting from the reduction in the number of outstanding shares.

Required

Which of the rationales offered in the proposal are sensible (i.e., value-enhancing) reasons for repurchasing shares and which are not? Are there other (legitimate) reasons not given in Scomi's proposal for why a company might repurchase its own shares?

NOTES

1. In some cases, the issuing company can force conversion.

2. Some countries do not allow firms to hold repurchased shares in treasury. Instead, the shares must be canceled.

3. The term "vested" refers to full ownership rights. Once the options are vested, the employee has the right to exercise the option. In many companies, if employees leave before the end of the vesting period, all rights to the options are lost.

Investments

17

Companies often purchase the shares of other companies. In this chapter, we discuss the accounting for these investments. Unless otherwise stated, the discussion applies equally to US GAAP and International Financial Reporting Standards (IFRS). Also, we focus on equity investments, although brief mention is made of debt instruments. To illustrate the concepts, we draw on the financial statements of Microsoft, the US-based software giant.

Introduction

When companies own shares in other businesses, the accounting follows one of three methods, depending on the degree of influence or control that the investor exerts over the other company. Three levels of influence/control are possible:

- **Passive.** In this case, the investor is assumed to exert no influence over the investee company. Generally, passive investment is assumed when the investor owns less than 20% of the outstanding voting shares of the investee. Such investments are "marked to market" at the end of each accounting period, with unrealized gains or losses appearing on the income statement or as adjustments to shareholders' equity. The accounting treatment depends, in part, on management intent and also on whether the reporting entity uses US GAAP or IFRS.

- **Significant influence.** Here, the investor is assumed to own enough of the investee (usually called an "affiliate" or "associate") to exert significant influence over operating activities and dividend policy. Generally, such influence is assumed when the investor owns between 20 and 50% of the affiliate's outstanding voting shares. In such cases, the "equity method" of accounting must be used.

- **Control.** Control is presumed if the investor owns more than 50% of the outstanding voting shares of the investee. If control is established, the proper accounting treatment is "consolidation." In other words, the accounts of the investee (or, in this case, the subsidiary) are combined with those of the parent company and other subsidiaries to produce the group accounts.

In this chapter, we deal primarily with passive and equity-method investments, although consolidation is addressed in a brief section at the end. As we will see next, there are two basic issues that determine the accounting for equity investments: (1) how investment income is recognized, and (2) the carrying value of the investment on the balance sheet.

Investments at Microsoft

Before introducing the market, cost, and equity methods, consider the asset section of Microsoft's balance sheet from fiscal years 2016 and 2017 shown in Table 17.1.

Table 17.1   Microsoft's Assets for Fiscal Years 2016 and 2017 (in Millions, US$)

	2016/06/30	2017/06/30
Assets		
Current assets		
Cash and equivalents	$6,510	$7,663
Short-term investments	**106,730**	**125,318**
Total cash and short-term investments	**113,240**	**132,981**
Accounts receivable, net	18,277	19,792
Inventories	2,251	2,181
Other	5,892	4,897
Total current assets	139,660	159,851
Property and equipment, net	18,356	23,734
Equity and other investments	**10,431**	**6,023**
Goodwill	17,872	35,122
Intangible assets, net	3,733	10,106
Other long-term assets	3,416	6,250
Total assets	$193,468	$241,086

Investments are shown in three accounts: cash and equivalents, short-term investments, and equity and other investments. Cash and equivalents comprise mainly demand deposits (i.e., checking accounts and the like) and low-risk, highly liquid financial instruments such as short-term government bonds. Short-term investments (sometimes called "marketable securities") contain mostly fixed-income securities, including longer-term government bonds. Notice that in Microsoft's case, the amounts are huge ($113.240 billion for 2016 and $132.981 billion for (2017), a level of liquidity that is found nowhere else, apart from tech giant Apple.

Equity and other investments ($10.431 billion for 2016 and $6.023 billion for 2017) comprise long-term investments, both in the shares of other companies and in debt instruments that are not classified as current. The term "equity" implies that a significant portion of the total covers investments that are accounted for under the equity method, meaning that Microsoft has a large minority stake.

Investments in subsidiaries (i.e., those companies that Microsoft controls) are consolidated across all accounts, and are therefore reflected in the consolidated amounts appearing on the above balance sheet. For example, the accounts receivable balance of each subsidiary is added to that of the parent to produce the consolidated balance (after eliminating any transactions among the subsidiaries and the parent). Likewise for inventories, property and equipment, and any other balance sheet account.

Debt and Passive Equity Investments

Passive equity investments are recorded at their fair value as of the balance sheet date. (We discuss how fair value is determined later in the chapter.)

Debt securities, such as corporate and government bonds, are also reported at fair value, if management intends to dispose of the bond before maturity. However, if management expresses its intent to hold a bond until maturity, it can select the held-to-maturity option. In such cases, the bond is reported on the balance sheet at amortized cost. For example, if a government bond is acquired at a discount to par (or maturity) value, the bond is initially recorded at acquisition cost, which is lower than the expected cash proceeds on the maturity date. The amount of the discount, i.e., the difference between par value and cost, is amortized over the life of the bond. In this way the carrying value of the bond gradually converges to par value such that the two are equal at the precise moment of maturity. Interest revenue in any given period equals the interest earned based on the bond's coupon (or stated) interest rate, adjusted for the amortization of the bond's discount or premium. For example, in the case of the government bond bought at a discount (meaning that the market interest at purchase must have been greater than the coupon rate), the interest revenue in a given year will equal the bond's stated interest rate plus the portion of the bond discount that was amortized in that year. For a bond sold at a premium to par, interest revenue equals the stated interest rate *minus* the portion of the bond premium amortized in that year.

For passive equity investments, dividend payments are reported as "dividend income" on the income statement.

For cost-method investments, no other income statement effects are possible except in the case of impairment or if the shares are sold or otherwise disposed of. In the latter case, the difference between the proceeds from the sale and the book value of the investment is treated as a realized gain or loss. For example, if Microsoft pays $50 million for the shares of another company, a subsequent sale of those shares for $60 million results in the following journal entry:

Cash	$60 million	
Investments		$50 million
Gain on sale		$10 million

where "gain on sale" is an income statement account.

However, if an investment is marked-to-market at the end of each period (i.e., the shares are accounted for under the market method), other income statement effects are possible, even while the shares are still owned. Returning to the above example, assume that the shares acquired by Microsoft are publicly traded. If the value of the shares on the balance sheet date is $60 million, Microsoft reports that amount on the balance sheet. How Microsoft treats the $10 million unrealized (i.e., unsold) holding gain depends on whether the investment is designated as:

- **available-for-sale (AFS)** or as

- **a trading security**.

AFS securities are marked-to-market investments that management intends to hold for dividend income and capital gains, although the shares might be sold if the price was attractive enough or the company was strapped for cash. Trading securities are those that management intends to actively buy and sell for short-term trading profit. Frequent buying and selling usually indicate a trading security.

For most companies AFS securities are far more common than trading investments. In fact, many businesses, even large ones, do not have trading securities. There are two major reasons for this:

- First, short-term trading in securities is not considered a core competency outside the financial services sector and, therefore, is an activity largely avoided by other businesses.

- Second, AFS is a default category. Any investment that cannot be classified as either trading or held-to-maturity must, by default, be classified as AFS.

The distinction between AFS and trading is an important one because it determines how the unrealized holding gain or loss is treated. In the case of the former, any changes in market value recognized at the end of the accounting period are reported directly in the balance sheet through "other comprehensive income" (OCI), a shareholders' equity account. Gains and losses in market value are recognized in the income statement only when securities are sold. In other words, realized gains and losses appear on the income statement, but unrealized gains and losses do not.

In contrast, changes in market value for trading securities are reported in the income statement. This difference in treatment implies that the classification of passive equity investments as trading securities can have a sizable impact on the volatility of earnings. Any change in market value is shown in the income statement, even if the gain or loss is unrealized. In general, the greater the proportion of investments classified as trading, the greater the volatility of earnings.

In the above example, if shares costing $50 million have a market value of $60 million on the balance sheet date, the following entry would be required if the investment is classified as AFS:

Investments	$10 million	
OCI		$10 million

where OCI is a shareholders' equity account.

Although we ignored taxes in this example, the increase to OCI is made net of expected tax effects. As the investment is sold, or otherwise disposed of, the amount in OCI is transferred to the income statement.

If the investment is classified as a trading security, the journal entry would be:

Investments	$10 million	
Unrealized gain		$10 million

where unrealized gain is reported on the income statement.

Transaction costs (brokers' commissions, etc.) are considered part of the acquisition cost of the investment. For example, if a firm acquires shares in another company for $150,000, incurring $5,000 in brokers' commissions, the acquisition cost of the investment is the total cost, $155,000.

It should be noted that US GAAP has recently undergone an important change in the accounting for passive equity investments. In January 2016, the Financial Accounting Standards Board issued an Accounting Standards Update (2016-01) that eliminates the available-for-sale (AFS) classification. The update took effect at the end of 2017, and now requires that all passive equity investments be accounted for in the same manner as trading securities (although the term "trading" is no longer be used). IFRS remains unchanged, meaning that the distinction between AFS and trading still applies.

The Fair Value Hierarchy

We now address the issue of how to determine fair value. Although our discussion focuses on equity and debt securities, the principles apply equally to any assets or liabilities that are reported at fair value, including property, plant, and equipment. Under US GAAP (FAS 157), fair value is defined as "the price that would be received to sell an asset or paid to transfer a liability in an orderly transaction between market participants at the measurement date." Fair value is defined similarly under IFRS as the amount for which an asset could be exchanged, or a liability settled, between knowledgeable, willing parties, in an arm's length transaction. The problem, of course, is determining price, especially when easily observable data are not available.[1] For this reason, US GAAP and IFRS rely on a three-level fair value hierarchy. The nature of the hierarchy, in which the first two levels result in "mark-to-market" accounting, is that it prioritizes observable inputs over unobservable inputs.

A Level 1 fair value is one where an active market exists for identical assets. For example, an equity investment in a company traded on the New York Stock Exchange would fall into this category, as would US treasuries or UK gilts. If such inputs are available, they must be used. If Level 1 data are unavailable the next step is to seek out Level 2 inputs. Here, the asset in question may be traded, and therefore prices are observable, but the market is inactive with only sporadic quotes. Or, similar assets are traded in an active market, but the assets are not identical to the ones being valued. Many real estate assets would fall into this category. An active and liquid market may exist, especially in large commercial centers, but each parcel of real estate is unique.

If Level 2 inputs are unavailable, the entity must resort to the bottom tier, Level 3. At this point, the process of determining fair value is no longer considered "mark to market," because there is no market, and therefore no observable market prices. Because Level 3 inputs are unobservable, this approach is often referred to as "mark to model" in the sense that a valuation model of some sort is required. The model can be based on discounted cash flows, multiples (e.g., price/earnings or price/sales ratios), replacement cost, or any other approach acceptable to the firm's auditors. Simply put, Level 3 fair values are based not on a market price but rather a prediction of what the market price would be if a market existed. Understandably, much of the controversy and debate in fair value accounting centers on this issue.[2]

To assist the financial statement reader in the analysis and interpretation of fair value assessments, the FASB and the IASB recently issued joint guidelines on fair value disclosures. These requirements include the following:

- Companies must disclose the amounts of, and reasons for, significant transfers between Level 1 and Level 2, as well as those into and out of Level 3. Transfers into a level must be disclosed separately from transfers out of the level.

- For Level 2 and Level 3 measurements, a company must disclose information about inputs and valuation techniques used in both recurring and nonrecurring fair value measurements. If a valuation technique changes, the company must disclose the change and the reason for it.

- Activity in Level 3 fair value measurements must be reconciled from the beginning of the period to the end. Information should be presented separately for significant purchases, sales, issuances, and settlements on a gross basis. This means that the changes that took place during the year cannot be lumped together in one number.

- Fair value measurement disclosures must be presented by class of assets and liabilities, including their classification in the fair value hierarchy. The practical implication of this requirement is that the financial statement reader should expect to see a detailed breakdown of all fair value assets and liabilities according to whether their measurements were determined using Level 1, Level 2, or Level 3 inputs.

Equity Method

Investments with significant influence must be accounted for using the equity method. Significant influence is assumed when the investor holds 20% or more of the voting power (directly or through subsidiaries).

However, use of the equity method is possible in cases where the holding is less than 20% if significant influence can be clearly demonstrated. The existence of significant influence by an investor is usually evidenced in one or more of the following ways:

- representation on the board of directors of the investee;

- participation in the policy-making process;

- material transactions between the investor and the investee;

- exchanges of key managerial personnel; or

- the provision of essential technical information.

The main features of the equity method are as follows:

- Investments are initially recorded at acquisition cost.

- Dividends are not treated as income, as they are for passive investments. Instead, dividends are treated as a recovery of the investment and, therefore, reduce the balance in the investment account.

- The investor reports income or loss equal to its percentage ownership share of the affiliate. For example, if the affiliate reports net income of $20 million, and the investor owns 25% of the affiliate's shares, it reports $5 million of equity income on its own income statement. A loss of $20 million by the affiliate results in a $5 million equity loss on the income statement of the investor.

- The investment is not marked to market as it would be under the market method although there is an exception (as discussed at the end of this section).

The equity method came into existence mainly to counter a particular form of manipulation.[3] The concern is that a company with significant influence can use it to affect the affiliate's dividend policy. For example, if the investor needs a boost in current earnings to achieve profit growth targets, it could simply impose higher dividend payouts on the affiliate. Because dividends are treated as income (in the absence of the equity method), the investor would report higher earnings. The equity method removes this potential for earnings management by making the recognition of income independent of dividend policy. The amount of income reported by the investor is based entirely on the percentage of total equity owned and the amount of net income or loss. Dividend policy has no influence on income because dividends are treated as returns, or recoveries, of the investor's stake in the affiliate.

Of course, as so often happens in financial reporting, where one loophole is closed, another is opened. Investors have sometimes manipulated their ownership percentages in other companies depending on whether the affiliates are reporting profits or losses. For example, in the early 1990s, when the UK was in the midst of a recession, several British companies brought the ownership interests in their investee companies just below the 20% threshold to avoid having to report their share of losses being reported by these companies. The lesson for analysts is clear: year-on-year changes in ownership interests, and their effects on the financial statements, should be closely monitored. It should also be noted that manipulation can occur at the other end of the ownership spectrum. For example, companies can choose to consolidate an affiliate's financial statements, or not, depending on whether the ownership interest is just above or just below the 50% threshold. To illustrate, Douglas Ivester, then the chief financial officer and later the CEO of Coca-Cola, created Coca-Cola Enterprises (CCE), a bottling giant, by consolidating several smaller, independent bottlers. By ensuring ownership was below 50%, or what Ivester called "the 49% solution," Coca-Cola did not have to consolidate the billions in debt held by the bottler. But while the parent did not consolidate, it certainly exercised the prerogatives of a full owner, at least in CCE's early days. Ivester had himself appointed chairman, while several other Coca-Cola veterans served on the board. There was little doubt as to who was really in charge.[4]

To illustrate how the equity method works, assume that Microsoft purchases a 30% interest in a supplier, ABC Software, paying $50 million in cash.[5] Microsoft records the purchase as follows:

Equity investments	$50 million	
Cash		$50 million

At the end of the year, ABC Software reports $20 million in net income and pays $10 million in cash dividends. To report its share of net income, Microsoft makes the following entry:

Equity investments	$6 million	
Equity income		$6 million

This entry records Microsoft's 30% share in the profits of ABC Software. The equity income account appears on the current period's income statement and will therefore boost Microsoft's earnings.

Microsoft also receives a dividend of $3 million, equal to 30% of the total dividends paid by ABC Software. The journal entry is:

Cash	$3 million	
Equity investments		$3 million

Notice that the dividend reduces the carrying value of the investment on Microsoft's balance sheet. Notice, too, that the dividend itself has no bearing on Microsoft's earnings for the year.

At the end of the first year, the balance sheet total for the investment in ABC Software equals the acquisition cost ($50 million), plus equity income ($6 million), minus dividends ($3 million), for a total of $53 million. This figure is not marked to market unless there is evidence of a significant and permanent impairment. In that case, the carrying value of the investment would be written down to fair value.

In the above example, ABC Software reported net income. What if the affiliate reported net losses instead? Microsoft would then have to recognize its proportionate share of the losses on its own income statement under the account title, equity loss. If Microsoft's share of ABC's losses equals or exceeds its interest in ABC (i.e., the balance in the investment account is brought to 0 because of the equity losses), Microsoft would stop recognizing its share of further losses. However, if Microsoft has incurred any legal or constructive obligations on behalf of ABC, a provision (liability) would have to be recognized.

Fair value accounting does not apply to equity method investments. However, under certain conditions, companies can elect a fair value option for investments that would otherwise be accounted for under the equity method.

The rules under US GAAP and IFRS differ slightly, but both allow the fair value option only on a specified election date. This date arises when any of the following events occur: (1) the firm acquires an investment that is eligible for equity method treatment, (2) the investment becomes subject to the equity method of accounting (for example, ownership is increased past the 20% threshold), or (3) the investor ceases to consolidate a subsidiary.

In these cases, and assuming the fair value option is chosen, the firm treats the investment in the same way as it would if it was classified as a passive trading security. This means that the investing firm does not report its proportionate share of the affiliate's profits and losses on its own income statement. Dividends received flow directly to earnings, and are not treated as a reduction in carrying value on the balance sheet. Also, unrealized gains and losses from changes in fair value are reported on the investor's income statement.

Any time this option is chosen, the election becomes irrevocable. In other words, the investing company is not permitted to switch to the equity method at a future date.

A Further Look at Microsoft's Investments

The disclosure from Microsoft's 2017 Annual Report shown in Table 17.2 provides a detailed breakdown of its investments. The total for the final three columns corresponds to the amounts reported on the balance sheet shown in Table 17.1.

Table 17.2   Detailed Breakdown of Microsoft's Investments (in Millions), June 30, 2017

	Cost basis	Unrealized gains	Unrealized losses	Recorded basis	Cash and equivalents	Short-term investments	Equity and other investments
Cash and securities							
Cash	$3,624	$—	$—	$3,624	$3,624	$–	$–
Mutual funds	1,478	—	—	1,478	1,478	—	—
Commercial paper	319	—	—	319	69	250	—
Certificates of deposit	1,358	—	—	1,358	972	386	—
US government and agency securities	112,119	85	(360)	111,844	16	111,828	—
Foreign government bonds	5,276	2	(13)	5,265	1,504	3,761	—
Mortgage-backed securities	3,921	14	(4)	3,931	—	3,931	—
Corporate notes and bonds	4,786	61	(12)	4,835	—	4,835	—
Municipal securities	284	43	—	327	—	327	—
Common and preferred stock	2,472	3,062	(34)	5,500	—	—	5,500
Other investments	523	—	—	523	—	—	523
Total	$136,160	$3,267	$(423)	$139,004	$7,663	$125,318	$6,023

Let's consider the cash and equivalents balance, $7,663 million. Table 17.2 shows that this account consists mainly of cash, foreign government bonds, mutual funds, commercial paper, and certificates of deposit. Small amounts of corporate notes and municipal (i.e., city and state government) securities are included too. Notice that the holding gains and losses for this category of investment are modest. This result is expected. First, some items, including cash and certificates of deposit, are not marked to market. Obviously, if the company has $3,624 million in cash, the market value of that cash is the same amount. Even those instruments that are marked to market, such as mutual funds and commercial paper, show only small changes in value. Given that all instruments in this account are highly short-term in nature (with nearly all expiring within 90 days), their market values are not highly sensitive to changes in interest rates. And given that changes in interest rates are the only factors that lead to changes in value for fixed-income instruments, any unrealized holding gains or losses should be modest.

Notice also that some mutual funds and certificates of deposit are included in the short-term investments account. The main distinction between the two classifications, cash and equivalents vs. short-term investments, is one of maturity. Mutual funds, mainly in the form of money-market funds, are classified as cash or cash equivalents if they function as demand deposits (i.e., checking accounts). Otherwise, they are classified as short-term investments.

As for short-term investments, $125,318 million, all of the components are in the form of fixed-income instruments, with US government bonds, foreign (non-US) government bonds, corporate bonds, and municipal securities representing the primary components. This breakdown is expected, given that managing short-term equity portfolios is not part of Microsoft's business model. For this reason, none of its equity investments are classified as short-term. Note also that because all of the instruments in short-term investments are due to mature within the next few months, their values are not heavily influenced by changes in interest rates. As a result, holding gains and losses are small. Also, it is highly likely that many of these bonds are classified by Microsoft as "held-to-maturity" securities, which means that they are not marked to market.

Equity and other investments, $6,023 million, are mainly in the form of common shares. However, Microsoft does not disclose the portion of the total that comprises common shares accounted for under the equity method and the portion accounted for as passive investments.

Table 17.3   The Investing Activities Section of Microsoft's Cash Flow Statement

Investing activities	2015	2016	2017
Additions to PP&E	(5,944)	(8,343)	(8,129)
Acquisitions of companies, net of cash acquired	(3,723)	(1,393)	(25,944)
Purchase of investments	(98,729)	(129,758)	(176,905)
Maturities of investments	15,013	22,054	28,044
Sales of investments	70,848	93,287	136,350
Securities lending payable	(466)	203	(197)
Net cash from investing	(23,001)	(23,950)	(46,781)

Table 17.4   The Income Statement Effects from Microsoft's Investing Activities (in Millions)

Year ended June 30	2015	2016	2017
Dividends and interest income	$766	$903	$1,387
Interest expense	(781)	(1,243)	(2,222)
Net recognized gains on investments	716	668	2,583
Net losses on derivatives	(423)	(443)	(510)
Net gains (losses) on foreign currency remeasurements	335	(121)	(164)
Other, net	$(267)	$(195)	(251)

Finally, given that Microsoft does not have any securities classified as "trading," all unrealized gains and losses for 2017, $3,267 million and $423 million respectively, are included in other comprehensive income. None of those gains or losses is included in 2017 net income.

Further information on Microsoft's investing activities can be learned from the investing activities section of the cash flow statement shown in Table 17.3.

The cash flow statement reveals that $25,944 million was spent on acquiring other companies, nearly all of which was devoted to the acquisition of social networking site LinkedIn. Also, $176,905 million was spent on investments. But notice that $28,044 million of cash was raised from the maturity of investments (i.e., bonds or notes coming to the end of their contractual lives) and $136,350 million from the sale of investments.

Finally, a note from Microsoft's Annual Report (see Table 17.4) shows the income statement effects of investing activities. Focusing on 2017, we see that Microsoft reported $1,387 million in dividends and interest.[6] Net gains on investments were $2,583 million. These net gains relate only to securities sold in fiscal year 2017.

Consolidation

When one company owns more than 50% of the voting shares of another company, the investor (or parent) is assumed to control the other (i.e., the subsidiary). US GAAP and IFRS require that the parent combine the financial statements of all majority-owned companies with its own, in consolidated financial statements. It should be noted that recent changes have resulted in a new, and more expansive, definition of control. The practical effect of these changes is that consolidation may be required from large minority holdings where other shareholdings are widely dispersed, and the investor holds significantly more voting rights than any other shareholder.

Consolidated, or group, financial statements exist because of the "substance over form" rule. Technically, a shareholder in the parent is investing in just a single company. But because the parent controls other companies, the shareholder is indirectly investing in those too. For the financial statements to be useful in guiding capital allocation decisions by investors, they should be based on the underlying economic reality of the business. Even though the parent and each subsidiary are separate legal entities, they operate as one centrally controlled economic entity. This is the economic reality that needs to be captured by the financial reporting process.

We do not intend to discuss the detailed mechanics of consolidation in this chapter. The process is highly technical and complicated. However, any reader of the financial statements needs to understand three fundamental concepts behind the consolidation process:

1. Consolidated financial statements are not simply a matter of adding together the accounts of the parent and its subsidiaries. The major complicating factor is the presence of intercompany transactions. Parents sometimes lend money to subsidiaries, or vice versa. Also, one legal entity within the corporate group may sell products or services to another. The guiding principle is that consolidated financial statements reflect the results that the group would report if it were a single company. The consolidated accounts should therefore reflect only those transactions between the consolidated group of entities and outsiders. Any intercompany transactions – including loans, receivables, payables, and sales – must be eliminated. For example, if a parent reports sales of $100 million, its subsidiary reports sales of $30 million, and $10 million of the parent's sales were to the subsidiary, the consolidated income statement would show sales of $120 million. The $10 million of intercompany sales are eliminated during the consolidation process.

2. Parents often do not own 100% of their subsidiaries. The consolidation process must therefore acknowledge the ownership interest held by minority shareholders. For example, assume that a subsidiary reports net income of $10 million and the parent owns 70% of the entity. Because the parent has operational control over the entire entity, 100% of all balance sheet and income statement accounts are consolidated with those of the parent (after removing any intercompany transactions). Therefore, the parent recognizes the full $10 million of net income on its own income statement. However, it must also acknowledge that external parties have claims on 30% of the subsidiary and are thus entitled to 30% (or $3 million) of the profits. This claim is shown on the income statement as "noncontrolling interest." If the parent reports total net income of $50 million, the income statement might look something like this:

Consolidated net income	$50 million
Less net income – noncontrolling interest	3 million
Net income attributable to parent company	$47 million

Noncontrolling interest, previously called "minority interest," is also recognized on the balance sheet. Here, noncontrolling interest represents external interests in the shareholders' equity of subsidiaries. In the past, it was found between the liability section and the shareholders' equity section. Recent changes in accounting rules now require that it be classified as shareholders' equity. In any case, most analysts consider noncontrolling interest to be a form of equity.

3. The process by which one company acquires another nearly always gives rise to "goodwill." Consider the following example. Microsoft acquires ABC Software for $100 million. For the sake of simplicity, assume that the acquisition is for 100% of ABC's shares (i.e., no

noncontrolled interests). The purchase price is first allocated to tangible and financial assets (e.g., inventories, receivables, PP&E, etc.) at fair value as of the acquisition date. The same is done with liabilities. In this example, we assume that the fair value of the tangible assets is $80 million and the fair value of liabilities is $25 million. The resulting net of $55 million is $45 million less than the total purchase price. By default, $45 million must be allocated to intangible assets. This is done by determining all "identifiable" intangibles – such as trademarks, brand names, patents, copyrights, customer lists, Internet domain names, franchise and royalty agreements, software, databases, and trade secrets. Each intangible is measured at its fair value.[7] If identifiable intangibles are valued at $31 million, that still leaves us $14 million short of the purchase price. That difference is allocated to goodwill, which is simply the popular term for unidentifiable intangibles.

Until a few years ago, goodwill was amortized like other assets, but no longer. Instead, companies test goodwill for impairment at least once a year. As long as the goodwill is deemed unimpaired, no goodwill charge is made. But if the goodwill is deemed to be impaired, an estimate of the magnitude of the impairment is required. Goodwill is then written down to this amount, and an impairment loss is recognized on the income statement.

"Negative" goodwill is possible too, though far less common than positive goodwill. In this event, the target company is bought for a price lower than the fair value of the acquired assets, net of debts assumed. The amount of negative goodwill is then recognized as a gain on the income statement in the year of the acquisition. In effect, negative goodwill implies a bargain purchase. However, such companies often come with costly strings attached. For example, the buyer may be forced to guarantee a specified number of jobs for a specified number of years. Or a minimum level of capital investment may be required. In short, the acquired company might not be a bargain after all.

KEY LESSONS FROM THE CHAPTER

- When companies own shares in other businesses, the accounting depends on the degree of influence or control that the investor exerts over the other company.

- Passive investors are assumed to exert no influence over the investee. Generally, passive investment is assumed when the investor owns less than 20% of the outstanding voting shares of the investee.

- When investors own between 20 and 50% of voting shares, they are assumed to exert significant influence over operating activities and dividend policy of the investee. The equity method of accounting is then required.

- Control is presumed if the investor owns more than 50% of the outstanding voting shares of the investee.

- When one company owns more than 50% of the voting shares of another company, the parent must combine the financial statements of all majority-owned companies with its own, in consolidated financial statements.

- Under IFRS, passive investments fall into three basic categories: debt securities held to maturity, trading securities, and available-for-sale securities. The last of these is the default category. As of 2018, US GAAP requires that all passive equity investments be accounted for using the same approach as trading securities under IFRS.

- Passive equity investments must be reported at fair value as of the balance sheet date.

- For trading and available-for-sale securities under IFRS, investments must be marked to market at the end of the year. The difference between the two methods lies in the treatment of the resulting unrealized holding gains and losses. In the case of the former, the gains and losses appear in that period's income statement. For the latter, the gains and losses are recorded directly in the shareholders' equity section of the balance sheet.

- Among IFRS-compliant companies, available-for-sale securities are far more common than trading investments. Trading securities are rarely found outside of financial services.

KEY TERMS AND CONCEPTS FROM THE CHAPTER

Passive investment	Consolidation	Fair value hierarchy	Held-to-maturity
Significant influence	Available-for-sale securities	Mark to market	securities
Equity method	Trading securities	Mark to model	Goodwill

QUESTIONS

1. What is the difference between available-for-sale securities and trading securities? How do the accounting treatments differ under IFRS?

2. True or false: Debt securities can be classified as available-for-sale or for trading purposes.

3. In the aftermath of the banking and economic crisis of 2008 and 2009, several banks reclassified investments from trading securities to held-to-maturity securities. What motive might they have had for doing this?

4. For equity investments, which classification is more common for industrial firms reporting under IFRS, available-for-sale or trading, and why?

5. Describe the fair value hierarchy.

6. Why are unrealized holding gains and losses on trading securities included in net income while unrealized holding gains and losses on available-for-sale securities are included in accumulated other comprehensive income?

7. What determines whether investments are classified as current or noncurrent?

8. Why was the equity method established? What purpose does it serve?

9. Can you think of an example where a company owns more than 20% of the outstanding equity of another company but does not use the equity method?

10. How is use of the equity method subject to manipulation? How might a financial statement reader detect such behavior?

PROBLEMS

17.1 Classification of Long-Term Investments

The following note was taken from the fiscal year 2011 Annual Report of Group Air France-KLM. (Note that the Group's fiscal year runs from 1 April to 31 March.) It refers to the initial public offering (IPO) of Amadeus IT, a Spanish travel-reservations technology company. At the time of its IPO, the company was majority-owned by WAM Acquisition, whose shareholders included two London-based private equity firms, and the carriers Iberia, Deutsche Lufthansa, and Air France.

Required

a. The note reports that as a result of the two actions undertaken by the Group, the Group's holdings in WAM decreased from 22 to 15%. In addition, "the governance of WAM was changed." What exactly does the Group mean by these statements and what were the financial reporting ramifications of these changes?

b. What entry did Group AirFrance-KLM make to record the holding gain from its investment in WAM?

c. The note says, "After this operation, the . . . shares . . . were reclassified as 'assets available for sale.'" What does this mean, and what effect did this change have on the financial statements?

On April 29, 2010, the company WAM (Amadeus) was the subject of an Initial Public Offering (IPO) on the Madrid stock exchange. This operation was executed in two stages:

1. A capital increase reserved to the market, to which the Group did not subscribe;

2. The concomitant sale of a portion of the shares held by the Group.

After the operation, the Group's holding decreased from 22% to 15%. At the same time, the governance of WAM was changed. These two items involved the loss of significant influence for the Group as well as a change in the valuation method of the remaining shareholding.

As a consequence, consistent with IFRS, since the April 29, 2010 IPO, the shares held by the Group have been valued at their market value (market price).

The overall profit recorded in the income statement amounting to €1030 million breaks down as follows:

- gain on disposal of shares: €280 million, including €193 million of cash received;

- valuation at the market price of the remaining shares held by the Group: €750 million.

After this operation, the WAM (Amadeus) shares held by the Group were reclassified as "assets available for sale" (in "other financial assets noncurrent"). The value of the shares is updated at each closing period as a function of the share price. The counterpart of this revaluation is recorded in other comprehensive income.

17.2 The Effect of Transaction Cost on Marketable Securities and Investments

Early in 2017, Yoon Industries purchased marketable equity securities for $5 million. These securities are classified as "available for sale." To acquire the securities, the company incurred transaction costs of $30,000 in addition to the $5 million. The securities had a fair value on 31 December 2017 of $4.6 million. None of these shares were sold during 2017.

Required

a. What amount would appear in the asset account when the securities are bought?

b. Make the journal required at the end of 2017 to reflect the fair value of the securities.

17.3 Journal Entries and Analysis Under the Equity Method

At 31 December 2005, Abbott Laboratories, Inc. owned 50% of TAP Pharmaceutical Products Inc. under a joint venture agreement with Takeda Pharmaceutical Company, Limited of Japan. TAP develops and markets pharmaceutical products for the US and Canada, and is an important strategic investee for Abbott Labs. Abbott appropriately accounts for the investment in TAP using the equity method.

The Investment in affiliate account is reported by Abbott Labs in its 31 December 2005 balance sheet at $167 million. Abbott received $343, $638, and $606 million dividends from TAP in 2005, 2004, and 2003, respectively. TAP declared income of $883, $1,290, and $1,303 million in 2005, 2004, and 2003 respectively. At 31 December 2005, TAP's balance sheet reports assets of $1,470 million, liabilities of $1,136 million, and shareholders' equity of $334 million.

Required

a. Reconstruct the journal entries made by Abbott Labs to account for its investment in TAP in 2005 using the equity method.

b. Assuming that Abbott acquired the investment in TAP at the beginning of 2003, how much did Abbott pay for the investment?

c. In a risk analysis of Abbott Labs, most analysts will calculate Abbott's debt-to-equity ratio. In this case, the debt-to-equity ratio may not capture an important element of Abbott's risk.

What is that risk, and why doesn't Abbott's balance sheet capture it?

d. Assume that the $167 million investment in TAP represents only a 10% (passive) interest, Abbott classifies the investment as available-for-sale, the $343 million dividends received by Abbott are a result of having a 10% interest, shares of TAP are actively traded, and TAP's *total* market capitalization at 31 December 2005 is $2000 million. Compute the effects of this investment on Abbott's 2005 income.

17.4 Review Problem

For each item listed below, indicate the effect of the transaction or accounting change on current period net operating profit after tax (NOPAT), end of the current period invested capital (ending IC), and current period cash flow from operations (CFFO). Set up your answer in the following format:

Item #	Effect on NOPAT	Effect on IC	Effect on CFFO
(a)			
(b)			
(c)			
(d)			
(e)			
(f)			
(g)			
(h)			
(i)			
(j)			

Write "Increase," "Decrease," or "No effect" in each column. When you are done, you should have 30 total answers.

Items to analyze

a. The company recorded the increases in market value of their passive investments in available-for-sale securities.

b. Estimates of expected salvage (or residual) values used in straight-line depreciation methods for delivery vans were decreased.

c. A large amount of production machinery was sold for cash at more than book value.

d. The company sold equipment inventory on credit to a regular customer in the normal course of business.

e. Cash dividends were declared and paid.

f. A 50% stock dividend was declared and distributed.

g. Land was revalued upward as permitted by IFRS rules. No prior write-ups or write-downs had occurred.

h. On the last day of the year, interest-bearing convertible bonds were converted to shares of common stock.

i. The company delayed payments to factory workers, normally due on the last day of the year, by several days.

j. In prior years, new lease signings were treated as capital leases. Similar new leases signed at the beginning of this year are treated as operating leases.

17.5 Mark-to-Market Accounting for Trading Securities

At the end of 2017, Huber Company had investments in trading securities as follows (amounts in thousands of euro):

	Cost	Market value
Renaud Company	1,000	1,300
Helsing, Ltd	900	1,100
Neilsen Financial	1,100	900
	3,000	3,300

The shares for each company were acquired during 2017. The market values shown above are based on market prices as of the close of trading on 31 December 2017.

Required

a. Record whatever journal entries are required to implement mark-to-market accounting for Huber Company at the end of 2017.

b. Based on the above information, what type of business would you expect Huber Company to engage in, and why? Industrial? Trading and distribution? Retailing? Finance?

17.6 The Equity Method and the Statement of Cash Flows

The statements of cash flows for the SAP Group are shown below.

Required

Based on these statements, answer the following questions:

a. What were the entity's two major sources of cash in each year?

b. What were the entity's two major uses of cash in each year?

c. How much was the company's bad debt expense in fiscal 2009?

d. Did accounts receivable increase or decrease in 2009? Explain.

e. Did the company report gains or losses from equity method investees in fiscal 2009? Your response here should be "gains" or "losses," not "yes" or "no." Briefly support your answer, indicating why these are added or subtracted on the cash flow statement.

f. Does the company appear to be in growth or contraction mode during the period covered by their cash flow statement? Support your answer.

Consolidated Statements of Cash Flows of SAP Group as at December 31,

€ millions	2009	2008	2007
Profit after tax	1,750	1,848	1,908
Adjustments to reconcile profit after tax to net cash provided by operating activities:			
Depreciation and amortization	499	539	262
Gains/losses on disposals of noncurrent assets	−11	11	−1
Gains/losses on disposals of financial assets	−2	−16	−1
Impairment loss on financial assets recognized in profit	10	15	8
Decrease/increase in sales and bad debt allowances on trade receivables	64	76	0
Other adjustments for noncash items	14	52	45
Deferred income taxes	−39	−91	8
Decrease/increase in trade receivables	593	−48	−521
Decrease/increase in other assets	205	−12	−277
Decrease/increase in trade payables, provisions and other liabilities	−116	−277	375
Decrease/increase in deferred income	48	61	124
Net cash flows from operating activities	3,015	2,158	1,932
Purchase of noncontrolling interests	0	0	−48
Business combinations, net of cash and cash equivalents acquired	−73	−3,773	−672
Repayment of acquirees' debt in business combinations	0	−450	0

€ millions	2009	2008	2007
Purchase of intangible assets and property, plant, and equipment	−225	−339	−400
Proceeds from sales of intangible assets or property, plant, and equipment	45	44	27
Cash transferred to restricted cash	0	−448	−550
Use of restricted cash	0	1,001	0
Purchase of equity or debt instruments of other entities	−1,073	−396	−778
Proceeds from sales of equity or debt instruments of other entities	1,027	595	1040
Net cash flows from investing activities	**−299**	**−3,766**	**−1,391**
Dividends paid	−594	−594	−556
Purchase of treasury shares	0	−487	−1,005
Proceeds from reissuance of treasury shares	24	85	156
Proceeds from issuing shares (share-based compensation)	6	20	44
Proceeds from borrowings	697	3,859	47
Repayments of borrowings	−2,303	−1,571	−48
Purchase of equity-based derivative instruments (hedge for cash-settled share-based payment plans)	0	−55	0
Proceeds from the exercise of equity-based derivative financial instruments	4	24	75
Net cash flows from financing activities	**−2,166**	**1,281**	**−1,287**
Effect of foreign exchange rates on cash and cash equivalents	**54**	**−1**	**−45**
Net increase (decrease) in cash and cash equivalents	**604**	**−328**	**−791**
Cash and cash equivalents at the beginning of the period	**1,280**	**1,608**	**2,399**
Cash and cash equivalents at the end of the period	**1,884**	**1,280**	**1,608**

Interest paid in 2009, 2008, and 2007 amounted to €69 million, €105 million, and €6 million, respectively, and interest received in 2009, 2008, and 2007 amounted to €22 million, €72 million and €142 million, respectively. Income taxes paid in 2009, 2008, and 2007, net of refunds, were €722 million, €882 million, and €811 million, respectively.
The accompanying Notes are an integral part of these Consolidated Financial Statements.

Case Study

17-1 Stora Enso: Accounting for Investments

Stora Enso is an integrated paper, packaging, and forest products company producing publication and fine papers, packaging boards and wood products. Sales were €12.4 billion in 2004. Headquartered in Helsinki, the group has about 45,000 employees in more than 40 countries. Customers are large and small publishers, printing houses and merchants, as well as packaging, joinery, and construction companies. The company's shares are listed in Helsinki, Stockholm, and New York, and its accounts are prepared in accordance with International Financial Reporting Standards (IFRS).

Investments at Stora Enso

Apart from affiliates, which are accounted for under the equity method, all of Stora Enso's investments are classified as long-term and "available-for-sale." Most of these investments are in other forestry firms or in suppliers of Stora Enso.

The carrying value of investments on the end-of-2003 balance sheet was €368.5 million. The acquisition cost of the investments was €288.0 million. The difference, €80.5 million, was classified as other comprehensive income in the shareholders' equity section of Stora Enso's balance sheet.

During 2004, the following transactions took place:

- The company made additional investments costing €13.2 million.

- Securities with an acquisition cost of €31.3 million were sold for €32.8 million.

Stora Enso's holdings were marked to market at the end of 2004 and estimated to have a fair value of €352.9 million.

Required

a. Specify the journal entries to record the transactions that occurred in Stora Enso's investment account in 2004.

b. What journal entry should be made to mark Stora Enso's investments to market at the end of 2004?

c. Suppose Stora Enso reclassified the investments as "trading securities." How would the accounting change as a result of the reclassification? Specify the journal entries required for 2004.

Case Study

17-2 Coca-Cola and Coca-Cola Enterprises: The Equity Method in Practice

Coca-Cola Enterprises (CCE), the world's largest bottler of Coke, was formed in 1986 from the consolidation of several bottling companies. At inception, Coca-Cola, Inc. owned 49% of CCE, allowing it to exert significant influence over operations without having to include CCE's large debts in its own balance sheet. Coca-Cola's investment in CCE has gradually declined, reaching about 36% by 2003. The investment has always been accounted for under the equity method.

On its end-of-2003 balance sheet, Coca-Cola reported the carrying value (i.e., book value) of its investment in CCE at $1,260 million.

During 2004,

- CCE reported net income of $596 million and paid $76 million in dividends to its shareholders.

- Through a variety of cooperative agreements, Coca-Cola increased its net investment in CCE by $121 million. Because of capital increases in CCE, these investments did not materially affect Coca-Cola's percentage ownership.

CCE is traded on the New York Stock Exchange. At the end of 2004, Coca-Cola's stake in CCE had a market value of about $3.5 billion (based on the market capitalization of CCE's shares).

Required

a. Make whatever journal entries are required to implement the equity method for Coca-Cola's investment in CCE for 2004.

b. What should be the carrying value for the CCE investment on Coca-Cola's end-of-2004 balance sheet?

NOTES

1. The standard on fair value applies equally to liabilities, but the focus in this chapter is on assets.

2. Another important controversy centers on the role that mark-to-market accounting may or may not have played in the recent global financial crisis. The charge is that accounting rules forcing banks and other financial institutions to write down assets led to catastrophic contagion effects – massive sell-offs led to plummeting prices, forcing banks to sell more assets to meet capital requirements, causing asset prices to fall still further, and so on. We believe that the contribution of accounting to the crisis has been seriously overstated, but the subject is beyond the scope of this book.

3. Mark-to-market accounting had not yet come into existence when the equity method was established.

4. By 2010, Coca-Cola's ownership stake in CCE had declined to 33%. It then bought out CCE's North American bottling assets and redeemed its remaining shares. CCE, therefore, has a far greater degree of operating independence than it had in Ivester's day.

5. This example assumes that there is no goodwill associated with the investment.

6. This book ignores the accounting for derivatives (i.e., options, futures, swaps, etc.). Therefore, we do not discuss the net losses on derivatives.

7. This difficult and controversial process is beyond the scope of this book.

Accounting for Mergers and Acquisitions

18

Introduction

Mergers and acquisitions (M&A), or "business combinations," bring together separate companies or businesses into one reporting entity. In this chapter we focus on the financial reporting issues that arise in such transactions. Since 2005, IFRS and US GAAP have mandated that all business combinations be accounted for as acquisitions, a transaction where one of the combining entities obtains control over the other. Simply put, all corporate control transactions are assumed to be acquisitions; mergers are not recognized for financial reporting purposes.

To illustrate the accounting for acquisitions, we refer to Microsoft's acquisition of LinkedIn, the business- and employment-oriented social networking site. On December 8, 2016, Microsoft completed its acquisition of all issued and outstanding shares of LinkedIn for a total purchase price of $27.0 billion.

Both IFRS and US GAAP require the "purchase method" of accounting. This method allocates the purchase price of the acquisition to all identifiable assets and liabilities on the basis of fair value. The remainder, i.e., nonidentifiable intangible assets, is captured in "goodwill." The following sections focus on the key features of the purchase method.

Purchase Price/Cost of Acquisition

The first step in accounting for M&A is to determine the acquisition cost. This exercise is fairly straightforward when the acquisition is a cash transaction. The cost of acquisition equals the amount of cash or cash equivalents paid. Determining the acquisition cost is more complex when the consideration involves an exchange of shares.

Under IFRS, shares issued by the acquirer as consideration are recorded at fair value at the date of the exchange – the date on which the acquirer obtains control over the acquired company's net assets and operations. When the acquisition occurs in stages, the fair value of the shares issued is determined at each exchange date. In an active market, the published price of a share at the date of exchange is the best evidence of fair value. The determination of fair value in the absence of an active market (as is the case for privately held companies) is more complicated.

Under US GAAP, shares issued as consideration are measured at their market price over a reasonable period of time (i.e., a few days) before and after the parties reach an agreement on the purchase price and the proposed transaction is announced.

An excerpt of Microsoft's filings with the Securities and Exchange Commission (SEC) is shown in Box 18.1 below.

BOX 18.1   Report by Microsoft Regarding LinkedIn Acquisition Cost

On June 11, 2016, Microsoft Corporation, a Washington corporation (the "Company"), entered into an Agreement and Plan of Merger (the "Merger Agreement") with LinkedIn Corporation, a Delaware corporation ("LinkedIn"). At the effective time of the Merger, each share of LinkedIn Class A common stock and Class B common stock issued and outstanding immediately prior to the effective time will be automatically cancelled and converted into the right to receive $196.00 in cash, without interest.

Contingent Consideration

To ensure the success of the transaction, and to protect the acquirer from paying too much, business combinations are sometimes structured with a subsequent earn-out payment that will be made to the seller if certain measures are achieved.

If part of the purchase consideration is contingent on a future event, such as achieving specified profit levels, US GAAP and IFRS require an estimate of the amount to be included as part of the cost at the date of the acquisition where it is probable that it will be paid and it can be reliably measured. Any revision to the estimate is subsequently adjusted against goodwill.

Recognition and Measurement of Identifiable Assets

Once the purchase price is determined, it is then allocated to the target's identifiable assets and liabilities.

Current Assets, Liabilities, and PP&E

Exhibit 18.1 shows LinkedIn's balance sheet just prior to Microsoft's acquisition of the company. As we would expect, the assets are reported using a variety of measurement approaches, including historical cost, net realizable value, lower-of-cost-or-market, and cost less depreciation. However, regardless of how these items were measured in the past, all assets (and liabilities) must be recognized on the acquirer's balance sheet at fair value as of the date of acquisition.

Intangible Assets

In general, intangible assets developed internally are not recognized as assets on a company's balance sheet. However, at the time of acquisition, the acquirer is expected to value any intangibles acquired and record them as assets. An intangible asset is recognized separately from goodwill if it represents contractual or legal rights, or is capable of being separated or divided and sold, transferred, licensed, rented, or exchanged. Microsoft reported what is shown in Box 18.2 regarding LinkedIn's intangibles.

| Exhibit 18.1 | LinkedIn Corporation Consolidated Balance Sheets (In Thousands, Except Share Data) |

	December 31,	
	2015	**2014**
Assets		
Current Assets:		
Cash and cash equivalents	$ 546,237	$ 460,887
Marketable securities	2,573,145	2,982,422
Accounts receivable (net of allowance for doubtful accounts of $17,970 and $11,944 at December 31, 2015 and 2014, respectively)	603,060	449,048
Deferred commissions	87,706	66,561
Prepaid expenses	62,992	52,978
Other current assets	61,949	110,204
Total current assets	3,935,089	4,122,100
Property and equipment, net	1,047,005	740,909
Goodwill	1,507,093	356,718
Intangible assets, net	373,087	131,275
Other assets	148,925	76,255
Total Assets	$7,011,199	$5,427,257
Liabilities, Redeemable Noncontrolling Interest, and Stockholders' Equity		
Current Liabilities:		
Accounts payable	$ 162,176	$ 100,297
Accrued liabilities	316,792	260,189
Deferred revenue	709,116	522,299
Total current liabilities	1,188,084	882,785
Convertible Senior Notes, Net	1,126,534	1,081,553
Other Long-Term Liabilities	201,128	132,100
Total liabilities	2,515,746	2,096,438
Commitments and Contingencies (Note 12)		
Redeemable Noncontrolling Interest	26,810	5,427
Stockholders' Equity (Note 13):		
Class A common stock, $0.0001 par value; 1,000,000,000 shares authorized, 117,500,405 and 116,468,385 shares issued and outstanding, respectively, at December 31, 2015 and 110,291,709 and 109,259,689 shares issued and outstanding, respectively, at December 31, 2014	12	11
Class B common stock, $0.0001 par value; 120,000,000 shares authorized, 15,580,510 and 15,782,261 shares issued and outstanding at December 31, 2015 and 2014, respectively	1	2
Additional paid-in capital	4,588,578	3,285,705
Accumulated other comprehensive income (loss)	9,124	(198)
Accumulated earnings (deficit)	(129,072)	39,872
Total stockholders' equity	4,468,643	3,325,392
Total Liabilities, Redeemable Noncontrolling Interest, and Stockholders' Equity	$7,011,199	$5,427,257

See notes to consolidated financial statements.
Source: The Gillette Company 10-K SEC filing for year ended December 31, 2004.

BOX 18.2 Microsoft's Reporting on LinkedIn's Intangibles

Following are the details of the purchase price allocated to the intangible assets acquired:

	Amount (In millions)	Weighted Average Life
Customer-related	$ 3,607	7 years
Marketing-related (trade names)	2,148	20 years
Technology-based	2,109	3 years
Contract-based	23	5 years
Fair value of intangible assets acquired	$ 7,887	9 years

In-process Research & Development (IPR&D)

At the time of acquisition, the acquired company may have ongoing (i.e., in-process) R&D projects. Acquired IPR&D is recognized as a separate intangible asset if it meets the definition of an intangible asset, and its fair value can be measured reliably. In transactions involving research-intensive, hi-tech companies, IPR&D is often the largest asset acquired.

Restructuring Provisions

At the time of the announced combination, management will often announce a postmerger restructuring plan to assist with the integration of the parent and target companies. IFRS states that the acquirer may recognize restructuring provisions as part of the acquired liabilities only when the target company has an existing liability for restructuring as of the acquisition date. US GAAP, on the other hand, does allow the acquiring company to recognize provisions beyond those already recognized by the target. However, several conditions are imposed, including the need to produce detailed restructuring plans.

Contingent Liabilities

The most common contingent liabilities are lawsuits and environmental liabilities. An acquirer must recognize separately the target's contingent liabilities at the acquisition date as part of allocating the cost, provided fair values can be measured reliably.

Goodwill

Goodwill arises as the difference between the cost of the acquisition and the fair value of identifiable assets and liabilities (including contingencies). Goodwill can result from name recognition, superior management, employee and customer loyalty, or any other attribute that makes net assets more valuable taken as a whole. In other words, because of potential synergies with Microsoft, LinkedIn may be worth more than the sum of its individual parts. Additionally, combining the two companies' assets may provide economies of scale, thereby making LinkedIn's assets more valuable to Microsoft than their individual fair values.

The accounting treatment for purchased goodwill is to capitalize it as an intangible asset. Goodwill is nonamortizable, but must be reviewed for impairment at least annually.

In Box 18.3, Microsoft reports the allocation of the acquisition purchase price for LinkedIn. The journal entry recorded by Microsoft for the LinkedIn acquisition is shown below (in millions):

Cash and cash equivalents	$1,328	
Short-term investments	2,110	
Other current assets	697	
Property and equipment	1,529	
Intangible assets	7,887	
Goodwill	16,803	
Short-term debt		1,323
Other current liabilities		1,117
Deferred income taxes		774
Other liabilities		131
Cash		27,009

Of course, the actual journal entry recorded by Microsoft included a more detailed listing of assets and liabilities. For example, current assets would have been broken down into cash, marketable securities, accounts receivable, inventory, and prepaid assets.

Negative Goodwill (Bargain Purchase)

Goodwill arises whenever the purchase price of the acquisition exceeds the fair value of identifiable net assets (assets – liabilities). When the opposite situation occurs, "negative goodwill" (also known as a "bargain purchase") is the result. According to IFRS, if there is any excess of fair value over purchase price, the acquirer should reassess the identification and measurement of the acquired company's identifiable assets and liabilities. If negative goodwill remains after the reassessment, the excess is recognized immediately as profit on the income statement. This means that the term "negative goodwill" should never be seen on a corporate balance sheet.

BOX 18.3 Microsoft's Allocation of the Acquisition Cost for LinkedIn

The allocation of the purchase price to goodwill was completed as of June 30, 2017. The major classes of assets and liabilities to which we allocated the purchase price were as follows:

(In millions)

Cash and cash equivalents	$ 1,328
Short-term investments	2,110
Other current assets	697
Property and equipment	1,529
Intangible assets	7,887
Goodwill[a]	16,803
Short-term debt[b]	(1,323)
Other current liabilities	(1,117)
Deferred income taxes	(774)
Other	(131)
Total purchase price	$ 27,009

[a]Goodwill was assigned to our Productivity and Business Processes segment. The goodwill was primarily attributed to increased synergies that are expected to be achieved from the integration of LinkedIn. None of the goodwill is expected to be deductible for income tax purposes.
[b]Convertible senior notes issued by LinkedIn on November 12, 2014, substantially all of which were redeemed after our acquisition of LinkedIn. The remaining $18 million of notes are not redeemable and are included in long-term debt on our consolidated balance sheets. See Note 12 – Debt for further information.

Similarly, US GAAP defines a bargain purchase as the excess of fair value of acquired net assets over purchase cost and results in a gain recognized in the period in which the acquisition occurs. Also, like IFRS, US GAAP requires the acquiring entity to double-check its calculations before concluding that a bargain purchase exists. If the same conclusion is reached, any further excess is recognized as a gain in the income statement. The gain is calculated as the excess of the fair value of the net assets acquired over the sum of (1) the fair value of the consideration transferred, (2) the fair value of any previously held equity interests, and (3) the fair value of any noncontrolling interests.

While not expected to be common, a bargain purchase may occur if, for example, the acquired entity is purchased in a forced liquidation or distress sale.

Subsequent Adjustments to Acquired Assets and Liabilities

IFRS permits adjustments against goodwill to the provisional fair values recognized at acquisition provided those adjustments are made within 12 months of the acquisition date.

Adjustments after the 12-month period must be recognized in the income statement as gains or losses. US GAAP is broadly similar to IFRS on this issue.

Box 18.4 shows what Microsoft had to say regarding subsequent adjustments for its acquisition of LinkedIn.

Goodwill Impairment

Both IFRS and US GAAP require periodic reassessments of goodwill, although there are some differences in the approaches required by each accounting regime. IFRS requires a one-step impairment test. The recoverable amount of the business unit in question (i.e., the higher of its net selling price and its value in use) is compared with its carrying amount on the balance sheet. An impairment loss is recognized if the carrying value exceeds the recoverable amount.

Under US GAAP, a two-step impairment test is required:

1. The fair value and the carrying amount of the reporting unit, including goodwill, should be compared. If the fair value of the reporting unit is less than the book value, goodwill is considered impaired; then

---

BOX 18.4   Microsoft's Comments on Subsequent Adjustments for its Acquisition of LinkedIn

We are in the process of finalizing the allocation of the purchase price to the individual assets acquired and liabilities assumed. The preliminary allocation of the purchase price included in the current period balance sheet is based on the best estimates of management. To assist management in the allocation, we engaged valuation specialists to prepare independent appraisals. The completion of the purchase price allocation may result in adjustments to the carrying value of LinkedIn's recorded assets and liabilities, revisions of the useful lives of intangible assets and the determination of any residual amount that will be allocated to goodwill. The related depreciation and amortization expense from the acquired assets is also subject to revision based on the final allocation.

2. The goodwill impairment should be measured as the excess of the carrying amount of goodwill over its implied fair value. The implied fair value of goodwill should be determined by allocating fair value to the various assets and liabilities included in the reporting unit in the same manner as goodwill is determined in a business combination. The impairment charge should be included in operating income.

In either case, goodwill impairment is recognized as follows:

Loss from goodwill impairment	XX	
Goodwill		XX

"Loss from goodwill impairment" is an income statement account. Until recently, goodwill was amortized like other intangibles, such as patents or copyrights. Goodwill charges would therefore reach the income statement in a stable, predictable way. But now that goodwill amortization is banned, goodwill reaches the income statement in a far less predictable fashion. Goodwill affects earnings but only when it is written off. For the typical company, expenses related to goodwill are zero in most years, but high (and in some cases, enormous) in years when write-offs are made.

Noncontrolling Interest

In the previous chapter, we introduced the concept of "noncontrolling interest" (NCI). NCI is the portion of equity in a subsidiary not owned, directly or indirectly, by the parent. At the time of acquisition, NCI is calculated as follows:

$$NCI = \text{Fair Value of Acquired Subsidiary}$$
$$\times \text{Percentage of Subsidiary Equity Not Owned by Parent}$$

To illustrate how this works, let's return to Microsoft's acquisition of LinkedIn, but now assume that Microsoft acquires only 80% of the outstanding stock for a price $21.6 billion. Because Microsoft owns more than 50% of LinkedIn, MSFT consolidates LNKD's financial results with its own. The 20% of LinkedIn's equity that Microsoft does not own is recorded at fair value on Microsoft's balance sheet. The fair value of the NCI is calculated as follows:

$$[(\text{Parent Purchase Price} \div \text{Parent's Controlling Interest}) \times NCI]$$
$$= [(\$21.6 / 80\%) \times 20\%] = \$5.4 \text{Billion}$$

The journal entry that would be recorded at the time of LinkedIn's acquisition is:

Cash and cash equivalents	$1,328	
Short-term investments	2,110	
Other current assets	697	
Property and equipment	1,529	
Intangible assets	7,887	
Goodwill	16,794	
Short-term debt		$1,323
Other current liabilities		1,117
Deferred income taxes		774
Other		131
Cash		21,600
Noncontrolling interest		5,400

NCI is recorded in the shareholders' equity section of the parent's balance sheet, separate from the parent's equity. The amounts of consolidated net income attributable to the parent and to the noncontrolling interest must be clearly identified and presented on the consolidated income statement.

KEY LESSONS FROM THE CHAPTER

- The first step in accounting for M&A is to determine the acquisition cost.

- To ensure the success of a transaction, and to protect the acquirer from paying too much, business combinations are sometimes structured with a subsequent earn-out payment made to the seller if certain performance measures are achieved. The presence of an earn-out clause complicates the determination of the acquisition cost.

- Once the purchase price is determined, it is allocated to the target's identifiable assets and liabilities, including current assets and liabilities, PP&E, intangible assets, in-process research and development, restructuring provisions, and contingent liabilities.

- Goodwill is the difference between the cost of the acquisition and the fair value of identifiable assets and liabilities.

- Goodwill can result from name recognition, superior management, employee and customer loyalty, and any other attribute that makes net assets more valuable taken as a whole.

- Negative goodwill arises when the purchase price of the acquisition is less than the fair market value of the net identifiable assets.

- All business combinations must be accounted for using the purchase method. In other words, it is assumed that one company is acquiring another company. Merger accounting no longer exists.

- When less than 100% of a controlling interest is acquired, a noncontrolling interest must be acknowledged. This interest appears in the shareholders' equity section of the balance sheet apart from the parent's equity. The portion of net income belonging to the noncontrolling interest must be identified on the consolidated income statement.

KEY TERMS AND CONCEPTS FROM THE CHAPTER

Purchase price	Goodwill	Negative	In-process research and
Identifiable assets	Contingent consideration	goodwill	development

QUESTIONS

1. What is goodwill?

2. How is goodwill determined?

3. What happens to goodwill after it has been recognized?

4. True or false: "Mergers" are not recognized under current financial reporting practice.

5. When one firm acquires another firm, the former records the assets of the latter at fair value on the acquisition date, not the target's historical cost. Why?

6. What is "negative" goodwill, and how is it recognized?

7. Can you think of specific instances in which negative goodwill, or a bargain purchase, might occur?

PROBLEMS

18.1 Journal Entry for an Acquisition

Tan Trading Company purchased all of the outstanding shares of Lau Chemicals on December 31, 2017. Just before the purchase, the condensed balance sheets of the two companies appeared as follows:

	Tan Trading	Lau Chemicals
(amounts in $000)		
Current assets	1,480	435.5
Property, plant, and equipment, net	2,100	676
	3,580	1,111.5

	Tan Trading	Lau Chemicals
Current liabilities	578	92.5
Share capital – common shares	1,950	525
Retained earnings	1,052	494
	3,580	1,111.5

The fair value of Lau Chemical's assets and liabilities is approximately the same as book value.

Tan Trading paid $1,225 in cash to acquire the shares of Lau Chemicals. For the excess of the purchase price over the fair value of Lau Chemicals' net assets, $86 is attributed to PP&E, and the remainder to goodwill.

Required

Prepare the entry for Tan Trading's acquisition of Lau Chemicals.

18.2 Analysis of an Acquisition

The 2003 Annual Report for Microsoft Corp. includes the following note:

In fiscal 2003, Microsoft acquired all of the outstanding equity interests of Navision a/s, Rare Ltd., and Placeware, Inc. Navision, headquartered in Vedbaek, Denmark, is a provider of integrated business solutions software for small- and mid-sized businesses in the European market that is part of the Microsoft Business Solutions segment. Navision, Rare, and Placeware have been consolidated into our financial statements since their respective acquisition dates. The estimated fair values of the assets acquired and liabilities assumed at the date of the acquisitions for fiscal 2003 are as follows:

	Navision July 12, 2002	Rare Ltd. September 24, 2002	Placeware April 30, 2003
(in millions)			
Current assets	$240	$25	$30
Property, plant, and equipment	8	8	7
Intangible assets	169	75	30
Goodwill	1,197	281	180
Total assets acquired	1,614	389	247
Current liabilities	(148)	(12)	(32)
Long-term liabilities	(1)		(13)
Total liabilities assumed	(149)	(12)	(45)
Net assets acquired	$1,465	$377	$202

Required

a. How much did Microsoft pay for Navision A/S?

b. What percentage of the Navision deal was for goodwill? What exactly is goodwill? How should Microsoft account for goodwill, at the time of acquisition and in subsequent periods?

c. How did the acquisition of Navision affect Microsoft's statement of cash flows?

18.3 Accounting for an Acquisition: Carrefour and BLC (China)

In the notes to its 2010 Annual Report, retail giant Carrefour disclosed the following acquisition:

On July 15, 2010, Carrefour entered into an agreement to acquire 51% of Baolongcang (BLC), a chain of 11 hypermarkets located in the Chinese province of Hebei (with two subsequently sold, as was initially planned), for a value of 35 million euros. At the end of 2009, Baolongcang held 9.4% market share in Shijiazhuang, the provincial capital. Baolongcang's founders retained a 49% interest in the joint venture. The transaction closed at the end of August 2010, and the approval of the local authorities was obtained in September 2010. Goodwill in the amount of 33 million euros was recorded as of December 31, 2010. Baolongcang is fully consolidated.

Supplemental information from the acquisition is provided below (all amounts are in millions of euro):

	Book value	Market value
Fixed assets	9	8
Inventories	4	1
Trade payables	(2)	(2)
Other liabilities	(2)	(3)
Net assets	9	4
Price paid		35
Fair value of net assets acquired*		2
Goodwill		33

*(51%).

For this acquisition, Carrefour did not value noncontrolling interests at fair value.

Required

a. Prepare the journal entry for the acquisition of Baolongcang.

b. Carrefour made the acquisition of Baolongcang shortly after the IFRS standard on minority interest was changed. During the transition period (between adoption of the standard and the date when the standard becomes mandatory), the company chose to use the old method, in which minority interest (noncontrolling interest) is reported at book value, while the majority investor's holdings are recorded at fair value. What entry would Carrefour have made if it elected to use the new approach?

18.4 Business Combinations at Tesco

On June 18, 2010, the Group acquired certain assets and liabilities of 2 Sisters Food Group, Inc. for consideration of £52m. On July 19, 2010, the Group acquired 100% of the ordinary share capital of Wild Rocket Foods, LLC for consideration of £64m. The table below sets out the provisional analysis of the net assets acquired and the fair value to the Group regarding these two acquisitions.

	Preacquisition carrying values £m	Fair value adjustment £m	Provisional fair values on acquisition £m
Noncurrent assets	45	7	52
Current assets	9	(1)	8
Current liabilities	(6)	(1)	(7)
Noncurrent liabilities	(8)	(11)	(19)
Net assets acquired	40	(6)	34
Goodwill arising on acquisitions			82
			116
Consideration:			
Cash			45
Noncash			76
Total consideration			116

The goodwill represents the benefit of supply chain efficiencies, production economies, the ability to develop new and innovative products, and further third-party revenue potential.

Required

a. How were the two transactions financed? What impact would the financing have on the three principal financial statements?

b. Explain the potential reasons for the adjustment in the values of net assets acquired.

c. What is goodwill and what percentage of the transactions does it constitute?

18.5 AB InBev acquires SABMiller

On 11 November 2015, the boards of AB InBev and SABMiller plc ("SABMiller") announced that they had reached an agreement on the terms of the proposed business combination between SABMiller and AB InBev (the "Combination").

The Combination was implemented through a series of steps and completed on the 10th of October. During the final step of the proposed structure, Anheuser Busch InBev SA/NV, the holding of the AB InBev group, merged into Newbelco SA/NV (Newbelco), which was formed for the purpose of effecting the Combination, so that following completion of the Combination, Newbelco became the new holding company for the combined AB InBev and

SABMiller group. Newbelco has been renamed Anheuser-Busch InBev SA/NV.

Under the terms of the Combination, each SABMiller shareholder was entitled to elect to receive 45.00 pounds sterling in cash in respect of each SABMiller share (subject to the terms and conditions of the Combination). The Combination also included a partial share alternative (the "Partial Share Alternative"), under which SABMiller shareholders could elect to receive 4.6588 pounds sterling in cash and 0.483969 restricted shares in respect of each SABMiller share in lieu of the full cash consideration to which they would otherwise be entitled under the Combination (subject to scaling back in accordance with the terms of the Partial Share Alternative and the other terms and conditions of the Combination).

The Partial Share Alternative was limited to a maximum of 326,000,000 restricted shares and 3.1 billion pounds sterling in cash, Altria Inc. and Bevco Ltd. which held in aggregate approximately 40% of the ordinary share capital of SABMiller, had given irrevocable undertakings to AB InBev to elect for the Partial Share Alternative in respect of their entire beneficial holdings in SABMiller.

On 6 October 2016, Newbelco issued 163,276,737,100 ordinary shares ("Initial Newbelco Shares") to SABMiller shareholders through a capital increase of 85,531m euro equivalent to 75.4 billion pound sterling, as consideration for 1,632,767,371 ordinary shares of SABMiller pursuant to a UK law court-sanctioned scheme of arrangement (the "UK Scheme"). Following completion of the tender offer, AB InBev acquired 102,890,758,014 Initial Newbelco Shares tendered into the Belgian offer. Based on the terms of the UK Scheme, all Initial Newbelco Shares not tendered to AB InBev in the context of the Belgian offer (i.e. 60,385,979,086 Initial Newbelco Shares) were reclassified into 325,999,817 restricted shares, in accordance with the mechanism by which any Initial Newbelco Shares that were retained after closing of the Belgian offer were automatically reclassified and consolidated.

The restricted shares are unlisted, not admitted to trading on any stock exchange, and are subject to, among other things, restrictions on transfer until converted into new ordinary shares. Subject to limited exceptions, the restricted shares will only be convertible at the election of the holder into new ordinary shares on a one-for-one basis with effect from the fifth anniversary of completion of the Combination. From completion of the Combination, such restricted shares rank equally with the new ordinary shares with respect to dividends and voting rights. Following completion of the combination, AB InBev acquired 105,246 SABMiller shares from option holders that had not exercised their option rights prior to the completion of the combination for a total consideration of 5m euro. Following this transaction AB InBev owns 100% of the SABMiller shares.

The SABMiller purchase consideration is calculated as follows:

	Newbelco number of shares	Newbelco valuation in million pound sterling	Newbelco valuation in million euro
Tender offer (cash consideration)	102,890,758,014	46,301	52,522
Converted to restricted shares	60,385,979,086	29,099	33,009[i]
	163,276,737,100	75,400	85,531

Total equity value at offer in million euro	85,531
Purchase from option holders	5
Total equity value in million euro	**85,536**
Total equity value in million US dollar	**95,288**
Foreign exchange hedges and other	7,848[ii]
Purchase consideration	**103,136**
Add: fair market value of total debt assumed	11,870
Less: total cash acquired	(1,198)
Gross purchase consideration	**113,808**

[i]The restricted share valuation is based on the valuation of the Newbelco shares that were not tendered into the Belgian offer and has regard to the AB InBev share price of the day of the closing of the SABMiller transaction, adjusted for the specificities of the restricted shares in line with fair value measurement rules under IFRS.

[ii]During 2015 and 2016, AB InBev entered into derivative foreign exchange forward contracts, as well as other non-derivative items also documented in a hedge accounting relationship, in order to economically hedge against exposure to changes in the US dollar exchange rate for the cash component of the purchase consideration in pound sterling and South African rand. Although these derivatives and non-derivative items were considered to be economic hedges, only a portion of such derivatives could qualify for hedge accounting under IFRS rules. Since inception of the derivative contracts in 2015 and upon the completion of the combination with SABMiller, 12.3 billion US dollar negative mark-to-market adjustment related to such hedging were recognized cumulatively over 2015 and 2016, of which 7.4 billion US dollar qualified for hedge accounting and was, accordingly, allocated as part of the consideration paid. The settlement of the portion of the derivatives that did not qualify as hedge accounting was classified as cash flow from financing activities in the consolidated cash flow statement.

On 10 October 2016, AB InBev announced completion of the Belgian merger and the successful completion of the business combination with SABMiller.

As a result of the Belgian merger, the former Anheuser-Busch InBev SA/NV (the "former AB InBev") has merged into Newbelco SA/NV ("Newbelco"), and Newbelco has become the holding company for the combined former AB InBev and SABMiller groups. All assets and liabilities of the former AB InBev have been transferred to Newbelco, and Newbelco has automatically been substituted for the former AB InBev in all its rights and obligations by operation of Belgian law. Newbelco has been renamed Anheuser-Busch InBev SA/NV, and the former AB InBev has been dissolved by operation of Belgian law.

The shares in the former AB InBev were delisted from Euronext Brussels, the Bolsa Mexicana de Valores and the Johannesburg Stock Exchange. The new ordinary shares were admitted to listing and trading on Euronext Brussels, the Johannesburg Stock Exchange and the Bolsa Mexicana de Valores at the opening of business in each market on 11 October 2016. In addition, ADSs trading on the New York Stock Exchange, each of which used to represent one ordinary share of the former AB InBev, now each represent one new ordinary share, effective as of the opening of business in New York on 11 October 2016.

The share capital of AB InBev now amounts to 1,238,608,344 euro. It is represented by 2,019,241,973 shares without nominal value, of which 85,540,392 are held in treasury by AB InBev and its subsidiaries. All shares are new ordinary shares, except for 325,999,817 restricted shares.

AB InBev financed the cash consideration of the transaction with 18.0 billion US dollar drawn down under the 75.0 billion US dollar Committed Senior Acquisition Facilities agreement dated 28 October 2015, together with excess liquidity resulting from the issuance of bonds in 2016. See Note 24 *Interest bearing loans and borrowings*.

The transaction costs incurred in connection with the transaction, which include transaction taxes, advisory, legal, audit, valuation and other fees and costs, amounted to approximately USD 1.0 billion. In addition AB InBev incurred approximately USD 0.7 billion of costs in connection with the transaction-related financing arrangements.

In accordance with IFRS, the merger between the former AB InBev into Newbelco is considered for accounting purposes as a reverse acquisition, operation by which Newbelco legally absorbed assets and liabilities of former AB InBev. As a consequence, the legal acquirer (Newbelco) is considered as the accounting acquiree and the legal acquiree (former AB InBev) is considered the accounting acquirer. Therefore, the consolidated financial statements represent the continuation of the financial statements of former AB InBev. The assets and liabilities of former AB InBev remained recognized at their pre-combination carrying amounts. The identified assets, liabilities and non-controlling interests of SABMiller are recognized in accordance with IFRS 3 Business Combinations and have only been provisionally determined at the end of the reporting period.

The provisional allocation of the purchase price included in the balance sheet and detailed in the table below is based on the current best estimates of AB InBev's management with input from independent third parties. The completion of the purchase price allocation may result in further adjustment to the carrying value of SABMiller's recorded assets, liabilities and non-controlling interests and the determination of any residual amount that will be allocated to goodwill.

The following table presents the provisional allocation of purchase price to the SABMiller business:

Million US dollar	Provisional fair values
Non-current assets	
Property, plant and equipment....................	9,060
Intangible assets...	20,040
Investment in associates...............................	4,386
Investment securities.....................................	21
Deferred tax assets..	179
Derivatives..	579
Trade and other receivables.........................	59
Current assets	
Inventories..	977
Income tax receivable....................................	189
Derivatives..	60
Trade and other receivables.........................	1,257
Cash and cash equivalents...........................	1,410
Assets held for sale..	24,805
Non-current liabilities	
Interest-bearing loans and borrowings.......	(9,021)
Employee benefits..	(195)
Deferred tax liabilities...................................	(5,801)
Derivatives..	(24)
Trade and other payables.............................	(146)
Provisions...	(688)
Current liabilities	
Bank overdraft..	(212)
Interest-bearing loans and borrowings.......	(2,849)
Income tax payable..	(4,310)
Derivatives..	(156)
Trade and other payables.............................	(3,520)
Provisions...	(847)
Net identified assets and liabilities..........	**35,253**
Non-controlling interests...........................	**(6,200)**
Goodwill on acquisition...............................	**74,083**
Purchase consideration...............................	**103,136**

The transaction resulted in 74.1 billion US dollar of goodwill provisionally allocated primarily to the businesses in Colombia, Ecuador, Peru, Australia, South Africa and other African, Asia Pacific and Latin American countries. The factors that contributed to the recognition of goodwill include the acquisition of an assembled workforce and the premiums paid for cost synergies expected to be achieved in SABMiller. Management's assessment of the future economic benefits supporting recognition of this goodwill is in part based on expected savings through the implementation of AB InBev best practices such as, among others, a zero based budgeting program and initiatives that are expected to bring greater efficiency and standardization, generate cost savings and maximize purchasing power. Goodwill also arises due to the recognition of deferred tax liabilities in relation to the preliminary fair value adjustments on acquired intangible assets for which the amortization does not qualify as a tax deductible expense. None of the goodwill recognized is deductible for tax purposes.

The valuation of the property, plant and equipment, intangible assets, investment in associates, interest bearing loans and borrowings, employee benefits, other assets and liabilities and noncontrolling interests are based on the current best estimates of AB InBev's management, with input from independent third parties.

The majority of the intangible asset valuation relates to brands with indefinite life, valued for a total amount of 19.9 billion US dollar. The valuation of the brands with indefinite life is based on a series of factors, including the brand history, the operating plan and the countries in which the brands are sold. The fair value of brands was estimated by applying a combination of known valuation methodologies, such as the royalty relief and excess earnings valuation approaches.

The intangibles with an indefinite life mainly include the Castle and Carling brand families in Africa, the Aguila and Poker brand families in Colombia, the Cristal and Pilsner brand families in Ecuador, and the Carlton brand family in Australia.

A deferred tax liability has been accrued on the fair value adjustments considering tax rates expected to apply to the period when the assets are realized or liabilities are settled, based on enacted tax rates in the relevant tax jurisdictions.

Assets held for sale were recognized in relation to the divestiture of SABMiller's interests in the MillerCoors LLC joint venture and certain of SABMiller's portfolio of Miller brands outside of the U.S. to Molson Coors Brewing company; the divestiture of SABMiller's European premium brands to Asahi Group Holdings, Ltd and the divestiture of SABMiller's interest in China Resources Snow Breweries Ltd. to China Resources Beer (Holdings) Co. Ltd. These divestments were completed on 11 October 2016.

Assets held for sale were also recognized in relation to the agreement to sell SABMiller's assets in Central and Eastern Europe (Hungary, Romania, the Czech Republic, Slovakia and Poland) to Asahi and the agreement to divest SABMiller's interests in Distell Group Limited in South Africa to the Public Investment Corporation (SOC) Limited. By 31 December 2016, these disposals had not closed. In addition, the company has announced its agreement to transfer SABMiller's Panamanian business to its Brazilian-listed subsidiary Ambev S.A. ("Ambev") in exchange for Ambev's businesses in Colombia, Peru and Ecuador, to allow Ambev to initiate operations in Panama through the established SABMiller business and further expand its businesses in Central America; however, no effect has been given to such asset exchange within the provisional allocation of the purchase price as all businesses will remain within the Combined Group.

Non-controlling interests recognized at acquisition date were measured by the reference to their fair values and amounted to 6.2 billion US dollar. The fair value of non-controlling interests were estimated by applying primarily a market-based multiple valuation and assumed adjustments because of lack of control or lack of marketability that market participants would consider when estimating the fair value of non-controlling interests in SABMiller's owned businesses. The Market Approach analyzes market conditions and transactions comparable to the subject asset being valued, and estimates the fair value where reliable and available data on guideline transactions can be found.

Following the completion date of the transaction, SABMiller contributed 3.8 billion US dollar to the revenue and 0.7 billion US dollar to the profit of AB InBev. If the acquisition date had been 1 January 2016 it is estimated that AB InBev's combined revenue and profit from operations would have been higher by 8.4 billion US dollar, and 2.2 billion US dollar respectively. The combined data includes certain purchase accounting adjustments such as the estimated changes in depreciations and amortization expenses on acquired tangible and intangible assets. However, the combined results do not include any anticipated cost savings or other effects of the planned integration of SABMiller. Accordingly, such amounts are not necessarily indicative of the results if the combination had occurred on 1 January 2016 or that may result in the future.

Appendix: Tables for Present Value and Future Value Factors

Future Value Factors for €1 Compounded at i% for N Periods

N	1%	2%	3%	4%	5%	6%	7%	8%	9%	10%	11%	12%	13%	14%	15%	20%
1	1.010	1.020	1.030	1.040	1.050	1.060	1.070	1.080	1.090	1.100	1.110	1.120	1.130	1.140	1.150	1.200
2	1.020	1.040	1.061	1.082	1.103	1.124	1.145	1.166	1.188	1.210	1.232	1.254	1.277	1.300	1.323	1.440
3	1.030	1.061	1.093	1.125	1.158	1.191	1.225	1.260	1.295	1.331	1.368	1.405	1.443	1.482	1.521	1.728
4	1.041	1.082	1.126	1.170	1.216	1.262	1.311	1.360	1.412	1.464	1.518	1.574	1.630	1.689	1.749	2.074
5	1.051	1.104	1.159	1.217	1.276	1.338	1.403	1.469	1.539	1.611	1.685	1.762	1.842	1.925	2.011	2.488
6	1.062	1.126	1.194	1.265	1.340	1.419	1.501	1.587	1.677	1.772	1.870	1.974	2.082	2.195	2.313	2.986
7	1.072	1.149	1.230	1.316	1.407	1.504	1.606	1.714	1.828	1.949	2.076	2.211	2.353	2.502	2.660	3.583
8	1.083	1.172	1.267	1.369	1.477	1.594	1.718	1.851	1.993	2.144	2.305	2.476	2.658	2.853	3.059	4.300
9	1.094	1.195	1.305	1.423	1.551	1.689	1.838	1.999	2.172	2.358	2.558	2.773	3.004	3.252	3.518	5.160
10	1.105	1.219	1.344	1.480	1.629	1.791	1.967	2.159	2.367	2.594	2.839	3.106	3.395	3.707	4.046	6.192
11	1.116	1.243	1.384	1.539	1.710	1.898	2.105	2.332	2.580	2.853	3.152	3.479	3.836	4.226	4.652	7.430
12	1.127	1.268	1.426	1.601	1.796	2.012	2.252	2.518	2.813	3.138	3.498	3.896	4.335	4.818	5.350	8.916
13	1.138	1.294	1.469	1.665	1.886	2.133	2.410	2.720	3.066	3.452	3.883	4.363	4.898	5.492	6.153	10.699
14	1.149	1.319	1.513	1.732	1.980	2.261	2.579	2.937	3.342	3.797	4.310	4.887	5.535	6.261	7.076	12.839
15	1.161	1.346	1.558	1.801	2.079	2.397	2.759	3.172	3.642	4.177	4.785	5.474	6.254	7.138	8.137	15.407
16	1.173	1.373	1.605	1.873	2.183	2.540	2.952	3.426	3.970	4.595	5.311	6.130	7.067	8.137	9.358	18.488
17	1.184	1.400	1.653	1.948	2.292	2.693	3.159	3.700	4.328	5.054	5.895	6.866	7.986	9.276	10.761	22.186
18	1.196	1.428	1.702	2.026	2.407	2.854	3.380	3.996	4.717	5.560	6.544	7.690	9.024	10.575	12.375	26.623
19	1.208	1.457	1.754	2.107	2.527	3.026	3.617	4.316	5.142	6.116	7.263	8.613	10.197	12.056	14.232	31.948
20	1.220	1.486	1.806	2.191	2.653	3.207	3.870	4.661	5.604	6.727	8.062	9.646	11.523	13.743	16.367	38.338
21	1.232	1.516	1.860	2.279	2.786	3.400	4.141	5.034	6.109	7.400	8.949	10.804	13.021	15.668	18.822	46.005
22	1.245	1.546	1.916	2.370	2.925	3.604	4.430	5.437	6.659	8.140	9.934	12.100	14.714	17.861	21.645	55.206
23	1.257	1.577	1.974	2.465	3.072	3.820	4.741	5.871	7.258	8.954	11.026	13.552	16.627	20.362	24.891	66.247
24	1.270	1.608	2.033	2.563	3.225	4.049	5.072	6.341	7.911	9.850	12.239	15.179	18.788	23.212	28.625	79.497
25	1.282	1.641	2.094	2.666	3.386	4.292	5.427	6.848	8.623	10.835	13.585	17.000	21.231	26.462	32.919	95.396

(Continued)

N	1%	2%	3%	4%	5%	6%	7%	8%	9%	10%	11%	12%	13%	14%	15%	20%
26	1.295	1.673	2.157	2.772	3.556	4.549	5.807	7.396	9.399	11.918	15.080	19.040	23.991	30.167	37.857	114.475
27	1.308	1.707	2.221	2.883	3.733	4.822	6.214	7.988	10.245	13.110	16.739	21.325	27.109	34.390	43.535	137.371
28	1.321	1.741	2.288	2.999	3.920	5.112	6.649	8.627	11.167	14.421	18.580	23.884	30.633	39.204	50.066	164.845
29	1.335	1.776	2.357	3.119	4.116	5.418	7.114	9.317	12.172	15.863	20.624	26.750	34.616	44.693	57.575	197.814
30	1.348	1.811	2.427	3.243	4.322	5.743	7.612	10.063	13.268	17.449	22.892	29.960	39.116	50.950	66.212	237.376
31	1.361	1.848	2.500	3.373	4.538	6.088	8.145	10.868	14.462	19.194	25.410	33.555	44.201	58.083	76.144	284.852
32	1.375	1.885	2.575	3.508	4.765	6.453	8.715	11.737	15.763	21.114	28.206	37.582	49.947	66.215	87.565	341.822
33	1.389	1.922	2.652	3.648	5.003	6.841	9.325	12.676	17.182	23.225	31.308	42.092	56.440	75.485	100.700	410.186
34	1.403	1.961	2.732	3.794	5.253	7.251	9.978	13.690	18.728	25.548	34.752	47.143	63.777	86.053	115.805	492.224
35	1.417	2.000	2.814	3.946	5.516	7.686	10.677	14.785	20.414	28.102	38.575	52.800	72.069	98.100	133.176	590.668
36	1.431	2.040	2.898	4.104	5.792	8.147	11.424	15.968	22.251	30.913	42.818	59.136	81.437	111.834	153.152	708.802
37	1.445	2.081	2.985	4.268	6.081	8.636	12.224	17.246	24.254	34.004	47.528	66.232	92.024	127.491	176.125	850.562
38	1.460	2.122	3.075	4.439	6.385	9.154	13.079	18.625	26.437	37.404	52.756	74.180	103.987	145.340	202.543	1020.675
39	1.474	2.165	3.167	4.616	6.705	9.704	13.995	20.115	28.816	41.145	58.559	83.081	117.506	165.687	232.925	1224.810
40	1.489	2.208	3.262	4.801	7.040	10.286	14.974	21.725	31.409	45.259	65.001	93.051	132.782	188.884	267.864	1469.772
45	1.565	2.438	3.782	5.841	8.985	13.765	21.002	31.920	48.327	72.890	109.530	163.988	244.641	363.679	538.769	3657.262
50	1.645	2.692	4.384	7.107	11.467	18.420	29.457	46.902	74.358	117.391	184.565	289.002	450.736	700.233	1083.657	9100.438

Present Value Factors (at i%) for €1 Received at the End of N Periods

N	1%	2%	3%	4%	5%	6%	7%	8%	9%	10%	11%	12%	13%	14%	15%	20%
1	0.990	0.980	0.971	0.962	0.952	0.943	0.935	0.926	0.917	0.909	0.901	0.893	0.885	0.877	0.870	0.833
2	0.980	0.961	0.943	0.925	0.907	0.890	0.873	0.857	0.842	0.826	0.812	0.797	0.783	0.769	0.756	0.694
3	0.971	0.942	0.915	0.889	0.864	0.840	0.816	0.794	0.772	0.751	0.731	0.712	0.693	0.675	0.658	0.579
4	0.961	0.924	0.888	0.855	0.823	0.792	0.763	0.735	0.708	0.683	0.659	0.636	0.613	0.592	0.572	0.482
5	0.951	0.906	0.863	0.822	0.784	0.747	0.713	0.681	0.650	0.621	0.593	0.567	0.543	0.519	0.497	0.402
6	0.942	0.888	0.837	0.790	0.746	0.705	0.666	0.630	0.596	0.564	0.535	0.507	0.480	0.456	0.432	0.335
7	0.933	0.871	0.813	0.760	0.711	0.665	0.623	0.583	0.547	0.513	0.482	0.452	0.425	0.400	0.376	0.279
8	0.923	0.853	0.789	0.731	0.677	0.627	0.582	0.540	0.502	0.467	0.434	0.404	0.376	0.351	0.327	0.233
9	0.914	0.837	0.766	0.703	0.645	0.592	0.544	0.500	0.460	0.424	0.391	0.361	0.333	0.308	0.284	0.194
10	0.905	0.820	0.744	0.676	0.614	0.558	0.508	0.463	0.422	0.386	0.352	0.322	0.295	0.270	0.247	0.162
11	0.896	0.804	0.722	0.650	0.585	0.527	0.475	0.429	0.388	0.350	0.317	0.287	0.261	0.237	0.215	0.135
12	0.887	0.788	0.701	0.625	0.557	0.497	0.444	0.397	0.356	0.319	0.286	0.257	0.231	0.208	0.187	0.112
13	0.879	0.773	0.681	0.601	0.530	0.469	0.415	0.368	0.326	0.290	0.258	0.229	0.204	0.182	0.163	0.093
14	0.870	0.758	0.661	0.577	0.505	0.442	0.388	0.340	0.299	0.263	0.232	0.205	0.181	0.160	0.141	0.078
15	0.861	0.743	0.642	0.555	0.481	0.417	0.362	0.315	0.275	0.239	0.209	0.183	0.160	0.140	0.123	0.065
16	0.853	0.728	0.623	0.534	0.458	0.394	0.339	0.292	0.252	0.218	0.188	0.163	0.141	0.123	0.107	0.054
17	0.844	0.714	0.605	0.513	0.436	0.371	0.317	0.270	0.231	0.198	0.170	0.146	0.125	0.108	0.093	0.045
18	0.836	0.700	0.587	0.494	0.416	0.350	0.296	0.250	0.212	0.180	0.153	0.130	0.111	0.095	0.081	0.038
19	0.828	0.686	0.570	0.475	0.396	0.331	0.277	0.232	0.194	0.164	0.138	0.116	0.098	0.083	0.070	0.031
20	0.820	0.673	0.554	0.456	0.377	0.312	0.258	0.215	0.178	0.149	0.124	0.104	0.087	0.073	0.061	0.026
21	0.811	0.660	0.538	0.439	0.359	0.294	0.242	0.199	0.164	0.135	0.112	0.093	0.077	0.064	0.053	0.022
22	0.803	0.647	0.522	0.422	0.342	0.278	0.226	0.184	0.150	0.123	0.101	0.083	0.068	0.056	0.046	0.018
23	0.795	0.634	0.507	0.406	0.326	0.262	0.211	0.170	0.138	0.112	0.091	0.074	0.060	0.049	0.040	0.015
24	0.788	0.622	0.492	0.390	0.310	0.247	0.197	0.158	0.126	0.102	0.082	0.066	0.053	0.043	0.035	0.013
25	0.780	0.610	0.478	0.375	0.295	0.233	0.184	0.146	0.116	0.092	0.074	0.059	0.047	0.038	0.030	0.010

(Continued)

N	1%	2%	3%	4%	5%	6%	7%	8%	9%	10%	11%	12%	13%	14%	15%	20%
26	0.772	0.598	0.464	0.361	0.281	0.220	0.172	0.135	0.106	0.084	0.066	0.053	0.042	0.033	0.026	0.009
27	0.764	0.586	0.450	0.347	0.268	0.207	0.161	0.125	0.098	0.076	0.060	0.047	0.037	0.029	0.023	0.007
28	0.757	0.574	0.437	0.333	0.255	0.196	0.150	0.116	0.090	0.069	0.054	0.042	0.033	0.026	0.020	0.006
29	0.749	0.563	0.424	0.321	0.243	0.185	0.141	0.107	0.082	0.063	0.048	0.037	0.029	0.022	0.017	0.005
30	0.742	0.552	0.412	0.308	0.231	0.174	0.131	0.099	0.075	0.057	0.044	0.033	0.026	0.020	0.015	0.004
31	0.735	0.541	0.400	0.296	0.220	0.164	0.123	0.092	0.069	0.052	0.039	0.030	0.023	0.017	0.013	0.004
32	0.727	0.531	0.388	0.285	0.210	0.155	0.115	0.085	0.063	0.047	0.035	0.027	0.020	0.015	0.011	0.003
33	0.720	0.520	0.377	0.274	0.200	0.146	0.107	0.079	0.058	0.043	0.032	0.024	0.018	0.013	0.010	0.002
34	0.713	0.510	0.366	0.264	0.190	0.138	0.100	0.073	0.053	0.039	0.029	0.021	0.016	0.012	0.009	0.002
35	0.706	0.500	0.355	0.253	0.181	0.130	0.094	0.068	0.049	0.036	0.026	0.019	0.014	0.010	0.008	0.002
36	0.699	0.490	0.345	0.244	0.173	0.123	0.088	0.063	0.045	0.032	0.023	0.017	0.012	0.009	0.007	0.001
37	0.692	0.481	0.335	0.234	0.164	0.116	0.082	0.058	0.041	0.029	0.021	0.015	0.011	0.008	0.006	0.001
38	0.685	0.471	0.325	0.225	0.157	0.109	0.076	0.054	0.038	0.027	0.019	0.013	0.010	0.007	0.005	0.001
39	0.678	0.462	0.316	0.217	0.149	0.103	0.071	0.050	0.035	0.024	0.017	0.012	0.009	0.006	0.004	0.001
40	0.672	0.453	0.307	0.208	0.142	0.097	0.067	0.046	0.032	0.022	0.015	0.011	0.008	0.005	0.004	0.001
45	0.639	0.410	0.264	0.171	0.111	0.073	0.048	0.031	0.021	0.014	0.009	0.006	0.004	0.003	0.002	0.000
50	0.608	0.372	0.228	0.141	0.087	0.054	0.034	0.021	0.013	0.009	0.005	0.003	0.002	0.001	0.001	0.000

Future Value of Annuity Factors for €1 Compounded at i% for N Periods

N	1%	2%	3%	4%	5%	6%	7%	8%	9%	10%	11%	12%	13%	14%	15%	20%
1	1.000	1.000	1.000	1.000	1.000	1.000	1.000	1.000	1.000	1.000	1.000	1.000	1.000	1.000	1.000	1.000
2	2.010	2.020	2.030	2.040	2.050	2.060	2.070	2.080	2.090	2.100	2.110	2.120	2.130	2.140	2.150	2.200
3	3.030	3.060	3.091	3.122	3.153	3.184	3.215	3.246	3.278	3.310	3.342	3.374	3.407	3.440	3.473	3.640
4	4.060	4.122	4.184	4.246	4.310	4.375	4.440	4.506	4.573	4.641	4.710	4.779	4.850	4.921	4.993	5.368
5	5.101	5.204	5.309	5.416	5.526	5.637	5.751	5.867	5.985	6.105	6.228	6.353	6.480	6.610	6.742	7.442
6	6.152	6.308	6.468	6.633	6.802	6.975	7.153	7.336	7.523	7.716	7.913	8.115	8.323	8.536	8.754	9.930
7	7.214	7.434	7.662	7.898	8.142	8.394	8.654	8.923	9.200	9.487	9.783	10.089	10.405	10.730	11.067	12.916
8	8.286	8.583	8.892	9.214	9.549	9.897	10.260	10.637	11.028	11.436	11.859	12.300	12.757	13.233	13.727	16.499
9	9.369	9.755	10.159	10.583	11.027	11.491	11.978	12.488	13.021	13.579	14.164	14.776	15.416	16.085	16.786	20.799
10	10.462	10.950	11.464	12.006	12.578	13.181	13.816	14.487	15.193	15.937	16.722	17.549	18.420	19.337	20.304	25.959
11	11.567	12.169	12.808	13.486	14.207	14.972	15.784	16.645	17.560	18.531	19.561	20.655	21.814	23.045	24.349	32.150
12	12.683	13.412	14.192	15.026	15.917	16.870	17.888	18.977	20.141	21.384	22.713	24.133	25.650	27.271	29.002	39.581
13	13.809	14.680	15.618	16.627	17.713	18.882	20.141	21.495	22.953	24.523	26.212	28.029	29.985	32.089	34.352	48.497
14	14.947	15.974	17.086	18.292	19.599	21.015	22.550	24.215	26.019	27.975	30.095	32.393	34.883	37.581	40.505	59.196
15	16.097	17.293	18.599	20.024	21.579	23.276	25.129	27.152	29.361	31.772	34.405	37.280	40.417	43.842	47.580	72.035
16	17.258	18.639	20.157	21.825	23.657	25.673	27.888	30.324	33.003	35.950	39.190	42.753	46.672	50.980	55.717	87.442
17	18.430	20.012	21.762	23.698	25.840	28.213	30.840	33.750	36.974	40.545	44.501	48.884	53.739	59.118	65.075	105.931
18	19.615	21.412	23.414	25.645	28.132	30.906	33.999	37.450	41.301	45.599	50.396	55.750	61.725	68.394	75.836	128.117
19	20.811	22.841	25.117	27.671	30.539	33.760	37.379	41.446	46.018	51.159	56.939	63.440	70.749	78.969	88.212	154.740
20	22.019	24.297	26.870	29.778	33.066	36.786	40.995	45.762	51.160	57.275	64.203	72.052	80.947	91.025	102.444	186.688
21	23.239	25.783	28.676	31.969	35.719	39.993	44.865	50.423	56.765	64.002	72.265	81.699	92.470	104.768	118.810	225.026
22	24.472	27.299	30.537	34.248	38.505	43.392	49.006	55.457	62.873	71.403	81.214	92.503	105.491	120.436	137.632	271.031
23	25.716	28.845	32.453	36.618	41.430	46.996	53.436	60.893	69.532	79.543	91.148	104.603	120.205	138.297	159.276	326.237
24	26.973	30.422	34.426	39.083	44.502	50.816	58.177	66.765	76.790	88.497	102.174	118.155	136.831	158.659	184.168	392.484
25	28.243	32.030	36.459	41.646	47.727	54.865	63.249	73.106	84.701	98.347	114.413	133.334	155.620	181.871	212.793	471.981

(Continued)

N	1%	2%	3%	4%	5%	6%	7%	8%	9%	10%	11%	12%	13%	14%	15%	20%
26	29.526	33.671	38.553	44.312	51.113	59.156	68.676	79.954	93.324	109.182	127.999	150.334	176.850	208.333	245.712	567.377
27	30.821	35.344	40.710	47.084	54.669	63.706	74.484	87.351	102.723	121.100	143.079	169.374	200.841	238.499	283.569	681.853
28	32.129	37.051	42.931	49.968	58.403	68.528	80.698	95.339	112.968	134.210	159.817	190.699	227.950	272.889	327.104	819.223
29	33.450	38.792	45.219	52.966	62.323	73.640	87.347	103.966	124.135	148.631	178.397	214.583	258.583	312.094	377.170	984.068
30	34.785	40.568	47.575	56.085	66.439	79.058	94.461	113.283	136.308	164.494	199.021	241.333	293.199	356.787	434.745	1181.882
31	36.133	42.379	50.003	59.328	70.761	84.802	102.073	123.346	149.575	181.943	221.913	271.293	332.315	407.737	500.957	1419.258
32	37.494	44.227	52.503	62.701	75.299	90.890	110.218	134.214	164.037	201.138	247.324	304.848	376.516	465.820	577.100	1704.109
33	38.869	46.112	55.078	66.210	80.064	97.343	118.933	145.951	179.800	222.252	275.529	342.429	426.463	532.035	664.666	2045.931
34	40.258	48.034	57.730	69.858	85.067	104.184	128.259	158.627	196.982	245.477	306.837	384.521	482.903	607.520	765.365	2456.118
35	41.660	49.994	60.462	73.652	90.320	111.435	138.237	172.317	215.711	271.024	341.590	431.663	546.681	693.573	881.170	2948.341
36	43.077	51.994	63.276	77.598	95.836	119.121	148.913	187.102	236.125	299.127	380.164	484.463	618.749	791.673	1014.346	3539.009
37	44.508	54.034	66.174	81.702	101.628	127.268	160.337	203.070	258.376	330.039	422.982	543.599	700.187	903.507	1167.498	4247.811
38	45.953	56.115	69.159	85.970	107.710	135.904	172.561	220.316	282.630	364.043	470.511	609.831	792.211	1030.998	1343.622	5098.373
39	47.412	58.237	72.234	90.409	114.095	145.058	185.640	238.941	309.066	401.448	523.267	684.010	896.198	1176.338	1546.165	6119.048
40	48.886	60.402	75.401	95.026	120.800	154.762	199.635	259.057	337.882	442.593	581.826	767.091	1013.704	1342.025	1779.090	7343.858
45	56.481	71.893	92.720	121.029	159.700	212.744	285.749	386.506	525.859	718.905	986.639	1358.230	1874.165	2590.565	3585.128	18281.310
50	64.463	84.579	112.797	152.667	209.348	290.336	406.529	573.770	815.084	1163.909	1668.771	2400.018	3459.507	4994.521	7217.716	45497.191

Present Value of Annuity Factors (at i% per Period) for €1 Received per Period for Each of N Periods

N	1%	2%	3%	4%	5%	6%	7%	8%	9%	10%	11%	12%	13%	14%	15%	20%
1	0.990	0.980	0.971	0.962	0.952	0.943	0.935	0.926	0.917	0.909	0.901	0.893	0.885	0.877	0.870	0.833
2	1.970	1.942	1.913	1.886	1.859	1.833	1.808	1.783	1.759	1.736	1.713	1.690	1.668	1.647	1.626	1.528
3	2.941	2.884	2.829	2.775	2.723	2.673	2.624	2.577	2.531	2.487	2.444	2.402	2.361	2.322	2.283	2.106
4	3.902	3.808	3.717	3.630	3.546	3.465	3.387	3.312	3.240	3.170	3.102	3.037	2.974	2.914	2.855	2.589
5	4.853	4.713	4.580	4.452	4.329	4.212	4.100	3.993	3.890	3.791	3.696	3.605	3.517	3.433	3.352	2.991
6	5.795	5.601	5.417	5.242	5.076	4.917	4.767	4.623	4.486	4.355	4.231	4.111	3.998	3.889	3.784	3.326
7	6.728	6.472	6.230	6.002	5.786	5.582	5.389	5.206	5.033	4.868	4.712	4.564	4.423	4.288	4.160	3.605
8	7.652	7.325	7.020	6.733	6.463	6.210	5.971	5.747	5.535	5.335	5.146	4.968	4.799	4.639	4.487	3.837
9	8.566	8.162	7.786	7.435	7.108	6.802	6.515	6.247	5.995	5.759	5.537	5.328	5.132	4.946	4.772	4.031
10	9.471	8.983	8.530	8.111	7.722	7.360	7.024	6.710	6.418	6.145	5.889	5.650	5.426	5.216	5.019	4.192
11	10.368	9.787	9.253	8.760	8.306	7.887	7.499	7.139	6.805	6.495	6.207	5.938	5.687	5.453	5.234	4.327
12	11.255	10.575	9.954	9.385	8.863	8.384	7.943	7.536	7.161	6.814	6.492	6.194	5.918	5.660	5.421	4.439
13	12.134	11.348	10.635	9.986	9.394	8.853	8.358	7.904	7.487	7.103	6.750	6.424	6.122	5.842	5.583	4.533
14	13.004	12.106	11.296	10.563	9.899	9.295	8.745	8.244	7.786	7.367	6.982	6.628	6.302	6.002	5.724	4.611
15	13.865	12.849	11.938	11.118	10.380	9.712	9.108	8.559	8.061	7.606	7.191	6.811	6.462	6.142	5.847	4.675
16	14.718	13.578	12.561	11.652	10.838	10.106	9.447	8.851	8.313	7.824	7.379	6.974	6.604	6.265	5.954	4.730
17	15.562	14.292	13.166	12.166	11.274	10.477	9.763	9.122	8.544	8.022	7.549	7.120	6.729	6.373	6.047	4.775
18	16.398	14.992	13.754	12.659	11.690	10.828	10.059	9.372	8.756	8.201	7.702	7.250	6.840	6.467	6.128	4.812
19	17.226	15.678	14.324	13.134	12.085	11.158	10.336	9.604	8.950	8.365	7.839	7.366	6.938	6.550	6.198	4.843
20	18.046	16.351	14.877	13.590	12.462	11.470	10.594	9.818	9.129	8.514	7.963	7.469	7.025	6.623	6.259	4.870
21	18.857	17.011	15.415	14.029	12.821	11.764	10.836	10.017	9.292	8.649	8.075	7.562	7.102	6.687	6.312	4.891
22	19.660	17.658	15.937	14.451	13.163	12.042	11.061	10.201	9.442	8.772	8.176	7.645	7.170	6.743	6.359	4.909
23	20.456	18.292	16.444	14.857	13.489	12.303	11.272	10.371	9.580	8.883	8.266	7.718	7.230	6.792	6.399	4.925
24	21.243	18.914	16.936	15.247	13.799	12.550	11.469	10.529	9.707	8.985	8.348	7.784	7.283	6.835	6.434	4.937
25	22.023	19.523	17.413	15.622	14.094	12.783	11.654	10.675	9.823	9.077	8.422	7.843	7.330	6.873	6.464	4.948

(Continued)

N	1%	2%	3%	4%	5%	6%	7%	8%	9%	10%	11%	12%	13%	14%	15%	20%
26	22.795	20.121	17.877	15.983	14.375	13.003	11.826	10.810	9.929	9.161	8.488	7.896	7.372	6.906	6.491	4.956
27	23.560	20.707	18.327	16.330	14.643	13.211	11.987	10.935	10.027	9.237	8.548	7.943	7.409	6.935	6.514	4.964
28	24.316	21.281	18.764	16.663	14.898	13.406	12.137	11.051	10.116	9.307	8.602	7.984	7.441	6.961	6.534	4.970
29	25.066	21.844	19.188	16.984	15.141	13.591	12.278	11.158	10.198	9.370	8.650	8.022	7.470	6.983	6.551	4.975
30	25.808	22.396	19.600	17.292	15.372	13.765	12.409	11.258	10.274	9.427	8.694	8.055	7.496	7.003	6.566	4.979
31	26.542	22.938	20.000	17.588	15.593	13.929	12.532	11.350	10.343	9.479	8.733	8.085	7.518	7.020	6.579	4.982
32	27.270	23.468	20.389	17.874	15.803	14.084	12.647	11.435	10.406	9.526	8.769	8.112	7.538	7.035	6.591	4.985
33	27.990	23.989	20.766	18.148	16.003	14.230	12.754	11.514	10.464	9.569	8.801	8.135	7.556	7.048	6.600	4.988
34	28.703	24.499	21.132	18.411	16.193	14.368	12.854	11.587	10.518	9.609	8.829	8.157	7.572	7.060	6.609	4.990
35	29.409	24.999	21.487	18.665	16.374	14.498	12.948	11.655	10.567	9.644	8.855	8.176	7.586	7.070	6.617	4.992
36	30.108	25.489	21.832	18.908	16.547	14.621	13.035	11.717	10.612	9.677	8.879	8.192	7.598	7.079	6.623	4.993
37	30.800	25.969	22.167	19.143	16.711	14.737	13.117	11.775	10.653	9.706	8.900	8.208	7.609	7.087	6.629	4.994
38	31.485	26.441	22.492	19.368	16.868	14.846	13.193	11.829	10.691	9.733	8.919	8.221	7.618	7.094	6.634	4.995
39	32.163	26.903	22.808	19.584	17.017	14.949	13.265	11.879	10.726	9.757	8.936	8.233	7.627	7.100	6.638	4.996
40	32.835	27.355	23.115	19.793	17.159	15.046	13.332	11.925	10.757	9.779	8.951	8.244	7.634	7.105	6.642	4.997
45	36.095	29.490	24.519	20.720	17.774	15.456	13.606	12.108	10.881	9.863	9.008	8.283	7.661	7.123	6.654	4.999
50	39.196	31.424	25.730	21.482	18.256	15.762	13.801	12.233	10.962	9.915	9.042	8.304	7.675	7.133	6.661	4.999

INDEX

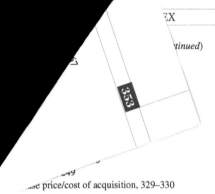